First World War
and Army of Occupation
War Diary
France, Belgium and Germany

34 DIVISION
Divisional Troops
152 Brigade Royal Field Artillery
1 February 1916 - 31 July 1919

WO95/2445/3

The Naval & Military Press Ltd
www.nmarchive.com
Published in association with The National Archives

Published by

The Naval & Military Press Ltd

Unit 10 Ridgewood Industrial Park,

Uckfield, East Sussex,

TN22 5QE England

Tel: +44 (0) 1825 749494

www.naval-military-press.com

www.nmarchive.com

This diary has been reprinted in facsimile from the original. Any imperfections are inevitably reproduced and the quality may fall short of modern type and cartographic standards.

© **Crown Copyright**

Images reproduced by permission of The National Archives, London, England, 2015.

Contents

Document type	Place/Title	Date From	Date To
Heading	WO95/2445/3		
Heading	34th Division 152nd Brigade R.F.A. Jan 1916 July 1919		
War Diary			
War Diary	Lynde	01/02/1916	17/02/1916
War Diary	Gris Pot	18/02/1916	29/02/1916
Miscellaneous	152 R.F.A. Vol 3		
War Diary	Grispot	01/03/1916	09/04/1916
War Diary	Lynde	10/04/1916	11/04/1916
War Diary	Setques	12/04/1916	30/04/1916
Miscellaneous	Right Group Orders (Scheme A) & Scheme A Coy G.O.C. 103 Inf Bde	08/03/1916	08/03/1916
Operation(al) Order(s)	Centre Group Operation Order No. 4		
War Diary	Sectques	01/05/1916	31/05/1916
War Diary	Officer Commanding 152 Brigade R.F.A.	19/05/1916	19/05/1916
Miscellaneous	O.C. 152 Bde. R.F.A.	15/05/1916	15/05/1916
Miscellaneous	G.H.Q. O.B. 818 163 (9)	06/05/1916	06/05/1916
War Diary	Behencourt	01/06/1916	06/06/1916
War Diary	Albert	07/06/1916	11/06/1916
War Diary	Bellevue Fme	12/06/1916	16/06/1916
War Diary	Albert	17/06/1916	23/06/1916
War Diary	W 30.a.9.0	24/06/1916	30/06/1916
Operation(al) Order(s)	Operation Order No. 4 Centre Group Orders For "Z" Day		
War Diary	Each Of The Above Will Take With Him The Following	18/06/1916	18/06/1916
Miscellaneous			
Miscellaneous	Instructions For "U" Day		
Miscellaneous	Instructions For "V" Day		
Miscellaneous	Instructions For "W" Day		
Miscellaneous	Instructions For "X" Day		
Miscellaneous	Instructions For "Y" Day		
Operation(al) Order(s)	Centre Group Operation Order No. 3	22/06/1916	22/06/1916
Miscellaneous	Centre Group Instructions	24/06/1916	24/06/1916
Miscellaneous	Reference Instructions For "V" Day Para 2 (C)		
Miscellaneous	Time Table B		
Miscellaneous	H.Q. Right Group	24/06/1916	24/06/1916
Miscellaneous	Artillery Instructions No. 13	26/06/1916	26/06/1916
Miscellaneous	Appendix VI Issued With 34th Divisional Arty Operation Order No. 10	29/06/1916	29/06/1916
Miscellaneous	Artillery Instructions No 18 28.6.16	29/06/1916	29/06/1916
Miscellaneous	The Following Raids Are To Take Place On Centre Group Front Tonight	29/06/1916	29/06/1916
Heading	War Diary Headquarters 152nd Brigade R.F.A. July 1916		
War Diary	W.30.a.8.0	01/07/1916	31/07/1916
Operation(al) Order(s)	Centre Group Operation Order No. 5	06/07/1916	06/07/1916
Miscellaneous	Reference Centre Group Order No. 5	06/07/1916	06/07/1916
Operation(al) Order(s)	Operation Order No. 6 Centre Group Orders	13/07/1916	13/07/1916

Type	Description	From	To
Heading	34th Divisional Artillery 152nd Brigade Royal Field Artillery August 1916		
War Diary	Albert X 30 A.8.0 Sheet 57 Dse 1/20,000	01/08/1916	14/08/1916
War Diary	Albert	14/08/1916	19/08/1916
War Diary	Beaucourt	20/08/1916	21/08/1916
War Diary	Croix Du Bac 9 5.c.1.2 1/20000 Sheet 36 N W	22/08/1916	24/08/1916
War Diary	H 17 D 3.3 1/20000 36 N W	25/08/1916	31/08/1916
Operation(al) Order(s)	L.K. Group Operation Order No. 7	04/08/1916	04/08/1916
Operation(al) Order(s)	L.K. Group Operation Order No. 8	08/08/1916	08/08/1916
Operation(al) Order(s)	L.K. Group Operation Order No. 9	10/08/1916	10/08/1916
Operation(al) Order(s)	L.K. Group Operation Order No. 10	12/08/1916	12/08/1916
Operation(al) Order(s)	L.K. Group Operation Order No. 11	16/08/1916	16/08/1916
Operation(al) Order(s)	L.K. Group Operation Order No. 12	16/08/1916	16/08/1916
Operation(al) Order(s)	Right Group Operation Order No. 13	28/08/1916	28/08/1916
Miscellaneous	General Instructions Right Group	29/08/1916	29/08/1916
Heading	War Diary Of 152nd F.A. Brigade From 1st To 30th Sept. 1916 Volume 9		
War Diary	Armentieres H.17.d.3.1/2 4	01/09/1916	04/09/1916
War Diary	Armentieres	05/09/1916	29/09/1916
War Diary	Armentieres H 17.d 3.1/2. 4	30/09/1916	30/09/1916
Operation(al) Order(s)	Right Group Operation Order No. 15	08/09/1916	08/09/1916
Miscellaneous	Right Group Memorandum Reference Right Group Operation Order No. 17	17/09/1916	17/09/1916
Operation(al) Order(s)	Right Group Operation Order No. 18 A	21/09/1916	21/09/1916
Operation(al) Order(s)	Right Group Operation Order No. 18	22/09/1916	22/09/1916
Operation(al) Order(s)	Right Group Operation Order No. 19	24/09/1916	24/09/1916
Operation(al) Order(s)	Right Group Operation Order No. 20	26/09/1916	26/09/1916
Operation(al) Order(s)	Right Group Operation Order No. 22	27/09/1916	27/09/1916
Heading	War Diary Of 152nd Brigade R.F.A. From 1st To 31st Oct. 1916 Volume 10		
War Diary	Armentieres H.17.d.35.40	01/10/1916	31/10/1916
Operation(al) Order(s)	Right Group Operation Order No 22		
Operation(al) Order(s)	Right Group Operation Order No 24	11/10/1916	11/10/1916
Operation(al) Order(s)	Right Group Operation Order No 25	12/10/1916	12/10/1916
Operation(al) Order(s)	Right Group Operation Order No 26	15/10/1916	15/10/1916
Operation(al) Order(s)	Right Group Scheme No 26	31/10/1916	31/10/1916
Heading	War Diary Of 152nd Brigade R.F.A. From 1st November To 30th Nov. 1916 Volume 10		
War Diary	Armentieres H 17.d.35.40	01/11/1916	30/11/1916
Operation(al) Order(s)	Right Group Scheme No. 27	01/11/1916	01/11/1916
Miscellaneous		02/11/1916	02/11/1916
Operation(al) Order(s)	Right Group Operation Order No. 28		
Miscellaneous		04/11/1916	04/11/1916
Miscellaneous	A Form Messages And Signals		
Operation(al) Order(s)	Right Group Operation Order No. 29		
Operation(al) Order(s)	Right Group Operation Order No. 30	06/11/1916	06/11/1916
Operation(al) Order(s)	Right Group Operation Order No. 31		
Operation(al) Order(s)	Right Group Operation Order No. 32		
Operation(al) Order(s)	Right Group Operation Order No. 33	12/11/1916	12/11/1916
Operation(al) Order(s)	Right Group Operation Order No. 35	19/11/1916	19/11/1916
Operation(al) Order(s)	Right Group Operation Order No. 37	21/11/1916	21/11/1916
Heading	War Diary Of 152nd Brigade R.F.A. From 1st To 31st Dec 1916 Volume XI		
War Diary	Armentieres H 17.d.35.40	01/12/1916	19/12/1916
War Diary	Armentieres	20/12/1916	21/12/1916
War Diary	Armentieres H 17 D 35 40	21/12/1916	28/12/1916

Type	Description	Start	End
War Diary	Armentieres	29/12/1916	30/12/1916
War Diary	Armentieres H 17.d.35.40	30/12/1916	31/12/1916
Operation(al) Order(s)	Right Group Operation Order No. 37	29/12/1916	29/12/1916
Miscellaneous	Right Group RA Reference Operation Order No. 37	30/12/1916	30/12/1916
Miscellaneous	Artillery Scheme In Conjunction With Raid By 10th Lincolns	19/12/1916	19/12/1916
Diagram etc			
Miscellaneous	Right Group R.A.	02/12/1916	02/12/1916
War Diary	Armentieres H 17.d.35.40	01/01/1917	31/01/1917
Operation(al) Order(s)	Right Group Operation Order No. 38	15/01/1917	15/01/1917
Diagram etc	Right Group R.A.		
Miscellaneous	34th Divisional Artillery Return Of Positions Zones, Night, Lines		
Miscellaneous			
Operation(al) Order(s)	Right Group R.A. Operation Order No 39	23/01/1917	23/01/1917
Operation(al) Order(s)	Right Group R.A. Operation Order No 40	25/01/1917	25/01/1917
Miscellaneous	Right Group R.A. Scheme For 24-1-17	23/01/1917	23/01/1917
Miscellaneous	Right Group R.A. Liaison & S.O.S. Barrages	24/01/1917	24/01/1917
Miscellaneous	152 Brigade Vol 3		
War Diary	Steenwerck	01/02/1917	13/02/1917
War Diary	Neuf Berquin	14/02/1917	19/02/1917
War Diary	Steenbecque	19/02/1917	19/02/1917
War Diary	Molinghem	20/02/1917	20/02/1917
War Diary	Cauchy a la Tour	21/02/1917	21/02/1917
War Diary	Bours	22/02/1917	31/03/1917
War Diary	Battle Field Of Arrds (Rochlincourt Area)	01/04/1917	30/04/1917
War Diary	H. Qrs H 17 d 3.0 Ref Sheet 51 B N.W. France	01/05/1917	03/05/1917
Heading	34th 152nd Bde. R.F.A. Vol 2		
War Diary		04/05/1917	31/05/1917
War Diary	Area Gavrelle	01/06/1917	26/06/1917
War Diary	Fampoux	27/06/1917	28/06/1917
War Diary	Area Fampoux	28/06/1917	30/06/1917
War Diary	Arras Sector	01/07/1917	06/07/1917
War Diary	Peronne District	07/07/1917	09/07/1917
War Diary	Hargicourt Sector	10/07/1917	29/09/1917
War Diary	Peronne	30/09/1917	08/10/1917
War Diary	Proven Area	09/10/1917	14/10/1917
War Diary	Wijdendrift	15/10/1917	18/10/1917
War Diary	Wijdendrift Area	18/10/1917	27/10/1917
War Diary	Wijdendrift	28/10/1917	31/10/1917
War Diary	Broembeek	01/11/1917	10/11/1917
War Diary	Heninel	11/11/1917	17/11/1917
War Diary	16 Div Area	17/11/1917	28/11/1917
War Diary	Heninel	29/11/1917	31/01/1918
Operation(al) Order(s)	Right Group Operation Order No. 28. Appendix 1	27/12/1917	27/12/1917
Operation(al) Order(s)	Centre Group Operation Order No. 29 Appendix 2. Appendix 2	01/01/1918	01/01/1918
War Diary	Heninel	01/02/1918	08/02/1918
War Diary	Ficheux	09/02/1918	09/02/1918
War Diary	On The March	10/02/1918	11/02/1918
War Diary	Wamin	12/02/1918	28/02/1918
Miscellaneous		26/01/1918	26/01/1918
Operation(al) Order(s)	Centre Group Operation Order No. 30 Appendix 3	08/01/1918	08/01/1918
Operation(al) Order(s)	Centre Group Operation Order No. 34. Appendix 4	15/01/1918	15/01/1918
Operation(al) Order(s)	Centre Group Operation Order No. 36	21/01/1918	21/01/1918
Operation(al) Order(s)	Centre Group Operation Order No. 37 Appendix 6		

Type	Description	From	To
Operation(al) Order(s)	Centre Group Operation Order No. 37 Appendix 1		
Operation(al) Order(s)	Centre Group Operation Order No. 38 Appendix 2	02/02/1918	02/02/1918
Heading	34th Divisional Artillery War Diary 152nd Brigade Royal Field Artillery March 1918		
War Diary	Wamin	01/03/1918	01/03/1918
War Diary	On The March	02/03/1918	02/03/1918
War Diary	St Ledger	03/03/1918	22/03/1918
War Diary	Henin	22/03/1918	22/03/1918
War Diary	Moyenville	23/03/1918	27/03/1918
War Diary	Adinfer	27/03/1918	27/03/1918
War Diary	Ransart	28/03/1918	31/03/1918
Heading	34th Divisional Artillery War Diary 152nd Brigade Royal Field Artillery April 1918		
War Diary	Ransart	01/04/1918	03/04/1918
War Diary	Gouy	04/04/1918	04/04/1918
War Diary	On The March	05/04/1918	09/04/1918
War Diary	On The Move	10/04/1918	12/04/1918
War Diary	Le Tir. Anglais	13/04/1918	30/04/1918
Operation(al) Order(s)	152nd Brigade R.F.A. Order No. 2 Appendix 1	23/04/1918	23/04/1918
Operation(al) Order(s)	152 Brigade R.F.A. Order No. 11 Appendix No. 6	30/04/1918	30/04/1918
Miscellaneous	Amendment To 152 Brigade R.F.A. Order No. 2	23/04/1918	23/04/1918
Miscellaneous	152nd Bde. No. NF/1 Appendix 2	25/04/1918	25/04/1918
Operation(al) Order(s)	152nd Bde. R.F.A. Order No. 4 Appendix 3	25/04/1918	25/04/1918
Operation(al) Order(s)	152nd Bde. R.F.A. Order No. 6 Appendix 4	26/04/1918	26/04/1918
Operation(al) Order(s)	152nd Bde. R.F.A. Order No. 9 Appendix 5	28/04/1918	28/04/1918
War Diary	Le Tir. Anglais	01/05/1918	08/05/1918
War Diary	Wittes	09/05/1918	16/05/1918
War Diary	Le Parc	17/05/1918	31/05/1918
Diagram etc	Sheet 30 A 1/10,000		
Operation(al) Order(s)	152 Bde Order No. 15 Appendix No. 1	04/05/1918	04/05/1918
Miscellaneous	152nd Bde. R.F.A. Order No. 14/1. Reference 152nd. Bde. R.F.A. Order No. 14 Attached.	04/05/1918	04/05/1918
Operation(al) Order(s)	152nd Bde. R.F.A. Order No. 14 Appendix 2	03/05/1918	03/05/1918
Miscellaneous	Left Group Order No. 1. Reference 5th Divl. Arty. No. HBM/15/24 Appendix 3	16/05/1918	16/05/1918
Miscellaneous	Left Group Order No. 5 Reference 5th D.A. Order No. 176 Appendix 4	19/05/1918	19/05/1918
War Diary	Le Parc	01/06/1918	03/07/1918
War Diary	On The March	04/07/1918	05/07/1918
War Diary	Houtkerque	06/07/1918	14/07/1918
War Diary	On The March	15/07/1918	18/07/1918
War Diary	Vemars	19/07/1918	19/07/1918
War Diary	On The March	20/07/1918	22/07/1918
War Diary	Vierzy	23/07/1918	27/07/1918
War Diary	Buisson de Hautwison	28/07/1918	28/07/1918
War Diary	Bois St Hilaire	29/07/1918	31/07/1918
War Diary	Oulchy La Ville	01/08/1918	01/08/1918
War Diary	Bois Monceau	02/08/1918	06/08/1918
War Diary	Droglandt	07/08/1918	12/08/1918
War Diary	Handekot	13/08/1918	22/08/1918
War Diary	Ypres	23/08/1918	31/08/1918
Operation(al) Order(s)	Right Artillery Brigade Operation Order No. 4 Appendix 1	31/08/1918	31/08/1918
War Diary	Ypres Sector	01/09/1918	01/09/1918
War Diary	Dickebusch Sector	02/09/1918	06/09/1918
War Diary	Dickebusch	07/09/1918	29/09/1918

Type	Description	Start	End
War Diary	Dickebusch Sector	29/09/1918	30/09/1918
Operation(al) Order(s)	Left Artily Brigade Operation Order No. 10 Appendix No. 1	07/09/1918	07/09/1918
Operation(al) Order(s)	Left Group Operation Order No. 12 Appendix No. 2	09/09/1918	09/09/1918
Operation(al) Order(s)	152nd Brigade R.F.A. Operation Order No. 19 Appendix No.3	26/09/1918	26/09/1918
Miscellaneous	Issued With 152nd Brigade O.O. No. 19. Programme Of Fire WIth Incendiary Shell Table "A"		
Miscellaneous	Issued With 152nd Bde R.F.A. O.O. No. 19. Programme Of Fire In Support Of Infantry Advance By Day.		
Miscellaneous	Addenda to 152nd Brigade R.F.A. O.O. No. 19	27/09/1918	27/09/1918
War Diary	Section Wervicq	01/10/1918	14/10/1918
War Diary	Sector Menin	15/10/1918	16/10/1918
War Diary	Wevelghem	17/10/1918	18/10/1918
War Diary	Belleghem	19/10/1918	20/10/1918
War Diary	Rolleghem	21/10/1918	23/10/1918
War Diary	Sector Rolleghem	24/10/1918	24/10/1918
War Diary	Moen	25/10/1918	25/10/1918
War Diary	Eelbeke	26/10/1918	27/10/1918
War Diary	Deerlyck Vichte	28/10/1918	31/10/1918
Operation(al) Order(s)	152 Brigade R.F.A. Operation Order No. 20	01/10/1918	01/10/1918
Operation(al) Order(s)	152nd Brigade. RFA Operation Order No. 21	02/10/1918	02/10/1918
Operation(al) Order(s)	152nd Brigade. RFA Operation Order No. 27	11/10/1918	11/10/1918
Operation(al) Order(s)	152nd Brigade R.F.A. Operation Order No. 29	12/10/1918	12/10/1918
Miscellaneous	Addenda No. 3 To 152nd Brigade R.F.A. O.O. No. 28	13/10/1918	13/10/1918
Operation(al) Order(s)	152nd Brigade R.F.A. Operation Order No. 28	12/10/1918	12/10/1918
Miscellaneous	Addenda No. 1 To 152nd Brigade R.F.A. Operation Order No. 28	12/10/1918	12/10/1918
Miscellaneous	Addendum No. 2 To 152nd Brigade R.F.A. Operation Order No. 28	12/10/1918	12/10/1918
Operation(al) Order(s)	152nd Brigade R.F.A. Operation Order No. 34	23/10/1918	23/10/1918
Operation(al) Order(s)	152nd Brigade R.F.A. Operation Order No. 35	24/10/1918	24/10/1918
Operation(al) Order(s) Miscellaneous	152nd Brigade R.F.A. Operation Order No. 37	26/10/1918	26/10/1918
Operation(al) Order(s)	152nd Brigade R.F.A. Operation Order No. 39	30/10/1918	30/10/1918
Miscellaneous	152nd Brigade R.F.A. Instructions No. 1	30/10/1918	30/10/1918
War Diary	Sector Ingoyghem	01/11/1918	03/11/1918
War Diary	Menin (Wevelghem)	04/11/1918	07/11/1918
War Diary	Deerlyk	08/11/1918	11/11/1918
War Diary	Menin (Wevelghem)	12/11/1918	15/11/1918
War Diary	St Genois	16/11/1918	16/11/1918
War Diary	Arc Ainieres	17/11/1918	18/11/1918
War Diary	Oeudechien	19/11/1918	11/12/1918
War Diary	Ollignies	12/12/1918	13/12/1918
War Diary	Thoricourt	14/12/1918	15/12/1918
War Diary	La Louviere	16/12/1918	16/12/1918
War Diary	Courcelles	17/12/1918	17/12/1918
War Diary	Pont De Loup	18/12/1918	18/12/1918
War Diary	Franiere	19/12/1918	31/12/1918
War Diary		01/02/1919	28/02/1919
War Diary	Seigburg	22/03/1919	19/05/1919
War Diary	Troisdorf	21/05/1919	21/05/1919
War Diary		04/05/1919	28/05/1919
War Diary		07/05/1919	28/05/1919
War Diary		12/05/1919	18/05/1919

War Diary		03/05/1919	25/05/1919
War Diary	Siegburg	19/05/1919	19/05/1919
War Diary	Hennef	23/05/1919	30/05/1919
War Diary	Siegburg	02/06/1919	14/06/1919
War Diary	Hennef	24/06/1919	24/06/1919
War Diary	Siegburg	01/07/1919	07/07/1919
War Diary	Wahn	08/07/1919	17/07/1919
War Diary	Siegburg	18/07/1919	31/07/1919

WO 95/24453

34TH DIVISION

152ND BRIGADE R.F.A.
JAN 1916 – ~~DEC 1918~~
1919 TLS

Army Form C. 2118.

WAR DIARY
or
INTELLIGENCE SUMMARY.
(Erase heading not required.)

Instructions regarding War Diaries and Intelligence Summaries are contained in F. S. Regs., Part II. and the Staff Manual respectively. Title pages will be prepared in manuscript.

Place	Date	Hour	Summary of Events and Information	Remarks and references to Appendices
LYNDE	FEB 1st		Brigade inspected in billets area by Major General WILLIAMS Comdg 34th Divn, who expressed himself as satisfied with the appearance of horses - men - billets generally.	
"	2nd 3rd		Training & recreation continued.	
	4th		Bde returned from forward area. Officers & NCOs instructed to forward area (2.3.Div)	
	7th		Training, instruction & harness cleaning continued.	
	8th		C.O. 152nd Brigade inspected Bde on marching order.	
	9th		One section each of A. & B. Batteries proceeded to forward area, employed at forward by 2.3.Divn	
			2nd Lieut R.F.R. Allen returned from two first + back to 152 B.C.	
	10.		(C.O. 152 wd. proceeded to forward area	
	11.		Remaining sections of A + B Batteries proceeded to forward area. Lt. Battery inspected by LORD KITCHENER. G.O.C. R.A. 34th Divn W. MAJOR FLD. my Head not turned out.	
	12.		A. + B. Batteries returned at 9 p.m. Dinners 3.6. M.W. 7.30 a.m.s + A.3.3. 4.5.3. Lieut W.MAC. JOHNSTONE R.F.A	
	14.3rd		Training in vicinity of LYNDE for following three weeks two	
	15.F.		One section of H.K.C + D Bty proceeded to reserve line of Bde of 108th Bd. R.F.A. 23rd D.W.	
			which they are to relieve	
	16.F.		Bde Amm Col proceeded to forward area and took over rear pitch G.5.a. 10.8	

2353 Wt. W2544/1454 700,000 5/15 D. D. & L. A.D.S.S. Forms/C 2118.

Army Form C. 2118

WAR DIARY
or
INTELLIGENCE SUMMARY
(Erase heading not required.)

Instructions regarding War Diaries and Intelligence Summaries are contained in F.S. Regs., Part II. and the Staff Manual respectively. Title Pages will be prepared in manuscript.

Place	Date	Hour	Summary of Events and Information	Remarks and references to Appendices
LYNDE	17th		Remaining Section of C & D Bty proceeded to wagon lines at Bellerui which they relieve Bde Hd Qrs moved to wagon line of "B" Bty 152nd Bde.	
GRIS POT	18th		Very quiet day - no observation possible on account of mist - heavy rain started in afternoon	
"	19		Took over at 10 am from 103rd Bde R.F.A. - Quiet day. Observation very bad owing to mist and rain - Our Field Bty fired 29 rounds. Enemy fired a few rds to keep in the swing and a number of 4.2 hows shells into BOIS GRENIER line to damage being done. Weather very bad.	
"	20th		Fine clear morning after cold night. Wind N.N.E. - Enemy aeroplanes on our needs nearly all the day, which hampered our firing - Enemy Artillery active against BOIS GRENIER and 47 Bty Wind N.N.E.	
"	21st		"B" Bty wagon lines Enemy shelled BOIS GRENIER line and an O.P. in nearly heavily in morning. Fine day - he retaliated on enemy front trenches & strongpoint or selected pont in our lines in morning and afternoon. Enemy causing one man slightly wounded. carrying of hicks to "B" Bty O.P Wind N.E	
"	22nd		Fine in early morning, but clouded over about 9 am and snowed till 1 pm. Fine afternoon Lt NEAKLIAM admitted to hospital - Wind N N E	
"	23rd		Snow all day, nothing of interest importance. Wind N.N.E.	
"	24		2/L RANSON posted to B.Bty vice 2/L JOHNSTONE killed - was admitted to hospital GOC 34 Divison took over command of front from G.O.C. 23rd Div. little activity False Gas alarm at night	

1875 W. W593/826 1,000,000 4/15 J.B.C. & A. A.D.S.S./Forms/C. 2118.

WAR DIARY or INTELLIGENCE SUMMARY

Army Form C. 2118

Place	Date	Hour	Summary of Events and Information	Remarks and references to Appendices
GRIS POT	25.15		2/Lr MILLIGAN joined and posted temporarily to "B" By. Hard frost, bak light & snow rendering operations almost impossible. Little activity on either side. Wind NNE	
"	26th		Very quiet day - hard light. False gas alarm at night. "A" By 16 o firing some 20 rounds	
"	27th		G.O.C. 34th next round gun position in morning. "B" 160 shelled during morning but no damage done. Enemy Artillery somewhat more active firing about 100 shells chiefly 77 -	
"	28.15		A very quiet day - day is very hot for observation. Only few rounds fired by enemy and ourselves. Wind ESE. Barr 29.38	
"	29.		Aeroplanes very active. Enemy Artillery somewhat active in our area - especially in afternoon when they fired about 100 5.9 shells at 8" Howr which had been shooting at a cupola in German front trenches about I.26.c.7½.2. Our Batteries reported a good many hostile Battns 2nd Ammo Dt Schrt LIETTRES (bullet flight) C B5 . Gr SHORTHOSE left for 1st Army 2nd Schrt LIETTRES (bullet flight) C B5. Gr HEPPENSTAAL wounded. General fin under Since taking over place in line Battery has been very busy improving their position registering targets & reconnoitring alternative positions for them	

K. Kincaid ... Maj RJA
Comdg 1st ? Bde RJA

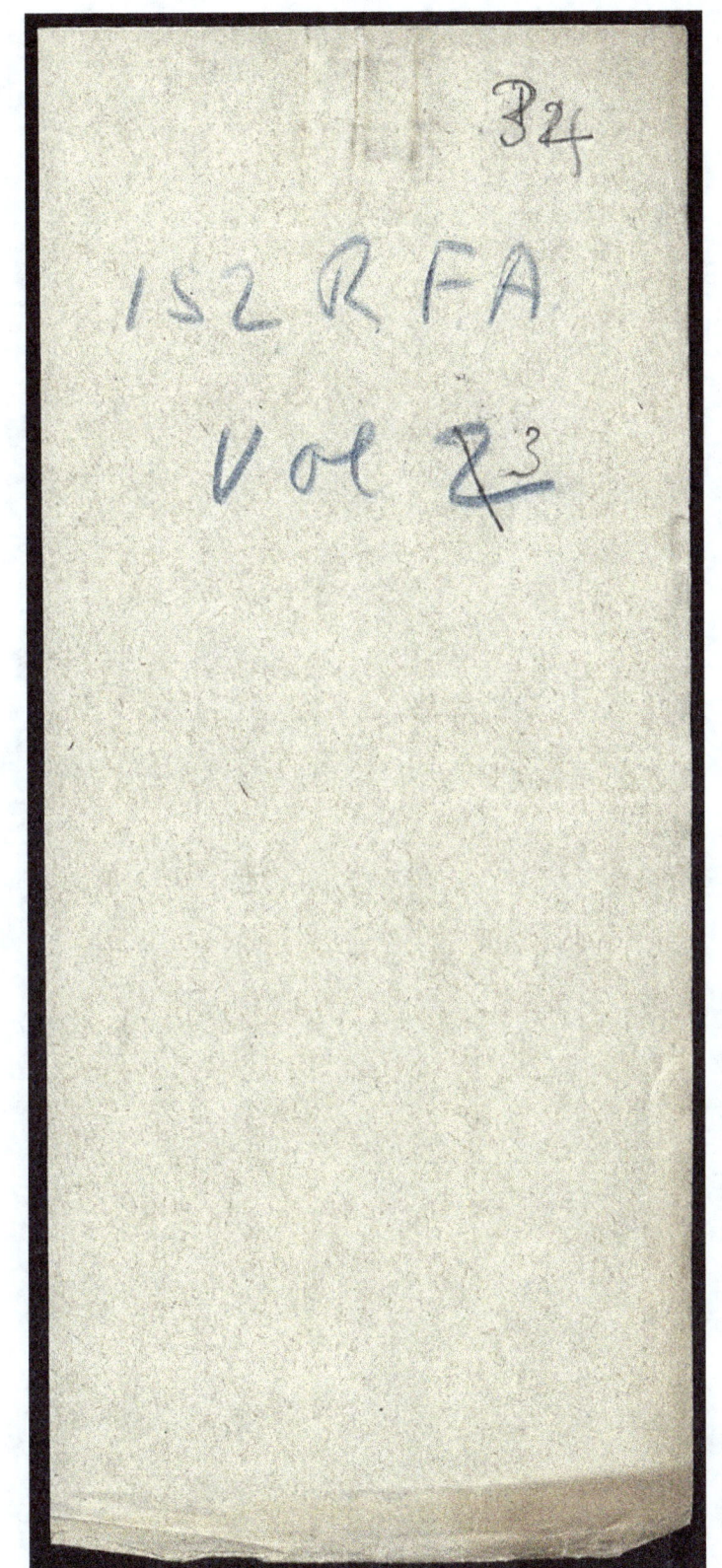

324

152 RFA

Vol 3

WAR DIARY

Army Form C. 2118

INTELLIGENCE SUMMARY

(Erase heading not required.)

152nd Bde.   R.F.A.

Place	Date March	Hour	Summary of Events and Information	Remarks and references to Appendices
GRIS POT.	1st		Fine day. Wind ESE - "B" 160 fired 20 rds. harrassing scheme, at enemy screen. "D" also. I 32 C 7.1 - Inf. Bde M.G's having been laid on tgts. with care &c - Direct hit on screen was obtained. Little enemy artillery activity. Signalling class started under 2/Lt MALTBY, B.A.C.	
GRIS POT.	2nd		A changeable day, falling barometer. Light not very good in morning but improved later. G.O.C. 34th Div. visited Bde Hd Qrs. Enemy artillery fired on 4 small batches of shells. On it were a quiet day. Own artillery was quiet & registered a few rounds. 2 large working parties were seen for a short time about J.31.C.5.5 & were dispersed by 176 Bde. C.O. attended conference of Group Commanders. Lieut. GARNETT & 2/Lt CHADWICK joined for 10 days course. No aeroplanes seen.	
GRIS POT.	3rd		Misty in morning with HE. wind. Enemy Artillery quiet & only fired a few shells in small areas excepting 30 firrd at MOAT FARM + vicinity "B" Bde 15.2 Bde retaliated on enemy trenches opposite I 31.d. "C" Bde cut wire in I 27.d.4.7. making an appreciable gap. 2/Lt RAWSON w/joined. 2/Lt FERNIE joined & posted to A. By from hospital.	
GRIS POT.	4th		Heavy snow all morning with a fairly strong N. wind. Very cold. Cleared up about 2.15'6pm when light improved. In morning "B" Batterie fire at third concentrating of Inf. in points selected by C.C. Enemy artillery very quiet until about 4.30.pm when they fired a few rounds. "B/152 registered on enemy's bomb. about O.I.a.2.7., "D"35 at I.d.4.3. & fired further rounds I.31.H. Fine morning but light not good at c/152 cut wire. B registered 3 bombs on enemy's barget + D retaliated at request of infantry. Enemy artillery quiet. Casualties Sergt Worrill killed & Sergt Law & the Spencer wounded (all 9 exclusively at A BW).	
GRIS POT.	6th		Heavy snow during night & morning. Lory. Light very bad. Enemy's balloons up morning + afternoon. Enemy very quiet. a B/152 cut wire in B Bdy tract machine gun emplacement obtained direct hit.	
GRIS POT.	7.		Snow during night + snow still showers during day. C. Howitzers was Successful in knocking down 6 foot light &/152 cut wire in front of I 31.d. 6.6. Result good. Enemy very quiet.	

Army Form C. 2118

WAR DIARY
or
INTELLIGENCE SUMMARY
(Erase heading not required.)

Instructions regarding War Diaries and Intelligence Summaries are contained in F. S. Regs., Part II. and the Staff Manual respectively. Title Pages will be prepared in manuscript.

Place	Date MARCH	Hour	Summary of Events and Information	Remarks and references to Appendices
GRIS POT.	8.		A fine day after heavy snow during night. Light had fell 10-30am. Wright Group Scheme A carried out, result successful. C/152 cut wire at I.26.d.5.7. B/160 at I.26.2.3.5. D/152 searched communication trench I.24.c.9.5. attached to I.24.c.2.4. D/146 destroyed tap from I.26.b.4.0.— A Enemy's Artillery quiet. Enemy's aeroplanes active. Conferences of Bde commanders at 152 Bde Hd. Qrs. Bde. Gen. Ruby present.	Scheme A attached.
"	9.		A fine day after hard frost during night. Light Rad. Enemy's quiet but but about 6.0, a 2 hrs. men return on Rue de CHARLES. no damage. A/152 cut wire. B.5 cut wire. F.B.4 cut a post opposite men return in O11 cu. 8. A.B cut wire (Middlesex). Light very bad & things generally quiet. A/146 cut a battn trench in O11 cu.8. A.B cut wire (Middlesex). Light very bad & observation very difficult. Right section of A.B4 enfiladed trenches for left troops (I.22a.5.9.) B.C. cut wire at I.31.C.9.5.1½. C. enlarged breach in enemy parapet at I.26.d.3.5. Enemy fairly quiet.	
"	10.			
"	11.			
"	12.		A fine day. Enemy's artillery much more active. Bois GRENIER & vicinity freely shelled. Retaliation carried out. B.By dispersed Boys working party & obtained direct hits on buildings in which they take cover.	
"	13.		A fine morning but light bad in early part of day. Enemy Artillery more active & fired a good many shells into BOIS GRENIER & vicinity & SHAFTESBURY AVENUE. "A" By cooperated with LEFT GROUP in enfilading trenches. "C" B4 enlarged gap in parapet at I.26.d.3.5.	
"	14.		A fine day & light good especially during afternoon. Enemy fairly active with Artillery & aeroplanes but no damage caused. Our batteries retaliated when asked.	
"	15.		A beautiful day. "B" By by bombardment & killed heavily bombarded & badly knocked about. Enemy's aeroplanes very active also. Casualties. Sergt Howells (A.B4) & G. EDWARDS (B.B4) wounded.	
"	16.		Light very good all day but everything fairly quiet until the reception of hostile aircraft which two Enemy Batteries in this group only fired S.O.S. Tests on receipt of hostility flights with satisfactory results.	
"	17.		A fine day but very quiet. That unga power laye which was shown as difficult. A.By Retaliated F...... to	

1875. Wt. W593/826 1,000,000 4/15 J.B.C. & A. A.D.S.S./Forms/C. 2118.

WAR DIARY
INTELLIGENCE SUMMARY
(Erase heading not required.)

Army Form C. 2118

Instructions regarding War Diaries and Intelligence Summaries are contained in F. S. Regs., Part II. and the Staff Manual respectively. Title Pages will be prepared in manuscript.

Place	Date	Hour	Summary of Events and Information	Remarks and references to Appendices
GRIS POT.	18	—	An exceptionally quiet day. Light very good. "C" & "D" B/152 registered Turplio guns by aeroplane. Enemy's artillery quiet in this area. A co CA aeroplane very busy.	
"	19	"	A beautiful day but quiet. B/152 successfully registered on target guns by aeroplane. Enemy's artillery active on friends & Savoy. Killed 118 R.F.A. without causing damage.	
"	20	"	Very little to report. 2 & 3 Howitzer Batteries attached to this group. A certain amount of retaliation was asked for by Infantry. "A" & "B" Bty replied.	
"	21	"	Very misty & observation impossible except from front line trenches. C" Bty 152. fired on enemy wire. Captain D. Liggan. C/152 killed.	
"	22	"	Thick & misty all day & observation almost impossible. Practically nothing doing. "A" Bty only fired a few rounds. C.O. attended conference of Group commanders at 11.96. Hd Qs Q/152 & B/160 fired a few rounds.	
"	23	"	A very cold day. Exceptionally quiet. Batteries fired a few rounds in retaliation or in support of infantry. Heavy snow during most of the day which made observation impossible. Quiet.	
"	24	"	Schems B carried out with good results. There was no retaliation. Very cold day.	Schems B. attached.
"	25	"	Fine day, gunshop but very quiet. The Cenbra group was differently attacked & A/108 B/160 Left A Groups. A/152 received position marked by B/160. C/152 night section beat own A/152 emplacement in return.	
"	26	"	B/62 took new position evacuated by B/160. They were relieved by 77 mm. batting with a burst then killed & did other damage. Batteries concentrated on I. 33. T. Q. 42. with satisfactory results. One battery did a little shooting & C/152 successfully strafed my outposts firing a comb tower which was recognised. A watenkilly inactive day though much more argument was observed on the East of the enemy. A + C Btys/152 only fired a few rounds.	
"	27	"		

Army Form C. 2118

WAR DIARY
or
INTELLIGENCE SUMMARY
(Erase heading not required.)

Instructions regarding War Diaries and Intelligence Summaries are contained in F. S. Regs., Part II. and the Staff Manual respectively. Title Pages will be prepared in manuscript.

Place	Date	Hour	Summary of Events and Information	Remarks and references to Appendices
G.R.is Pot	29	-	A fine day but light not good in the early part of the day. Enemy's artillery was more active on front line trenches. Several times over retaliation had the desired effect – stopping the enemy's fire. B/51 charged R section of Ammunition position.	
G.Ris. Pot	30	-	Light my [?] all day. A lot of movement observed but not much doing. Enemy's observation balloons busy. Our retaliation fire[?] effective.	
"	31	-	Still a lot of movement seen behind enemy's lines but not a great deal of hostile shelling in this area – though on right a battery fired now was being shelled Our batteries busy, retaliation requested. C/152. Breastwork brought at point where suspected M.G. was.	

R. Macintosh? Lt. Col. R.A.
Comdg 152 Bde R.A.

1875 Wt. W593/826 1,000,000 4/15 J.B.C. & A. A.D.S.S./Forms/C. 2118.

152 RFA

Army Form C. 2118

XXXIV

WAR DIARY
or
INTELLIGENCE SUMMARY
(Erase heading not required.)

Instructions regarding War Diaries and Intelligence Summaries are contained in F. S. Regs., Part II. and the Staff Manual respectively. Title Pages will be prepared in manuscript.

Place	Date April	Hour	Summary of Events and Information	Remarks and references to Appendices
GRISPOT	1.4.16		A very fine day & considerable activity on both sides. Scheme "B" was carried out successfully in conjunction with Infantry (103). All batteries were busy & a good deal of retaliation was required. Enemy shelled BOIS GRENIER pretty heavily during evening. No damage reported	SCHEME B attached.
"	2.4.16		A fine day but owing to a ground fog a light "A" & "B" & "D" batteries fired a few rounds only in retaliation & registering. On the whole a very quiet day.	
"	3.4.16		A fine day but very quiet on part of Enemy's Artillery. Our batteries fired 163 rounds in retaliation for activity on front line trenches & registering.	
"	4.4.16		A very dull day with bad light & quiet in consequence. C.O. 4 B4 commander of 1st Australian Bde arrived & arranged to take over.	
"	5.4.16		Fine day but hazy. Scheme C. successfully carried out. Considerable damage was done and an occupied house at LE QUESNE was set on fire. Enemy shelled BOIS GRENIER pretty heavily in evening. Our batteries effectively replied. Sergt MOSELEY B.Bty wounded.	SCHEME C attached.
"	6.4.16		Light very bad all day which was quiet in consequence. L. BRADLEY, "A" Bty wounded.	
"	7.4.16		Light very bad. Altogether an extraordinary quiet day.	
"	8.4.16		Fine day. Enemy artillery more active during day and again between 8.30–9 pm. Our batteries effectively retaliated "B" Bty had good results on firing at working party.	
"	9.4.16		One section of each Battery moved to LYNDE & 1 section of 11, 17, 18, 12, Bgs. F.A.A.I.F. took over. A fairly quiet day but Enemy got away in evening round BOIS GRENIER.	
LYNDE	10.4.16		Remainder of Brigade moved to LYNDE, which was reached in good time & without any casualty.	
"	11.4.16		Battery exercise, cleaning & overhauling harness & transport.	

Army Form C. 2118

WAR DIARY
or
INTELLIGENCE SUMMARY
(Erase heading not required.)

Instructions regarding War Diaries and Intelligence Summaries are contained in F.S. Regs., Part II. and the Staff Manual respectively. Title Pages will be prepared in manuscript.

Place	Date	Hour	Summary of Events and Information	Remarks and references to Appendices
SEZQUES	12.4.16		Moved to reserve area at SEZQUES. Very wet & cold. Good turn out & Brigade moved in without casualty & in good time.	
"	13.4.16		Battery Spring training commenced.	
"	14.4.16 to 30.4.16		Battery & Brigade training continued. On 24 & 30 April Divisional attack as per Operation order 100 in conjunction with 101, 102, 103 Infantry Brigades.	

P Stewart.
Lieut.
[stamp]

30.4.16.

Right Group Orders (Scheme A) + Scheme A by G.O.C. 103 Inf Bde in consultation with O.C. Right Group.

March 8th 1916.

1. Three 18 pounder Batteries to cut gaps in enemy's wire between I.26.b.7.0 + I.26.d.3.5. Three gaps could probably be cut.

2. One howitzer Battery to devote its attention to the sap running out towards our line from point I.26.b.7.0.

3. One 18 pounder Battery to fire at the communication trench between I.27.c.7½.½ to I.27.c.2.4.

4. One 4.7 Battery to stand by for counter Battery work.

5. Machine Guns from parapet, + others giving overhead fire, to play on gaps during night.

Right Group Orders (Scheme A)

Reference Scheme "A" by G.O.C. 101st Inf Bde.

Tasks. 1. The following tasks are allotted to Batteries of Right Group.

  A. Wire Cutting.

   C. 152 to cut a lane in enemy's wire at I.26.b.7.0.
   B. 160   "   "   "   "   "   "   "   I.26.d.5.7.
   A. 160   "   "   "   "   "   "   "   I.26.d.3.5.

   Ammunition 55 A + 5 AX per Battery

  B. D. 152 to search communication trench with Shrapnel between I.27.c.7½.½ and I.27.c.2.4.

  C. D. 176. to destroy sap running towards our line from point I.26.b.7.0.

  D. 118 Bty. R.G.A. will stand by ready for counter Battery work.

2. Firing to commence at 11.30 a.m. if observation is practicable but Right Group will telephone to Units concerned at 11.15 a.m. in any case, confirming or otherwise, the time at which firing is to commence.

SECRET   Copy No 12

Centre Group Operations Order No 4

1. "A" and "B" Batteries 160 Bde R.F.A. and "A" Bty 175 Bde R.F.A. will be withdrawn from Centre Group on night 25th/26th and 26th/27th in accordance with orders issued by R.A. Headquarters.

2. In consequence of the above the following moves will take place:

   (a) "A" Bty 152 Bde will take over the position at present occupied by "A" Bty 160 Bde, as follows:

   Bty Hdqurs and Left Section on night of 25th/26th.

   Right Section   "   "   26th/27th.

   (B) "C" Bty 152 Bde will send Section to relieve Right Section of "A" Bty 152 Bde on night of 26th/27th.

3. Moves to commence at 7.15 p.m. each evening.

4. <u>Ammunition:</u>

   "A" & "B" Btys 160 Bde will take all ammunition in gun positions with them.

   "A" Bty 152 Bde will therefore arrange to transfer to its new position all ammunition at present kept in gun positions.

5. The front will be covered as follows on completion of moves:

   "B" Bty 152 Bde.   I31.1 & I31.2.

   "D"   "   "   I31.3, I31.4, & I31.5.

   "A"   "   "   I32.1, I26.1, & I26.2.

   "C"   "   "   Right Section. Enfilading Section.

                            Left   "   I26.3 & I26.4.

   D   "   176   To cover whole front.

6. All existing Telephone lines will be left as they are at present from the positions which will become vacant and caretakers will be provided by Batteries to occupy the Telephone dug-outs as follows:

   "A" Bty 152 Bde will provide caretakers for position evacuated by B 160.

   "C"   -   -   -   -   -   -   -   -   -   -   -   -   - A 152.

7. Acknowledge.

                                               P. Stewart.   Lieut & Adjutant
                                                                  Centre Group.

Copies to:

No 1   File
   2   A 152 Bde
   3   B "   "
   4   C "   "
   5   D "   "
   6   A 160 "
   7   B "   "
   8   A 176 "
   9   D "   "
10 to 12 spare.

WAR DIARY or INTELLIGENCE SUMMARY

Army Form C. 2118

152 Bde R.F.A. Vol 4

Place	Date	Hour	Summary of Events and Information	Remarks and references to Appendices
SECQUES	MAY 1st		Operation order No 9 received for move (May 1st), Bde Training	
	2nd		Operation order No 100 repeated with infantry	
	3rd 4th		Battery training continues.	
	4 + 5		Brigade entrained at Dieppe for forward area, detrained at Longeau & billeted at BEHENCOURT. Bde HQs followed the next day, billeting at BEHENCOURT night 6/7	
	6		Batteries moved into forward area into wagon lines E.16.d near ALBERT. Operations order No 7 issued.	
	8th 16th		Batteries preparing Gun Positions & O.P.s	
	16th		G.H.Q letter No O.B.818 carried out. Amalgamation of B.A.C.s into D.A.C.	Appendix attached
	17th & 21st		Batteries preparing Gun Positions & O.P.s	
	21st		2/Lieut A.W. BAXTER evacuated to Hospital to undergo operation for Appendicitis	Div Arty Order 117/2
	22nd		G.H.Q letter No O.B.818 carried out. A/152 becomes A/146, D/152 becomes A/146, C/146 (Howitzer) becomes D/152, D/152 Remain in action at W.29.a.y.2. (Shot S4°S.E) under Lt Stevenson attached Left Group	
			Capt H.H. BADELEY, Lieut G. HOWITT, 2/Lieut J.R BUDD, 2/Lieut D.WALLIS & 2/Lieut G. FERNIE posted from A/152 to A/146. Capt P.H. FERGUSON, Lieut E.H GREEN, 2/Lieut P.W. LAURIE, G.W MEAKIN, H.W PULFREYMAN were taken on Strength from C/146 & posted to D/152. G/322 received re move to BEHENCOURT.	
	23rd 24th		Work on Gun Positions + O.P.s	
	25		G/322 carried out Tony LL A,B + C Btys moved into billets at BEHENCOURT. Details left behind to carry on work on gun pits etc firing practice on the 28th ready to commence	
	26 - 27		Div Memo No 934/9 received under scheme. Batteries carried out drill in the full	
	24th		Bde H.Q moved into BEHENCOURT	
	28		A & B Btys carried out firing practice in the field 6am to 8am. CRA present	
	29th		2/Lieut D.N. SHORTHOSE posted to V/34 Heavy Trench Mortar Bty	
	30nd		B + C Btys carried out firing practice between 6am & 8am. Brigadier Gen. Kirby, C.R.A present	
	31st		A + C Btys carried out firing practice in the field 6am to 8am. CRA present A,B + C Btys + Bde H.Q. Sig O carried out inf action as a brigade. C.R.A. present	

K. Minchin Lt Col
2.6.16
Cmdg 152 Bde RFA

Officer Commanding
152 Brigade R.F.A.   34th Divn R.A. 1172/A.

1. G.H.Q. Letter O.B/813 directs that the Divl Artly is to be re-organized as follows.

   A. One Howitzer Battery will be substituted for one 18 pdr. Battery in each of the 18 pdr Brigades.

   B. The three 18 pdr Batteries thus displaced will form the fourth Brigade under the former How Bde H.Q.

2. To give effect to the above scheme, Batteries will be transferred and re-numbered as follows.

   a. | Battery | Transferred to |
       |---------|----------------|
       | A. 176. | 160 4th Bde. |
       | C. 176. | 152 nd Bde. |
       | D. 176. | 175 th Bde. |
       | A. 152. | 176 th. Bde. |
       | B. 160. | - do - |
       | C. 175. | - do - |

   b. | Battery | New Designation |
       |---------|-----------------|
       | A. 176. | D. 160. |
       | D. 160. | B. 160. |
       | C. 176. | D. 152. |
       | D. 152. | A. 152. |
       | D. 176. | D. 175. |
       | D. 175. | C. 175. |
       | A. 152. | A. 176. |
       | B. 160. | B. 176. |
       | C. 175. | C. 176. |

3. The above transfers and re-numberings will take effect from 11 a.m. 22nd inst.

4. Wagon lines will be changed accordingly. All Tarpaulins and Tents will be left standing.

5. No alterations in personnel or equipment are to be ma

R.A.H.Q.
19-5-16

(Sgd) A. Beal
Captain
Staff Captain R.A.
34 Division

SECRET.   31st Div Arty No 1131/A

O.C. 152 Bde. R.F.A.

1. The necessary changes in accordance with the attached
   G.H.Q. letter No. O.B. 818 will be carried out on 16th inst.
2. At 11 a.m. on that day the Officer Commanding 31st
   Divl Amm Coln. assumes command of the reconstructed
   Div Amm Col.
3. Before this date, Brigades will transfer the necessary
   personnel in Gunners, Drivers and horses to complete
   the Battery Establishments from their Bde Amm Col.
4. The Bde Amm Cols of the 152nd, 160th, & 175th
   F.A. Brigades will become Nos 1, 2 & 3 Sections
   respectively of "A" Echelon. No 2 Section Div Amm Col
   will form the nucleus of No 1 Section "B" Echelon.
   N.C.O's, men, horses and mules to bring "A" & "B" Echelons
   to establishment will be drawn from the 176th
   Bde Amm Col and Nos 1 and 3 Sections Divl Amm Col.
5. Captain. H. F. Barker. 175th Brigade Amm Col will
   command all Details remaining.
   Captain. W. P. Robertson will command No 3. Section.
6. A state showing residue of Officers, N.C.O's Artificers
   Gunners & Drivers, Animals and vehicles will be
   rendered to this Office on 21st instant.
7. All Ammunition will be retained.
8. Units will continue to occupy their present Billets.
9. Nos 1, 2, & 3 Sections will be affiliated to their
   former Brigades for Ammunition supply and in the
   event of a Brigade being detached, will follow
   their affiliated Brigade.
10. Acknowledge.

15.5.16.   (Sgd) A. Beal
                                              Captain
                                        Staff Captain R.A.
                                           31st Division

SECRET   Copy   G.H.Q. O.B. 818
                                                                163 (9)

4th Army.

         In continuation of G.H.Q. letter No O.B 818, of the 28th April, the following further measures of re-organisation in connection with the Divisional Artillery will be undertaken.

a. _____

b. <u>Re-organisation of the system of ammunition supply with the Division.</u>

       In order to meet the changed conditions consequent on the growth of the Army, & to provide an organization which will be more manageable and more economical than that at present existing, the Commander-in-chief has decided:-

a. to abolish the Brigade Ammunition Columns as such.

b. to re-constitute the Div Amm Columns in Divl Columns, of two echelons each, composed as follows.

Headquarters.

"A" Echelon, consisting of 3 sections (Nos 1, 2 & 3 sections)

"B"   "   "   "   1   "   (No 4 section)

The Headquarters and "A" Echelon are designed to accompany the Division closely at all times.

"B" Echelon will follow the Division if circumstances permit, but is detachable under Corps control when necessary.

       Tables showing the new War Establishment of a Divisional Ammunition Column are attached.

       This re-organization will be commenced forthwith, the surplus personnel, horses and vehicles, being disposed of under orders to be issued by the Adjutant General and Quartermaster General.

General Headquarters   (Sgd) R. Butler. M.G.
6th May. 1916.   for Lieut General
                                                           G.G.S.

Army Form C. 2118
JUNE
XXXIV /152 Bde RFA Vol 5

WAR DIARY
or
INTELLIGENCE SUMMARY
(Erase heading not required.)

Instructions regarding War Diaries and Intelligence Summaries are contained in F.S. Regs., Part II. and the Staff Manual respectively. Title Pages will be prepared in manuscript.

Place	Date	Hour	Summary of Events and Information	Remarks and references to Appendices
BEHENCOURT	1.6		No foreign practice – Officers attended a practice infantry attack, carried out by one Brigade	
"	2.6		8th Divn and one Brigade of the 34th Divn. Lieut P. STEVART (Adjt) struck off strength – (Sick in England) A.B.C Batteries carried out frame practice as a Brigade.	
"	3.6		2/Lt A.W. BAXTER "C" Bty struck off strength (app'd cdwh) – M.O proceeded on leave. A.B.C Bty carried out frame practice as Bde. D.152 Rt Sect relieved by D.175. A.B.C Bty carried out frame practice as Bde (6am–8am) relief of D.152 by D.175 completed	
"	4.6		A. B. C & D Bty carried out frame practice as Bde	
"	5.6		A. B. C. D Bty " " " " "	
"	6.6		A. B. C. D Bty " " " " " C.R.A present each day during fire practice Brigade moved up to began lines at VIVIER MILL after dark	
ALBERT	7.6		Capt. RAMSDEN (C.Bty) evacuated to CORBIE for dental treatment Bde employed on work at gun positions	
"	8.6		Batteries commence to dump ammunition at gun positions (1500 rds per gun)	
"	9.6		Operation Order No 8 partly carried out – Section of A B & C 152 Bde relieving Section of A B & C 160. Capt. RAMSDEN returned, owing to no cases in orders as preceding to have for dental treatment	

Army Form C. 2118

WAR DIARY
or
INTELLIGENCE SUMMARY
(Erase heading not required.)

Instructions regarding War Diaries and Intelligence Summaries are contained in F.S. Regs., Part II. and the Staff Manual respectively. Title Pages will be prepared in manuscript.

Place	Date	Hour	Summary of Events and Information	Remarks and references to Appendices
ALBERT	JUNE 11th		Operation Order No 8 complete.	
BELLEVUE FME	12th	9.30am	Bar 29.22. Ther 54. Wind N. 2nd Lt K. Kincaid-Smith took over command of Right Group from 2nd Lt WARRINGTON. Dull indifferent all day. Small group scheme carried out in conjunction with French Mission. Rt Sect D.152 relieved Rt Section D.175 - Quiet day.	
"	13th		BM/SP/ 14 - 15 + 17 received. Considerable movement of wagons seen opposite CONTALMAISON TROIS ARBRES - Enemy shelled OP's in area W2q d 5.5 at 6 am + 10 c.1 4 pm.	
"	14th		Bar 29.42 - Ther 55 - Wind W - BM/SP/20 recd. Small group scheme carried out with effective results, planks & hay thrown into own Clock advanced one hour at 11 p.m. Op. Order No. 9 received.	
"	15th		Bar 29.05 - Ther 59. Wind N.N.W. Small group scheme carried out satisfactorily, but failure in conjunction with French Mission postponed. Op. Order No 9 received, and no Section of A.B.C. relieved of Section of A.B.C. when of A.B.C. 16.0. Ber.	

Army Form C. 2118

WAR DIARY
or
INTELLIGENCE SUMMARY

/52 Bde RFA

(Erase heading not required.)

JUNE

Place	Date	Hour	Summary of Events and Information	Remarks and references to Appendices
AUBERT BELLEVUE FME	16th		Bar 29.12 Ther 58. Wind N.E. Enemy some what active. Relief of A.B.C. 152 by A.B.C. 160 completed. Guns of 152 Bde gone into positions held not for defence of line. 2/Lt A. B. CONLEY joined from D.A.C. + posted to "C" By.	
ALBERT	17th		Bde HQrs returned to 49 RUE BAPAUME in what of 160 Bde. Batteries commenced registration from new gun positions. Calibration of Ordn No 1 carried out. (Quadrant Inclination)	"A"
	18th		Work on new gun positions continued. - registration continued in afternoon. R.A. O.F. Ordn No 10 received and Cable for p of Ordn No 2 issued to Bdes.	
	19th		Appendices 5 to R.A. O.F. Ordn No 10 received - registration and work on new positions continued	
	20th		Registration + general work on new positions continued Lieut BELL transferred to Bde from D.A.C. and posted to "A" By Lieut BISHOP " " - DAC	
	21st		At Instructions No 1 & L.T.A. O.F. Ordn No 10 received. No 18 + Amendment No 1 Registration to work on gun pits continued	

Army Form C. 2118

WAR DIARY
INTELLIGENCE SUMMARY
(Erase heading not required.)

152 Bde RFA

Place	Date	Hour	Summary of Events and Information	Remarks and references to Appendices
ALBERT	22nd		At Ihebuhen. No q received, Appendix V and supplementary App V, New 1st Phase for Z day, Amendment for Z day received. Registration to continued. 2/Lieut. G.B. MILLIGAN transferred from B.E.C. & 2/Lieut CONLEY from C. GRNS. Centre Group OP Order No 3 issued to Btys, also instructions for U.V.W.X.Y.	"B" + "C"
"	23rd		At Ihebuhen 10 - 11 received - Batteries continued registration. C/152 new position shelled by 5.9 Hows. Several shots hit in underground passage entrance to detonator depot. Lieut HARVEY R.A. Signals wounded and sent home. Bde HQ An enemy anti-aircraft gun in forward position close to Batteries. Day nb. 20 ft Klm Summit. - Very hot night.	
			"U" day Preliminary bombardment commenced. Batteries completed registration and cut one throughout the day. Observation extremely difficult on account of haze, and ammunition to 8 pm full line being/greatly cut. Enemy fire weak. Casualties - Driver D.S.C. CREIGHTON wounded, also Sergt JAMES from C. Bty. Ammn expended from noon to 8 pm. 633A, 98AX, 338BX. Gas attack & raid ordered for the night but cancelled. A 176 came under orders of Centre Group. Centre Group Instruction received to BTYS.	"D"
N 30 a.9.0.	24th			

WAR DIARY or INTELLIGENCE SUMMARY

Army Form C. 2118

152 Bde R.F.A.

Place	Date	Hour	Summary of Events and Information	Remarks and references to Appendices
N30 a.9.0	25/6		**V day.** Fine day, observation good. V day instructions cannot out. Bm/SP/49 issued to Btys. Gas was entered for this night (V) but at late hour, was postponed. Ammn expended 8pm 24/6 to 12 noon 25/6 = 368 A, 165 Bx = 874 A, 353 AX, 398 BX } 152 Bde " " noon 25/6 to 8pm Two raids were attempted during the night, the enemy being found ready in "NO MANS LAND"	E
"	26/6		Copy arty Instructions 13. issued to Btys. **W day.** Weather changeable. General instruction for W day carried out. Difficulties were met carried out during special bombardment, but the Salvoes much interfered with by French Mortar fire. Enemy Artillery more active. Ammn expended 8pm 25/6 to 12 noon 26/6 = 543 A, 570 AX, 428 BX } 152 Bde " " noon 26/6 to 8pm = 757 A, 11 AX, 603 BX	F
"	27/6		**X day.** Weather fair. General instructions for X day carried out. Special "K" bombardment carried out Zero time being 10pm, effect good, as enemy extremely heavy upon the Capt BAXTER A.176 wounded left arm, leg, and down the side whilst observing from front trench, and Gnr MILLER (slightly) at forward gun position. Ammn expended 8pm 26/6 – 12 noon 27/6 1448 A, 307 AX, 230 BX. " " 12 (noon) 27 – 8 pm 1302 A, 679 AX, 302 BX Following amendments received. Nos. 2 & 3 R & F Order No 10.	

Army Form C. 2118

WAR DIARY
or
INTELLIGENCE SUMMARY
(Erase heading not required.)

152 Bde R 7a

Instructions regarding War Diaries and Intelligence Summaries are contained in F.S. Regs., Part II. and the Staff Manual respectively. Title Pages will be prepared in manuscript.

JUNE

Place	Date	Hour	Summary of Events and Information	Remarks and references to Appendices
W30a.9.0	28th		"Y" day Weather rainy in morning, but improved in afternoon. General instruction for Y day carried out. – Z day postponed for 48 hours. Enemy fire somewhat more brisk, chiefly against front line trenches. Guns shew distinct signs of wear, chief defects being buffer springs and spring cases. Ammn expended 8pm 27th – 12noon 28th = 1012 A, 443 AX, 411 BX " " " " 8pm " = 1427 A', 45 AX, 379 BX.	
"	29th		"Y1" day Weather fine and observation good. General work in wire cutting carried out. + Special bombardment At Inst No18 19 received – Appendix VI & Art Op Order No10 received + issued to Btys. "G" + "H" Gen Sir H GOUGH & B.Gen STRONG visited our gun positions Gas enlarged about X21a2.9.1 Ammn expended 8pm 28 – 12noon 29 15 = 907 A, 13 AX, 248 BX " " " " 8pm 30 15 = 965 A, 446AX, 487 BX Enemy fire considerably heavier than on preceding days. Wire in enemy front line very difficult to cut in places, especially about X20a.0.5 to X20a.4.3. Orders (Centre Group) for raid issued to Btys	"I"

WAR DIARY
INTELLIGENCE SUMMARY

152 Bde. RFA

Army Form C. 2118

Place	Date	Hour	Summary of Events and Information	Remarks and references to Appendices
W20d.9.0	JUNE 30.	"Y2" day.	Fine morning. Patrols which went out during the night found wire very strong still, abt. X20 a.0.5 & X20 a 4.5. 2.18 pm Ballières and 4.5 How Bty shortling their attention to this throughout day. Many Lachrymating shells in TARA VALLEY, effects of which disbwith fell in M.Q. for day out. Enemy retaliation on BECOURT WOOD at front line very heavy at times throughout the day. Special Order of the day from 34th Division - expressing the satisfaction of the Army and Corps Comdr with the Division 30.6.16.	

R. Kincaid Smith Lt Col RFA
Comdg 152 Bde RFA

"A"

Operation Order No 4.   SECRET

Centre Group Orders for "Z" day

Operation Order No 2 is cancelled & should be returned.
1. Zero time will be notified later. In all probability it will be after daylight.
2. There will be eight phases as follows:—

1st PHASE.	2. 18 pdr. Btys.	Front Line.
	A+C, 152.	X.20.a.8.3 — X.20.b.2.5.
		Communication Trenches
Time. — 1·5 to 0		X.20.a.8.8 — X.14.d.4.5.
		X.21.a.7.9 — X.15.b.8.1.
		Front Line.
	A/176.	X.20.b.2.5 — X.20.b.4.3.
		Communication Trenches.
	B/152.	{ X.20.b.3.8 — X.14.d.7.2.
		X.20.b.7.6 — X.15.c.8.9.
		X.14.b.4.2 — X.14.b.8.7.
		Front Line.
— 1·5 to 0·2. }	D/152.	X.21.c.1.6 to X.20.d.9.3.
(then on to BLUE)		
— 0·10 to 0·2.	BECOURT GUN. 1·18 pdr.	Salient X.20.d.8.9 to 9·9.
		(H.E. only)

(3) Cont'd.

2nd PHASE

0.0 TO 0.3.

A/152. Trench X.14.c.5.1 — X.20.b.3.8.
B/152. do X.20.b.3.8. — X.20.b.7.6.
A/176. do X.20.b.7.6. — X.21.a.3.6.
C/152. Communication Trenches X.15.c.2.4. to X.15.c.8.9.
" " " . X.15.c.9.2 to X.15.b.3.1.

BLUE LINE

along road   X.16.a.1.3 to X.16.a.2.8.
" "   X.16.a.1.3 to X.16.a.7.4.

D/152. Trench X.20.b.3.8 — X.21.a.2.6.
and point X.14.d.9.2.

0.0 to 0.2. BECOURT Gun Salient X.20.d.8.9. — X.20.d.9.9. (H.E. only)

Batteries lift from BLUE line at +0.3, going back 150 yards at a time, reaching YELLOW line at +0.4.

3rd PHASE

0.4 to 0.12

A/176 Trench X.14.d.4.5 — X.14.d.9.2.
C/152 " X.14.d.9.2 — X.21.a.4.9.
A/152 " X.21.a.4.9 — X.21.a.7.9.
B/152 Com'n Trench X.15.d.2.5 — X.15.b.8.1 and
Cross Roads X.16.a.1.3 — X.16.b.1.8.

YELLOW LINE

D/152 Points X.14.d.9.2, X.21.a.7.9, X.15.c.9.2, X.15.c.2.4.

BECOURT GUN Points X.15.c.9.2 and search along trench towards X.15.b.8.1.

Batteries start lifting from YELLOW line at 0.12, 150 yards at a time reaching GREEN at 0.17.

4th PHASE

0.17 to 0.25

C/152 Trench X.15.a.5.2 — X.15.a.8.0.
A/152 " X.15.a.8.0 — X.15.d.2.5.
A/176 " X.15.d.2.5 — X.15.d.4.1.
B/152 Com'n " X.15.d.2.5 — X.15.b.8.1.
" " X.16.b.2.7 — X.11.c.1.6.
D/152 " X.16.a.1.3 — X.16.b.2.5 and

GREEN LINE

Point X.15.b.8.1.

BECOURT GUN. STOP FIRING at 0.17.

Batteries start lifting from GREEN at 0.25, 100 yards at a time reaching BROWN at 0.30.

5th PHASE	C/152 Trench	X.15.b.4.5	– X.15.b.8.1.
0.30 to 0.48	A/152 "	X.15.b.8.1	– X.15.d.9.8.
	A/176 "	X.15.d.9.8	– X.16.c.1.5.
BROWN LINE	B/152. Com" "	X.16.a.1.3	– X.16.b.2.5.
	D/152 BAILIFF WOOD (X.16.a)		

Batteries start lifting from BROWN at 0.48, 100 yards at a time reaching ORANGE at 1.8.

6th PHASE	C/152 Trench	X.10.c.7.2	– X.16.a.8.9.
C 1.8 to 1.25	A/152 "	X.16.a.8.9	– X.16.a.9½.5.
	A/176 "	X.16.a.9½.5	– X.16.d.2.9
ORANGE LINE	B/152	CONTALMAISON WOOD	

Batteries start lifting from ORANGE at 1.25, going back 100 yards at a time reaching LIGHT BLUE at † 1.50.

7th PHASE	C/152	Western edge of MAMETZ WOOD. from X.17.d.8.5 Northwards.
1.50 to 2.15	A/152	Cutting at X.17.a.5.5.
LIGHT BLUE.	A/176 } B/152 }	In observation on MAMETZ WOOD

Batteries lift direct from LIGHT BLUE to CRIMSON at 2.15

8th PHASE	C/152 }	Barrage WEST side MAMETZ WOOD	To allow Infy Patrols to reconnoitre German 2nd line. Lift of 500 yds will be carried out at 2.45 p.m. using H.E. only.
2.15.	A/152 }	X.17.d.8.5 to X.18.a.3.4.	
CRIMSON LINE.	A/176 } B/152 }	In observation	

At 3.30 they reopen on CRIMSON LINE (W side MAMETZ WOOD

4. The Infantry will have 3 objectives viz:-
(A) X.9.c (Central) – X.15.b.8.2 – X.22.a.4.0.
(B) X.10.a.8.6. – X.16.b.1.5 – X.22.b.8.2.
(C) X.5.c.4.5. – X.11.b.7.0 – X.17.d.5.4.

101st & 102nd Infantry Bdes will capture & consolidate A + B on their respective fronts.
103rd Bde is allotted (C) objective.

5. LIAISON with Infantry.

On the night Y/Z the following Officers will report at Btln HqQrs of A & C Btlns 103rd Infantry Bde viz
2nd Lieut. THOMPSON. A. Bty. with 'A' BTLN.
2nd Lieut. RAWSON. B Bty. with 'C' BTLN.

5 Cont.d Each of the above will take with him the
following :- 1 - NCO
2 - Telephonists
1 - Linesman

together with telephone & cable, trench signalling lamp
signalling shutter etc.

They will remain with "A" & "C" B'tns H.Qrs respectively,
accompanying them on the advance until ordered to
rejoin their batteries.

Special instructions will be issued to them regarding
keeping up communications with the Brigade.

6. All ranks will wear as a distinguishing mark, an
Equilateral Triangle of Yellow Cloth (16 inch sides)
attached to the back.

7. The position of our troops will be indicated
by the lighting of flares at 15 seconds interval.
FLARES will only be lit by Troops in the Front Line

8. It is expected that the 152 Bde (less D Bty) will
advance about 3 hours after Zero time, and take
up a position about X 15 b.

9. Visual signalling will be established as follows :-
101st Bde — Adv Report Centre W 30 d 2· 4½·
102nd Inf Bde — DRESSLERS POST
103rd "   — KINFAUNS STREET

There will also be divisional visual signalling stations at :-
E 8 c 2·2
E 5 b 2·3
E 16 b 2·5.

10. Batteries when advancing, will take firing
battery & 1st line wagons, and will dump the contents
as soon as possible after coming into action, sending
back wagons to refill from gun pits or Advanced
Dump at W 29. d 4·6.

After refilling wagons should return as soon as possible
to the battery positions

(11) Advanced Brigade Wagon lines will be established at E 4 c 6.6.

(12) 2 men per battery will be left at battery positions when Bde advances. They should know the whereabouts and quantity of ammunition left behind, and must safeguard it until handed over to battery wagons or D.A.C. when they will return to their wagon lines.

(13) <u>All Iron Rations</u> (except that already in possession of the men) must be taken forward when advancing.

(14) Route from present gun positions over our front trenches has been prepared, and will be indicated to Bty Comdrs.

(15) Acknowledge.

G Farr Lieut & Adj for
O.C. Centre Group

18-6-16

"B" SECRET

<u>Instructions for "U" Day</u>

(1) As much wire cutting as possible to be done.
(2) Outstanding registration to be completed.
(3) Night firing on wire cut- and approaches.

SECRET

Instructions for "V" Day.

(1) Wire cutting, and bombardments by all natures will take place throughout the day.

(2) In addition the following special bombardments will take place:—

(A) (1) At 10 a.m. every Gun & Howitzer of the Corps Heavy Artillery will open fire simultaneously on POZIERES Village — and fire at their highest rate for 12 minutes when fire will stop.

(2) At 10-30 a.m. exactly similar procedure will be followed as regards CONTALMAISON.

34th Division Artillery will take no part in bombardment A(1).

They will Co-operate in Bombardment A(2) as shewn in Table A (attached)

(B) At 4 p.m. the Artillery will open exactly as arranged in every particular (except rate of fire), for the intense bombardment prior to Zero on "Z" day.

At 4-15 pm FIRE will be lifted to BLUE Line
" 4-45 pm "   "   "   " " PINK & YELLOW Line
" 4-55 pm "   "   "   " from PINK to GREEN
" 5-5 pm   "   "   "   " from YELLOW to GREEN
" 5-15 pm Special bombardment will cease and the ordinary deliberate bombardment resume.

{ Rate of fire not to exceed 1 round per gun every 2 minutes H.E. only }

(C) If GAS is used on V/W night the following will be the action of the Artillery:—

Taking "O" as the hour at which the GAS is enlarged

O-3. 18prs will a heavy shrapnel barrage on the German front Trenches along the whole line (Except at the LA BOISSELLE Salient where the Barrage will be as near the front Trenches as safety permits).

Barrage to last for 1 minute.

Instructions for "V" Day (Continued)

(2) (c) cont^d

1.27. Above Barrage will be repeated. Rockets will be sent up at that hour to induce the enemy to man his parapet. Barrage will last 5 minutes.

2.0. Bombardment to cover our raiding Parties will begin. Special orders for this will be issued later.

2.20. Fire will be lifted and our Raiding Party will go in.

Normal procedure will be carried on between 0.3 and 1.27 — and 1.32 and 2.0.

TABLE A

Time	Group	Battery	Objective
10.30 am to 10.42 am	Right	1 - 18p. B.ty	Barrage along Road X.16.d.6.0 - X.17.a.9.0
		1 - 18p. B.ty	Trench X.22.b.6.8 - X.17.d.0.5
		2 - 18p. B.tys	Shrapnel area enclosed by Points X.17.a.5.5 - 9.3 — X.16.d.9.3 - 8.4
		1 - 4.5 B.ty	Cutting on Road X.17.a.5.5 - 8.9
		1 - 4.5 B.ty	BAILIFF Wood
	Centre	4 - 18p. B.tys	Area enclosed by points X.16.b.2.3 - X.16.d.9.0 - X.16.d.4.1
		1 - 4.5 B.ty	Trench junction X.16.b.2.7 - X.16.b.25 - 23
	Left	4 - 18p. B.tys	Area X.16.b.23 - 25 — X.17.a.5.5 - X.16.b.9.0
		1 - 4.5 B.ty	Comⁿ Trench X.16.b.8.4 to X.17.a.7.4

In accordance with above, Area allotted to Centre Group will be divided as follows:—

Time			
10.30 am to 10.42 am	C/152 RFA	X.15.b.2.3 - X.16.b.3.0 - X.16.b.5.0
	A/152 RFA	X.16.b.3.0 - X.16.b.5.0 - X.16.d.4.6 - X.16.d.5.6
	B/152 RFA	X.16.d.4.6 - X.16.d.5.6 - X.16.d.4.3 - X.16.d.7.3
	A/176 RFA	X.16.d.4.3 - X.16.d.7.3 - X.16.d.4.1 - X.16.d.9.0
	D/152 RFA	Trench Junction X.16.b.2.7 X.16.b.25 - 23

SECRET.

Instructions for "W" Day.

1. General work will be carried out as on "V" day.
2. Following special bombardments will take place:—
   At 9 a.m. the artillery will open fire on Blue Line exactly as in the final bombardment at 0.3 on Z day.
   At 9.25 a.m. fire will be lifted to PINK and YELLOW Line
   " 9.45 am " " " " from PINK to GREEN line
   " 9.50 am " " " " from YELLOW to GREEN
   " 10.10 am " " " " " GREEN to BROWN
   10.20 am Special bombardment will cease, and ordinary bombardment will be resumed.
   Trench mortars will be used on the front line
3. Should the GAS not have been enlarged on V/W night but postponed to W/X night, the bombardment arranged for the Gas on "V" day will be carried out.
4. If the wind permits, discharges of Smoke will take place during the last 10 minutes of Special Bombardment.
   Time "W" day. 10-10 am to 10-20 am
   On all occasions on which this Smoke Barrage is discharged, the following will be carried out:—
   Taking the hour at which the Special bombardment ceases as Zero (0.0)
   0.3 All Guns will fire a Rapid burst (1 round) as in Phase 1 on Z day
   0.5 Above will be repeated
   During Special Bombardments H.E only to be used

Instructions for "X" Day.

1. General Work as on "W" Day.
2. The following Special bombardments will take place:—
   (A) At 4-30 am. The Artillery will open fire on the Orange Line exactly as in the Final bombardment on Z day.
   At 5 am Fire will be lifted on to BLACK Line
   " 5.10 am " " " from BLACK to LIGHT BLUE line
   " 5.20 am " " " from LIGHT BLUE to CRIMSON Line
   " 5.50 am The Special bombardment will cease, and ordinary bombardment will be resumed
   (B) At 6.30 pm The Artillery will open fire on the front line
   " 6.35 pm Fire will be lifted on to BLUE Line
   " 6.38 pm " " " from BLUE Line to PINK & YELLOW
   " 6.40 pm " " " from PINK to GREEN
   " 6.52 pm " " " from YELLOW to GREEN.
   " 6.55 pm " " " " GREEN to BROWN
   " 7 pm this special Bombardment will cease, and ordinary deliberate bombardment will be resumed.
   (C) At 7-30 pm Fire will recommence on the PINK and YELLOW LINE
   " 7-50 pm The whole fire will lift on to GREEN Line
   " 8-10 pm Fire will cease, and ordinary bombardment will be resumed.
3. If the GAS attack has been postponed to this night, the arrangements detailed in "V" day Instructions will be carried out.
4. If the wind permits, discharges of smoke will take place during the last 10 minutes of Special Bombardments
   Time "X" Day 5-40 am to 5-50 am
   On all occasions on which this smoke Barrage is discharged, the following will be carried out:— Taking the hour at which the Special bombardment ceases as Zero (0.0)
   0.3 All guns will fire a Rapid burst (1 round) as in Phase I on Z day.
   0.5 Above will be repeated
   During Special Bombardments H.E. only to be used.

Instructions for Y Day.

1. General work will be carried out as on preceding days.
2. The following special bombardments will take place:—
(A) At 6 am Fire will open as for opening of intensive Bombardment on Z day.
   at 6-35 am fire will lift on to BLUE Line
   " 6-55 am "   "   "   " PINK and YELLOW Line
   " 7-10 am "   "   "   " GREEN Line
   " 7-20 am This special bombardment will cease, and ordinary deliberate bombardment will be resumed.
(B) At 4-5 pm Fire will open on BROWN Line.
   " 4-15 pm " " lift on to MAUVE and ORANGE line
   " 4-25 pm " " " from MAUVE to ORANGE line.
   " 4-55 pm " " " " ORANGE to BLACK
   " 5-10 pm " " " " BLACK to LIGHT BLUE Line
   " 5-15 pm Fire will cease and ordinary bombardment will be resumed.

Rate of fire not to exceed 1 round per gun every 2 minutes

3. The Heavy Artillery will during this day completely destroy:—
   Salient X20 d y.2 – HELIGOLAND – Y Gap.
4. If the wind permits, discharges of Smoke will take place during the last 10 minutes of Special Bombardment. Time "Y" Day 7-10 am to 7-20 am

On all occasions on which this smoke Barrage is discharged, the following will be carried out:—
Taking the hour at which the Special Bombardment ceases as Zero (0·0)
0·3 All Guns will fire a Rapid burst (1 round) as in Phase 1 on Z day.
0·5 Above will be repeated.
During Special Bombardments H.E only to be used.

SECRET   CENTRE GROUP.   "G"   PAGE 1.

Operation Order No 3.   22.6.16.

Reference 34th Div Arty Operation Order No 10 of 18.6.16.

1. Operation Order No 1. is cancelled and the following substituted.

2. The following Wire-cutting tasks are allotted to 18 pr. Batteries of the Centre Group on U, V, W, X & Y days, and should be carried out as far as possible at times stated, when the Heavy Artillery will not fire in the vicinity of the area:—

U. Day.
- A.152 } 3 pm { X.15.c.0.½ — X.21.a.3.8.
- C.152 } 6 pm { X.21.a.4.8 — X.21.a.6½.8.
- A.176 } 3 pm { X.14.d.7.7 — X.15.c.2.4.
- B.152 } 6 pm { X.14.d.4.4 — X.14.d.8½.2.

V. Day.
- 2 - 4 pm { X.14.c.8.3 — X.14.c.9½.4.
- 6 - 7 pm { X.14.d.3.3 — X.14.d.4.5.

W. Day.
- A.152 } 3 pm to 4 pm   X.20.b.6.6. — X.21.a.3.5.
- C.152 }   X.20.a.5.9½ — X.20.b.3.7.
- A.176 } 4.30 pm to 6.30 pm   X.20.b.3.7½ — X.20.b.6.6.
- B.152 }

X. Day.
Any necessary repetition.

Y. Day.
- A.176 } 12.30 pm to 3.30 pm   X.20.a.7.3 — X.20.a.1.5
- B.152 }   X.20.b.1.5 — X.20.b.-.-

3. When the wire allotted has been cut, it is expected that Batteries will cut good lanes in all wire they can see in their zones up to the first Infantry objective. (BLUE lines on map already issued)

4. The special tasks of B.152 on these days will be to deal with following points.

     X.15.b.3.1.
     X.15.b.7.2.
     X.14.d.9.2.
     X.15.c.3.9.
     X.15.a.3.0.
     BAILIFF WOOD.
     X.14.b.4.5.

In addition to taking part in any special Bombardments which are ordered.

5. The general task of the 18 pr Batteries during these days in addition to wire-cutting will be.

(1) Preventing repair at night to wire cut, to strong points and hostile defences broken down by our Heavy Artillery.
(2) Shelling Communication Trenches and approaches at intervals.

Page 2.

(1) Taking part in practice and intense bombardments as ordered.

(2) The average rate of fire during all practice bombardments will not exceed one round per gun per minute.

6. Batteries must pay particular attention to following points during these days.

(1) S.S.11a. Note on care of guns during prolonged bombardments.

(2) Proper system of reliefs for personnel.

7. Each Battery must have an Officer at the Wagon Line during the whole period.

8. Watches must be Synchronized with Signal Time at 9 a.m., 12 noon & 6 p.m. daily, and in addition, immediately before any special bombardment.

9. Any outstanding registration must be completed on U day.

10. Night will be considered as from 9 p.m. to 5 a.m. during which time the expenditure of Ammunition should not exceed 20 rounds per gun. (Excluding any special bombardment)

11. No restrictions as to amount of Ammunition to be expended during the day.

12. No firing to take place between the following hours, to enable the R.F.C. to take photographs.

  V day.   5.30 p.m. to 6 p.m.

  W "   " p.m. to 4.30 p.m.

  X "   3 p.m. to 3.30 p.m.

  Y "   12 noon to 12.30 p.m. and 5.30 p.m. to 6 p.m.

13. Commencing on 'U' day the following reports will be required, and must reach Group Hd. Quers by 6.15 p.m.

(A) General situation — Wire cut — general effect of our fire — Intensity of enemy fire — any barrages noticed, or points concentrated on by him.

(B) Casualties. (unless previously reported)

(C) State of equipment and ammunition (if unusual)

During the bombardment, the method of supply of Ammunition will be as at present.

  Amm. Refilling point. D.23.d.5.8.
   Dump.   E 20 (Central)
  Railhead.   CONTAY

(15) Horses will only be exercised on the exercise ground flagged out in J24, and will proceed there in small batches by the track crossing railway at E.15.c.0.3.

(16) Indents for H.E. material will be submitted in ordinary way.

(17) Sketch map (Appendix A) showing route for ammunition wagons is attached.

(18) Acknowledge & return operation order No 1. to this office

S. Varr Lieut and Adj for
O.C. Centre Group.

"D"

Centre Group Instructions 24-6-16

~~Additional Instructions~~

SECRET

Reference Instructions V day para 2 (c)

① The 103rd Inf Bde will carry out the Raid in above mentioned instructions.
This may be carried out on U/V night or any favourable subsequent night. On the day on which a favourable wind is probable a message will be sent out about 6 pm. saying "WARN ROGER".
If the wind continues favourable the Zero hour at which discharge of gas will commence, will be sent as follows. "ROGER tonight — (Time)"
Artillery Action will then be as already ordered.

② Points of entry into German Trench will be.
 (A) Raid A near X20.a.5.6.
 (B) Raid B near X19.b.9.9.

③ Trench Mortars. O.C. Trench Mortar Group will cut the hostile wire along the Hostile Front Line in vicinity of these points. He will bombard points according to instructions issued as under with medium Trench Mortars.
 + 2.5. Commence Bombardment.
 + 2.16. Stop.
 + 2.55. Ordinary Night programme may be resumed. Except that no fire is to be opened on the raid objective or vicinity before +3.5.

④ Artillery Should it be found necessary to continue the bombardment (PHASE II) beyond +2.55 orders will be issued by R.A.H.Q. "Continue Second PHASE".

(5) Every endeavour must be made to locate the position of any barrage the enemy put up during or subsequent to the discharge of GAS.
The direction from which fire comes and nature of Gun should also be noted if possible and reported to R.A.H.Q soon as possible.

(6) Following will be the precautions against our own Gas. All men in occupation of the USNA - TARA line and EAST of it will wear their Gas Helmets on. Any man who should become slightly gassed should be kept as quiet as possible.

(7) Acknowledge.

S Farr Lieut & Adj
Centre Group.

Reference Instructions for "V" day para 2.(c)

① Time Table (B) attached gives details of bombardment to be carried out in accordance with para 2. c.

② If the wind is unfavourable for GAS on V/W night, this Time Table will hold good for the night on which it is subsequently enlarged.

③ Raiding Party will enter German Trenches at +2.25, and leave again so as to be back in our line at +2.50.

④ Once the 2nd Phase has commenced, no gun will fire WEST of line X.13.d.7.2 — X.14.c.0.3 — X.14.c.3.1 — X.20.a.8.3 — X.20.a.9.5 until +3.30.

⑤ Batteries not detailed to take part in this operation will continue their usual night programme, except that no Battery not detailed should fire WEST of a line X.13.d.9.7 — X.14.c.5.3 — X.20.b.3.8 — X.20.b.4.3 between +2 and +3.30.

⑥ Zero hour will be notified later.

⑦ Acknowledge.

SECRET

TIME TABLE. D.
(Reference Instructions for V day para 2 (c))

GROUP	UNIT	Time of Commencing	Objective	Time of Lift	REMARKS
	1st PHASE				
CENTRE	C. 152 A. 152	+2.0	Front trench X20.a.8.3 – X20.a.4.5 – X20.a.3.6 " X20.a.5.7 – X20.a.3.9 (exclusive) ✱ Support line to line X20.a.9.5 – X20.a.8.8 X14.c.5.1 – X14.c.3.1 – X14.c.2.3 – X14.c.0.3.	+2.20	Risking backwards and forwards from end to Support line ✱. Front take back to begin at +2.20 after and no fire is to be put on front trenches
	B 152	+2.10	X20.a.8.3 – X20.a.9.5 – X20.b.3.8	+2.25	Barrage.
	II 152 1 Section	+2.10	X13.d.8.4 – X13.d.7.4 – X13.d.6.3 – X13.d.7.2	+2.55	} Slow rate of fire
	II 152 1 Section	+2.15	X20.a.9.5 – X20.d.3.8.	+2.35	
	2nd PHASE				
	C. 152 A. 152	+2.22	Support line X20.a.9.5 – X20.a.8.8 – X14.c.5.1 (exclusive)	+2.55	Final take of 1st Phase artificial commences at +2.20 and must reach this line at +2.22.

Other guns and Howitzers as in 1st PHASE.

SECRET   "E" B.M/S.P./49.
                                              24.6.16.

H.Q. Right Group.
     Centre Group.
     Left Group.
     Forward Group.

Following is a rough Guide to Ammunition expenditure on Z day.

(A) 18 pdrs.
Times
-1.5 to -0.10.   1 round per Gun per 2 minutes.
-0.10 to -0.1.   3   "   "   "   " 1   "   .
Zero to 0.3.   3   "   "   "   " 1   "   .
0.3 to 0.12   3   "   "   "   " 1   "   .
0.12 to 0.25   3   "   "   "   " 1   "   .
0.25 to 3.30   1   "   "   "   " 1   "   .

Which works out at about 320 rounds per Gun. This is keeping up high pressure, and the G.O.C, R.A. does not consider that many batteries will fire more than 250 Rounds per Gun.

(B) 4.5 Howitzer.
        Expenditure Z day 200 rounds per Gun.
                Other days 120 rounds "   "

This is a guide only.

                        (Sgd) H.B. Waller.
                              B.M. R.A.
                              34 Div Artly.

O.C.   /
    Centre Group.

        For your information and guidance.

                        S. Farr. Lieut & Adjt.
25.6.16.   Centre Group.

"F"

Copy No. 2.

SECRET

Artillery Instructions No 13. 26.6.16.

1. From receipt of this, gas will be liberated at any time of day or night when the wind is favourable.

If this takes place in daylight it will be accompanied by ½ hour smoke all along the Divisional Front.

"WARN ROGER" will be sent ½ hours before.

The ½ hour smoke will commence from the ZERO hour named for "ROGER".

Starr Lieut & Adjutant.
Centre Group.

APPENDIX VI.

Issued with 4th Divisional Artty Operation Order No 10.

(1) The supplementary S.O.S. Signal to be employed on Z/Z1 and subsequent days will be single Red Rockets to be fired at short intervals until acted upon by the Artillery.

As it does not appear practical for Rockets for this purpose to be carried forward by Battalions in the initial advance they will be taken forward when Brigade Headquarters move, and will be sent forward by the Relay Posts in C. Communication Trench as opportunity offers, to the most advanced line occupied.

(2) The O.C. 18th Bn. Northumberland Fusiliers, will also arrange during Z day to send forward not less than 36 Rockets to the Relay Post to be established at Trench Junctions X.14.d.9.2. and X.15.c.0.1. (in C. Communication Trench). The personnel at this post are to be warned to carry these Rockets forward when taking messages to BLYTH Relay Post X.15.a.8.0. Runners 103rd Infantry Brigade will in turn carry Rockets forward from this point to the new advanced Report Centre 103rd Infantry Brigade.

(3) In event of Rockets failing to reach any portion of our Advanced Line Red Flares will be substituted as the S.O.S. Signal.

To avoid any misunderstanding Red Flares to indicate the S.O.S. Signal will, however, only be employed during the hours of darkness.

To ensure their being seen by F.O.O.'s they will be placed as high as possible prior to being lit.

29-6-16

S. Law Lieut R.F.A.
152 Bde R.F.A.

SECRET.

Artillery Instructions No 18. 28.6.16.

There will be a special bombardment tomorrow 29ᵗʰ inst as follows:—
at 4 pm. fire will open on Front Line.
" 4.45 pm. " " lift on to Blue "
" 5.20 pm. Special bombardment will cease.

Rate of fire 18 pdrs will be one round per Gun per two minutes. Except 4.45 - 4.47 pm which will be 4 rounds per Gun per minute.

S. Haw. Lieut & Adjutant.
Centre Group.

O.C.

From examination of German prisoners it has been elicited that owing to our shelling of the enemy's avenues of approach to his front system nightly, it has often been impossible and always difficult for supplies etc to be brought up.

The G.O.C, R.A, congratulates the Divisional Artillery on their good work, and trusts that no efforts will be spared to make the enemy's night more difficult and dangerous.

He suggests occasional rounds over the ground between approaches & communication trenches as well as the usual bombardment along them.

29.6.16.

S. Haw Lieut & Adjutant.
Centre Group.

I

The following raids are to take place on Centre Group front TONIGHT:-

(a) X20 b 9.1 to X20 a 8.3.
 Time when raiding party leaves our parapet and will return will be telephoned later, between which times no firing on above front line.

(b) Raid on Salient X20 a 3.6 to X20 a 4.5
 Party leave our trenches at 11 p.m and re-enter trenches at 11-45 p.m.
 No firing on front X20 a 3.9 to X20 a 8.3 between 11 p.m & 12 midnight.

                    D. Tan Lieut R??

29-6-16

34th Div.
III. Corps.

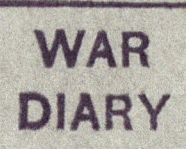

Headquarters,

152nd BRIGADE, R.F.A.

J U L Y

1 9 1 6

WAR DIARY or INTELLIGENCE SUMMARY

Army Form — Vol 6

152 Bde — R.F.A. 3rd Unknown — R.F.A.

Place	Date	Hour	Summary of Events and Information	Remarks and references to Appendices
W.30 a 8.0	July 1st		"Z" day. Misty till about 9 am, fine later. Zero hour was fixed for 7.30 am. The heavy bombardment commenced at 6.25 am in accordance with R.A. Time Table. The forward gun in BECOURT moved firing over 105 rounds. At 7.30 am the 101st & 102nd Inf Bdes. assaulted and were soon out of sight over the ridge. The 103rd Inf Bde. who followed in reserve were met by heavy hostile machine gun and rifle fire, and some battalions were unable to reach the enemy front line. Practically no further movement was seen until about 10.30 am when parties of our men were observed to be withdrawing from the Contalmaison X.15.d.5.2 – X.20.a.3.8. From this line the situation appeared to develop into our men holding the following portion of enemy front X.20.a.4.5 – X.20.a.8.3 – X.20.a.4.5 – X.20.a.9.4. At 10 pm a special bombardment of LA BOISSELLE was ordered, preparatory to an attack by the 58th Bde at 19:15. Air. Not to prepare was made. All accounts testified that the line in front of enemy trenches had been held out left of the 18 pr Battleon (Inkerpuill, located noted in BATH)	
			Casualties: No 46826 Dr. CARBURY H.Qrs missing " 11131 Gr. RODGERS "D" 185 wounded " 8235 " WILLIAMS " " 81,32 By ALLEN B " " 8119 " MEATS "	
			Ammn expended: 8 pm 30th to 12 noon 1st : 1024 A, 1042 AX, 647 BX 12 Am 1st 8 pm " : N2 A, 92 AX, 220 BX	

WAR DIARY or INTELLIGENCE SUMMARY

Army Form

34th DIVISION — 152 Bde. F.A. (2)

Place	Date	Hour	Summary of Events and Information	Remarks and references to Appendices
N30a 8.0	July 2nd	—	Very good day for observation. Infantry consolidating position held by them in enemy front support line S. of LA BOISSELLE. 16" Siu took front & support line to point X20a 8.8, X20a 8.4 - 5.6. enemy No Mans Land to trench 19" Siu took front & support line to point X20 a 3.6, thence bombing their way N.N.W. arrived at IE which came at about 20 yds from X20 a 3.6. 18pr Batteries. Amn expended 8pm 1st — 12 noon 2nd : 161 A, 410 AX, 554 BX, 466. 653 A, 913 AX, 744 BX. " 2nd — 8pm : OVILLERS being very heavily bombarded from H.A. to which enemy replied with strong barrage on No MANS LAND from OVILLERS to BECOURT wood.	
"	3rd	—	A good day for observation. 16" Siu attacked LA BOISSELLE from S.E. at 4pm. Position in LA BOISSELLE deemed to be as follows — enemy kept holding in X14c 8.9 - 2.6, 4.7; 5.3, 5.1. L - X20 a 9.8 — X20 c 3.8 - 7.6. Our inf. advanced this morning 6 x mc 4.9, 7.7. W- Which subsequently to former line (11am) which they consolidated. Our 18pr Bty hit a heavy barrage on X8c.d from which divisions expected for renewed adv on B4. (A152) knocked out a machine gun at X8c 3.4 with machine gun fire also being kept up on enemy communication trenches & approaches. Amn expended 8pm 2nd — noon 3rd : 1423 A, 362 AX, 353 BX. noon 3rd — 8pm — 855 A, 117 AX, 305 BX	
"	4th	—	Bar 29.27 Bombing by our infantry who worked their X14d 4.5 — X14c 9.5 by 10am. Forward gun withdrawn from BECOURT trench & motion as battery position 2/Bty observation, which left advancing of English as they pursuit themselves vomiting in active cooperation against enemy communication trenches and approaches. 34 Div Cdr O.O 6 N.W received Amn expended 8pm 3rd — 8am 4th : 1078 A, 534 AX, 570 BX 4th — 8pm — 188 A, 367 AX, 319 BX	

Army Form C. 2118

WAR DIARY
or
INTELLIGENCE SUMMARY

(Erase heading not required.)

153 Bde FA 3

Place	Date	Hour	Summary of Events and Information	Remarks and references to Appendices
X.30.a.8.0	July 5th		Bar. 29.37. Ther. 60°. (9am)	
			Operation Order No 11 cancelled. (Relief of 34th Div Art. by 23rd Div Art.)	
			Enemy shelled LA BOISSELLE with 5.9" from 2:30 to 3:30 pm heavily, otherwise enemy artillery normal.	
			Our inf made two brisk attacks at 2 pm, preceded by heavy bombardment.	
			Ours battalion at other times (approx) which were engaged as they presented themselves.	
			One battalion chiefly in domain.	
			At 6 pm. X.15.d.2̄.0, X.21.a.5.6 - 7.4 - X.21.d.2.7. (Howitzers) in action, & numbers of prisoners seen surrendering.	
			A/176, C/175 & D/175 placed under Cole front.	
			At 9.h.t No 22 received - 8pm R - 12mm 5th 9·15A, 168AX, 248BX	
			nm 5th - 8pm 5th 743A, 575AX, 499BX	
			Amm expended.	
	6th		Bar. 29.60. Ther. 61.	
			A good day for observation - neither fire recent 2 18 pr. (B4) to observation to trust (the secondary) of enemy (caught on they presented themselves) on enemy communication trenches and approaches	Op. Order No 5
			Cole front Op. Order No 5 issued.	
			Amm expended. 8pm 5th - 12 nm 6th 954 A, 101AX, 268 BX	
			nm 6th - 8pm - 336 A, 69 AX, 37 BX	
	7th		Bar. 29.25. Ther. 56.	
			111th & 112th Inf Bdes relieved 102nd & 103rd ~ in 34th Div.	
			Op. Order No 5 carried out - Attack taking place at 8 am.	
			CONTALMAISON occupied but subsequently evacuated.	
			Line held X.14.b.7.5 - X.15.a.8.0 - X.15.d.1.3.	
			F.O.O. sent forward kept in communication by signalling shutter with O.P.	
			Hostile Art was active - LA BOISSELLE and Country to S.E. heavily shelled.	
			Amm expended. 8pm 6th - 12 nm 7th 1468 A, 658 AX, 664 BX } 152 BX
			12 nm 7th - 8pm 7th 814 A, 47 AX, 227 BX }
			30 Thermite

WAR DIARY
or
INTELLIGENCE SUMMARY

Army Form C.

152 Bde FA 4

Place	Date	Hour	Summary of Events and Information	Remarks and references to Appendices
N 3 a 8.0	8th July		Bar. 29.15 – Ther. 62.50. Centre group kept up intermittent fire on enemy communication trenches in X 10 a and various selected points.	
			Ammn expended. 8pm 7th – 12 noon 8th: 922 A, 4 AX, 224 BX. 12 noon 8th – 8pm: 334 A, 48 AX, Nil.	
			During day barrage was successfully received by our infantry who shortly after 7.0.0 am on CONTALMAISON. Our Inf. again occupied CONTALMAISON but subsequently withdrew. Hostile Artillery very active throughout day along rd from front and support line from OVILLERS L X 20 b.	
" " "	9th		Bar. 29.47 Ther 59°	
		9. am	Inf reported field following line at 9 am x 86 5.3 – x 9 c 4.6 – x 9 c 9.1 – X 15.b.8.1 – x 23 d 4.7 – X 24 c 1.7	
			Heavy hostile shelling X 20 b – X 14 c	
		4.30 pm	Enemy reported advancing in line X 16 a 2.8 – X 9 d 4.5" Contn: front pm trenches X 9 c 9.8 – X 16 a 2.8 & trenches X 9 d – X 10 a r c	
		5.55 pm	Enemy reported advancing X 16 a could.. barrage increased to X 16 a for 5 mins.	
		7.2 pm	Our Inf reported in trenches X 9 d – barrage lifted to X 16 a 2.8 – X 4 c 7.4 and CONTALMAISON woods Capt. WALLER BM 34th Bde 2nd Lt reported wounded in Thigh	
			Ammn expended 8pm 8th – 12 noon 9th: 902 A, 92 AX, 182 BX. 12 noon 9th – 8pm: 789 A, 166 AX, 423 BX.	
			Operations of 69th Bde Inf. reduced to 6 pm, subsequently opened, but carried out as below.	

Army Form C. 2118.

152 Bde. FA 3

WAR DIARY
or
INTELLIGENCE SUMMARY
(Erase heading not required.)

Place	Date	Hour	Summary of Events and Information	Remarks and references to Appendices
N30 a 8.0	July 10th		Bar. 29.50. Ther 58°	
			Fine & warm - a very good day for observation.	
		1:15am	Our Inf. prepn. oversleds line X9b06 - X3d31 - X3c9.3, X3c5.1 - 0.2	
			23rd Div. of under No 53 and. so 34th 2nd Art Inst No 2.2 - Group- 2nd Brandenia	
			Cert. Group to barrage between 4 - 6.3pm	
			A r C 152 - X10c 6.3 - X10d 1.1	
			B 152 r A76 Ront r X10d 5.3 - X10b 4.9	
			C 152 - X10b 9.7 - X10b 4.9	
			D 152 - Clash R.E. - X10c 6.3 - X10c 4.6	
			D 152 - French - X 4d 1.1 - X5c 2.2	
		7pm	Reported our Inf. occupy CONTALMAISON & outskirts E.N. & E.- This is confirmed by aerial message from F.O.O.	
		9:15pm	Counter attack reported from direction of CONTALMAISON reported - Inf. brought up & fire to 2 much	
			Orders for 11th June issued	
			A r C 152 in chronolaw 9pm to 6.1 am	
			B 152 r A 76 X 16 b 1.8 - X 16 a 9.5 thence X 10 c 6.3 - X 10 c 6.9 Till 1 am then in chronolaw	
			Rate of fire 10 r.p.g. for 2 mins to 10.30pm. Then 15 r.p. gun for 5 mins	
		11:15pm	Situation when letter under	
			25" Div. - X 8 a 9.7 - S.1, 6.1, X 8c 3.9, 7.7, 8.3, X 8 b 0.1, 1.2, 4.2, 5.3, X 8 d 7.5, 8.9	
			34" - X 9 d 4.5, 5.4, 7.3, 8.2 - X 10c 1.0, 1.4.	
			23" ~ = X 16 a 1.3, 7.3, X 16 b 2.5, 7.2, 9.5, 4.5, X 17 a 3.1, X 17c 2.8, 4.1	
			Amm. expended 8pm-9th = 12 noon 10th = 730 A, 66 AX, 302 BX ⎫ 152 Bde	
			noon 10th - 8pm - = 952 A, 171 AX, 22.1 BX ⎭	

Army Form C. 2118.

WAR DIARY
or
INTELLIGENCE SUMMARY
(Erase heading not required.)

152 Bde/54 6

Place	Date	Hour	Summary of Events and Information	Remarks and references to Appendices
N30a 8.6	July 11th		Bar. 29.64 - Ther. 58° Fine day. Observation post - Mobile Artillery not so active.	
		9.25am	Enemy replied to occupy Xqd 3.4.	
		10.30am	Enemy gun replied in neader X5b0.3 - D175 turned on to from 10 to 25 BX. Morning situation replied unbroken Our Inf. consolidating line X 8b9.0, Xqc 4.6.8.2, Xqd3.4,5.4, X10c.10, X16a2.8-1.3, X16b2.5.7.2.9.5, X17a4.1 X17c2.8	
		2.15pm	Enemy shelling LA BOISSELLE heavily. 2Lt LEWIS sprained ankle and got to maps line to rest. Amm expended 8pm 10th - noon 11th = 868 A, 113 AX, 330 BX noon 11th - 8pm 11th = 524 A, 494X, 75 BX	
" "	12		Bar. 29.65 - Ther. 60 Weather fine + threatening rain. Enemy shelled promenade throughout the day, not so round Sig. into ALBERT during afternoon. Our Inf. pushing forward to X10c6.9 - CONTALMAISON wood - X16b4.9. Cable front post to fire W 7 X10d 3.5.	
		8.45am	dept Bde. 3rd Div replied to hold CONTALMAISON wood - X10c6.3 cholm X16b2.7-4.9 - X10d.8.2 thence line down X16a7.3, X16b2.5, 4.2, 7.2, X17a.5.5. Bdy. sep. from except D'175 on ff" X5d 4.5, 6.7, 7.8, 8.7	
		11.30am	Slow heavy retreat on X10 central. X11 central. 1.2 p gm for 5 min.	
		12 noon	Barrage increased to 1.12 pm for 1 min.	
		12.15pm	A.C. 152 SOS firing	
		12.30pm 9pm	B152 - A176 9pm - 6.1am X10 central - X11b0.3- 6 rd p gun for hr, followed by Ordinal - night line mud. X106 4.0 X106 4.0 Branch of magazine intended (4 rd p gun p hr B152- A176 9pm - 6.1am - X5d0.0 C.175 X11a.2.3 - X5d0.0 D152 mod X106 1.0. X10b4.0 B152 - A176 Forms/C.2118/12. D'175 product X5d 4.5 - 6.7, 7.8 - 8.7 SOS p gun p hr	

WAR DIARY or INTELLIGENCE SUMMARY

152 Bde. F.F. 171

Place	Date	Hour	Summary of Events and Information	Remarks and references to Appendices
N 30 a 9.0	July 12th	10.14pm	Germans sent up many white rockets in vicinity of CONTALMAISON	
			Ammn expended 8pm 11th – noon 12th = 439 A, 54 AX, 125 OX	
			" " noon 12 – 8pm = 735 A, 44 AX, 170 BX	
			" " 8pm – noon 12 [sic]	
" "	13th	–	Bar 29.43. Ther 52.	
			18pr Bdes put in duty on zone X10 central – X116.0.3 in 4hr relief of 6 pm – 6 am to be	
		1.10 am	D 175 stopped firing. Centre Group 6 operation order No 6 issued.	OP.OR NO
		12.30pm	C 75 – limits & X 11a.9.0 – X116.8.9	
		9.15 am	B 152 ordd to lift to German 2nd line trench X Sd central	
			New zone for 34th Div Art issued	
		9.30pm	34th Div Art Instr No 26 issued – Centre Group 6 Order No 6 ind at 9.30pm	
			Ammn expended 8pm 12 – noon 13 = 280 A, 247 AX, 132 BX	
			" " noon 13 – 8pm " = 155 A, 14 AX, 24 OX	
" " "	14th	Bar 29.44 – Ther 58°	
			Reported that 21st Div on left mov through BAZENTIT LE PETIT wood	
			" 7th Div has captured BAZ LEPETIT & GRAND villages	
		7 am	" Cavalry entered through Mata HIGH wood	
		9.30 am	34th Div Cat Instr No 27 received + orders issued for Bde to F.B. Villers	
		2.15pm	Batteries slip firing in front + front & left to permit no aeroplane into R.A. Instr No 27	
		2.30pm	R.A.H.Q. " " order troops and show as smartly moving into attack	
		3.10pm	Centre group order given to slip from 4 at 6 pm	
		4 pm	Reported no less strong points all rnd OVILLERS and L.C. HIGH wood	
			Ammn expended 8pm 13 – noon 14 = 316 A, 1147 AX, 69 OX	
			" " noon 14 – 8pm = 21 A, 384 AX, Nil	

Army Form C. 2118.

WAR DIARY
or
INTELLIGENCE SUMMARY

(Erase heading not required.)

152 Bde FA (8)
34th DIVISION

Instructions regarding War Diaries and Intelligence Summaries are contained in F.S. Regs., Part II. and the Staff Manual respectively. Title Pages will be prepared in manuscript.

Place	Date	Hour	Summary of Events and Information	Remarks and references to Appendices
N30a8.0	July 15th		Bar 29.47. Ther 60°. Weather fine. Good day for observation. 34th Div. Oct. Instr. No 28 received re bombardment & attack on POZIERES.	
		10.30am	Reported by F.O.O. Heavy enemy barrage X10a - X10c - X16a - with 5.9", 4.2".	
		11.30am	Our H.A. shelling POZIERES steadily. Enemy shelling X8d3.2 & thereupon X15d - X10b0.5.	
		12 noon	About 70 enemy 4.2 fell about X30b of which only 3 burst.	
		1.30pm		
		6.30	Enemy retaliating about X9b, X10a - X10b.	
		11 pm	Aeroplanes reported over AUTHUILLE wood	
		12 m	Cuts from actual to shell main road POZIERES-BAPAUME between X4c7.4 - X4b7.2 till 6am. No firing SW of X4c7.4. Amm 17th until 15 rds to 18 pr Shrap. - 4.5 20 rds per gun. Amm expended 8pm 14th — noon 15th = 91A, 45AX, N.LBx hrs 15 - 8pm - = Nil	
" " "	16th		Bar 29.65. Ther 60°. Billious, came fine 6am. Weather fine; shower in afternoon, observation good	
		11.40am	3.0.0 upto date. Cutting X17a completed - bomb proofs - trench for POZIERES & S.W corner of	
		3pm	B LE PETIT has strong points held by enemy. Our H.A. shells POZIERES with all calibres 4 6.12"	
		8.30pm	Cuts from did not fire between 6am and 8.30pm	
			2/L LEWIS to hospital - doubtful fracture of left ankle. Amm expended 8pm 15th - noon 16th = 889A, N.LAX, 68Bx " 16th - 8pm - = Nil	

Army Form C. 2118.

WAR DIARY
or
INTELLIGENCE SUMMARY

(Erase heading not required.)

152 Bde FA (9)

34th DIVISION

Place	Date	Hour	Summary of Events and Information	Remarks and references to Appendices
N30&8.0	July 17th		Bar. 29.52 ... Ther 61°. Weather misty, clearing later, but rain in afternoon - Observation bad all day. 34th Div R.A. H.Q. in chev at MOULIN VIVIER and opens at 14 RUE DE BRAY ALBERT. C/175 leaves Centre front. Our Inf repulsed two held from German 2nd line up to X5d central. 34th Div Art. Instr. No 30 received re bombardment and attack n POZIERES. A.B+C/152 + A/175 - X4d 3.6 - X 5a 5.4. B/175 1 Sect - X 5a 1.5 - X 4b 6.0 D/152 " " - X 4d 3.8 - X5c 1.8 (orchard) Batteries carry out some target throughout. 6.30pm - 9pm. Remaining Sections of How Bty to fire Therm.t. shell, but did not arrive in time.	
		11.30pm	Operation re attack on POZIERES cancelled. Amm. expended 8pm 16th - noon 17th = 77 A, 81 AX, 80 BX " " noon 17 - 8pm " = 434 A, 116 AX, 77 BX	
" "	18th		Bar 29.54 - Ther 57°. Enemy shells LA BOISELLE constantly with 5.9's, 10pm 30 tons - trench morters shelling X 10 A - X 11 b.	
		1.30pm	D/175 leaves Centre front.	
		2.45pm	A/175 " " " G/152 received re Btns moving forward under their own C.O. B/152 supplies 300 rolls B.E. in front line. Amm. expended 8pm 17th - noon 18th = 173 A, 21 AX, Nil BX noon 18 - 8pm " = Nil 100 BX	

Army Form C. 2118.

152 Bde F.A. 1107

34th DIVISION

WAR DIARY
or
INTELLIGENCE SUMMARY
(Erase heading not required.)

JULY

Place	Date	Hour	Summary of Events and Information	Remarks and references to Appendices
W30a 8.0	19th		Bar 29.63. Ther 62°. Fine day for observation	
		7.45	B.M. R.A. ordered 2 Batteries 152 Bde to dig forward positions. Working parties of 2 guns from 13½ ordered up per	
			S gone forward to X16b 4.2, where position was pointed out by C.O. and A & C B⅟₄ Comdrs	
		3pm	Orders re forward position cancelled & digging parties recalled	
			D 152 moved up one Section left to position vacated by B 176. Heavy enemy shelling throughout day.	
			Amm expended 8pm 18th – noon 19th = 192 BX
			noon 19 – 8pm = 102 BX
" " "	20th		Bar 29.57 – Ther 59½° Fine day. observation good	
			A-C 152 ordered to fire 4 rounds per gun per hour on POZIERES. This made up to 8pm	
			D 152 moves up left Section to map position X30 b 1.5	
			1st Bde has repaired the X52 38, 6.9, X52 6.9 and lines of posts from N.W. corner of BAZENTIN LE PETIT Wood through S1d 0.4 & X 6.8 1.9	
			Amm expended 8pm 19th – noon 20th = 216 A
			noon 20 – 8pm = 174 A, 33 BX, 7 Common (Shorts)
" " "	21st		Bar 29.74 – Ther 59° Beautiful day. good observation	
			Major Livermore at 10 am to E 3 a.	
			POZIERES heavily shelled by our H.A. in evening	
			Batteries in Observation (Scrimsrith)	
			Amm expended 8pm 20th – 12 noon 21st = 9 A
			12 noon 21st – 8pm = 3 BX

2449 Wt. W14957/M90 750,000 1/16 J.B.C. & A. Forms/C.2118/12.

Army Form C. 2118

152 Bde FA (11)

WAR DIARY
or
INTELLIGENCE SUMMARY
(Erase heading not required.)

Instructions regarding War Diaries and Intelligence Summaries are contained in F.S. Regs., Part II. and the Staff Manual respectively. Title Pages will be prepared in manuscript.

Place	Date	Hour	Summary of Events and Information	Remarks and references to Appendices
N30a8.0	22nd July		Bar. 29.69. Ther 61°. Fine day. Observation good. 34th Div. Art. Op. Order No 31 received. 152nd Bde in attendance. Maj Gen E.C. Ingouville Williams Cdg 34 Div was killed byshell. Amm expended. 6pm 21st - noon 22nd Nil. noon 22 - 8pm - 19 BX - 7 Common	
" " "	23rd		Bar. 29.66. Ther 58°. Fine day. Int. observation good. Situation unaltered 11 pm. 4.8A Div occupy trenches W of POZIERES about X14a 3.4. 4th Australian Bde were relieved & went to attack W of POZIERES. Div & villages of POZIERES occupied & consolidated. Amm expended = Nil	
" " "	24th	9.30 am 3 pm	Bar. 29.66. Ther 59°. 7.0.0 reports heavy shelling of our own lines in POZIERES. impracticable to keep telephone line open. CO & ArC B&C both vacated & took positions in SAUSAGE valley. Situation midnight on phone. Own line X6a23, 3.1; X6c9.7 - SJd4.4, 8.4 - S2c3.4, 8.4 - S2d2.2, 5.4 - S8b6.9 - S3c4.5 - Sq a 2.3 - Sqc26 - Sad2.7 Amm expended = Nil	

Army Form C. 2118

152 Bde. F.A. 1/12

WAR DIARY
or
INTELLIGENCE SUMMARY

(Erase heading not required.)

Instructions regarding War Diaries and Intelligence Summaries are contained in F.S. Regs., Part II. and the Staff Manual respectively. Title Pages will be prepared in manuscript.

Place	Date	Hour	Summary of Events and Information	Remarks and references to Appendices
W30A 8.10	25th		Bar. 29.65 — Ther. 56° Tuesday. Observation good.	
		7.40am	F.O.O. reports Australians attacking in POZIERES, with object of occupying whole village & far N. of cemetery.	
			F.O.O. reports no attention — Nil	
		7.30pm	4th Bde held heads W. of POZIERES & to time line X4a3.7. When 2nd Bde. X4b6.8.	
			No rifle approaches reported to Right Bde.	
			Bn. D/152 recommendation & relief personnel of A & D/175 on 26.7.16	
			Ammn. expended = Nil	
" " "	26th		Bar. 29.66 — Ther. 61° Clear day. Observation good.	
			Bs. D/152 where personnel of A + D/175 coming into the relay to form of Lt. Fammel C/175th	
			Sub K. in. Att. of Order No 33 issued.	
			Heavy enemy barrage in POZIERES & approaches during afternoon.	
			Ammn. expended A + C Bty = Nil	
" " "	27th		Bar. 29.60 — Ther. 62° Fine day — observation good.	
			A + C/152 each section each to new position being dug at X15c6.6. in SAUSAGE valley.	
			Ammn expended = Nil	

Army Form C. 2118

152 Bde FA 1/3

WAR DIARY
or
INTELLIGENCE SUMMARY
(Erase heading not required.)

Instructions regarding War Diaries and Intelligence Summaries are contained in F. S. Regs., Part II. and the Staff Manual respectively. Title Pages will be prepared in manuscript.

July

Place	Date	Hour	Summary of Events and Information	Remarks and references to Appendices
N30a.8.0	28th		Bar 29. Ther 63° Fine day. Observation good.	
			Remaining Section A/C now up to rear gun position	
			A.C – D 152 did not fire	
			34th Div Art Op Order No 35 & amendment received	
			F.O.O refused Ammn. Rsn. 1st Gun now E. POZIERES	
			Ammn expended – Nil	
"	29th		Bar 29.84 – Ther 64°	
			Fine hot day	
		6.25am	R.M refused rd hostile works R.34.c.2.7 – R.34 central	
		8am	F.O.O refused 2.3." Ave Btn hill R33.d.8.4½ & NE & R34.c.4.8 & from there to cemetery – Brigade ~ Army W?	
			advanced bn could not maintain position	
		3pm	34th Div Art Op Order No 25 carried out	
		4.35pm	New German Trench X.56.77 – R35.d.7.0 3 rnds per gun per min	
		3ˢ –	" " " " " 1 " " " " "	
		3ˢ – E.33o.	" " " " " ½ " " " " "	
		9pm	"A" 152 ordered to keep up slow barrage on R35.a.6.11 – R35.d.4.2 during night 1.2 pr gn pr 4 min	
			34th Div Art Op Order No 36 received	
			Ammn expended. 8pm 28th – noon 29th = Nil	}M.C. 152
			" " noon 29th – 8pm = Nil	
			" " 8pm 29th – " " = 260 A, 34 AX	

Army Form C. 2118

WAR DIARY
or
INTELLIGENCE SUMMARY
(Erase heading not required.)

152 Bde FA 114

Instructions regarding War Diaries and Intelligence Summaries are contained in F.S. Regs., Part II. and the Staff Manual respectively. Title Pages will be prepared in manuscript.

Place	Date	Hour	Summary of Events and Information	Remarks and references to Appendices
N30 a 8.0	July 20		Bar 29.82 - Ther 62°	
			Fine hot day. Too hazy for observation.	
			Op Order No 36 cancelled nil (repetition of O Order 35) between 4.40 am & 5.10 am	
			E.475 received (last man passing it 5.20 a.m.)	
			B/152 } with their guns when 2 B/s 175 Rd & came into 2nd Gr Positional	
			D/152 }	
		9.50am	Slow barrage started on trench from MARTINPUICH thro' S18 based Snell line (A.C/152) not i/position	
		10.45am	Barrage increased to 100 per gun per 3 minutes.	
			34th Div Art Op Order No 37 received.	
			A&C Bty & barrage area enlarged by following boundaries - between 5.40pm & 7.10pm	
			(1) drive 50yds W & new trench R35d 7½.4½ to R35d 6.7½	
		5.40pm to 7.10pm	(2) BAPAUME road R35d 6½.7½ - R35d 8.8½	
			(3) R35d 8.8½ - R36c 0.5	
			(4) R35c 0.5 - R35d 7½.4½	
		9.15pm	Slow barrage throughout night 1 rd per gun per 3 min R35d 3.5 - 4.2, to X 56.7.7 (C/152)	
		10.15pm to 12.1am	Heavy German bombardment in vicinity of POZIERES.	
			Lt ALLEN & 10 men DAC attached D/152 for instruction.	
			Casualties No 47928 Gr BOYD killed / No 42436 Gr HILL wounded	
			7930 " BEASLEY wounded 7972 " SPYRE "	
			7963 " ROSTOCK " 7931 " MASSEY "	
			Amm expended 3pm 2.5 - hour 30 h² = 682 A	
			hour 30 " - 9pm " = 902 A, 128 AX } A&C/152	

Army Form C. 2118

152 Bde FA 1/55

WAR DIARY
or
INTELLIGENCE SUMMARY
(Erase heading not required.)

Instructions regarding War Diaries and Intelligence Summaries are contained in F. S. Regs., Part II. and the Staff Manual respectively. Title Pages will be prepared in manuscript.

July

Place	Date	Hour	Summary of Events and Information	Remarks and references to Appendices
N30a.8.0	31st		Bar 29.69 Ther 65° Fine, hot day. In kept bombardment	
			Hostile Artillery quiet during night except for few shells into POZIERES and gas shells in SAUSAGE valley.	
			Capt KNOX evacuated to hospital from Kilo Balloon, his communication trench being dug from trench 6.	
			The whole battery position not unpassable ground.	
			F.O.O with A Coy BE withdrawn.	
	10.54pm		SOS Signal observed (GREEN rockets) and B4 Coy opened fire, but were stopped by C.O's order.	
			Ammn expended 8pm 30th – 12noon 31st = 109 A, 75 A.X.	
			12 noon 31st – 8pm " = Nil	
			Ammn expended 8pm 30th – 12noon 31st = 109 A, 75 A.X.	

1.8.16.

R. Kincardine TMR RFA
OC 152 Bde RFA

To OC. A./152 RFA.

Centre Group Operation Order No 6.
5.7.16

Intention
① The 4th Army will continue the attack tomorrow, the objective of the 3rd Corps being.

The cutting (X17.a Central) CONTALMAISON — BAILIFF WOOD (X16.a.5.0) French Junction X15.a.8.0 — X15.c.5.5 — X15.c.0.1. The XVth Corps on our right will attack MAMETZ WOOD.

Batteries allotted to CENTRE GROUP.
② The following Batteries are allotted to Centre Group. 152 Bde.
C. Bty. 175 Bde.
D. Bty. 175 Bde.
A. Bty. 176 Bde.

③ There will be 3 Phases in the Operations and the tasks of Batteries will be as follows.

1st PHASE.
—0.40 to ZERO.

A.176.	X15.c.2.4 — 3.4 to X15.a.8.0.	
A.152. } C.152 }	X14.d.5.8 to X15.c.2.4.	
B.152	X15.d.3.4 to X15.a.8.0.	
C.175	X16.a.9.9 — X10.c.6.3, 8.4, 9.1.	
D.152	X15.b.4.4 — 4.6 — 5.5 — 5.3.	

—0.70 to —0.40
D.175. X4.c.7.4 (Thermit Shell)

—0.40 to ZERO.
D.175. X16.b.9.5 to X17.a.5.5.

Rate of fire —40 to —10. Two rounds per gun per minute.

—10 to Zero. Three " " " ".

2nd PHASE.   A.176.   X9.c.8.2 — X15.b.5.5.
 ZERO to   A.152. }
 +1.30.   C.152. }   X15.a.8.0 — X14.b.9.4.

            B.152.   X9.d.6.7, X10.a.5.3, X9.d.7.6, —
                      & X10.a.3.0, 7.2.
            D.152.   As in 1st PHASE.
            D.175.   Cutting X10.d.3.1 — 2.2. 3.3, X16.b.4.9.
            C.175.   As in 1st PHASE.
            Rate of fire. One round per gun per 2 minutes.

3rd PHASE. A.176.   X9.c.8.2 — X9.d.5.8.
 +1.30   B.152.   As in 2nd PHASE.
  to
 End.   A.152.   X10.c.6.3 — X10.a.8.5.
            C.175.   X10.c.6.3 — X16.a.9.9.
            C.152.   X14.b.9.4 — X15.a.3.3.
            D.152.   X10.c.1.0 — X9.d.9.2. — 9.4.
            D.175.   X10.c.6.3 — X10.c.1.9.
            Rate of fire. 1 round per gun per 3 minutes.

(4) ZERO hour will be notified separately.
(5) Acknowledge.

                                P. Fox. Lieut & Adjutant
                                         Centre Group.

To
O.C
A/152 R.F.a

Reference Centre Group order No 5.
6-7-16.

Zero Hour will be 8 a.m.

P. Van Lieut & Adj.
Centre Group.

OPERATION ORDER. No. 6

Centre Group orders
―――――――――――

(1) The 13th & 15th Corps are attacking the enemy's second line between LONGUEVAL and BAZENTIN LE PETIT wood on July 14th.

(2) The task of the Centre Group will be to barrage the enemy's 2nd line on its own front viz X5.d.4.7 – X11.c.8.9.
  No firing S.W. of this line.

(3) Batteries which can reach this line will open fire at 3 a.m. at a rate of one round per gun per minute and continue at that rate till 3.20 a.m. From 3.20 to 3.25 a.m. they will fire at their highest possible speed after which they will gradually reduce their rate to one round per gun per two minutes and will continue at this rate till 5.30 a.m.

(4) The object to be obtained is to create an impression of an attack on the line X.12.c.9.6 – POZIÈRES.

(5) Up to 3 a.m. ordinary night firing will continue.

(6) Acknowledge.

                                      E. Farr. Lieut & Adjutant.
                                                Centre Group.

13.7.16.

34th Divisional Artillery

152nd BRIGADE

ROYAL FIELD ARTILLERY

AUGUST 1916

L.K. GROUP Operation Orders attached.

Army Form C. 2118

WAR DIARY
or
INTELLIGENCE SUMMARY

152 Bde RA VOL I

(Erase heading not required.)

Instructions regarding War Diaries and Intelligence Summaries are contained in F. S. Regs., Part II. and the Staff Manual respectively. Title Pages will be prepared in manuscript.

Place	Date	Hour	Summary of Events and Information	Remarks and references to Appendices
ALBERT. X 20 A 6.0 Sheet 57D SE 1/20,000	AUG 1st		Bar 29.75, Ther 67°. A beautiful hot day but hazy for observation, unable to register by Balloon. Ammn Exp. — A, 140 AX. (A+C/152) During evening 1½" Several gun rockets were reported at different times & much artillery action on both sides followed but no other results were reported.	
	2nd		Bar 29.73 Ther 66°. A beautiful hot day, but hazy for observation, unable to register by Balloon Ammn Exp = 43A, 185 AX, (A+C/152) 34th Div Arty Opr Order No 38 recd.	
		Zero 3pm	to X 5a 4.7 — X 5a 8½.6. Zero hour 3pm.	
		0.18	Time & rate of fire :- Fire will commence at a rapid rate (not more than 3 rds per gun per min) as close in front of infantry as possible & search back to the Sunken Line at the pace of assault. Fire will then be continued at a rapid rate on Sunken Line.	
		0.25	Fire will lift 300 yds beyond the Sunken Line searching the ground during the lift & at 0.30½ come back on to the Sunken Line with one Salvo. Stops firing. The pace of assault will be taken at 2½ miles per hour i.e. lift 25 yds every 20 secs. The search back will commence after one round Battery fire has been fired at the shortest range, and carry back to enemy trenches. Owing to nearness of our own Infantry to German Line along this objective, the 34th Div Arty will commence their fire on enemy front line & — not short of it. 34th Div Arty Opr Order No 39 recd. (Special Bombardment to be repeated at 5am 3-8-16	
		9pm	152 RA ordered night barrage on road leading to MARTINPUICH M31D, A/152 turned on till 1am, C/152 from 1 - 5am, rate 6 rds per gun per hour.	
		9.20pm	Batteries report fire rockets & movements hostile to our own fire, this was reported to 152 RA who at 9-40pm ordered barrage on X 35 d 6.0 N to BAPAUME ROAD. A+C/152 turned on for 10 mins, rate 6 rds per gun 4 mins. Then the remainder night turns.	

WAR DIARY or INTELLIGENCE SUMMARY

Army Form C. 2118

Page 2

152. F.A.B.de

Place	Date	Hour	Summary of Events and Information	Remarks and references to Appendices
ALBERT X30a 8.0 Sheet 57d SE 1/20,000	Aug 3rd		Bar 29.9", Ther 61°. Beautiful hot day. Too hazy for Balloon observation. Ammn Exp 20A, 410 AX (ArC/152) BM 29 rnds RC 34 Div consisting of Points S2c 8.2½ - S2c 8.4 Opd Lines made by RMRA. nords. R35a 8.5 - 4.2. ArC/152 in turn 4 bdrs ea, yats 100 pds yds 5 mins. WOF line R35 Central, R35a 8.5 - 4.2. ArC/152 in turn 4 bdrs ea, yats 100 pds yds 5 mins. 34° Div Arty No 39 carried out (repetitions of 34° Div Arty Opn Order No 35)	
	4th	5 am	Bar 29.7", Ther 64°. Fine day but cooler. Too misty for ships to hoppers sudden line of Visibli. Ammn Exp 112A, 224 AX (ArC/152) 9/465 RCC temporary transferred to BTYS 34° Div, CrD/175/where 15rD/152 on the 6" west who go to inform Lieut Col Cotter 176 Bn to rest. 34° Div Arty Opn Order No 40 rds. LK Group Opn Order No 7 issued. 40ArC/152. BMQ2 = BMQ7 both ammunicate to 34° Div Arty Opn Order No 40 rds. BMRA reports 23rd Div held count street from S2c5.3 to road about S2c4½.5.	L.K.Opn Order N7.
	5th		Bar 29.83", Ther 60°. Fine Day. Ammn Exp 683A, 670 AX (ArC/152) BMQ2 report we sites hunt R34 29.9 - x 5 6.3.6 + junction of TORR Trench with 1st + 2nd line rose conducting with all possible speed, we occupy 20 yds of TORR Trench towards MUNSTER ALLEY in property. We site Witamite.	
		5-10p	BMRA report 1st Anzacs we begin. Prisoners report trenches were running from 09.2 line at R34 2.1.2 to COURCELETTE to a serum prison + two dug-outs in it. Last night a company other comdr attacked war him Balloon registered by Aeroplane today. 1 - OR wounded by 60 pdr premature.	
	6th	6.30p	Bar 29.75", Ther 58°. Fine warm day, observation good. DAC now attached to bth reported by another officer to min Watches + fatteurs be synchronged at rockets from aeroplane. rockets not seen Ammn Shop 103A, 269 AX (ArC/152)	
			9/465 carried out CrD/195 return. 13 rD/152 who went to wayn line Night line Ship map rnds with Square letters. BMRA order night lines on T, M + L, ArC/152. Turnds on side + one per gun per hour, where water has been shelled sufficient to induce enemy to take to country, the country to be swept with bursts of five, half H.E., half Shrapnel	

Army Form C. 2118.

WAR DIARY
or
INTELLIGENCE SUMMARY.
(Erase heading not required.)

50 F.A. Bde

Place	Date	Hour	Summary of Events and Information	Remarks and references to Appendices
ALBERT X.30.a.8.0 Sheet 57DSE 1/20000	Aug 7.	6.30am 5.00am	BM RA orders LK Group to be prepared to form Barrage during night at request of Australians on R.25 Central to R.35.d.6.6. Bar. 29.73, Ther 57°, a beautiful fine day. Amm Exp 624 A, 639 AX (A+C/152)	
			BM RA ordered Barrage on line R35 Central to X.5.6 g½.f½. A+C/152 therefore to 2 Div and report. Rifle Bde report enemy attack 0.8.1 + 0.6.2. 1/6 No3 Windmill & heavy approach observed. 1.20am Staff Inf were driven out & 50 prisoners captured, the report had to attack 5 of Bapaume Rd. situation appears normal. 800 in cemetery & barking party heads in advance of T & R found. to connect X 26 27 with left of 25th Div in quarter at left about X.5.7½.2½. Heavy shelling during night on front + South of 7 sausage Valley. Report delayed owing to wire being cut. Left Bde report 14 + 15 Batt'n attacked 4.30 am after heavy bombardment, & heavy casualties. Line old wire driven back, one officer & card of one captured report himself Jan delayed, wire cut.	
	8.	11-45am	Bar 29.75, Ther 62° a beautiful fine day. Amm Exp 210 A, 362 AX (A+C/152) BM 117 ack. LK to Barrage. R.35 u.9.1. - R.35 a.9.6 rate about 25 yards for 114 further A+C/152 tomorrow. 34 Div Arty Op. Order No 41 ack LK Group operation order No 5 issued to 4 and Div & 112 Div	LK O.O. No 8.
		3pm 3.30pm	BM 119 ack at 4.pm return to Barrage ordered in BM 118 120 mg Inf OM ing for 4th near 4-15pm A+C/152 times on a beautiful hot day. Bar. 29.78, Ther 60° BM 121 A, 6A7 AX (A+C/152)	
	9.	10.50am 11-55a	Amut Exp 134.1 A, 6A7 AX (A+C/152) BM 123 ack Hq Australian asks for lift of the Flowery Barrage will to former R.35.C.45 - R.36.e.5.3 LK Group take forward No 3 Bapaume Road. BM 124 A+C/152 informed BM 125 ack Inf counter enquired, therefore to continue till further asked. A+C/152 informed BM 126 enquired Enemy to dug in, trench to X 60 68. Groups will keep up steady fire Mon French Hq Land 12 midnight by Divisional General R.36 c 04 to North of them fired, rate of fire will be increased between 12 midnight & 1am. A+C/152 informed BM on not count report Their line now R.34 b 24 - R.34 b 74 - 5.3 - 4.3 - R.34 c.4.5. BM R.A. ordered same Barrage as last night A+C burst or 25 nods for firm hour, afterwards rebuild to 2 orders for Battery per hour	
	10.		Bar 29.70 Ther 6.3° a dull day rain in morning Amm Exp 420 A 353 AX (A+C/152)	

2353 Wt. W2514/1454 700,000 5/15 D.D. & L. A.D.S.S. Forms/C 2118.

Army Form C. 2118.

152 F.A.Bde

4

WAR DIARY
or
INTELLIGENCE SUMMARY.
(Erase heading not required.)

Instructions regarding War Diaries and Intelligence Summaries are contained in F.S. Regs., Part II. and the Staff Manual respectively. Title pages will be prepared in manuscript.

Place	Date	Hour	Summary of Events and Information	Remarks and references to Appendices
ALBERT. X 30 a 8.0 Sheet 57 D SE Photos	AUG 10 a.m.		34" Div Arty Instr No 42 recd. Relief of 1st Div Batteries by 176 Bde R.F.A. 34" " " After Order No 43 recd. 34" " " Instr No 44 recd. no barrage day or night in conjunction with 160 Bde. LK Group O.O. No 9. Operation Order No 9 issued. B.M.133 recd. Australians now report that our forward men are along line X 5 d 8.3 to R 35 d 2.3.	
	11th	1.40pm	Bar 29.70 Ther 69° A fine day Ammn Exp. 262 A, 282 A X (A+C)/152 4/152 had raid last on gun by Wing Sargt, cannot through open at front of pit, though still damaging fire. 2 killed, 2 wounded (one afterwards died). Infantry want BM/141 theta Infantry report taking X5d 7.3, X5b 6.5, X5b 4.6, X5b 3.9. all firing to be beyond this line. From BM Trubrett Order B/152 to start barrage position tomorrow.	
	12th	2.50pm	Bar 29.58 Ther 62° A fine Day Ammn Exp. 337 A 239 A X 23 9 A X (A+C/152) 34° Div Arty Oper Order No 10 issued D.O. No 10. LK Group Oprl Order No 10 issued BM/152 recd. Liason officer with Australians to be found today, A+C/152 to do this. Ther 65° Bar 29.40 A fine day Ammn Exp 418 A, 376 A X (A+C/152)	
	13th	12-1pm	BM 157 recd. 15" Div ask for increased fire in New Trench Bapaume Road to have 4"+RE increased shell fire 84" Div RA alter their Code from Y C D to F J 4"+RE Kind Bardon + party replaced (?) A C eluded for instruction.	
		12 noon	BMRA reports: Australians hole shot bombs about X5d 7.4, 6.4½, 5½, 5½, 5.7½, - then on to 0.9.2, Hny Lane dug in trench No of Dalhousie into 0.9.2 line further North R34.4.0 - 2.4 - R34 a 8.2 - 3° - R33, R8.7 - 55 - 1.3 - R33 c 8.1 - c 4.7 - 1.4 Aust report Bomb gun post opposite last night. 15° Div captured w new hotels switches line	
		10.55pm	from MUNSTER ALLEY to elbow about S 1.2.9, Right of 15" Div attack failed BM 162 recd. of fighting. LK. Div battery started barrage up Maan line from X 5 b 9.9½ to R 36 e 5.½, with occasional bursts. One section of Bapaume Rd NE from R 35 d 8.9½, burst of fire, A+C/152	
	14th	9.5pm	Bar 29.35 Ther 65° A fine day. Rain in evening Ammn Exp 306 A, 470 A X (A+C/152)	

Army Form C. 2118.

WAR DIARY
or
INTELLIGENCE SUMMARY.
(Erase heading not required.)

162 F.A.Bde.

Place	Date	Hour	Summary of Events and Information	Remarks and references to Appendices
ALBERT.	14th & 15th	9-2pm	RM 162 recd. Australians are continuing their advance towards M.H. LK group increase rate of fire of barrage across BAPAUME road from 10pm to 11pm. At C Btys O complete. RAHQ closed at RUE de BRAY at 6pm. & reopened at W.26.c.3.3. at same hour No 2893 Francis Staff Sergeant & Underwood thered by F.6.C.M. B/ordered of Brig. Gen. AD Kuty R.A.	
	116°	Bar 29.36 Ther 62° Rainy day with a little rain at intervals. Ammn. Expd. 400 A, 626 AX (A+C/152) Opn Order N° 11	O.O. N° 11.
			34° D.w. arty Opn Order N° 9 rect., LK Opn brau N° 11 revd. (practice semtainned)	
			34° " " " " 50 " " Regt Opn attack No 12 does not participate	O.O. N° 12.
			34° " " " " 51 " " LK Opn order N°12 revd, which by 44 Bde on 31 D.w. & not D°	
	116°	Bar 29.26 Ther 62° Morning fine Later dull with little rain.	
			Ammn. Expd. 79 + A 797 AX (A+C/152)	
			34° D.w. arty Opn Order N° 42 recd, copy sent to Btys, Relief of 30° D.w. arty by 50° D.w. arty	
	117°	Ammr Expd. 1868 A, 1301 AX (A+C/152)	
			34° D.w. arty Opn Order N° 52 recd, attack by 1st & 15th Dw on 18th inst.	
	118°	Snow, rain during morning & afternoon Ammn Expd E 939 A, 954 AX ((A+C/152)	
			A/152 withdrew to wagon line to one section D/152 were ordered to assist to wagon line (O.O. N°46)	
			remaining Battery to continue barrage thereline, C/152 complete	
	119°	Showery, both morning & afternoon. Bar 29.29 Ther 57.5. Ammn Expd 388 A, 438 AX (C/152)	
			SC/195 recd ammunition to 34° D.w. arty Opn Order N° 48, LK Bar to Bths at Beaucourt	
			owing to wet weather	
			2/Lieut J A RADFORD awarded Military Cross.	
			C/152 withdrew to wagon line, remaining section of D/152 returd, at Q/152 marched to billets at BEAUCOURT.	
BEAUCOURT	20°	Headquarters, C + D Batteries marched into billets at BEAUCOURT	
"	21st	Batteries marched as far time table (34° O.O. N° 48) to entrain at LONGEAU, Headquarters to SALEUX station.	

WAR DIARY or INTELLIGENCE SUMMARY

Army Form C. 2118.

152. F.N.Bde.

6

Place	Date	Hour	Summary of Events and Information	Remarks and references to Appendices
CROIX DU BAC Q.S.C.1.2. from Sheet 36 NW	AUG 22nd		Batteries attacked at BAILLEAU. Hdqrs at STEENBECQUE marched into Camp near CROIX DU BAC	
	23rd		34" Div Arty Opn Order No 73 recd. Relief of 12" Div Arty by 34" Div Arty on nights 24/25 & 25/26. C.O. with relieving battery positions of 63Bde H.Q. & 85" Bde	
	24th		Systems of batteries A,B & C/152 relieved sections of Batteries A,B & C. 85" Bde. Also sect D/152 relieved sect D/84. Rifle guns were relieved both 4.2 Hows were exchanged with D/84	
H.17.2.3. from 36 NW	25th		Renewing sections of Batteries 85" Bde relieved – D/84. Bde HQ 152 relieved Bde HQ 85" at 11p.m	
	26th		Bar 29.30. Thr 64°. Fine day. Barometer mostly misty in morning. Later good. Quiet Day. Exp. 25"A M12 AX, 288X. Hostile Aeroplanes over. Batteries refirming	
	27th		Bar 29.42. Thr 60°. Fine day. Information from — Quiet, very little hostile fire. Batteries refiring. Armn Exp. 63A 76X. 34" Div Arty Opn Order No 54 received relieving 31" Div Arty from 4 to 6 p.m. 19" Bde Batteries to be completed by 12 noon 28-7-16. Orders issued by 1/152 Bde re-reconstruction. 10/21 Bde Opn Order No 53 rec'd (Relief) — Nights 28/29, 29/30.	
	28th		Bar 29.40. Thr 64°. Fine day. Observation misty in air later good. Hostile Arty Quiet Little Hostile movement seen. At noon 152 Bde who command to 3-6 Bn Rifle Battn. R7148 — 4-5 Hows Left (Opn Order No 59) "D" O.C. Kincaid Smith CMG, DSO was appointed into 2 Groups Right 9 Groups under A/175. 6.C. 8 O.C. groups Asswer No 13 issued — Right Group Opn Orders No 13 issued responsibility at 12 noon.	O.O. N°13
	29th		Bar 29.41. Thr 61°. Observation bad. Grey and soft hazy thunderstorm also heavy rain in vicinity. Quiet day. Enemy still non-existent. Sectors 4050 & White City thinly I31.c, I31.A. Batteries carried out a little refiring, light difficult. Right Group General instruction issued of 152 Opn Orders No 13 issued. Armn Exp. 31A, 8AX.	Geman Larr
	30th		Bar 29.26. Thr 58°. A very quiet day. Light very bad most of the day. Heavy rain little Hostile movement seen. No aircraft activity reported. Batteries registered a little. but light bad.	

Army Form C. 2118.

152 F. A. Bde - 7

WAR DIARY
or
INTELLIGENCE SUMMARY.

(Erase heading not required.)

Place	Date	Hour	Summary of Events and Information	Remarks and references to Appendices
H17 d 3.3. 1/20,000 Sheet 36NW	31st		Bar 29.76 Ther 54° cloudy up to 9 a.m. Good for rest of day. Very quiet day, 5 enemy planes seen, large working party on hand about O.12.c.8.8. (and 1 day) reported to RAHQ, disappeared quickly at 5.5 f—. Battery reporting. Ammn. Exp. noon 30th to noon 31st 46A. Lieut F. Stein joined from H.Q. 176 + was posted to D Bty.	

2.9.16.

K. Kincaid-Smith Lt-Col. RFA
Comdg. 152 Bde. RFA

L.K. Group. Operation Order No 7.

1. 2nd Australian Divn will attack German Line O.G.1 and O.G.2. from Tramline X5.A.9.5 and from R35.c.8½.½ to R34.A.9.1 and R34.D.1.2 respectively. The left flank from R34.A.9.1 to R35.d.8.5 will be held as a defensive flank.

   1st Objective is O.G.1.
   2nd " " O.G.2.

2. Smoke will be emitted on Left Flank at certain points

3. There will be bombardment by H.Arty commencing at - 4.15.
   From - 0.15 to ZERO there will be a period of silence with no Artillery bombardment.

4. The tasks of Batteries L.K. Group will be as follows:
   A & C. Batteries, 152 Brigade. R.F.A.
   0 to 0.3. Bombard O.G.1. from BAPAUME ROAD to X5.A.9.6.
   0.3 to 0.13. Bombard O.G.2. from BAPAUME ROAD to Tramline
   0.13 to 0.15. Lift 50 yards.
   0.15 to 0.17 " further 50 yards
   0.17 " " " " and establish final barrage from ALBERT-BAPAUME road to Railway X5.B. both inclusive.

   Rates of fire.
   0 & 0.3 3 rounds per gun per minute.
   0.3 to 0.30 2 " " " " "
   0.30 onwards. 1 " " " " " .

   If still firing at midnight, all fire will lift 500 yards beyond O.G.2 from 12 midnight to 12.45 a.m.
   Ammunition 2/3rds Shrapnel. 1/3rd. H.E.

5. In case of hostile Counter-attack existing S.O.S. signal of 3 Red Rockets will be used, and in addition Very lights will be fired in quick succession in groups of 3 along front enemy is attacking.
   In such case Artillery will maintain barrage 150

yards in rear of O.G.2.
  GREEN lights are not S.O.S. signals and will be used occasionally to indicate position of infantry.
6. ZERO hour is being notified separately.
7. Acknowledge by wire

4.8.16.   Starr. Lieut & Adjutant.
6.30 p.m.   L.K. Group.

SECRET.

L.K. Group Operation Order No. 8

1. The 4th Australian Division will carry out an operation tonight with the object of pushing forwards towards MOUQUET FARM.

   (A) Objective a line R.34.B.2.4 - R.34.D.0.4 - R.34.A.7 - R.34.A.5.3 - R.34.A.1.2 - R.33.d.9.9 - R.33.d.8.7.

   (B) 12th Division on the left will co-operate by seizing R.33.d.7.8 - R.33.d.8.9 (inclusive).

2. 34th Divisional Artillery will co-operate on right of 4th Australian Division.

   L.K. Group.
   A & C/152 Barrage R.35.A.9.1 - R.35.d.4.6.

   Times & rate of fire.
   ZERO to 0.15.   1 round per gun per minute.
   0.15 & remainder of night. 25 rounds per Bty per hour.
   Ammunition 2/3rds H.E. 1/3rd Shrapnel.

   NOTE. Present barrage will be maintained at present rate until ZERO.

3. Signals. Green flares will be shown in front line at 5.30 am, 8.30 am, & 10.30 am. Tomorrow.

4. ZERO hour is 9.20 am.

5. Watches will be synchronized at 8.30 pm.

6. Acknowledge.

Issued at.
8.18 pm.
8.8.16.

G. Ian Reid   Adjutant
152 Brigade R.F.A.

SECRET.

L.K. Group. Operation Order N° 9.

1. In order to isolate a portion of the switch line preparatory to an eventual attack, the following barrage will be kept up day & night viz:—
Portion of switch line between MUNSTER ALLEY and Tramline (X6.A.4.7 & Tramline)

2. Batteries will undertake this as follows:—
   2 p.m. – 6 p.m. 10th.   "C". Bty. 152.
   6 p.m. – 10 p.m.   "   . "A".   "   ".
   10 p.m. – 10 a.m. 11th.   160 Bde.
   10 a.m. – 2 p.m.   "   . "C". Bty. 152.
   2 p.m. – 6 p.m. 11th.   "A".   "   ".
   6 p.m. – 6 a.m. 12th.   160 Bde.
   and so on.

3. Rate of fire.
   1 rounds per gun per 3 min by day.
   1   "   "   "   " 2 " by night.
   Ammunition 70% Shrapnel. 30% H.E.

4. The battery not in above barrage will keep up irregular bursts of fire on the new trench.
   A 35.d.7.7 to A 5.c.0.4.
   12 rounds per Bty per hour. (70% H.E. 30% Shr)

5. Present position of our Infantry.
   23rd. Div. - X 6.A.1.4. up MUNSTER ALLEY.
   Australian. - X 5.B.8.3 – A 35.d.2.3.

6. Acknowledge.

10.8.16.

S. Law Lieut & Adjt.
L.K. Group.

SECRET.

L.K. Group Operation Order No. 10.

1. 4th Australian Division is attacking on night 12/13 along the following line.
M34.A.8.6, 6.5, 0.5. M33.B.6.5, 3.2.
15th Division will attack SWITCH LINE from S1.d.9.9 to junction of MUNSTER ALLEY.

2. 34th Divisional Artillery will barrage BAPAUME Rd inclusive to 50 yards S. of tramline.

3. L.K. Batteries (A & C 152) will barrage new trench X.35.d.4.6 to M35.d.8.3.

4. Time and rate of firing.
   0.0 to 0.5.   4 rounds per gun per minute.
   0.5 to 0.10.   2   "   "   "   "   " .
   0.10 to 1.0.   1   "   "   "   "   " .
   1.0 & onwards ordinary night firing on same barrage (12 rds per Bty per hour.)

5. Ammunition. 2/3rds. Shrapnel. 1/3rd. H.E.

6. ZERO hour. 10.30 p.m.

7. Watches will be checked at 10.0 pm.

8. Acknowledge.

12.8.16.   S. Farr Lieut & Adjutant
 6.20 pm.   L.K. Group.

SECRET.

L.K. Operation Order. No 11.

1. With a view to future operations a practice bombardment will be carried out this afternoon by 34th & 47th Divl Arty.

2. A & C. Btys 152 Bde will take part as follows:
   (A) 0.0 to 0.1. "A". 152. barrage tramline.
       A.36.c.4.0 — A.36.c.8.2.
       "C". 152. Barrage tramline.
       A.36.c.8.2 — M.31.d.5.5.
   (B) 0.1 to 0.3. "A" 152. Barrage.
       A.36.c.6.1 — S.1.B.5.0 & search to N.E.
       "C". 152. continue as in "A".
   (C) 0.3 to 0.5. Both Btys as in "B".
   (D) 0.5 to 0.9.   "   "   "   "   "B".
   (E) 0.9. Cease firing.

3. Rate of fire throughout — 3 rds per gun per min.
4. Ammunition. 2/3rds H.E. 1/3rd Shrapnel.
5. ZERO hour 4 pm.
6. Watches will be synchronized at 3.30 pm.
7. Acknowledge.

16.8.16.
S. Fan Lieut. Adjt.
L.K. Group.

SECRET.

L.K. Group Operation Order No 12.

1. On the 17 inst the 44th Infantry Brigade is attacking the German Switch line from the ELBOW (S1.d.4.8) Westwards.

2. A & C Btys. 152 Bde. will take part as follows:

   (A) 0.0 to 0.1. "A" Bty. Barrage Tramline.
       A36.c.4.0 to A36.c.8.2.
       "C" Bty. Barrage Tramline.
       A36.c.8.2. – M31.d.5.5.

   (B) 0.1 to 0.5. "A" Bty. Barrage
       A36.c.5.1 to S1.B.6.0 & search to N.E.
       "C" Bty. Barrage Tramline as in (A)

3. Rates of fire.
   0.0 to 0.5. = 3 rounds per gun per minute.
   0.5 to 0.15. = 2   "   "   "   "   " .
   0.15 onwards = 1   "   "   "   "   " .

4. Fire will be continued at this rate till further orders.

5. Ammunition. 2/3rds Shrapnel. 1/3rd. H.E.

6. An officer from Group Headquarters will call at Battery positions to synchronise watches about 7 a.m.

7. Acknowledge.

16.8.16.   S. Jan. Lieut & Adjutant
9.30 a.m.   L.K. Group.

Right Group Operation Order No 13

SECRET   28-3-1916.

Composition. (1) The Right Group will consist of the
re-constituted 152 Bde R.F.A. together with A/175.

Allotment of Front (2) The German Front allotted to the Group
is :-   O1.a.6.9 to I27.a.1.9.
which is sub-divided for Batteries as follows:
B 152.   " O1.a.6.9. - I32.c.½.7½.
C   "   " I32.c.½.7½. - I26.c.8½.½.
A   "   " I26.c.8½.½. - I26.b.8.2.
A 175.   " I26.b.8.2. - I27.a.1.9. (2 Sections)
          1 Section enfilading Left Group front.
D 152.   Whole front.

Liaison Duties (3) A liaison officer will be detailed to
remain at Btn Hd Qrs of each Battalion holding
the Line from 8 pm to 8 a.m.
They will be provided as follows :-
Right Bttn.   B & C/152.   On alternate nights.
Left Bttn.   A/152 & A/175   "   "

These Officers must know full details with regard to
front covered by the Batteries they represent, position
of night lines, and will frequently test their
communications to Group Hdqrs and Batteries.

(4) Batteries will complete the attached
table giving various information as to positions of guns,
arcs of fire etc, and return to Group Headquarters
with as little delay as possible.

(5) During hours of daylight an officer must
always be in the Battery O.P.

(6) 200 rds per gun will be kept at Gun
position.

(7) There will always be a look out man on duty
at each Gun position watching for enemy aeroplanes
during daylight, & no firing is to take place from a
gun position when an enemy plane is in the vicinity
unless operations are in progress.

                                    S. ??? Lieut R.F.A.
                                    Adjutant. ???

SECRET.

General Instructions
"Right Group"

__Work with Aeroplane.__ (1) Squares are allotted to Batteries as follows:—

    D. 152.   I.34.
    C. ",   I.31, I.32, I.33.
    B. ".   O1, O2, O3, O7, O8.

__Retaliation for Enemy Minenwerfer.__ (2) On receipt of message "MINNIE" R or L from Infantry Brigade or either Battalion holding line D.152 will fire forthwith 2 salvos as follows:—

"MINNIE Right." = STRAWBERRY HOUSE O1.b.3.6
       and OYSTER FARM. I.32.c.2.4
"MINNIE Left" = LE QUESNE. I.27.c.8.0. & I.26.b.0.2.

and will then report to Group Headquarters for further orders.

__GAS and S.O.S.__ (3) Attention is drawn to para 12 of 34th Div. G.S./22/118 of 24.8.1916. which has been circulated to Batteries which gives the instructions for the guidance of Battery Comdrs, who must act on their own initiative, and then report to Group Headquarters.

__Returns__ 4 Due care must be taken to render punctually and accurately the returns, a list of which has been sent to all Units.

29-8-1916.

S. Farr Lieut. & Adjutant
Right Group.

vol 8

Confidential
War Diary
- of -
152nd F.A. Brigade
From 1st to 30th Sept. 1916

Volume 9

Army Form C. 2118.

WAR DIARY or INTELLIGENCE SUMMARY. 152nd Bde. R.F.A.

(VOL I)

(Erase heading not required.)

Place	Date	Hour	Summary of Events and Information	Remarks and references to Appendices
ARMENTIERES H.17.D.55.A	Sept 1st	4 P.M.	Fine day. The 60th Bar 2893. From day's good observation Right Grps. to have carried out an operation and 101st Infantry Brigade were ready pretty much although somewhat ruled out by our own who shelled two of C Right Bty's Batteries and 370 & 270 rounds respectively apparent to be very effective. The enemy artillery was exceedingly quiet and we made the 7th M.H. appeared to be very effective. The enemy artillery was exceedingly quiet and we made H2", C9, M.H. any B-D battery positions and alarm zones. The Field Litz Locale. O 010 89. Intermittent amount of German air activity and no patrols in range. Ammunition Expended A 122 13 x 87.	
	Sept 2	9.30 AM	Bar 29.85. The 60. Fine day. 10 men seen carrying material apparently from Batley Houses. 02.C.5.25. & deep situation O.5.A.2.8. Men seen digging in the trench area. About 30 houses and few tree entrances 27,46,49 + 30. Our batteries were fairly quiet along. A Hostile aeroplane seen flying over A battery positions & parts of C.H day. Ammr. Expended. A.262, BX.44.	
	Sept 3	10 AM	About 30 British aeroplanes flew over the lines. Day was heavy. Little wind no enemy rifle fire but without any visible. Hostile guns fronts were located at 0.15.C.2.2. + 0.15.C.6.8. The batteries did a little registration. Ammunition Expended. A 67	
	"		Bar 29.52. Ther 54°. A quiet day by artillery on both sides. Saw aircraft were seen many day read I.36.D.13 & I.36.D9.1. Ammr. Expended A.49, A.X.6. B x 13.	

WAR DIARY or INTELLIGENCE SUMMARY.

Army Form C. 2118.

Instructions regarding War Diaries and Intelligence Summaries are contained in F. S. Regs., Part II. and the Staff Manual respectively. Title pages will be prepared in manuscript.

(Erase heading not required.)

Place	Date	Hour	Summary of Events and Information	Remarks and references to Appendices
ARMENTIERES	SEPT. 5		Bar. 29˙34. Ther. 53°. Rainy & cool day for observing. Hostile artillery very quiet. Small parties of our own on enemy seen from RADINGHEM & BONTEMS. Ammnt. expended A.3.3, Ax.5.	
	SEPT 6		BAR. 29.92. Ther. 54°. Overcast day, in afternoon a few small working parties put on a vegetable arm carried by enemy in trenches. Artillery (hostile) was not active during the day. Ten enemy aeroplanes were observed. Ammnt. expended A.11.	
	SEPT 7		BAR. 30.05. Ther. 53°. Fair day (reconnaissance). Considerable movement taken every time Left Group carried out a shoot. Ration role No.56. Enemy retaliated with 77mm & 4.2 on trench No. S83.59 and also on ARMENTIERES. Ammnt. expended. A.91. Ax.15. Gr. MORGAN. B Battery. Warrant Sergeant.	
	SEPT 8		Bar. 30.05. Ther. 53°. Friday, good observation. Several parties of enemy were seen to leave their lines & dispersed by our artillery.	
		5 P.M. Zero hour.	Right Gr. Group Oper. Order. No 74 carried out not considered result is damage to enemy front line & parapet. No destruction. Havre Gunnery party. Ammunition Expend A. 66. Ax 26. Right Group O.O. 15° issued.	
	SEPT 9		Bar. 29.95. Ther. 56°. Too windy for good observation. Men seen carrying coats to & at O.2.C.A5.25° they were dispersed by our fire. Three hostile aeroplanes were flying over.	

2353 Wt. W2514/1454 700,000 5/15 D. D. & L.   A.D.S.S./Forms/C. 2118.

Army Form C. 2118.

WAR DIARY
or
INTELLIGENCE SUMMARY.
(Erase heading not required.)

Instructions regarding War Diaries and Intelligence Summaries are contained in F. S. Regs., Part II. and the Staff Manual respectively. Title pages will be prepared in manuscript.

Place	Date	Hour	Summary of Events and Information	Remarks and references to Appendices
ARMENTIERES	Sept 9		GROUP SCHEME. At 1.55 A.M. the batteries as detailed opened rapid bursts of fire lasting 2 minutes on enemy front line & parapet, which had been damaged by us the preceding afternoon. Hostile Artillery very quiet. Answer. Enfilador A 32; AX 139. BX 91.	
	Sept 10		2½°J.S. Bell attached H&v. o 9th. M° Thomas attached A Battery. Bar. 29.55. Ther. 60°. No movement seen behind enemy line during 2 event. Enemy artillery very quiet. Counter Enfilador A 21. BX 7.	
	Sept 11		BAR 29.82, Ther 57°. A dull day's observation on 2 event. Two working parties seen & fired on. Our hostile Artillery up. Enemy artillery shelled our C & D batteries. against Battery	
			N°32337 9/B F°. WYKES A. KILLED 9 D/15.2	
			N°32323 9/B. STANHOPE. H.A. WOUNDED 9 D/15.2.	
			Ammunition. Enfilador A 30. AX 4.	
	Sept 12		Bar. 29.70. Ther 58°. 9B/152 noticed that the Germans in I.31.D centre have been relieved by 75% Regiment and have got riflemen [?]. Hostile Artillery was active. a 4.2 Battery was located at O.11.C.5.9. a 5.9 battery at O.10.B.99. Batteries chiefly engaged in wire cutting & registering. 3rd Div. Art. Brdr. orders No 382 Ammunition received. Right Group 201 days. Arm: Enfilador A 213. AX 15. BX 31 ordered. N°16. issued. Bombardments 2 & 1 days.	

Army Form C. 2118.

WAR DIARY
or
INTELLIGENCE SUMMARY.
(Erase heading not required.)

Instructions regarding War Diaries and Intelligence Summaries are contained in F. S. Regs., Part II. and the Staff Manual respectively. Title pages will be prepared in manuscript.

Place	Date	Hour	Summary of Events and Information	Remarks and references to Appendices
ARMENTIERES	SEPT/13.		Wagon line move to A.19 & A.21.	
	Sep/14		Dull day & bad observation raining & windy. Our artillery carried out wire cutting on the Right Group Ops. Gds. No 16 with satisfactory results. Two enemy working parties were seen & dispersed. Men were seen shelling trench along tram line. They were fired upon until good round obtained or until they ceased. 3rd Div. Arl Observ. Gds. No 57 received Right group Ops. Gds. No 17 xxxx raids Enemy Trenches at A.199, AX.38, BX.6. Bar. 29.75. Ther 51.	-1 day
			Our artillery fired according to plan & with a para 9. A great deal of gas shell fire was being replied to & guns were muzzled entangled and accused of being. The bur'l war too free with respect to gas shell. Normal registration was also carried out by battus. Four Torpedoes A.603, A.X.103. B.X.58	
	Sep/15		Bar. 29.29. The 1st. Scheme for zero day carried out. By Richar & encounter good. To battns carried out our cutting. Men seen in enemy's back area about O.2.A.7.1. Men also seen to be digging a long line of trenches. O.8 and they were fired at and circuit timber were thrown up.	

2353 Wt W2544/1454 700,000 5/15 D. D. & L. A.D.S.S. Forms/C. 2118.

WAR DIARY
or
INTELLIGENCE SUMMARY

Army Form C. 2118.

Place	Date	Hour	Summary of Events and Information	Remarks and references to Appendices
ARMENTIERES	15	2.15 p.m.		
		2.17 p.m.	Burst of rapid fire was carried out by all batteries, shortly repeated it be very accurate by enemy. The Artillery are busy out their reply to this in this & unneeded fire was C. Coy which which a front on Coys trenches telegraphic & the report of that. Artillery reply also telephone on Sp/9 was also very damaged. Ammunition expended A.755, AX 102, BX 47.	
	Sept 16		Bar 29.83. Ther 53°. Sodden pt 71 day now current out. During at days the batteries fired a steady rate in at rate at day time & also no few hours below when rounds are seen. The Sher Inf sent forward very infantry. In no place the pppp was breached throwing over of top on round cannot much south on for several operations, & probably have beneath French road near materials clearing at night & 15:50 & 15:24 "But now the 8 or 9 persons can take a serious what was formed the Ammunition "Expended A 73, AX 91, BX 24.	
	Sept 17		Bar 30 Ther 45°. The batters chiefly fired a regards to on was carrying to the night road of 42 day. Sa it Morning Devenue an seen at STRAWBERRY HOUSE & FARM HOUSE & alles home been in her Coy & by letter Brig Genl Crossy manno 17 Lieut	

WAR DIARY
or
INTELLIGENCE SUMMARY.
(Erase heading not required.)

Army Form C. 2118.

Place	Date	Hour	Summary of Events and Information	Remarks and references to Appendices
ARMENTIERS			During the morning two hostile aeroplane were up & flew well behind our lines one Kite Balloon	
			Hand grenades dropped on front H.3.D.3.0, the same as yesterday	
	6/152		Had when the pin was to life	
		12.50AM	Raid on 2 days carried out by 10th Royal Scots. Zero time 12.50am 15.9.16. The batteries carried out an intense bombardment on enemy's parapet W.20.0+2 who wire entanglements. The Trench Mortars also maintained the fire of heavy trench shells at w.20.0+2 the artillery left a gap in the enemy's parapet through which the infantry afterwards entered. The infantry advanced immediately bombing & capturing trenches, etc, in the enemy trench they also went along the trench for some distance also into the enemy line & took 2 prisoners and after exploring two counter mines in our wire and one returned. The enemy retaliated on the support lines and 77 and 342 were no own casualties	A 15·40. BX. 347
Commenced Barrage at 2^h 6.Rd A 15.40   BX 24
A 75, AX 91,
Parry at 5y 6.Rd	
	Sep. 15.		Ban. 30. Thr. 65°. Light had scarcely fallen 6.Pm. A very quiet day, the artillery a bit active, hardly fired at all. Snipers were silence owing from trenches BLANK CORNER, 27 sentries pound new post	

Instructions regarding War Diaries and Intelligence Summaries are contained in F. S. Regs., Part II. and the Staff Manual respectively. Title pages will be prepared in manuscript.

WAR DIARY
or
INTELLIGENCE SUMMARY.
(Erase heading not required.)

Army Form C. 2118.

Place	Date	Hour	Summary of Events and Information	Remarks and references to Appendices
			direct hits were obtained and a column of smoke resulted did not clear away for several minutes. Gen Kirby goes on leave & Lt Colonel Kincaid Smith temporarily takes over CRA. Lieut Colonel Furnivall takes command of the right group in his absence. Ammunition Expended. A 99. BX 25	
	Sept 19		Bar. 29.6 Ther. 45. Raining & bad for observation. The batteries fired very little during the day. Working parties were reported by the infantry at I.26.D.8.2 his batteries dispersed same. Three hostile aeroplanes were flying over during the morning. The usual small amount of traffic was seen on the ridge behind the German lines between HADINGHAM & LANNETIERES. Also smoke was seen rising from house O.10.D.7.8. five direct hits were obtained on this building. Ammunition Expended. AX 32 BX 15.	
	Sept 20		BAR. 29.62 Ther. 50. The batteries were wire cutting most of the day. A lane was cut with satisfaction @ I.26.C.9½.1½. Work was seen to be in progress at buildings O.2.A.2½.7. They were fired on by our Hows. several direct hits being obtained, timber etc was thrown into the air. Smoke was seen rising from house O.10.D.5.7, five direct hits were obtained. Two large 4.2 anti aircraft guns were firing from O.21.A.9.3 they were fired on by our Hows & have not fired since. Ammunition Expended. A. 106. AX. 15. BX 10.	

2353 Wt. W2544/1454 700,000 5/15 D. D. & L. A.D.S.S. Forms/C 2118.

WAR DIARY
or
INTELLIGENCE SUMMARY

(Erase heading not required.)

Army Form C. 2118.

Place	Date	Hour	Summary of Events and Information	Remarks and references to Appendices
ARMENTIERES	Sept 21		Bar. 29.79. Ther. 49°. Our Artillery cut wire & damaged the enemy's parapet @ I.26.B.8.3½. New night wire was reported by B/152 @ C/152. 14 Rounds were fired at hours 0.2.A.7.2 & several others fired was at hours 0.2.B.5.0 & 0.8.D.F.6.5. Other buildings were fired at. 34th Div. Operation Order No 63 received, under A/152 & 155th Bde withdrawn from the line & began at night at its wagon line. They were temporarily attached to "FRANK'S FORCE" commanded by Major Gen. G. Frank. & the Bde. acceptd. They were at its at lie at ARMENTIERES. Lt. Colonel Ferguson Left at 15.30 & Major J. Hogan Bryant Cap. FERGUSON 7D/152 was temporary [illegible] at 15.30. Bdr. D.O.W. 18 [illegible] No 1648	
	SEPT 22		Bar. 30.1. Ther. 46°. Our batteries chiefly fired a regular new night line & forms a new. Sounds was seen near the FARM HERISSON this was first on & the evening but Tracers were thrown slanting & Station 0.26.D.7.6.7.c.6. many times the next occs, & some truck enumerated & seen Gunners movement went across C. BATTERIES. Who butting was piercd R. Two M2 Rounds arrived from O.F.C.F.6 they did not fire light & registered by our. they did not fire again shortly Eight [illegible]	
	Sept 21			

Army Form C. 2118.

WAR DIARY
or
INTELLIGENCE SUMMARY.
(Erase heading not required.)

Instructions regarding War Diaries and Intelligence Summaries are contained in F.S. Regs., Part II. and the Staff Manual respectively. Title pages will be prepared in manuscript.

Place	Date	Hour	Summary of Events and Information	Remarks and references to Appendices
ARMENTIERES	Sept 22		Eight enemy aeroplanes were observed to be flying over station about 6 P.M. Spooner Order No 18 received. There was an intense [?] about by the 10th Cavalry. Our own batteries responded. A.77. A.X.30. B.X.64. M = Ammunition Expended. [?]	
	Sept 23		The 2nd Leinsters 2nd R.Br. Fusiliers [?] were sent forward from Reserve Trenches. Two batteries [?] are now [?] was observed working at C.14.D.17.60. This point was [?] at 12C.77 & 2 P.M. The [?] range was on [?]. Carriages appeared on road [?] the movement ceased. During the day 3 Field aeroplanes were [?] about 12 W.15.2. [?] on back W.7.7.62. Ammunition Expended A.164, A.X.F. B.X.64.	
	Sept 24		Bar 29.78. Ther 45°. Very cloudy. A good fire [?]. Spooner Order No 18 was carried out at 3.30 P.M. with exception [?] T.T.M.'s expecting doing much damage to be at enemy front [?] [?] fire 150 rounds. Hr. 9 [?] no damage to [?] o T 31.B.57 & reply [?] shelled in many places. T.22.C.2.9. 90 [?] [?] [?]	

2353. Wt. W2544/1454. 700,000. 5/15. D.D.&L. A.D.S.S. Forms/C 211b.

WAR DIARY or INTELLIGENCE SUMMARY

Army Form C. 2118.

Place	Date	Hour	Summary of Events and Information	Remarks and references to Appendices
ARMENTIERES	24"		Meanwhile the batteries were firing & beyond extent the trenches, two half doz Howitzers got on every apparently & fired well was seen hitting enemy front line. Effect not timed No 3". This was the G and T He & spinning of batts was thrown up. The enemy retaliates rarely for Regtl Group O.O No 19 issued Moment was seen on fort & Tain at I 35 c 2.7 This front was inactive.	
		9.30 AM	Our hostile aeroplane flew over our lines but was immediately chased off by our aeroplane. A S.S. Pt Manager's aeroplane was brought back but had not our own Immunition to hover a O No 19 issued.	
	23rd		Bev 29.77 Ten. 48 Light gun Decress to Morning the battery fired on regesting front and aeroplane. The enemy fired one thousand & five Towed Jenny were quiet apparently to usus. Some infusion on O Pat. 03 032 90. this front was fired at a ten times into Stones. Moment var you were or O.I.R. S.O. Ten to two seas fire ___ Two own aeroplane on eighteen was carried, apparently on ammunition dump. The hostile aeroplanes were steered during the day. Ammunition Expended, A.H, A X 66, B X 32	

Place	Date	Hour	Summary of Events and Information	Remarks and references to Appendices
ARMENTIERES	Sept 26		Bar 29.5 Ther 53 Observation bal. NE 2 P.M. Left Camp 10.0 10 onward	
			The battery carried out a registration on targets in war Table in chart, this not registration.	
			A Working Party was observed at O.2.c.9.5. they were fired upon & dispersed. Six Enemy Aircraft guns were seen to fire.	
			From Road O.14.B.5.6. to O.14.B.3.2.6.	
			There were many little shellings by the enemy that am Barrages A.37.A.x.22.B.x.24.	
			Bar 29.5.3 Ther 58. The G.O.C R.A. return from leave at Chatham small	
			[illegible] at 12.30 HRs T. Fane took his place he was on leave in	
			Belgium. They left our own trenches & passed unseen & got to their trenches	
			in the morning. From 3 o c 3.30 P.M 2CL batteries fired in conjunction with Trench	
			Mortar School. The T.M. fired in front as limit & barrage to watch they were	
			accurately clear up. There were being carried out of Iron trenches & several places	
			Tanks & armoured cars come up as well as The battalions & half [illegible] supper	
			& communication trench, gate & Cigale Farm & Place House, over the long	
			string on it latter by ct Moir. The aerial roman ammunition personnel	
			was seen on it Somewhere - Enemy gun seen	

WAR DIARY
or
INTELLIGENCE SUMMARY.

(Erase heading not required.)

Army Form C. 2118.

Instructions regarding War Diaries and Intelligence Summaries are contained in F.S. Regs., Part II. and the Staff Manual respectively. Title pages will be prepared in manuscript.

Place	Date	Hour	Summary of Events and Information	Remarks and references to Appendices
ARMENTIÈRES	Sep 27		During the afternoon a smart fire was opened on Armentières	
		6 PM	A hostile aeroplane fallen into hands of flew over our lines it was shot at by our Anti-aircraft & finally very low down flares by air of air aeroplane. Rgt'l Group D O W 22 used. Ammunition Expend A 53 A X 1. B X 14	
	Sep 28	Bar 29.52	The 52.S.F. A.coy. busy day of B registration. No firing after 4.30 P.M. Sh. all batteries fired till 4.30 P.M. ammunition exp't cont. T.M. Shot damage wasted & over & hopes in many places expend. part I. 31 D.5.5. This was carefully sent in telephs today the hole of 52.S.F. A.coy chiefly in Supplies 2nd Lieut. M.D. WERE wounded by shell fire 6/15-2 RFA. Ammunition Expended A 77 A x 36 B x 5-4	
	29th	Bar 29.48	The 52' Observation very good all day. Very little firing done by the batteries. reregistration carried out during the afternoon on Frelen & on OOSTERN=O Ke. 14.74. A.coy slept about 30 H.E. in T. and 47. Ammunition Expended A 70 A X 45 B X 40	

WAR DIARY or INTELLIGENCE SUMMARY

Army Form C. 2118.

Place	Date	Hour	Summary of Events and Information	Remarks and references to Appendices
ARMENTIERES H17.d.3.7.	Sep/30		Bar. 29.57. Ther 51° A coy from Rly. The 34th Div. Art. horseshow held at Croix du Bac. Very successful good turn out. Weather very good. The following prizes were won by the Brigade. 1st Jug. Officers Charger. Capt Mybergh. A battery. 1st N.C.O. Jumping. B.S.M. Bradbent. A battery. 1st Machine gun Maxinne. Brigade Headquarters. 2nd Jug. Team 76 hours and wagon. A battery. 2nd Driving completed. C/D battery. 1st N.C.O. Jumping. B.S.M. D/battery. Very little firing was done during the day. A Bty Kept up gun fire at 07A 9.5.6. The forgeur chapsau and Bridge were in action at O.M.A.7.B	
		12.M.M	21.12. quadruped its time and fired bucks on line In reply enemy of 6.E.I.h Speckenick No 22 gun cases out. November Eshems on A.27.A.8.7. BX 3-1	

K. Vincent Mackenzie Mr
Cy 152 Bde R.F.A.

1.10.16

SECRET.

RIGHT GROUP Operation Order No 15.

1. <u>Objective</u>. A combined shoot in conjunction with Trench Mortars followed by a dummy raid to obtain identifications, will take place ~~tomorrow~~ Today Sept 8th on German front line between T.26.c.8.0 – T.26.d.0.2½ and strong points in rear.

2. <u>Tasks</u>. The Tasks of Batteries, Right Group will be as follows:

A/152 on Front line and wire between T.26.c.3.0 – T.26.d.0.2½.
C/ " on strong point. T.32.a.4.7.
B/ " "   "   " T.26.d.3.5.1.5.
D/ " "   "   " T.33.d.1.3.

A/175 will stand by ready to take advantage of any target which may present itself.

   Ammunition. 15 rounds per gun.

3. <u>Trench Mortars</u>. Medium Trench Mortars, 2 guns on front line T.26.c.8.0 – T.26.d.0.2½.
   Ammunition. 20 rounds per gun.

4. <u>Time</u>. Zero 5 p.m. Shooting to finish by 5.30 p.m.
   Time will be checked at 4 p.m.

5. <u>Dummy Raid</u>. Machine guns will fire from dark until 1 a.m. where any damage may have been done, and at 1.55 a.m. a rapid burst of fire lasting two minutes will be fired by following Batteries.

A/152 on T.26.c.8.0 – T.26.d.0.2½ (4 guns)
C/ " "   do   do.   (4 guns)
B/ " "   T.32.a.9.9 – T.26.d.1.2 (4 guns)

Rate of fire. 6 rounds per gun per minute.
Time will be checked at 1. a.m. 9.9.16.

6. <u>Acknowledge</u>.

8.9.1916.   G. Turr Lieut & Adjutant
                              Right Group

Copy No.

Right Group Memorandum

Reference Right Group Operation Order No 17

(1) Zero Time will be 12.50 am 18-9-16.

(2) Lieut Howitt R.F.A. will report to O.C. 16th Royal Scots at his advanced Hd Qrs near JOCKS JOY at 11pm. He will have telephonist & linesman with him and be in direct communication with Right Group Hd Qrs.

(3) OC. "Z" TM Battery will have his mortars ready to fire on point I 26 c 8.0, and opposite BRIDOUX SALIENT if called upon to do so by the Left & Right Battln Commanders respectively.

S. Farr Lieut & Adjutant
Right Group.

17-9-16

SECRET

Right Group Operation Order N° 12ᴬ

1. A/152 & A/175 are withdrawing to wagon lines tonight

2. <u>Ammunition</u> A/152 & A/175 will move with their Echelons full (fill up from Battery Position) C/152 will take over ammunition remaining in A/152 positions & B/152 will take ammunition left behind by A/175. All ammunition at detached sections A/152 & A/175 should be removed tonight

   Receipts to be obtained of A & AX handed over & sent to Right Group H.Q. A/152 will report no quantity of A & AX in their Echelons.

3. O.C. Batteries will report completion of their withdrawal to Group H.Q.

4. Captain P.H. Ferguson will assume command of Right Group 34th Divisional Artillery from 6 am 22nd September 1916.

5. For withdrawals no movement will take place before 8 pm tonight.

6. A/152 & A/175 will leave behind 1 N.C.O & 3 men, one to be a lineman, to keep positions in repair & patrol telephone lines.

7. B/152 will find Liaison Officer & telephonist with Right Battalion — C/152 ditto with Left Battalion.

8. Attached D.A.C. men to remain behind for work on O.Ps

9. At 7 pm tonight:—
   B Battery 152 Bde will cover trenches 48, 49, 50, 51,
   C " " " " " " " 52, 53, 54, 55
   (& part of 56) marked on German trenches as "
   B/152 O1a 6.9 to road T 32 a 5.3.
   C/152 T 32 a 5.3 to I 26 b y 5.30.

10. Acknowledge

S. Farr Lieut & Adjut
Right Group.

21-9-16

Secret

Right Group Operation Order No 18.

Objective 1. A Bombardment of Enemy Defences will be carried out tomorrow by Right Group in co-operation with 101st Infantry Brigade.

Tasks 2. The task of Batteries Right Group will be as follows:-

C/152 to fire on wire & front trench I26c8.0 to I26d0.2

B/152 to fire on communication trench I32a90.70 to T32b75.20

D/152   2 guns on T.32 b 2.1

         2 " " LE QUESNE.

Trench Mortars. Trench Mortars, Medium Trench Mortars 2 guns on front line I26c8.0 to I26d0.2

Ammunition 3. Ammunition   18 pdrs 15 rounds per gun

                 4.5 Hows 5 rounds per gun

            Trench Mortars 20 rounds per gun

Time 4.   3 pm to 3-45 pm.

Watches will be synchronised with Right Group. H.Q at 2 pm.

Rate of Fire 5. Observed fire.

Identification Raid 6. An Identification Raid will be carried out the same night

S. Farr Lieut & Adj
Right Group.

22-9-16

Secret

Right Group Operation Order No 19

A Trench Mortar Shoot will be carried out this afternoon, commencing 3 pm.

Both Medium & Stokes Mortars will fire and are to continue firing either until it is dark or they have expended their ammunition.

The points to be engaged by the Trench Mortars are as follows:—

I 26 c 8.6   (a)
I 32 a 6.6   (b)
I 32 c 2.9   (c)
I 31 d 2.3   (d)

B/152 will co-operate with the Shooting c & d T.M. targets
C " " " " " " " a & b " "

These batteries will keep up a fire on suspected O.P's, front line & communication trenches during the time T.M's are firing in order to cover the fire of the T.M's

D/152 will fire at intervals on strong points behind enemy front line.

Ammunition   18 p'dr   **25** rounds per gun
             4.5"   **15**   "   " How.

Acknowledge

                     E. Jan Lieut & Adjutant.
                     Right Group.

24-3-16

Secret

Right Group Operation Order No. 20.

1. A bombardment of the enemy's defences will be carried out by Right Group Artillery in conjunction with 101st Brigade on Sept 27 & night 27/28th Sept.

2. **Right Group.** Time 3-0 pm to 3-30 pm
Medium Trench Mortars will bombard enemy front parapet & cut wire I26c8.0 - I26d0.3 & from I31d3.3 to I31d6.6 covered by 18 pdr fire on communication trenches etc.

B/152	Commn Trench	I26c8.0 to I32b6.2	2 Guns
B/152	Support Line	I31d2.2 to I31d6.3	
C/152	Commn Trench	I26d2.5 to I24c4.1	
D/152	Support Line	I26d5.5 to I32a8.6	

Ammunition
 20 rounds per Medium Trench Mortar
 15 " per 18 pdr
 20 " " 4.5 How.

3. 10-0 pm to 10-2 pm
B/152 bursts of fire on Road from Bois Blancs to I33a2.5½
C/152 do do I33a2.5½ to La Houssoie
D/152 do do Bois Blancs, Le Quesne, La Houssoie

10-15 pm to 10-16 pm
All batteries repeat 10-0 pm bursts.

2-0 am to 2-1 am.
Bursts of fire from all 18 pdr & 4.5 Hows. on enemy parapet from I26c8.0 - I26d0.3.
Ammunition for Night Bursts.
18 pdr 4 rounds per gun per minute
4.5 How 3 " " " " "

4. Time will be synchronized with Group H.Q at 2 pm & 8 pm
5. Acknowledge

S. Farr Lieut & Adj
Right Group

26-9-16

Copy No 10   SECRET.

RIGHT GROUP.
Operation Order No 22.

Intention. 1.   A raid on the enemy front trenches about the point I.31.d.5.5 will be carried out on the night of the

Artillery Tasks. 2.   The tasks of Batteries Right Group will be as follows:—

1st PHASE.   Zero to O+6.

B.152.   Enemy front line   I.31.d.25.30 to O1.A.6.9.
C.152.   "   "   "   I.31.d.85.65 to I.32.c.2.9.
D.152.   One gun.   BRIDOUX FORT.
     "   "   House O1.b.4.9.
     "   "   Support trench I.32.c.1.5.
     "   "   Point. I.32.c.2.9.

Rate of fire.   18 pdrs.   4 rds per gun per minute.
                 5. Hows.   3   "   "   "   "   "   " .

2nd PHASE.   O+6 to end.

Batteries remain on same objectives but rate of fire will be reduced to 2 rds per gun or howitzer per minute.

French mortars 3.   Two medium trench mortars will open fire at Zero hour on enemy front line 126.c.8.0 – 126.d.0.2.
Ammunition. 20 rds per mortar.
Rate of fire. As fast as possible.

Registration 4.   Registration will be carried out on Sept 29th & 30th and to avoid drawing special attention to I.31.d.5.5 Batteries will also register other points in their respective zones, and the O.C. Right Battalion must be warned before any registration of trenches opposite BRIDOUX salient take place.

Zero hour. 5.   Zero hour will be   approximately but the definite signal to open fire will be the explosion of a BANGALORE Torpedo.
Watches will be synchronized as follows with Group Adjutant.
         6 pm. by an Officer with watch from each Bty
        10 pm. by Telephone.

Liaison. 6. Lieut. G. HOWITT R.F.A. will report at advanced
Bttn Hd Qrs of Right Battalion Jocks Joy at
hour to be notified later accompanied by
telephonist and linesman, and will arrange
to be in direct communication with Group
Hd Qrs.

7. Acknowledge.

27.9.16. T. Howitt Lieut and Adjutant
Right Group.

Copies to
    No. 1. H.Q. R.A.
        2. 101st Inf Bde
        3. Left Group
        4. B. 152.
        5. C. 152.
        6. D. 152.
        7. Trench mortars.
     8 to 11. -spare.

Confidential

War Diary
- of -
152ⁿᵈ Brigade R.F.A.
From 1ˢᵗ to 31ˢᵗ Octr. 1916.

Volume 10

Army Form C. 2118.

WAR DIARY
or
INTELLIGENCE SUMMARY
(Erase heading not required.)

Instructions regarding War Diaries and Intelligence Summaries are contained in F.S. Regs. Part II and the Staff Manual respectively. Title pages will be prepared in manuscript.

Place	Date	Hour	Summary of Events and Information	Remarks and references to Appendices
ARMENTIERES H17.D.55.40	Oct 1st		Bar 1795. Temp 60.5° — During the night part of the morning Operation Order No 22 was carried out. A raid by C + D Coys Ladder on enemy trench at I.31.D.5.5. At morning a Bangalore Torpedo was taken out. They were each 78 feet long, and joining fields each 6 ft. Old. They were placed under the enemy wire as far as possible & well fused at 4.11 A.M. by charging they blew it out to pieces, but could not be fused quick for enough up. There was about 10 yards of very thick wire which came up & which the infantry could not cut & get through. They found no German who were in a sap head & took them partially turned by the explosion. They were met in a sap turn & have been wait. Back a bit. It was held & the reinforcements were brought up. It belonged to 82nd Bavarian Regiment. Immediately it took up position the tattoo fired a creeping barrage by H.E. and the T.Ms fired. One casualty was one officer slightly wounded.	

WAR DIARY

Army Form C. 2118.

Place	Date	Hour	Summary of Events and Information	Remarks and references to Appendices
ARMENTIÈRES H³⁷.D.35.40.	1/10/16		A H gun battery of H.E. AA. seen in action at 0.21.V.C. They were firing at our 18 pdr front trench to be out of range. A party of men working at house I.35.c.50.15 was fired on & dispersed. Registration was also carried out by 6/152 by the guns from Chez les Deux pots. At midnight 30/9/16 & 1/10/16 the time & chapes were put back to G.M.T. actual time from Summer time tonight, 1 hour. Ammunition Expended A.H.E. A × 320. B × 135.	
	2/10/16		Bar 29.81. Therm. 60°. Raining hard all day. Observation impossible. No retaliation by the enemy. Ammo Expended A.59.A × 5. B × 3	
	3/10/16		Bar 29.57. Therm. 57°. Observation impossible till 2 P.M. One working party shelled at L.32.c.7.4. they were first upon & dispersed. Ammo Expended A.2.	

WAR DIARY

Army Form C. 2118.

Place	Date	Hour	Summary of Events and Information	Remarks and references to Appendices
ARMENTIERES H.17.D.35/10	1/11/18		Bar. 29.65. Ther. 5-8°. Observation poor. The Battery fired one registration from H.M.P. 0.13.D.10.5, 0.5.B.50.95 & I.35.D.95. Tanks were observed from trees 0.7.0.20.05 & they have been kept on stand over 36 hours there. Ammunition Expended A.15. A×1. B×8	
	2/11/18		Bar. 29.60 Ther. 61. Little firing was done today by own artillery in support of infantry. Oxyle Farm was registered & the Howr. Large hour I.27.C.11 was fired on a registration at lay range of 2d Salvos. Marconie Tramway was cleared at the relay bet. LINSELLES FOSTER X-ROADS RD. Buffs to Queen's and S.C. to our troops M.G. The men were M.G. west Les. MAISNIL. Time was occasionally done. Relation by the men of our reserve lines I.31.3 & I.6.6.6.55.7. Rear e/r 21 Bdr. Cadres of BRADCASE & RATTRAY arrived & camp was made & their building's made our use & Rr. Amm. Expdr. A.15. A×1. B×8.	

WAR DIARY
INTELLIGENCE SUMMARY

(Erase heading not required.)

Army Form C. 2118.

Place	Date	Hour	Summary of Events and Information	Remarks and references to Appendices
ARMENTIERES	6/10/16		Bar. 29.72. Ther. 59°. Obtain letter	
H17 D 35.40			A Raiding Party on enemy at O.8.D.6.2. They are found my	
			dispersed and to party was observed @ I.27.c.11. They were	
			also fired on & dispersed.	
			Exp 13.75 Gun 250 rounds of ammunition. We attacked L	
			G.152, also an officer's detachment.	
			During the afternoon all batteries were on expected wire	
			T.M. Schlem Operation Order No.23. Enemy front lines of enemy	
			searched from I.26.C.80. to I. 26.C.73.05. & neighbouring	
			damaged @ I.26.D.02 & I.31.D.F.6. Also MR HAMMER WAFER has	
			trenches. A considerable amount of retaliation was done.	
			Got enemy on the RATTRAP & BIRDCAGE. wired 42.	
			Enemy Cocoand. A.15. 4 × 27. T.M. 266	
		7/10/16	Bar. 29.78 Ther. 56°. Obscure own arty cany it day	
			Moment was known lowered times awad front O.14.B.8.6.	
			He was fired on 3 times his kind of wire.	

Army Form C. 2118.

WAR DIARY
or
INTELLIGENCE SUMMARY
(Erase heading not required.)

Place	Date	Hour	Summary of Events and Information	Remarks and references to Appendices
ARMENTIERES H.17.D.35.20.	3/10/16		Men were trench unloading E.S. Wagons @ O.14.B.70.75. They were fired on at 7 a.m. was seen to work. A Working Party was on Metal at S.2.c.5.9. they were fired on & dispersed. Men were seen carrying materials from house O.14.B.66. The building was shelled. One hostile aeroplane was seen during the day. Very little shelling was done by the enemy. Enemy T.M. bursts at 17.A.4 x 17.B x 79. Elevator Pond. Bar 29/78 Ther 38° A fat. J.9. was seen working on screens among the trees @ I.33.D.25.75. 19 new armoured jacks at forty degrees a new MG affair again. Considerable movement was seen round house O.14.B.66. Three rounds were fired out the Lanterns Tel. 1. Having found were also boy fragments by A. Mons. I 27.c.74. DISTILLERY. I.3.5. D.5.9. GRAND MAISON Fm. Mmn 65° lat. A.33. A x 9. B x 6.	

2333 Wt. W2344/7454 700,000 5/15 D. D. & L. A.D.S.S. Forms/C. 2118.

WAR DIARY
or
INTELLIGENCE SUMMARY

Army Form C. 2118.

Place	Date	Hour	Summary of Events and Information	Remarks and references to Appendices
ARMENTIERES H.17.D.35.40	9/10/16		Bar. 29.93. 1 Ther 57°. Observation insufficient. Strong wind N.W. Our artillery chiefly put in retaliation at the request of the infantry & also on trench registration. Our Trench Party of 12 men was sent at I.33.D.3.9. This was fired on & dispersed. Two other large working parties were observed on F.O. & were reported & so they were caught last half & were dispersed. Red 60 yds. Several seen moving from a factory church towards BENTEMS. A big Naval shell was noted they fired at supposed I.L.32.1. Italy a 25 cm Heavy MINENWERFER H.E. Ammunition Expended A.32.A×3. B×24.	
	10/10/16		Bar. 29.92. Ther. 55°. Observation insufficient. T.M. fired & cut wire during the afternoon & latter part as a cover for them. Our enemy T.M. was observed firing from the EARTHWORKS. I.31.D.73. No hours fire & our observers amount of damage. Clothing was silenced. Ammunition Expended A.34. A×44. B×F.	

2353 Wt. W2544/1454 700,000 5/15 D.D.&L. A.D.S.S. Forms/C. 2118.

WAR DIARY or INTELLIGENCE SUMMARY

Army Form C. 2118.

Place	Date	Hour	Summary of Events and Information	Remarks and references to Appendices
ARMENTIERES H17 D 35 40	11/10/16		Bar 29.95. The 60°. Observation fair. Operation Order No. 24 was issued & attempt & carried out Tilleul Road, but was not a success. It was carried out by the Suffolks. The raiding party consisting of 3 Officers & 34 O.R. left our front line trench @ 12 midnight & lay out in NO MANS LAND till 5 A.M. The night was very moonlight, & there were several German Working Parties out repairing their wire & parapet & covered by strong Enemy Parties. At 5 A.M. the party returned having accomplished nothing. During the day our artillery fired from time to time T.Ms. Movement was viewed @ O.S.C.77. This spot was fired at 2-9. Rather more movement than usual was seen on ENVETIERES – ESCOBECQUES Road. Our artillery was fired at & fired a. c.	A-
		3.35 P.M.	Rockets were observed as follows – 2 Red, 2 White 9 Red. from concert party 3.27.9. PADIN SHEIM CHURCH. Weather Confused.	

A53. AX 69. 13 × 5.5.

WAR DIARY or INTELLIGENCE SUMMARY

Army Form C. 2118.

Place	Date	Hour	Summary of Events and Information	Remarks and references to Appendices
ARMENTIERES M.17.D.3.5.40	12/10/16	7.30 P.M.	Bar. 30.01 Ther. 60° Observation Good. Operation Order No. 25 was issued & carried out. Zero hour 7.30 P.M. Preliminary bombardment was carried out by the Artillery & Stokes guns & T.Ms. whilst the infantry lay out in "No Man's Land". At Zero + 3' the Artillery lifted & the Infantry advanced. The Infantry reported that the enemy wire was cut & bent back & that the bombardment & stationary barrage they laid down & threw it cut & also that all machine guns & rifle fire was silenced. The enemy threw up very into/satisfy & several Germans were seen to go on unseen further Bayler back. Our casualties Nil. Ammunition Expended A.56. A×102. B×57.	B-
	13/10/16		Bar. 30.01 Ther. 59° Observation good. Large working party of about 40 men seen at trench x.0.13.D.15.10. The party was heavily engaged & great damage was done to trench. Tabi Wires Stellen: cars were taken away. Later Smith was seen running from trench in rear. Several dead left in rear of trench.	Ammn Expended A.370. A×329. B×260

Army Form C. 2118.

WAR DIARY
or
INTELLIGENCE SUMMARY
(Erase heading not required.)

Instructions regarding War Diaries and Intelligence Summaries are contained in F. S. Regs., Part II. and the Staff Manual respectively. Title pages will be prepared in manuscript.

Place	Date	Hour	Summary of Events and Information	Remarks and references to Appendices
ARMENTIERES H.I.D. 35·40	14/10/16		Bar. 29.95. Ther. 50°. Working Party fired on & dispersed 2 O.S.B.25.00. also working party fired on & dispersed I 33.B.3.1. Several small parties of men wearing full pack seen going & coming on Road O 12.c.9.6 & O 5.D.44. Two Hostile aeroplane observed coming at day. One, Infant. reet. A 20.A.16. B×7.	C
	15/10/16		Bar. 29.39. Ther. 45°. Observation Post. Eight group columns 26th count. Working Party at O 4.B.57. fired on & dispersed. The following unit or regiments were there viz R.O.D.W.N.Z.E.M. 1 Red. 1 Whl. 1 recorded. 1 mo. Enemy aeroplane observed coming at day Allies Rifles. A 55 A×10. B×16	
	16/10/16		Bar. 29.95. Ther. 45". Working Party observed at O.27.C.9.5. fired on & dispersed. Hostile AA battery firing fire O 21.A.65.20 Harris & others fired on our Plane, which follow from behind it enemy lines. From lost plane 6 observation post. Harrison Coy. Cement Cropshin A 15. A×1. B×7.	
	17/10/16		Bar. 29.91. 9 ths 45°. Working Party O 02.C. F.S. fired on & dispersed. Fourth reported um.	

Army Form C. 2118.

WAR DIARY
or
INTELLIGENCE SUMMARY.
(Erase heading not required.)

Instructions regarding War Diaries and Intelligence Summaries are contained in F. S. Regs., Part II. and the Staff Manual respectively. Title pages will be prepared in manuscript.

10

Place	Date	Hour	Summary of Events and Information	Remarks and references to Appendices
ARMENTIERES				
H.Q. D.33.40	18/1/17		Observed Gas shells from Orient Bar before A.19.9x1. B x 9	
			Dec 30. The 45"	
	19/1/17	6.30AM	Pull in West front to 2 min'h reported at the front line.	
			Gas trap went off at 6.13 D.15. Stay in from a depression 3 long	
			Harry at day. Launched from the T.M. From the S.W.	
			Target Smith's DISTILLERY? MANAGERS HOUSE 6. From D.17. Box 10	
			Dec. 29.19. The 45°	
			Dec. 29.19. The 45° Fired 6 trips into A.9.H. A.9.H. A.5. B x 9 H.	
			External Bar. Was went seen over OXT, W.177 those where were fixed	
			Support Before A.9.H. A.9. B x 22	
	20/1/17		Bo. 29.19. The 45° All batteries fired as required – total 737 TM rds.	
			From our trench onto No Ball end the FOUR WESTERN HOUSES	
			to note Cupola Keep over before A.5, A.14 B.y 20.	
	24/1/17	10.30-11.00AM	T.B. on F.9.H. F.o.4.6. 6 pistols Ord. No 26 was successfully carried out by S Group	
			Y/157 & two of D/157 which be fired at Mill Ramp Salien	
			Movement was observed at OYSTER F.M.T. 6 Mobile blows observed	
			Approx. Enfee A790 AX67. B x 203	

2353 Wt. W2514/1454 700,000 5/15 D.D.& L. A.D.S.S. Forms/C. 2118.

WAR DIARY
or
INTELLIGENCE SUMMARY

Army Form C. 2118.

Place	Date	Hour	Summary of Events and Information	Remarks and references to Appendices
MAHEMERIES M.17.D.35.a.a	28/9/18		Lieut Colonel R Kincaid Smith CMG DSO from Bde. Senior Officers C.R.A. 25th Div. Lieut Col. M.S. Thorpe in take command of 152nd Bde R.F.A.	
		3 P.M.	All batteries made a T.M. shoot & enemy was prepared the machinery in order in trench places. Observed by A.F.O. A510. BX 35	
	29/9		Bar 29.85. Tem 46. Shoots on positions.	
		12 am	All batteries fired as enemy to T.M. hdr were very active & harbed was shown up for front. Materials Yseri A.96 A x 25. BX 55	
			Ammunition. Infantry has no movement this am	
	29/9		Bar 29.85. Tem. 45. Shoots on Ravines, exposed A 35. A x 16. BX 56	
	29/9		Bar 29.82. Tem. 45. Targets of opportunity A 35-9. M. PLOEG AN	
			Car report only that of Buffalo 013 D 18. Targets of opportunity from Enemy planes	
			Received flying. What every line registering on PLOEG AN A 36. BX 17	

WAR DIARY
or
INTELLIGENCE SUMMARY.
(Erase heading not required.)

Army Form C. 2118.

Place	Date	Hour	Summary of Events and Information	Remarks and references to Appendices
ARMENTIERES H.17.D.35.20	26/11/16		Bar. 29.06. There at observation very misty. Our artillery was disposed O.11.A.2.90 and at O.13.D.25. Armentieres Cupola A 35 B×17	
	27/11/16		Bar. 29.40. Ther 43. Elevator Fort. First scout encountered & have been there, they up and are engaging. Guns to take in all day & light T.M men observed fire from that. They were eventually silenced by our heavy Mortly Batty was dispersed from I.13 D & 9. Enemy shoots his own started with work.	
		3 PM	On EARTHWORKS I.3.D.30. All batteries suddenly suffering T.M's and letting in destruction and we any badly damaged I.31.D.95. & "Jacob" trenches I.26.C.70. Armentieres Cupola A 23. A×24. B×17	
	28/11/16		Bar. 29.35. Ther. 48. Observation indifferent. Enemy aeroplane over n ESCAUBEAUX CEMETERY as ROAD & on Monkey Puzzle wood. Influence for MARTINS CORNER. Our hostile artillery silent.	

Army Form C. 2118.

WAR DIARY
or
INTELLIGENCE SUMMARY.
(Erase heading not required.)

Instructions regarding War Diaries and Intelligence Summaries are contained in F. S. Regs., Part II. and the Staff Manual respectively. Title pages will be prepared in manuscript.

Place	Date	Hour	Summary of Events and Information	Remarks and references to Appendices
ARMENTIERES			regarding No 5 g battery in Bois GRENIER	13
M17 B 75 40		7.30 pm	RADINGHEM 15 pdr fired expose n LE QUESNE ROAD.	
			Ammunition Expect A8D 6x75, B8 11)	
	29/10/16		Bar 29·35° Ther 42° Thermometer Fair	
			Work. Pat. departure at I 32·c·5·1 & ne perpendicular 0·15·c·6·7	
			Considerable and has been done round CHOCOLATE HOUSE. Shown damage	
			RADINGHEM was later re watch 7 enemy activity BOIS GRENIER	
			Amount 7 Rockets ie 16A 12 AX 4 5 BX	
29/1/16		10 am	Bar 29·37 Ther 49° Thermometer Bad	
		11 am	No Work. Platoon expend at 0·1 A Z 5· Gun & other drains by I house been repaired a for Repair 0·15·c·2·3	
			Issues. ENFILES. Amount Expend 8 A 4 A X, 2 V 4·13X	
	29/1/16		Bar 29·45 Ther 53° Chinese sent	
		3.30 pm	All batteries fired in support most T 14·10·7 a for OPn Ord No 26.	
			6pm. Rng 10.f. an alarm was 0.5 T 7 B· I 30 DE LF gauge was also lately damaged also opn. activity cannot re-reply	

2353   Wt. W2514/1454   700,000   5/15   D. D. & L.   A.D.S.S./Forms/C. 2118.

Army Form C. 2118.

WAR DIARY
or
INTELLIGENCE SUMMARY.
(Erase heading not required.)

Place	Date	Hour	Summary of Events and Information	Remarks and references to Appendices
			(safety) pass etc. need to go on the suffocation much material was brought there via et ai 6 or Working Party now depend on RTC 7.5 Ambulance Refreshed 36A 9AX	

signed
Lieut. Col. R.F.A.
COMDG. 152nd (NOTTM.) BDE. R.F.A.

Copy N° 9.   A1. SECRET.

RIGHT GROUP
Operation Order N° 22.

Intention. 1. A raid on the enemy front trenches about the point I.31.d.5.5 will be carried out on the night of the 30th/1st Oct.

Artillery Tasks. 2. The tasks of Batteries Right Group will be as follows:

1st PHASE. Zero to O+6.

B.152. Enemy front line I.31.d.25.30 to O1.A.6.9.
C.152.   "   "   "   I.31.d.85.65 to I.32.c.2.9.
D.152.   One gun.   BRIDOUX FORT.
    "   "   House O1.b.4.9.
    "   "   Support trench I.32.c.1.5.
    "   "   Point I.32.c.2.9.

Rate of fire. 18 pdrs. 4 rds per gun per minute.
              4.5 Hows. 3 "   "   "   "

2nd PHASE. O+6 to end.

Batteries remain on same objectives but rate of fire will be reduced to 2 rds per gun or howitzer per minute.

Trench Mortars 3. Two medium trench mortars will open fire at Zero hour on enemy front line I26.c.8.0 - I26.d.0.2.
Ammunition. 20 rds per mortar.
Rate of fire. As fast as possible.

Registration 4. Registration will be carried out on Sept 29th & 30th and to avoid drawing special attention to I.31.d.5.5 Batteries will also register other points in their respective zones, and the O.C. Right Battalion must be warned before any registration of trenches opposite BRIDOUX salient takes place.

Zero Hour. 5. Zero hour will be   approximately but the definite signal to open fire will be the explosion of a BANGALORE torpedo.
Watches will be synchronized as follows with Group Hdqrs.
    6 pm. by an officer with watch from each Bty
    10 pm. by telephone.

Liaison. 6. Lieut. G. HOWITT R.F.A. will report at advanced Btn Hd Qrs of Right Battalion TOCHS TOY at hour to be notified later accompanied by Telephonist and Linesman, and will arrange to be in direct communication with Group Hd Qrs.

7. Acknowledge.

G. Howitt, Lieut and Adjudant for
Right Group.

Copies to
    No. 1.   H.Q. R.A.
        2.   101st Inf Bde
        3.   Left Group
        4.   B. 152.
        5.   C. 152.
        6.   D. 152.
        7.   French mortars.
   8 to 11.   spare.

SECRET   A   Copy No 9

RIGHT GROUP.
Operation Order No 24.

If the weather is favourable the 11th Suffolks will raid the enemy's trenches at I.26.c.95.15 on the night of 11th/12th Oct.

The raid will be a silent one, i.e., without Artillery bombardment which will be called for if necessary.

The object of the raid is to inflict as much damage as possible and identifications are of secondary importance.

Zero hour will not be before 2 A.M. on the 12th inst.

Batteries will get half an hours warning to stand to get layed. Until this warning is received batteries will remain on their ordinary night lines.

If required, guns will fire as follows, Zero being taken as the time fire commences.

C.152.	I.26.d.2.3	to I.26.d.3.7.
B.152.	I.32.A.80.75	to I.32.A.6.5.
D.152.	I.32.b.10.57	
	I.32.b.20.80	
	I.26.d.60.45	} 1 Gun on each.
	I.26.d.80.50	

Rate of fire. Zero to +6 mins.

18 pdrs.   4 rounds per gun per minute.
4.5 hows.   3   "   "   "   "   " .

60% H.E.   40% Shrapnel.

+6 until further orders.

18 pdrs.   2 rounds per gun per minute.
4.5 hows.   1   "   "   "   "   " .

Medium T.M's will stand by ready to fire 2 guns about I.31.d.5.5.

If Right Group R.A. open fire Z/34 will fire.

10 rounds per gun as fast as possible.

<u>Liaison</u>. Lieut. G. Howitt will act as Liaison Officer with O.C. Raid.

<u>Orders to open fire</u>. If the order to open fire is given it is essential that Batteries should start as quickly as possible. Lieut G. Howitt will be in direct telephone communication with D/152.

C & B Batteries will arrange to watch for the flash of D/152 and commence firing at once. The order to fire will also be transmitted by phone through Right Group H.Q.

Watches will be synchronized at 10 pm with Right Group H.Q.

<u>Acknowledge</u>.

S. Farr Lieut & Adjutant.
Right Group. R.A.

11. 10. 16.

Copies to.
    No 1. H.Q. R.A.
        2. 101st Infy Bde.
        3. Left Group.
        4. B/152.
        5. C/152.
        6. D/152.
        7. French mortars.
    8 to 10. spare.

SECRET   RIGHT GROUP B   Copy No 8

Operation Order No 25

A raid will be carried out tonight 12th/13th by the 11th Suffolks. Point of entry about I.26.c.95.15. Zero hour 7.30 pm.

Assault at + 3 mins.

Tasks are allotted to Batteries Right Group as follows:—

ZERO to + 3 mins.

B/152.   3 guns on front line I.32.A.6.5 to I.32.A.80.75. Remainder on front line wire I.26.c.8.0 to I.26.d.0.2.

C/152.   3 guns on front line I.26.d.2.3 to I.26.d.3.7. Remainder on front line wire I.26.c.8.0 to I.26.d.0.2.

D/152.   I.32.b.10.57.
         I.32.b.2.8.
         I.26.d.60.45.
         I.26.d.8.5.

+ 3 mins until cease fire.

B/152. all guns. I.32.A.6.5 to I.32.A.80.75
C/152. all guns. I.26.d.2.3 to I.26.d.3.7
D/152. No change.

Rate of fire.

ZERO to +10 mins. 18 pdrs. 4 rds per gun per minute.
                      4.5 hows. 3 "

+10 to cease fire. 18 pdrs 1 " " " "
                  4.5 hows. 1 " " " "

Orders to cease fire will be given by O.C. Raid.

Ammunition for front line I.26.c.8.0 to I.26.d.0.2.
        all shrapnel.
        Remainder 60% H.E.

O.C/ B152 & C/152 will arrange between themselves the best way to distribute their guns over the trench I26.c/8.0 to I26.d.0.2 from ZERO to +3.

Laision Lieut. G. Howitt will act as LAISION Officer with O.C. Raid.

Watches will be synchronized at 6.30 p.m.

6" How's are co-operating.

Heavy Artillery are standing by for Counter Battery work if required.

Acknowledge.

12.10.16.

Starr Lieut & Adjutant
Right Group.

Copies to
1. H.Q.R.A.
2. 101 Infy Bde.
3. Left Group.
4. B/152.
5. C/152.
6. D/152.
7. French Mortars.
8 to 10 Spare.

RIGHT GROUP. C   SECRET.
Operation Order No 26.A
Proposed Right Group Artillery scheme for Dummy Raid.

1. ZERO to +4.
    B/152.   I.32.A.6.2 To I.32.A.7.4.
    C/152. (less 3 guns) I.32.A.7.4 To I.32.A.8.5.
    D/152. (2 guns) { I.32.c.55.90.
                     { I.32.b.15.58.

2. +4 To +6.
    B/152.   } I.32.A.45.30 To I.32.A.6.6.
    C/152. less 3 guns }
    D/152.   No change.

3. +6 To +10.
    B/152. 3 guns. I.32.A.45.15 To I.32.c.30.92.
           3 guns. I.32.A.95.35 To I.32.A.75.12.
    C/152. (less 3 guns) I.32.A.80.95 To I.32.A.72.72.
    D/152.   No change.

+10 To +11.
        STOP FIRING.

+11 To +30.
    B/152.   I.32.A.45.30 To I.32.A.6.6.
    C/152 (less 3 guns) ——— do ———
    D/152.   No change.

Rate of fire.
    ZERO To +6.   18 pdrs. 4 rounds. ⎫
                  4.5 Hows. 3   "   ⎪
    +6 To +10.   18 pdrs. 3   "   ⎪ per gun
                  4.5 Hows. 2   "   ⎬ per
    +11 To +16.   ——— do ———   ⎪ minute.
    +16 To +24.   18 pdrs. 2   "   ⎪
                  4.5 Hows. 1   "   ⎪
    +24 To +30.   18 pdrs. 1   "   ⎭
                  4.5 Hows. 1   " per gun per 2 mins.

Estimate of Ammunition.
    A 330.   AX 330.   BX 74.

                            Statt Lieut. R.F.A,
15.10.15.   Adjt. Right Group.

Copy Nº 8   SECRET

Right Group Scheme Nº 26.

1. A shoot will be carried out by the French mortars today 31st inst.

   One gun on wire I.31.d.8.6. to keep open the lanes already made.

   One gun on new dug-out observed by iron girders in roof at I.31.d.w.w.

   Ammunition. 25 rounds per gun or as many as can be fired in 15 minutes.

2. B/152 will fire on support line.
      I.32.c.1.4 to I.31.d.5.3.

   C/152 Right half battery on front line trenches.
      I.31.d.9.6 to I.32.c.1.8.

   Left half battery on front line trenches.
      I.31.d.0.2 to I.31.d.30.35.

   D/152 on LA MOTTE HOUSSAIN FME (I.32.d.1.6) and suspected dump in trees behind.

3. Ammunition
      18 pdrs.   60 rounds per Battery.   50% H.E.
      4.5 hows. 30.   "   "   "   "

4. Time.   3.30 — 3.45 p.m.

5. Acknowledge.

31.10.16.   G. _____ Lieut. R.F.A.
                                                                      Right Group. R.A.

Copies to.
   1. H.Q. R.A.
   2. 101 Infy Bde.
   3. B/152
   4. C/ "
   5. D/ "
   6. French mortars
   7 to 9.   Spare.

Vol 10

Confidential

War Diary
— of —
152ⁿᵈ Brigade R.F.A.

From 1ˢᵗ November to 30ᵗʰ Novr. 1916

Volume 11

WAR DIARY or INTELLIGENCE SUMMARY

Army Form C. 2118.

152 F.A. Bde

Place	Date	Hour	Summary of Events and Information	Remarks and references to Appendices
ARMENTIERES H.17.d.35.40	NOV 1st	Bar 29.20 Ther 51	Observation hazy. Our Artillery fired chiefly in Retaliation at enemy's Artillery. Our Working Party was dispersed from trench O.15.c.6.9 & works not damaged. A Gun Tank (6 hour stay) was in good posn. I.5.c.6.c.5.5 times L.09.b.05. There was some shelling by the enemy today chiefly in our front line. Ammunition expn. A. 75, A.X. 75, B.X. 75.	
	2nd	Bar. 29.30 Ther. 48. 2.30 PM	Observation bad till 2 P.M. T. McCurnier at I.31.D.2.2 & I.32.c.1.5 again commenced annoying damage to parapet. Our Artillery fired on supposed location of enemy. Our Working Party was dispersed from O.8.C.7.8 to Ten Yards. Trams were seen going up Mess. The Enemy fired 9.4 Hows. Flares were seen during the day. Ammunition Expended. A.25. A.X.42. 13.X.17.	
	3rd	13m 29.40 Ther 51	Observation indistinct. Our Artillery fired in Retaliation of enemy of Infantry. Mills Trenchmortars seen passing along road. L.Sc.0.B.2.c.9.vb-3 - EW.7.05	

Army Form C. 2118.

WAR DIARY
or
INTELLIGENCE SUMMARY.
(Erase heading not required.)

152 F.A. Bde

Place	Date	Hour	Summary of Events and Information	Remarks and references to Appendices
ARMENTIERES. HQ at 33.d.40	Nov 3		1 hostile aeroplane appeared at h.q. Fire from anti-aircraft battery. Ammunition Expended A. 105, AX 50, BX 77.	
	4th		Bar. 29.30. Ther. 50. Observation misty. Operation Order No. 28 issued.	
		2.30 PM	In orders of 5/6 ct. One battery fired as a cover for a 7th Middlesex Infantry reported that our own curfew I.31.d.70.55 to I.32.c.0.75. Fire at I was today trained on several places. One hostile battery was disposed from I.31.d.52.0 rounds was expended at Fire hose wagon was seen near a road 0.12.d. Ammunition Expended A. 60. AX 15, BX 15.	
	5th		Bar. 28.90 Ther. 52. Observation good. Operation Order No. 29 issued. Little firing on either side. Batteries aim I have anything worth. Several aeroplanes flying at day nearly from school house in rear.	

Army Form C. 2118.

152 Fd A Bde

WAR DIARY
or
INTELLIGENCE SUMMARY.
(Erase heading not required.)

Place	Date	Hour	Summary of Events and Information	Remarks and references to Appendices
ARMENTIERES H.17.d.35.40.	NOV 5"		Tactical movement was seen in LE ENNETIERES - ESCOBECQUES Road. A 77MM battery was located firing from O.10.d.0.6. Ammunition Expended A.59 Ax 65, Bx47	
	6"		Bar. 29.20. The H.E. Operation Order No 29 was received and the record that wire was destroyed to 30yds round front. L.32.a.H.30. a.m. 90yds round Junct L.26.t.75-45. a.h.o.k. Target was ableity of trella to ground. There was evidently some shelling by enemy. Chiefly on our front line. Ammunition Expended A.106. Ax 91. Bx63	
	7"		Bar. 29.18. The. 45. Elevation had changed. May. Operation Order, No 30 was issued. a little agitation was carried out in the. No enemy movement seen to have taken place during the day. Ammunition Expended A.106. Ax 91. Bx63	

WAR DIARY or INTELLIGENCE SUMMARY

Army Form C. 2118.

152 Inf Bde

Place	Date	Hour	Summary of Events and Information	Remarks and references to Appendices
ARMENTIERES and area	Nov 7th	5.15 PM	Bar. 29.83 Ther 49. Observation Good. A raid was carried out by the Liff. Group as per Special Order No 30 in which B & D batteries of 4th part Lowerdale regiment were engaged. MARTIN'S CORNER & wood. Direct hits were observed on the buildings there. Enemy was seen at O.13.d.7.8 Men were seen entering a dug out at O.8.d.7.3. This spot was regarded as no further movement was seen. At various times during the day men were seen to enter from Gun pits at O.1.b.6.8 & 70 trench LAVALLEE 9 in every case returning in a few minutes. Party of a dig out was seen to enter Gun posts at A.263 & A.243 O.x.13%. Ammunition Expended A.263 A.243 O.x.13%.	
	9th	4.30 AM	Bar. 29.53. Ther. 42. Observation Fair. Reply to Enemy Operation Order No 32. carried & carried out. Information has been received from patrols etc that the enemy were on the lookout for Enemy up very early. Parties being changed—	

Army Form C. 2118.

152 F.A. Bde

WAR DIARY
or
INTELLIGENCE SUMMARY.
(Erase heading not required.)

Place	Date	Hour	Summary of Events and Information	Remarks and references to Appendices
ARMENTIERES H.17.d.35.40	Nov 7		At Ypres wire & trenches. One enemy party was dispersed from 0.15.c.65.90. Counted intermediate trench on road at point 0.26.a.2.1. A hostile balloon went up during the day & several planes flew on our lines. Ammunition Expended. A.105; AX 37. 13 x 36.	
		10:45	Bar 30. Ther 36. Observation very misty. Smoke seen rising from houses in O.2.c.99 & I.34t.30.15. had the things see three open On Bti along appeared to be being made at O.12.c.2.3. 9 prev S.S. Wagons were seen to unload but this was reported at times. One shell fell in two airplanes were seen during the day. Ammunition Expended. A 19. AX 67. 13 x 76.	
		11:5	Bar 30.19 Ther 46. Observation improved. One enemy party was observed at I.33.6.2.2 & feet up, but would never out be seen every 1 part. Ammunition Expended A 12. AX 4.	

WAR DIARY
INTELLIGENCE SUMMARY

152 2nd Bn

Army Form C. 2118.

Place	Date	Hour	Summary of Events and Information	Remarks and references to Appendices
ARMENTIERES H17d.35.60	Nov 12th		Bar 30. Ther 43. Observation bad. Offensive Cooperation No. 33 issued. Patrol was sent nearly from hour 0.2.C.6.4. This hour was fired upon the Fusch. Registration was carried out for O.G. 33 from Ref. A.6. A x 2.	
	13"		Bar 30.06 Ther 44. Observation fair. Offensive Cooperation No. 33. 4.30 A.M. wire examined & 9 A.M. a heavy raid in enemies wire & as a diversion the red hand carried out by Left Group. Targets A 34 A x 2. B X 44. Counter battery Targets A 34 A x 2.	
	14"		Bar 30. Ther 30. Observation good. A Working Party was seen to 0.2.C.5.5. & defence by our fire. Two other working parties were seen at 0.15.C.6.9. & at 5.5.d.9.2. these were fired upon & dispersed. Two Bats through gas were observed firing from 0.26.a.0.5.7. One balloon & 1 Aeroplane were seen over our lines. Objective 25 pdrs at B.69. 0 x 1. B x 2.)	

2353 Wt W2344/1454 700,000 5/15 D.D.&L. A.D.S.S./Forms/C. 2118.

Army Form C. 2118.

152 F.A.Bde

WAR DIARY
or
INTELLIGENCE SUMMARY.

(Erase heading not required.)

Instructions regarding War Diaries and Intelligence Summaries are contained in F. S. Regs., Part II. and the Staff Manual respectively. Title pages will be prepared in manuscript.

Place	Date	Hour	Summary of Events and Information	Remarks and references to Appendices
ARMENTIERES H.12.d.25.00	Nov 15		Bar. 29.70. Ther. 43. Observation bad. Guns at O.2.c.1.2. & O.7.b.5.9. were fired upon by an HV. What appears to be a lamp was seen signalling from O.12.d. Ammunition Exploded A.23.a.5.2, B.x.10.	
	16th		Bar. 23.81. Ther. 25. Observation bad. Operation Order No. 34 issued & carried out. This was a 7. H. shoot with all batteries firing as a enemy considerable damage was done at the end of I.28.c.50. 9 also fn 77yds some from I.26.b.7.5. Three hostile balloons, 1 airplane were seen during the day. Ammunition Exploded at A.1.a x 5. B.x.19.	
	17th		Bar. 30. Ther. 42. Observation Good. A hostile battery was located at O.15.c.6.8. & was engaged by D/152 and covered successes. Again 8 horses were seen at O.12.c.2.3 and batteries were notified, they proceeded down a track in the direction of Fournes	

2353 Wt. W5344/7454 700,000 5/15 D.D.&L. A.D.S.S./Forms/C. 2118.

WAR DIARY
or
INTELLIGENCE SUMMARY

Army Form C. 2118.

152 T.F.Bde

Place	Date	Hour	Summary of Events and Information	Remarks and references to Appendices
ARMENTIERES H.17.d.35.60	Nov 18		5" hostile aeroplanes came over lines during the day. Ammunition expended: A.35. A.X.41. B.X.50.	
	19	Bn. 29.70 Tr. 30	Ammunition expended. A.8.A.X.1. B.X.60.	
	19 d	Bn. 29.60. Tr. 46. 6 enemy aerial recco. scouts & reconnoissance. A T.M. started at L.26.c.8.1 when several shots were put in our arcs. We lost from L.26.c.4.70 to L.21.c.2.5.9 probably as our own men "Expended cases who reccer our wire attacked others. Enl at T.M. Saps. 8" of shell were fired at D.DISTILLERY enemy retaliating with all huns in area. The retaliating being very accurate both sides. Try to 7 range. The enemy arrangement sheds one T.M. & fire a "MINNIES" which always puts our own support lines & one close but 7 range of our T.M. Sentries in forward Ammunition Expended A. 17. from Q.1. L.5.5	

WAR DIARY
or
INTELLIGENCE SUMMARY.
(Erase heading not required.)

Army Form C. 2118.

152 Fd Bd

Place	Date	Hour	Summary of Events and Information	Remarks and references to Appendices
ARMENTIERES N19d 25.40	Nov 20		Bn. 289's. The Lt. Observer Group Spotter Ords. 011 35 reverses came out a T.M. shot between I.31.d.45 and I.31.d.9.7. who merely all enemy aus mg. emp. 9 four hind factory stokes in several places At lattice fired as a convoy. A Mg Party was seen at 09.c.05.40 & was disperses by our guns. Four flashes were seen from a 4 gun 77mm battery at. 0.13.c.6.5 from where twenty rounds were fired by no. 3 shoot. Hits observed on the houses. Host T.M. was observed firing from 0.11 h 65.95. O.M.L.H.F a wire defense. Also one T.M. fired from 0.11 b 65.70 & was silenced. They were fire after a which. There was a lot of our rebels by the enemy chiefly on on front line. Armenta Epitets I 32, AX 23, 58+40.	
	21		Bn. 39.27. Then 33. Chevalis Loos. The T.M. carried out a shot & did considerable damage to enemy wire by. at I 26c7.3.5 I26d.60.75. O.R.T.H. steamed to his far inside of 700mm land away 1/1/1. Armenta Epitets A.2.	

Army Form C. 2118.

152 F.A.Bde.

10

WAR DIARY
or
INTELLIGENCE SUMMARY.
(Erase heading not required.)

Place	Date	Hour	Summary of Events and Information	Remarks and references to Appendices
ARMENTIERES H110 d 25.40	NOV 22.		Bde. 29.60. The 43. Olivrah Lad. T.M. shell was noted over I 26 d 67a I 26 F 7.3 into enviable change on the rail CR batteries. Fine on a enemy ammunition dugout at 32, Ax 23, B x 10.	
	23.		Bde. 30.09. The 49. Olivrah good. O.T.M. shots on I 26 c 7145. when neutralising enemy activities, all batteries fired on a enemy 72/152 registration point in rear of aeroplane flash. T.M. was now firing for lower I 32 c 13.16. There were engaged G 8/152 a round burst hits on wood standed on battery Box hostile battery A 35, Ax 32, B x 30. Latter a 1 Aeroplane seen Ammunition Dugout A 337, Ax 313, B x 128.	
	24.		Bde. 29.78. The 43. Olivrah Fair. Enviable movement was seen along RADINGHEM - ESCOBECQUES Road enemy near F.S. Wagon 64 over a most touch was sent for any further into Ammunition Dugout A 337, Ax 313, B x 128.	

Army Form C. 2118.

1532 A.B..
11

WAR DIARY
or
INTELLIGENCE SUMMARY.
(Erase heading not required.)

Place	Date	Hour	Summary of Events and Information	Remarks and references to Appendices
ARMENTIERES H.770 15.40	NOV 25th		Bar. 29.69. Ther. 45. Observation good. Our artillery dispersed one working party from I.32.d.16. Ramparts Enfiladed 6 x 1.	
	26th		Bar. 29.36. Ther. 40. Observation good. Enemy party 70 of 7 men was seen digging a new trench running from railway embankment O.10.c.05.10 to O.10.c.s.3. Enemy working party observed at O.3.2.a.85.95. Sentrie exposed on Gable roofs were seen about noon. Two loopholes in 5 Aeroplane sheds observed obstacle duty. Ammn. Exped. A.22. 4 x 3.	
	27th		Bar. 29.90. Ther. 34. Observation good. Enemy lorry seen between ten & four from 6 posts. In addition large party (about one man every 4 yds) for 20 min. from O.2.c.5.5. From a wire fired enemy Hely was viewed G steeple for L.33.d.2.8. Ammn. Expend. A.14. A.2. P. 8 x 9.	

WAR DIARY
or
INTELLIGENCE SUMMARY

Army Form C. 2118.

152 F.A. Bde.

Place	Date	Hour	Summary of Events and Information	Remarks and references to Appendices
ARMENTIERES H.T.M 55.40	Nov 28		Bar 30. Ther 31. Okewahi lost. The men sent returned in the 26th in front after a went has been enlarged the during rest. Amount Topher. A.9. A×6. B×8	
	29th		Bar 30. Ther 31. Okewahi Topher. a T. Mortar on enis I.26.B.F.5. Targets Bang five rounds and certain no Bays on either side Job limit. During the shoot there was heard at the enemy lines Am. Bortar. A.F.	
	30th		Bar 30. Ther 33. Okewahi meig. a T. Mortar was carried out at front I.26.B.60 & considerable damage was done one on each side of the front. Our How fired on a enemy. Ammunite. Topher A×1	

Copy No 9   SECRET

Right Group Scheme No 27

1. A shoot will be carried out by the French mortars tomorrow 2nd inst.

   Target. Wire and parapet at the following points.

   One gun.   I.32.c.1.8.
   One gun.   I.31.d.20.25.

   Ammunition. As many rounds as time will allow.

2. B/152. will fire on front line I.31.c.70 to I.31.d.01. and support line I.31.d.10 to I.31.d.5.3.

   C/152. will fire on front line I.32.c.1.9 to I.32.A.6.5.

   D/152. One gun on "The Gap" 02.b.4.0.
   "   "   "Martens Corner" 07.b.0.7.
   Two guns. LE BAS HAU.

   If observation is impossible on these targets for 'D' Battery. Guns will fire on OYSTER FARM, BLANCO HOUSE, and LE BRIDOUX.

3. Ammunition.

   18 pdrs.   60 rounds per Battery.
   4.5 hows.   60   "   "   "

4. Time.   2.30 pm to 3.30 pm.

5. Acknowledge.

1-11-16.

G. Howse, Lieut R.F.A.
Right Group R.A.

Copies to:-
No 1   H.Q.R.A.
   2   101 Infy Bde
   3   B/152.
   4   C/ "
   5   D/ "
   6   French mortars
   7   Left Group
8 to 10 Spare

L. No 9
To.

SECRET
B326

With reference to the shoot for on the 2nd inst, the time will be altered, dividing the programme into two phases.
1st phase. 12.30 p.m. to 1 p.m.
2nd phase. 2.30 p.m. to 3 p.m.
Please acknowledge.

2-11-16.

E. Hart. Lieut. R.F.A
Right Group. R.A

Copies to
1. H.Q R.A.
2. 101 Bde
3. B/152.
4. C/152.
5. D/152.
6. 34 T.M.
7. Left Group.
8 to 10. Spare.

No 10   Secret

Right Group Operation Order No 28

A raid will be carried out by the 15th Royal Scots on the enemy trenches at I.32.c.2.9. The Raiding Party will capture 50 yards on either side of this point & remain in the trench for 30 minutes.

The Right Group Artillery will fire as below.

B/152   ZERO to +3 minutes
            Enemy Front line I.32.c.00.72 to I.32.c.30.94 }
            +3 till +13 minutes
            Support line between OYSTER FARM & BLANC HOUSE }

C/152   ZERO to +3 minutes
            3 guns on Front line I.32.c.00.72 to I.31.D.70.55 }
            3   I.32.A.42.00 to I.32.A.49.22 }
            +3 to +13 minutes
            Same target as from ZERO to +3

D/152   ZERO until requested to cease fire by
            1 gun   OYSTER FARM
            2 guns Junction of communication trench and Support line
                    at BLANCO HOUSE.
            1 gun. Front line at point I.32.A.46.30.

4/34. T.M. ZERO to +13 minutes
            1 gun on Front line at I.32.A.46.30
            2 guns   "   I.26.C.8.0 to I.26.D.05.20
                    to create a diversion

The Heavy Artillery will stand by on counter battery work.

night of 5/6

ZERO HOUR - will be notified later, also the date.

Ammunition. 18 pdr. 50% H.E.

RATE OF FIRE 18 pdr. ZERO to +3 minutes = 4 Rounds per Gun per Minute.
+3 to +13 minutes = 3 " " " "
+13 till further orders = 2 " " " "
4.5 Hows. ZERO till further orders. 3 " " " "
T. Ms Maximum rate

Where the full number of guns is not available in a battery the rate of fire of a section will be increased to make up the deficiency.

Lieut J. Firon will act as Liaison Officer for the Artillery & report to Infantry Battle H.Qrs. two hours before Zero hour.
ACKNOWLEDGE.

G. Hewitt B/Major
Roy. l. Group R.A.

1/16

Copies to
No 1   H.Q.R.A.
    2   101 Infy Bde.
    3   Left Group.
    4   D/152.
    5   C/.
    6   D/".
    7   Trench mortars
8 to 10. Spare.

To.   SECRET.
                                                             D361.

   Reference Right Group O.O. No 28 of Friday.
The raid will be carried out on night of 5/6th inst.
Please acknowledge.

4-11-1916.   G. Hooks Lieut. R.F.A.
                                      Right Group R.A.

"A" Form.
MESSAGES AND SIGNALS.

Army Form C.2121 (in pads of 100).

Reference Night [illegible] Operation Order No 28 [illegible] LEFO [illegible] 2 5 [illegible] am [illegible] will be [illegible] [illegible]

Copy No 8   SECRET

Right Group Operation Order No 29

On Nov **6**th in conjunction with Troops on our Right & Left.

1st PHASE.   Time   2 P.M. to 2.30 P.M.
    2/34 T.M.   1 gun from No 11 bd on   I.26.D.3.7.
         "   "   No 13 bd on   I.26.B.75.45.

2nd PHASE.   Time   3.30 P.M. to 4 P.M.
    2/34 T.M.   1 gun No 8 bd on   I.26.D.2.5.
         "   No 12   "   I.26.B.75.45.

B, C & D batteries 152nd Bde. will cover as follows.

    B/battery   4 guns   Hostile Front Line I.32.A.80.95
                                    to I.26.D.05.20.

    C/battery   6 guns   Front line I.26.B.6.0 to I.26.D.46.65.
                         & support line I.26.D.5.5 to I.26.D.4.2.

    D/battery   2 Guns on battery & communications at
                         LE BAS HAU   O.2.D.1.6
                 2 Guns on EARTHWORK I.33.D.1.5.

        Ammunition 18 pdr. 35 Rounds per battery per phase
                                50% each of A & AX
                    Hows 4.5" 30 Rounds per battery each phase
                    T.Ms   25 Rounds per gun per phase

Copy to:
1. H.R.A.   Acknowledge
2. 101 Infy Bde.
3. Left Group.
4. B/152.
5. C/152
6. D/152
7. 2/34 T.M.

Copy No 9   SECRET

Right Group Operation Order No. 30.

On the night of 7th Nov. the Left Group will raid Hostile lines. — Objective 121.c.62.15.

The Enfilade Section of B/152 and one section of D/152 will co-operate as follows:

B/152.   ZERO to +2 mins. Front Trench 121.c.5.1 – 25.00.

+2 mins to +30 mins. Support Line Trench 127.A.45.85 – 55.95.

D/152.   ZERO to +2½ mins. Points 121.c.5.1 + 25.00
+2½ mins to +30 mins. Points 127.A.45.85 and 121.c.25.00.

ZERO hour will be at 8.15 p.m.
Watches will be synchronized at 3.30 p.m. on 7th inst.

Rate of fire. 8.15 to 8.35 p.m. 18 pdrs & 4.5 hows.
3 rounds per gun per minute.
8.35 to 8.45 p.m. 18 pdrs & 4.5 hows.
2 rounds per gun per minute.
Cease fire at 8.45 p.m.

Acknowledge.

6-11-1916.
G. Howell Lieut. R.F.A.
Right Group. R.A.

Copies to
No 1. H.Q. R.A.
2. 101 Inf Bde
3. Left Group
4. B/152
5. C/ "
6. D/ "
7 to 9 Spare

SECRET.

Right Group Operation Order No 31.
(In conjunction with Right Group O.O. 30.)

As an additional diversion the Right Group will carry out the following bombardment.

ZERO to + 10 Minutes
B/152   4 guns Enemy Front Line
                I.32.A.80.90 to I.26.D.0.2.

C/152   4 Guns Enemy Front Line.
                I.26.D.37 to I.26.D.57.80
         2 Guns on Trench. I.26.D.5.5. to I.26.D.5.4.

D/152   1 Section on EARTHWORKS. I.33.D.1.5.

Z/34. T.M. 1 Gun.   Point.   I.26.D.3.7.

RATE OF FIRE.
    ZERO to +5 mins.   18 pdrs 4 Rounds per gun per minute
                        4.5 Hows. 2   "   "   "   "
                        T.Ms.   as fast as possible.
    +5 mins to +10 mins 18 pdrs 2 Rounds per gun per minute
                        4.5 Hows. 1   "   "   "   "
                        Z/34 T.M. As fast as possible.

Watches will be synchronised at 4 P.M. Nov 7th.

Copies to   Acknowledge.
1. H.Q. R.A.
2. 101 Infantry.
3. Left Group
4. B/152
5. C/152
6. D/152
7. Z T.M.

                                G. Rowatt Lt. Col.
                                Right Group R.F.A.

Copy No 10   SECRET

Right Group Operation Order No 32.

1. Information gained by patrols etc. indicates that the enemy brings up strong working parties after midnight to work on his front & support lines & wire & that these parties continue work until shortly before morning "Stand to".

2. To inflict loss on these parties a special hurricane bombardment will be carried out by 34th Div. Arty. S. Coys Mortar Batteries & available Lewis & Machine Guns will co-operate.

C/152		Enemy Front Line 40 yards each side of I.26.B.75.45
B/152	4 Guns	I.32.C.1.8 to I.32.C.1.9.
	Enfilade Section 1 Gun	= I.21.C.2.0 to I.21.C.50.0
	" " 1 Gun	= I.27.A.55.95 to I.27.A.85.95
D/152	2 Guns	I.32.A.46.30
	2 Guns	I.26.B.85.45
Z/34 T.M.	1 Gun	I.26.D.3.7
	1 Gun	I.26.C.8.0

ZERO HOUR.   4.30 A.M. Nov 9th & will continue for 3 min

RATE OF FIRE   18 pdr = 4 Rounds per gun per minute
               4.5 Hows = 3   "   "   "   "   "
               T.M. = Maximum Rate.

Watches will be synchronised with Right Group Headquarters @ 12.30 A.M. Nov 9th
Acknowledge
                                              G. Knight
                                                Bgdr.

Copies to
1. H.2.A.A.
2. B.M. 101
3. 34/152
4. C/152
5. B/152
6. D/152
7. Z/34
8. 10 Wes.

Copy No 10   SECRET

Right Group. Operation Order No 33.

In co-operation with the Left Group who are carrying out a raid, the following dummy raid will take place.

Time. ZERO hour 4.30 a.m. 13th Nov.

ZERO to +5.
  2/34. T.M's 1 Gun on wire I.26.c.85.00.
    As fast as possible.

ZERO to +3.
  B. Bty. 2 guns on front line I.26.c.85.00. — 9.1.
           2   "   "   "   "   I.32.a.60.50 — 65.65.
  C. Bty. 3 guns. I.26.c.9.1 — I.26.d.05.20.
           3   ".   I.26.d.2.5 — 3.7.

+3 to +5.
  B. Bty.   4 guns. I.32.a.6.5 — 65.65.
  C. Bty.   6   ".   I.26.d.2.5 — 37.

Rate of fire.
        B. Bty.   4 rounds per gun per minute.
        C. ".   3   "   "   "   "   " .

D. Bty. **ZERO to +5.**
  2 guns. I.32.b.1.6.
  1 gun.   I.26.d.68.50.
  1   ".   I.27.c.85.02.
  Ammunition 50 rounds.

2.11.1916.   [signature] Lieut. R.F.A.
                               Right Group. R.A.

Issued to.
  1. H.Q.R.A.
  2. 101 Bde.
  3. Left Group.
  4. B/152.
  5. C/ ".
  6. D/ ".
  7. 2/34 T.M.
  8 to 10 Spare.

Right Group Operation Order N° 35

1. The following shoot will take place today at 3-10pm to 3-25pm for the purpose of cutting wire & creating a false impression as to the objective of a raid to be carried out in the near future.

2. 101st T.M. Battery will bombard I 32 c 00.½ to I 32 c 2.9. To fire from 3-10 to 3-15 pm.
Rate of fire - 20 rounds per gun per min.

L/34 T.M. Battery will cut wire & fire on enemy parapet at I 26 b 8.1.
Rate of fire - As fast as possible

B/152 & C/152 will cover this as follows:-

B/152   2 guns enemy front line 20 yards on either side of pt. I 26 d 2.5
        2 guns (enfilade) support line I 27 a 05.15

C/152   6 guns 50 yards on either side of point I 26 b 6.5 front & support line.

D/152 - In observation for hostile T.M. activity

Ammunition 12 rounds per battery.

                 G. Farr Lieut & Adj
                 Right Group

19-11-16

Copy No 6   SECRET

Right Group Operation Order No 34.

The 16th Royal Scots are carrying out a raid on the night of the 23rd/24th. Point of entry I 26 c 83.04. The Infantry will lie up in "NO MANS LAND" & enter the German trenches as soon as possible after Zero. Their route across "No Mans Land" is along the track as far as I 26 c 83.36 thence direct to point of entry. The raiding party will leave enemy trenches at + 18 mins

Right Group R.A. will fire as follows :-

Zero to + 18 mins

Z/34 M.T.M — on Enemy parapet & wire at I 26 b 8.4
  Rate of fire :— as fast as possible.

C/152 R.F.A. — Zero to +3 :- Front line I 26 d 3.6 to I 26 d 60.85.
  +3 to +18 all guns concentrate on I 26 d 3.4.
  to I 26 d 60.85.

B/152 R.F.A — Zero to +3 - Front line I 26 d 18.34 to I 26 d 3.6
(4 guns)   +3 to +18 — Lift to Support line I 26 d 4.3
  to I 26 d 5.5.

Rates of fire :- Zero to +3   - 4 rounds per gun per min
(18 prs.)   +3 to +18 —   3   "   "   "   "
  +18 till asked } 2   "   "   "   "
  to stop by Infantry }

D/152 R.F.A — 2 guns - I 32 b 1.6
  1 gun - I 26 d 68.50
  1 gun - I 24 c 85.02.

Rate of fire — Zero to +18 - 3 rounds per gun per min
and at +18 ~~rounds to~~ stop ~~rounds per gun per min~~

Zero & synchronizing of watches to be notified later.

Acknowledge   S. Farr Lieut & Adj
                                            Right Group.
21-11-16

Confidential

War Diary

-of-

152nd Brigade R.F.A.

From 1st to 31st Dec 1916.

Volume 12.

Vol XI

WAR DIARY

Army Form C. 2118.

152 Bde RFA

Place	Date	Hour	Summary of Events and Information	Remarks and references to Appendices
ARMENTIERES H.17.D.3.5.4.0	DEC 1st 1916		Bar 29 H 5: Ter. 36. Observation imperfect. Our artillery fired on salvation in enemy T.M. at the request of infantry on front line trench effect ? 31.4.75: & Bianca House. One working party in front of enemy lines was reported by the infantry & H rounds were fired. also shown by our artillery. 2/34 T.M fired on unit at L.26.c.5.7. but extent of these shells unable owing to mist. Ammunition expended A.21. 4x17. 13x 37:	
	DEC 1st		Bar 29 H 2. Ter. 38. Observation bad. 2/3 2 T.M battery fired on aux at I 310 0.3 The result was good. Enemy retaliation was pretty heavy. Many T.H fired on Trenches in front of Wats Farm also on trenches corner White City where old trench was run the aus & moxity to high Principals were fired along the road from between Wats Farm & Bridoux Salient. Right group retaliated 9	

Army Form C. 2118.

WAR DIARY
or
INTELLIGENCE SUMMARY
(Erase heading not required.)

Instructions regarding War Diaries and Intelligence Summaries are contained in F. S. Regs., Part II. and the Staff Manual respectively. Title pages will be prepared in manuscript.

Place	Date	Hour	Summary of Events and Information	Remarks and references to Appendices
ARMENTIERES H.17.D.35.40	Dec 3		Silenced all enemy fire. Ammunition expended A×34 B×15 —	
			Bar. 30.1 Ther. 39	
			Observation impossible all day owing to mist. Ammunition expended A2/A×37 B×25.	
			Bar. 28.6 Ther. 35 - Observation Moderate	
			7/3.4.P.M. Fired fire at 1.45 P.M. on enemy snipers at L.31.a.4.5 & L.32.c.0.9. Snipers were active in that place. The right hand gun came for after 15-rounds	
	4		our front trenches being blown down by 5-9". At the detachment was subjected to rifle fire [?] between the canal was very much shaken. Right Group rations at MANNIE LEFT at enemy's infantry. Ammunition expended A2. A×40. B×13	

Army Form C. 2118.

WAR DIARY
or
INTELLIGENCE SUMMARY.
(Erase heading not required.)

Instructions regarding War Diaries and Intelligence Summaries are contained in F. S. Regs., Part II. and the Staff Manual respectively. Title pages will be prepared in manuscript.

Place	Date	Hour	Summary of Events and Information	Remarks and references to Appendices
ARMENTIERES H.17.D.35.40	Dec 5		Bar. 29.86. The 39 Observation Gard. 2/34 T.M. cut wire at L.26.d.15.50. Air. 1.30 pm High Exp. fire on Minnie wp. Several threw up. At report of Infantry. Two groups of men about 40 in each group seen about in 0.12.c towards L.19.0.5. About 20 men seen at 0.2.a.N.3. They were fired on & the Huns were dispersed. Movement was seen at House O.9.C.1.9. Our work had been done on Tuesday and this point they were fired on. Movement ceased & work was damaged. Ammunition Expended A.T. At. 51, 13 × 25.	
		6	Bar. 29. The 37 Observation Lapizzite 2/34 T.M. fired on wire at L.26.d.15.50 to cut wire was thrown up & hit on note 1.30 p.m. our Friday. Artillery fired as covering fire T.M.s & also Ps responsible	

WAR DIARY
or
INTELLIGENCE SUMMARY

Army Form C. 2118.

Place	Date	Hour	Summary of Events and Information	Remarks and references to Appendices

O.C. Left Group (B/152 Battalion Sector)
Ammunition Expended A10. AX4.6. B10. BX 21.

The following promotions & movement of officers in 152nd Bde:-

Capt. P.S. MYBURGH   A/152
W.G HULL   B/152-2 } to be acting Majors dated 6/12/16.
"   BERRY KNOX GORE C/152-2

Lt R THORPE   A/152
"   G.W. BAXTER B/ } To be acting Captains dated 2/8/16.
"   H.A. JOHNSTONE C/152   2/11/16.

Bar 29.42. The 37. Observator Infantry
Right Group fired on MINNIE LEFT at Signals of
Infantry.
Ammunition Expended A8. AX.14. 13 x 12.

WAR DIARY
or
INTELLIGENCE SUMMARY.

(Erase heading not required.)

Army Form C. 2118.

Place	Date	Hour	Summary of Events and Information	Remarks and references to Appendices
ARMENTIERES H.17.D 35.60	Dec 8		Bar. 29.03. Ther. 36. Observation Impossible throughout the day owing to thick fog. Ammunition Expended. AX19 13x12.	
	9		Bar. 29.40. Ther. 37. Observation Impossible throughout the day. Our Battery fired MINNIE left at 3.45 PM. Ammunition Expended. A8 AX 4s 13x17	
	10		Bar. 29.06. Ther. 38. Observation Good. A Morning light fog. Enemy working parties seen working at 0.7.a.7.8. they were fired on & dispersed. Smoke was seen rising from house at 0.7.a.9.6. 16 men were seen entering WEST. School Bldge in TRENCH map Sheet WEST. Target, & two heavy T.M. BEAUCAMP direction. Targets from T 31.6. 30. 25. (n army at arm human) were seen from T 31.6. 30. 25.	

WAR DIARY
or
INTELLIGENCE SUMMARY

Army Form C. 2118.

Place	Date	Hour	Summary of Events and Information	Remarks and references to Appendices
ARMENTIERES H.Q.P. 35.w.				
		7 P.M	Three T.M's. Amos Van Deventer . The Battery fired on the 2 also fired a retaliate on received out at enemy's Infantry. Ammunition Expend A 14 AX 97, BX 24.	
		1.30 AM	Bar. 29.22 Ther 39° O Barato Good. Enfilade Sector B/152. Fired in response to coil Raid by on LEIST group front.	
		2.15 P.M	Right Group fired on M.1.N.N.14-14.17.T a alarm enemy fire for our T.M shoot Movement was seen towards O.2.C 7.F six shells were fired Hostile T.M's were seen firing from behind trees in O.1.B 30.75. 2 also on heavy T.M. Upon general fire to this she of 1. 5 hostile aeroplanes flew over our lines during the day as opposed to have been seen to attempt to cross over their lines of the time over at BAC ST MAUR a again on their lines. Ammunition Expended A.96, AX 103, BX 5.	

Army Form C. 2118.

WAR DIARY
or
INTELLIGENCE SUMMARY.
(Erase heading not required.)

Place	Date	Hour	Summary of Events and Information	Remarks and references to Appendices
ARMENTIERES	12		Bar. 29.26. The 38. Observation Inefficient. Clear sky all day. Ammunition Expended A.16 AX.20. 13x M7.	
	13		Bar. 29.42. The 39. Observation bad. Smoke was seen rising from the rear of OYSTER FARM. Ammunition Expended A.6. AX.7. 13x.10.	
	14		Bar. 29.03. The 36. Observation Good. Capt. P.H. FERGUSON 3/152 was Promoted & Acting Lieut. Colonel Dated 14/12/15. Right Group Artillery was twice called upon for MINNIE LOTT. at North T.M. batteries were very active. Right Group Scheme No. 331 was carried out in very good form time just after dark. Smoke was seen rising from T/32.6.6.5. & 07.C.900.r. & 07.A.90.50. From Flashes of MINNENWURFER thrown friendly fire to be of short duration. T/32.6.50.95. this was regarded by 8/152 Armament Expended A.3. 13x15.	

Army Form C. 2118.

WAR DIARY
or
INTELLIGENCE SUMMARY.
(Erase heading not required.)

Instructions regarding War Diaries and Intelligence Summaries are contained in F. S. Regs., Part II. and the Staff Manual respectively. Title pages will be prepared in manuscript.

Place	Date	Hour	Summary of Events and Information	Remarks and references to Appendices
ARMENTIERES H.11.D.15.20	15th		Bar. 29.06. The 37 Observation Post Ore small party seen working in Ruined Farmhouse at O.4.c.7.8.9 our dispersed by our fire. Sand was seen issuing from Trench opposite A.135. AX 37. 8X.108. CHOCOLATE HOUSE	
	16th		Bar. 29.02. The 34 Observation Inspected. Guards hit to T.M. Hostile are observed coming from the ruins of reference G on Artillery Ammunition Sketch. A.26. AY.12. I 32.c.60.95.	
	17		Bar. 29.40. The 36 Observation Inspected. T.M. fired 10 rounds target at I. 32.9.3-3. much J.34 T.M. good result. The hostile T.M. Trench fires a cartridge on relation of Minnie Right. Ammunite Sketch A.9. AX.18. BX.20.	

2353 Wt. W3544/1454 700,000 5/15 D.D.&L. A.D.S.S./Forms/C. 2118.

Army Form C. 2118.

WAR DIARY
or
INTELLIGENCE SUMMARY.
(Erase heading not required.)

Instructions regarding War Diaries and Intelligence Summaries are contained in F. S. Regs., Part II. and the Staff Manual respectively. Title pages will be prepared in manuscript.

Place	Date	Hour	Summary of Events and Information	Remarks and references to Appendices
ARMENTIERES H17d.25.40	18"		Bar. 29.82. Tr. 35°. Observation insufficient owing to mist. Several men were seen in trench I.33.0l.1.5. working a pump, they were fired upon & dispersed. Smoke from them was seen rising in the ridge in O.12.c.9.d. 2/3rd T.M. fired at I.26.d.3.7. O I.26.d.2.5. Mr. was unsatisfactory as our first burst. Ammunition expended A×25. B×40.	
	19"		Bar. 29.09. Tr. 33. Light cast. 2/3rd T.M. fired a hate series at I.26.d.3.7 & I.26.d.2.5. All the first pair & three & one was cut through the wire. At the latter point a large gap also appeared & an enemy T.M. was active at times, & at infantry Retaliation for which T.M. was asked for times. Ammunition expended A×2.	

2353 Wt. W2544/1454 700,000 5/15 D.D.&L. A.D.S.S./Forms/C. 2118.

Army Form C. 2118.

WAR DIARY
or
INTELLIGENCE SUMMARY.
(Erase heading not required.)

Place	Date	Hour	Summary of Events and Information	Remarks and references to Appendices
ARMENTIERES	20th		Bar. 29.44 Ther. 36. Observation fair. Snace Working Party was seen digging at point I.33.c.9.5. Party was fired upon & dispersed. Smoke seen rising from Chimney in house I.34.c.2.1. also from trench O.7.d.6.4. Fresh registration was carried out by the Batteries & also registration by Aeroplane. Enemy aeroplanes were seen during the day. Ammunition expended A.39. AX 30. BX 46	
	21st		Bar. 29.62 Ther. 32. Observation Good. Large working party was dispersed at 0.10 a.m. they were chased away & three salvos were dropped up on an advance Guard of them. A party of about 100 men passed in single file under Railway Embankment at O.4.c.9.3. Hostile artillery was quiet until about during the day, but ceased firing after our Retaliation scheme. Registration for enemy never was carried out. Ammunition expended A.52. AX 30. BX 18.	

WAR DIARY or INTELLIGENCE SUMMARY

Army Form C. 2118.

Place	Date	Hour	Summary of Events and Information	Remarks and references to Appendices
ARMENTIERES. H.17.D.25.40	21"		A raid was carried out on Enemy trenches in which our Battery fired a programme for barrage. The Raiding Party 10 Leicesters failed to enter the enemy lines. O.O. 34.	
	22"		Bar. 2942. The 38. Observation Post. Motor Lorry & six transport wagons were seen passing along road O.12.d towards L'N4108. A large amount of shelled timber has recently been dumped at point in rear of new trench - Considerable further registration was carried out. Counter-Batteries Expended A.335, A.340, B.305.	
	23		Bar. 29.62. The 38. Observation Post reports everything the day. The hostile T.M. were fairly active during the day & retaliation was twice asked for by the Infantry, after the last retaliation they cause ammunition expended A.64, A.12.	

Army Form C. 2118.

WAR DIARY
or
INTELLIGENCE SUMMARY.
(Erase heading not required.)

Instructions regarding War Diaries and Intelligence Summaries are contained in F. S. Regs., Part II. and the Staff Manual respectively. Title pages will be prepared in manuscript.

Place	Date	Hour	Summary of Events and Information	Remarks and references to Appendices
ARMENTIERES H.17 d 3.5.40	Dec 24		Bar. 29.40. Thr. 33. Observation fair. Fresh registration was carried out by aeroplane on O.T. and green. The enemy shelled our front line about 970 & 5.7.9. & our retaliation was carried out on I.32.c.2.4. Also our retaliation on MINNIE RIGHT. Ammunition Expended 4 x 3.	
	25.		Bar. 29.41. Thr. 34. Observation Good. Smoke was seen rising from I.33.d.1.5. LE MAISNIL GRAND. There was available his movement seen a rear of enemy lines than usual on bright day. The Artillery fired a [?] upon A 1.2.3. A.17. B X 2.3. Right front taken	
	26.		Bar. 29.44. Thr. 33. Enemy the trenches [?] throughout the day owing to wet. MINNIE RIGHT was able to fire owing to the flying of the shells around [?]	

2353 Wt.W2344/1454 700,000 5/15 D.D.&L. A.D.S.S./Forms/C. 2118.

Army Form C. 2118.

WAR DIARY
or
INTELLIGENCE SUMMARY.
(Erase heading not required.)

Place	Date	Hour	Summary of Events and Information	Remarks and references to Appendices
ARMENTIERES H.17.d.15.40.	27"		Ammunition was fired 2/5H T.M. also fired on enemy second line & old communic. trenches. Ammunition. Fx pistol A.25, 9x3¾, B×4¾.	
			Bar. 29.96. Ther 51. Trenches dry. Fired on site Tarpelm all day. Three hostile aeroplanes were observed during the day. 2/5H T.M. fired 50 rounds on Enemy saps line between I.30.3.8. & I.32.c.1.6. Considerable damage was done. Much dirt material was thrown up. Ammunal — Rapidex A.40 A×120. B×104	
	28		Bar. 30.06. Ther 50. Observer reported my & enemy Two hostile Aeroplanes were seen during the day. Trench Mr Grp Artillery fired on to B.25 M.G. & the Ennep Salem. Ammunition. Rapidex N.16. A×64. 13×36.	

Place	Date	Hour	Summary of Events and Information	Remarks and references to Appendices
ARMENTIERES	29		Mar 30. The 33. Observation Good. Large working party of 30 to 40 men seen on trench 0.10 c.5.d. was fired on & dispersed. Four salvos were fired into party returning into camp. They were dispersed but on clear up were scanned & further. Men further fully active O.2.C. was fired on & ran. The Head of 3–15 cm How emplacement to the time bearing on 1325 of battery books. O.14.C. it was found but to be shown. Flares were also seen from a gun at 0.15.C.55.50. Immediate movement was noticed along our own & in rear. Ammunt exploded a 57, A×52, B×54.	
	30		Mar 29.17. The st. Observation Good. Party of 20 men seen working at trench. 0.2.6.4.5. They were fired upon & dispersed. Several pla were seen working in the vicinity of trench I: 3.5.4.56. House struck by 2 min. of fire in trench second.	

WAR DIARY
or
INTELLIGENCE SUMMARY.

Army Form C. 2118.

(Erase heading not required.)

Instructions regarding War Diaries and Intelligence Summaries are contained in F.S. Regs., Part II. and the Staff Manual respectively. Title pages will be prepared in manuscript.

Place	Date	Hour	Summary of Events and Information	Remarks and references to Appendices
ARMENTIERES M17d 3340.	Dec 30th	7/3.0 PM	Fired 40 rounds, treacle brooch a cut a lane through wire at I 26.6.8.1. Ammunition expended A.53. AX 56. BX 103.	
	31	Ba 29.	Then 41 Shrapnel Soon. Seen close to hale-p 17mm gun come to same line bearing 122° 10' for RENDEZVOUS. Seen from new informer I-om gun flashes plainly 4.2 how. having 0°45' R of Ploegstr Church from RENDEZVOUS. favorable moment. 3 small partir observed all day in 1 car. Our Artillery fired on the Group later in reply at Night. Ammunit.—Expended A 146. AX 116. BX 170.	

(signature) Lieut. Col. R.F.A.
Commdg. 152nd (NOTTM.) BDE. R.F.A.

SECRET   Right Group.   Copy No. 9

Operation Order No. 37

The following shoots will take place on the night of 30th/31st at times to be notified later.

Shoot 1 + 3.

18 pdrs. Shrapnel.

Roads.   B/152.   2 guns.   I.33.a.7.9 to I.33.b.9.2.
                           2 guns.   O2.d.10.66 to O2.d.7.0.
              C/152.   2 guns.   I34.c.9.7 to I34.d.60.10.
                           2 guns.   I35.c.10.10 to ENNETIERES.
                           2 guns.   O2.d.7.0 to 09.c.37.70.
              D/152.   Points. O2.d.10.67., 09.c.11.7.,
              I34.a.05.25., I34.a.28.uu., I34.c.74.62.

Shoot 2 + 4.

18 pdrs. 50% HE.

Tramlines.   B/152.   I32.d.7.9 to I33.c.12.38.   2 guns.
                            O2.c.8.7 to O2.d.55.00.   2 guns.
               C/152.   I32.b.32.55 to I32.b.68.20.   2 guns.
                            O2.a.2.6 to O2.c.8.7.   2 guns.
                            O2.d.55.00 to 09.c.03.80.   2 guns.
              D/152.   O1.b.60.65 to O2.a.15.10.
                       I32 Central to I32.b.62.15 and
                       point. O2.d.12.56.

Two salvos per Battery on each shoot.

This shoot is a repetition of the one which took place on the night of the 14th inst.

Batteries will report expenditure of ammunition separately.

Acknowledge

29.12.16.

                                             S. Farr. Lieut. R.F.A.
                                             Right Group R.A.

Copies to: 1.   H.Q.R.A.
                2.   H.Q. 101 Bde.
                3.   Left Group.   6.   C/152.
                4.   2nd Anzac Arty.   7.   D/152.
                5.   B/152.   8.   X/34.T.M.B.
                                      9 to 11.   Spare.

Copy No 8   SECRET

RIGHT GROUP RA.
REFERENCE OPERATION ORDER No 57

Shoot No 1 & 3 will take place at 5.5 pm, 7-20pm, 11-40pm

Shoot No 2 & 4 will take place at 5.50pm, 6-35pm & 11-5pm.

Ammunition 3 Salvoes per battery will be fired on each occasion.

Watches will be synchronized at 5pm

Copies to :-
1. HQ RA
2. HQ 103 Inf Bde
3. Left Group
4. New Zealand Bde
5. B/152
6. C/152
7. D/152
8 & 9. Spare

30-12-16

S. Farr. Lieut & Adj
Rgt RA Group. RA.

SECRET

O.O. 34

Artillery Scheme in conjunction
with Raid by 10th Lincolns.

Objective – Enemy front-line between
points I.26.d.3.7 and I.26.d.16.42.
Time of Entry +3 mins. Time of Exit. +18 mins.
18 Pdrs. 5 guns B/152 & 6 guns C/152.
 Zero to +3 min. – front line I.26.d.c.98.18
      to I.26.d.6.9.
 +3 mins to +23 mins. Centre 5 guns lift to
    Support line I.26.d.37.21 to I.26.d.61.63.
Rates of Fire.
 Zero to +3 mins. – 5 rounds per gun per min.
 +3 mins. to +18 mins. – 3 do. " " " "
 +18 " to +23 " – 2 do. " " " "

4.5" Hows. 6 guns D/152.
 Zero to +23 mins fire on following points.
 I.26.c.90.08 I.26.d.90.40.
 I.26.d.32.08 I.26.d.23.87.
 I.26.d.70.45 I.26.b.66.00.
Rates of Fire
 Zero to +3 mins. – 3 rounds per gun per min.
 +3 mins to +18 mins. – 2 do. " " " "
 +18 " to +23 " – 1 do. " " " "

Estimated expenditure Zero to +23 mins.
 315 A, 315 AX., 264 BX.
At +23 mins. Batteries cease fire & stand by for
further orders.
Heavy Artillery. 60 Pdrs. to be asked to stand by
for counter battery work.
Diversion From Zero to +4 mins. Z/34 Med. T.M. Battery
will fire on front line I.26.b.20.55 to I.26.b.85.70.
Rate of fire As fast as possible.

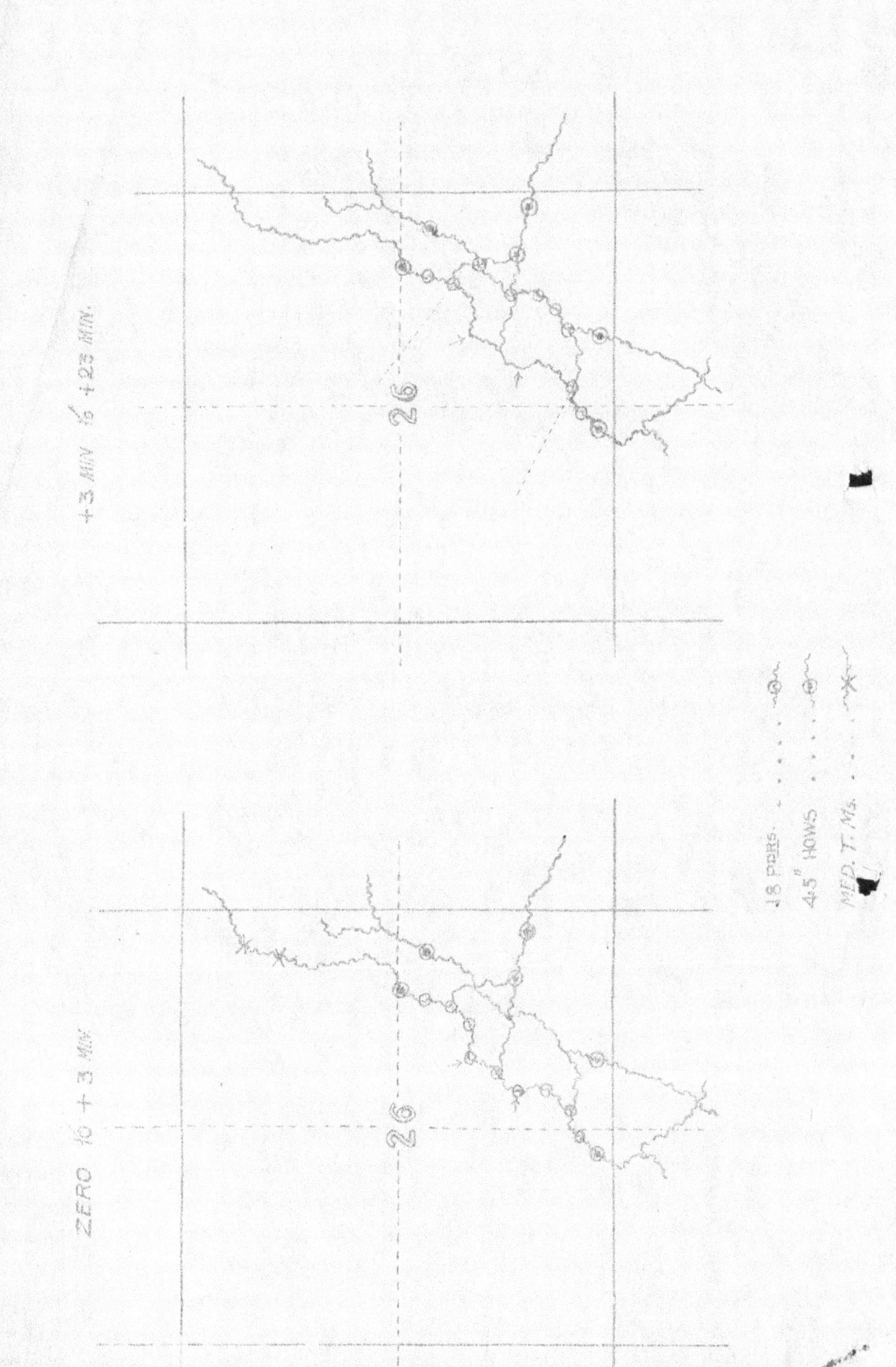

SECRET

RIGHT GROUP R.A.

"MINNIE RIGHT" or "MINNIE LEFT"

The above may be sent by Battalion Headquarters as a call for retaliation to Heavy Hostile Trench Mortars. "MINNIE RIGHT" or "MINNIE LEFT" will be passed to all batteries RIGHT II GROUP immediately on receipt at GROUP HEADQUARTERS. Batteries will concentrate on the following targets and report :-
READY TO FIRE to Group Headquarters.

MINNIE RIGHT   O I B 40·95

MINNIE LEFT   Houses about I 32 b 1·1

When all batteries have reported ready Group H.Q. will give the order to fire.
Fire will last one minute.
Ammunition 18 pdr 18 rounds per battery.
        4·5 How 12 rounds per battery

G. Farr Lieut + Adj
Right Group.

2-12-16

Army Form C. 2118.

WAR DIARY
or
INTELLIGENCE SUMMARY.
(Erase heading not required.)

152ND BDE. R.F.A.

Place	Date	Hour	Summary of Events and Information	Remarks and references to Appendices
ARMENTIERES H17d.35.m.	JAN 1. 1917	Bar. 29.25 Ther. 30. Observation Good	T/3 M. T. M. Battery fired 125 rounds on wire at I.31.N.8 & I.26.d.18.30. At the former point wire was seen cut & another lane partially cut. At the latter point six good lanes were cut. Our Artillery fired as a covering fire at 7 PM. Two hostile T.M's were observed firing from I.32.c.6.9. There were engaged by our 15 Pr. Batt. fire their again. Flashes of 15cm How were observed from O.14.C.3.2. D/152 engaged the battery. Hostile observation was to have a glimpse of this shot. Flashes of hostile guns were located at O.4 & 7.7 The 6"too & 60 pdr. were turned on to this spot Hostile Artillery were considerably more active during the day. Ammunition expended A.X.1, D.X 21	
	Jan 2nd	Bar. 29.30 Ther. 29. Observation Indifferent	Considerable movement was observed at O.2.C.7.7. Men were seen carrying timber, & French fire & all movement ceased.	

WAR DIARY or INTELLIGENCE SUMMARY

Army Form C. 2118.

Place	Date	Hour	Summary of Events and Information	Remarks and references to Appendices
ARMENTIERES H.1704.35.40			Considerable movement was seen at dawn in 0.10.a. Rapid fire on it dispersed. Hostile minnies were very active during the day. Their flash was seen at the Brewery near Chard at (Ammn Exped) A.14.B A.4.10.b. B.4.7.b	
	Jan. 3		Bar 29.32 Ther. 30 Observation Good. 6/52 cut a complete lane through wire at I.32.a.6.6. Partially entanded at same point. The Haslers of a 77m battery were observed 3" R" of RADINGHAM CHURCH (being the fm (on.w.22)) the position appears to be 0.15.a.7.1. The 60 pdr gunner fire order Tanks of a 7.m. was observed from I.28.d.9.2 (D)/152 batteries the 7.m. registered the spot. 2/34 T.M fired 5.3 rounds. A lane was cut at I.26.d.15.30 a german gun cttee of large size was blown up at I.26.d.5.7. two This was certain while a complete lane was cut in the front l[ine]	

Place	Date	Hour	Summary of Events and Information	Remarks and references to Appendices
ARMENTIERES H17d.35.10			Our battery fired on a carriage in A.7.M. Enemy retaliation by sly shots, chiefly on WHITE CITY. One hostile aeroplane observed. Reconnoitring Officers, Armourer, Engineers. In Military Orders in the diary received Military Cross in the New Year's Honour List. Capt. Ferguson command D/152, (now Lieut Col.) Major Perry knox-Gore awarded D/152. Capt. Thorp A/152, & Lt. KARR Adjutant, 152 RFA all for Work in the Somme.	
			Ammunition Expended A142 A×135, D×120	
	2nd		Bar 29.62 Ther 32 Observation fairly good. Ammunition seen Escoubecques Enfros R° all in snow patches. Smoke was seen rising from trench D.1.06.94 A Party of men laying telephone cable at 0.1.0C. seen firing upon & dispersed. Signalling by lamp i.c.t from trench from the Railway Embankment. L.O.H.0. L1. L 32. L 75.70 was noticed. 2/34 T.M. fired 10 5 rounds at area L26. L72. L 26.01.5.7. Strong	

Army Form C. 2118.

WAR DIARY
or
INTELLIGENCE SUMMARY.
(Erase heading not required.)

Instructions regarding War Diaries and Intelligence Summaries are contained in F. S. Regs., Part II. and the Staff Manual respectively. Title pages will be prepared in manuscript.

Place	Date	Hour	Summary of Events and Information	Remarks and references to Appendices
ARMENTIERES H.17.d.3.5/10			were after the shots of P/152 cut a wire through in about I.31 or 33.63. Enemy T.M. was Second Group F. 01.d.5.6. Minen Before A.38.7. A.X 25, B.X 89.6.	
	5th		Bar 29.78. Ther. 38° Observation good. No enemy movement observed throughout the day. Our Artillery fired on Petillon or Lequyl of Totaly. Ten Field Guns on m Saurage Minen Before A.15. A.X 60, B.X 42	
	6th		Bar 29.65. Ther 59°. Observation poor. Sniped received from obs. post I.33.01.1.5. Battery fire on I.33.01.15. (Gulop ammunition taken) 1 Field Gun fired Enemy Before A.X 26. B.X 49	
	7th		Bar 29.70. Ther 33° Observation sufficient. Enemy H.T.M. firing from O.1.b.5.6. was engaged by 9.2/152 (23 rounds) & silenced. Minnet Fire from I.33.6.3.9 annihilated 9.2/152	

Army Form C. 2118.

WAR DIARY
or
INTELLIGENCE SUMMARY.
(Erase heading not required.)

Place	Date	Hour	Summary of Events and Information	Remarks and references to Appendices
ARMENTIERES M.17.d.3.5.u0			Our batteries fired a creeping Barrage and left S.O.S. zones were accurate results. 2/34 T.M. fired 75 rounds on wire + parapet round I.31.c.1.5.5.o. with excellent results. Much material was damaged. L.R.H.A. battery was attacked & dispersed. One of our planes was brought down in flames, the observer was badly burnt but the pilot unwounded. Own Barrage AX47 Bx18.	
	Sat		Bar 29.24 The 31. Observation Post Sent was enemy fm CHOCOLATE HOUSE (10 rounds were fired out the battery) Night party 9.12 am fired on dispersing from 24.c.9.6. Our own Barrage at 0.W. a french was dispersed. 2/34 T.M. fired 35 rounds at I.33.c.2.9 and government 5.0.5; D/5.2 fired a creeping Barrage at 4 a.m. our enemy placed 9 left of front second. Our hostile Airplane stopped. Own Barrage AX335, Dx 89	

WAR DIARY or INTELLIGENCE SUMMARY

Army Form C. 2118.

Place	Date	Hour	Summary of Events and Information	Remarks and references to Appendices
ARMENTIERES H.17.d.3.40	9th	9am	Bar 29.27. Ther. 38. Overcast. Fine. 4.30 T.M fired on houses in OYSTER FARM, believed to be used by the enemy. 11 rounds on target; rail at I.31.d.75.60 & I.32.c.07 the target was very damaged. 90 rounds on cert. wire at I.31.d.7.8 & I.30.d.57.63. V/34 Heavy T.M battery was attached to the Brigade & fired 51 rounds at Le BRIDOUX, both M shots were covered by our artillery. Twenty-one were working at deep 0.10.a 10th Australian Brigade. Fired a dispersed. Seven Germ. Flares were seen at 05. c.6.5. T.M firing from I.33.a.7.1 was aggressive during 7D/1.22. German Trench at A.7 A.X 245, B.X 177	
		10pm	Bar 29.82 Ther. 32. Overcast. Poor. Work kept as close on to defence. Much more on road OYSTER FARM. Cold wire late. Enemy hostile Airplane over German Army H. Hay. German Trench A.19 A.X 160. B.X 24	

Army Form C. 2118.

WAR DIARY
or
INTELLIGENCE SUMMARY.
(Erase heading not required.)

Place	Date	Hour	Summary of Events and Information	Remarks and references to Appendices
ARMENTIÈRES H.17.d.75.40	JAN 11th		Bar. 29.20 Ther. 30. Cloud. 10d. Fired on Minnie Right a fresh rifle at regions Trap.G. Considerable gun activity by us & enemy. T. R.H.A. battery left 4th Group. D/152 engaged M.G. battery at O.9.Z.45.50. Gen. flashes were observed from O.3.c.6.5. No action was taken owing to mist. Amm. Exped. A.20. A.X.111. D.X 24.	
	12th		Bar. 29.76. Ther. 51. Observation Difficult. Layecham 7 dum rounds over the using fire O.25.c. T.M.A.S row inferno. Working Party 1 own gun out of action at O.10.d.9c. 9 new Dugouts 1 Tank 7 M.G.M's 1 own gun at I.32.d.62.9. I.32.c.5.8 fed the Minnis are dug in + silenced. 2/34 T.M. fired 103 rounds on enemy trenches at I.26.d.60.25 & I.2.b.6.75.10, were Shrapnel were scattered & Hits + 1 Oblique Places? direct trench mortar was thrown up. 1/34 T.M. fired 6 rounds on OYSTER FARM & support line + fort. Amm. Exped. A.Y.90. B.X.56	

2353 Wt.W.2344/454 700,000 5/15 D.D.&L. A.D.S.S./Forms/C. 2118.

WAR DIARY
or
INTELLIGENCE SUMMARY

Army Form C. 2118.

Place	Date	Hour	Summary of Events and Information	Remarks and references to Appendices
ARMENTIERES H.17.d.38.20	Jan. 13		Bar. 29. Observation bad. Moment our men got on charge @ 9.10 a. his men hurried to start. Fired on MINNIE WERFT & further retaliation. Hostile artillery were mostly on active during the day. Ann. Enfer. A×9.5, B×7.7.	
		10 p	Bar. 29.30 Ther. 51. Observation fair until Operation Order no. 58 was circulated. 2nd Lt W.A. LEWIS B. Battery posted to A battery also. Harkney attached to B batty. Capt. Micah Smith R.A.M.C. posted as M.O. to the Brigade. Our artillery fired a MINNIE WERFT & also a charge 9.10 a. Hostile batteries were very active especially on our support line & just 3 Jan 9.7.32 our J actor Enemies Torpedo A×1.32 B×7.7	

Army Form C. 2118.

WAR DIARY
or
INTELLIGENCE SUMMARY.
(Erase heading not required.)

Instructions regarding War Diaries and Intelligence Summaries are contained in F. S. Regs., Part II. and the Staff Manual respectively. Title pages will be prepared in manuscript.

Place	Date	Hour	Summary of Events and Information	Remarks and references to Appendices
ARMENTIERES N.17.d.35.20	JAN 15		Bar. 29.35. Ther 30. Observation Impaired. Tried on hostile T.M. at L.27.a.55 & L.52.0.51. 62d were returned. 2/2nd T.M. fired 10 times for OYSTER FARM & L.31.d.90.35. experimental of kind desired was then up 9 rounds his on farm. 1/3 M.T.M. fired instigation rounds on communication Trench at L.32.9.5.2. Enemy retaliated were heavy Trench Mortars Bursts A×72, B×99	
	16		Bar. 29.30. Ther 30. Observation fair. Hostile Battery (77mm) open fire from 05.C.18 upon our M.M.G. at L.27.a.5.5.2 much too Heavy were expended. Rounds Expended 175. 137.114.	
	17th		Bar. 29.36. Ther 22. Observation fair. Hostile Batts. N.17.25 carried out ___ on other N.17.d. ?/??? returned to N.17.? Bivouac. Our return 7 and battery ounces ?? myself ? 175, 112, 119. Enemy Bursts A X 1	

Army Form C. 2118.

WAR DIARY
or
INTELLIGENCE SUMMARY.

(Erase heading not required.)

Place	Date	Hour	Summary of Events and Information	Remarks and references to Appendices
ARMENTIERES	Jan 18th		Bn 29:30 The 30 Observation confirmed. V/34 HTM four rounds on front I.11.d.3.0 and good result. 7/24 Tr Fired 67 rounds on front I.26.c.15.30. M.77. A. BAXTER Wanted 4 Fd L.B/52. Ammunition Expend AX 3.	
H.Q.R.J.S.G.C.	19th		Bn 29 The 30 Observation indifferent. Generally fired upon opposite front batteries on Minnie Right 9 MN NW Trenton Defense on Enemy wire on Enemy fatigue party. No rounds fire deep sap. Ammunition Exp'd A.T. AX 57, BX 33 Cement Front Fair	
	20		Bn 29.69 The 31 Observation Fair. Field Artillery were unusually more active. Enemy wire cutter Large amount of Arty's deployed on I.31.30. Several rounds from 0.10.0.0. Gun fired slower for hatty 0.5.c.35.90.	

Army Form C. 2118.

WAR DIARY
or
INTELLIGENCE SUMMARY.
(Erase heading not required.)

Place	Date	Hour	Summary of Events and Information	Remarks and references to Appendices
ARMENTIERES H17.d.15.6.			This report was adopted. 1/13 M.R. Coy started a trench I.21.d.5.3 to I/12T.R. from 7.30 am on page I.33.c.1.9. a leader party on plan. Major Hollis M/1A. BAXTER wounded & helped carried. Snipers active A.12. A.X.1.2. B.X.1.2.7.	
	2/12		Bar. 29.32 Ther. 17. C.brant. To officers. Balloon fires at P. B.y.L.5.d.4. Enemy aeroplane seen at 0.2.5.9.P. (about 30 am.) Crews on fuzes arrangement. Nrampson taking day on at I.27.c.9.6. am shell. 2/1.T.M. officer + 2 runners at trench I.36.6.10. Quantities of wire & material over them top. Bomb officer A.3. A.X.14.1. B.7.3.7.	
	22		Bar. 29.24 Ther. 15. Went all day. Few or M.N. M.E. R.6.M.7. lifts oa.6. a. M.6. baked am.a.3.6.	

WAR DIARY or INTELLIGENCE SUMMARY

Army Form C. 2118.

Place	Date	Hour	Summary of Events and Information	Remarks and references to Appendices
HAMEL TREK HQ 2nd Div.	23		Too hot explain own shrine dump cl. 07. Command 2/ Rifles AX 206 BX 38.	
	24		Ba 29.22 Th M. Obimati torpude. H14HT June 5 Round a Commeret Round about 075. Command Bofoten AX 104 BX 52	
			Ba 28. Th.N. Obimati Jun. Our Artillery fire on Right Bays Salka gate a Bipotole. A light rar stream coming from a half opposite beef to a how at HAMEL 2/6UTN from 20 mm and at I 11 A 2.55. Lt H BELL M.C. & Mn Bomb Wounded. Ba rifle AX63 AX54	
	25		Ba 29.22 Th.N. Obimati Lote Own artillery fire on Two Right Bay Sol. Retaled on eye of Tyfoul.	

Army Form C. 2118.

WAR DIARY
or
INTELLIGENCE SUMMARY.
(Erase heading not required.)

Instructions regarding War Diaries and Intelligence Summaries are contained in F. S. Regs., Part II. and the Staff Manual respectively. Title pages will be prepared in manuscript.

/3

Place	Date	Hour	Summary of Events and Information	Remarks and references to Appendices
ARMENTIERES H.Q. 152 B.	26"		4. Hostile Airplane was observed flying E.S.E. of Armentieres at slight altitude and was fired on by a 15 cm battery at H.23 in a field of fire. An. E. of H. A.123 A×174, B×70.	
			Bom. 29. The 17 F Hostile Batteries were engaged by Bde batty at H.29L at signals from pickets up. Bdes were engaged for the above tasks and enemy at others we reg each batty was observed as as orders D. 200 4. In each engagement 27 by N. Zealand	
	27		Bom tasks A×D, B×St All Batteries engaged in various support ranges.	
	28		Hostiles at 15.00 am on 1 Rue de Bar. No. of tower H.A.6. A×36. B×3	
	-31		A, B & D. prepare further hypothetical task	

152 B. RFA

Copy No 13   SECRET

Right Group Operation Order No. 38.

1. The 175 Brigade R.F.A. and A/152 R.F.A. at present attached to 3rd Australian Division, will be relieved in the line by 3rd Australian Artillery, between 17th and 19th inst.

2. Reliefs will be carried out by Sections, one Section per night on the nights of 17/18th, 18/19th, 19/20th.
   A/152 R.F.A. will hand over Command on completion of relief on the night 19th/20th.
   Clerks, Telephonists of 152 Bde R.F.A. at present attached to Left Divisional Artillery will be relieved at 10 a.m. 20th inst. to rejoin their Units.

3. A/152 R.F.A. will march out with Echelons full. Surplus Ammunition will be handed over in the pits at 12 noon on the 19th inst.

4. No equipment will be changed.
   The following will be handed over: Telephone lines, maps, Planchettes, Aeroplane photographs, Registration Log books, and all trench stores.

5. On relief A/152 R.F.A. will march by sections to its position in Right Group area at H.13.b.48.63.
   A/175's section will relieve section of B/152 in Enfilade position H.30.a.05.35 on the night 17/18.
   B/152 R.F.A. Enfilade section withdrawing to position at H.23.a.7.5. Ammunition in Enfilade section will be handed over by B/152 to A/175, receipt obtained and forwarded to this office by 9 pm 17th.
   Completion of reliefs to be reported to this H.Q. by phone.

6. Batteries will register the guns on their new positions at first opportunity.

7. At 12 noon on 20th inst Batteries will be responsible for the zones they cover (as shown on position & zone report attached).

S.O.S. lines will be changed over by O.C. 101
Inf. Bde Signals in the morning. Batteries reporting
that this is correct at 12 noon.

8. A/175 will not be in direct communication with
the Infantry. In case of S.O.S. they will fire
as ordered by O.C. Right Group.

9. Liaison with Infantry.
The same officer to do liaison with the infantry
during its tour of the trenches. During this time
the battery concerned will find 3 telephonists with
telephone to be continually at Battalion H.Q.

Batteries will find Liaison Officers in the
following order:

LEFT BATTALION	RIGHT BATTALION
A/152 R.F.A.	B/152 R.F.A.
C.	D.
A.	B.
D.	C.
A.	B.
C.	D.
A.	B.
D.	C.

10. Acknowledge.

Enclosures: Sketch of Right lines and
Companies covered.

15/1/17.

S. Law. Lieut R.F.A.
Right Group, R.A.

Copies to.
No 1. H.Q.R.A.
2. H.Q. 101 Inf Bde.
3. Left Group.
4. O.C/175 Bde R.F.A.
5. A/175.
6. A/152.
7. B/152.
8. C/152.
9. D/152.
10. to 13. Spare.

– SECRET –

RIGHT GROUP R.A

SKETCH HEWING

(1) COMPANIES COVERED BY BATTERIES

(2) NIGHT LINES OF BATTERIES

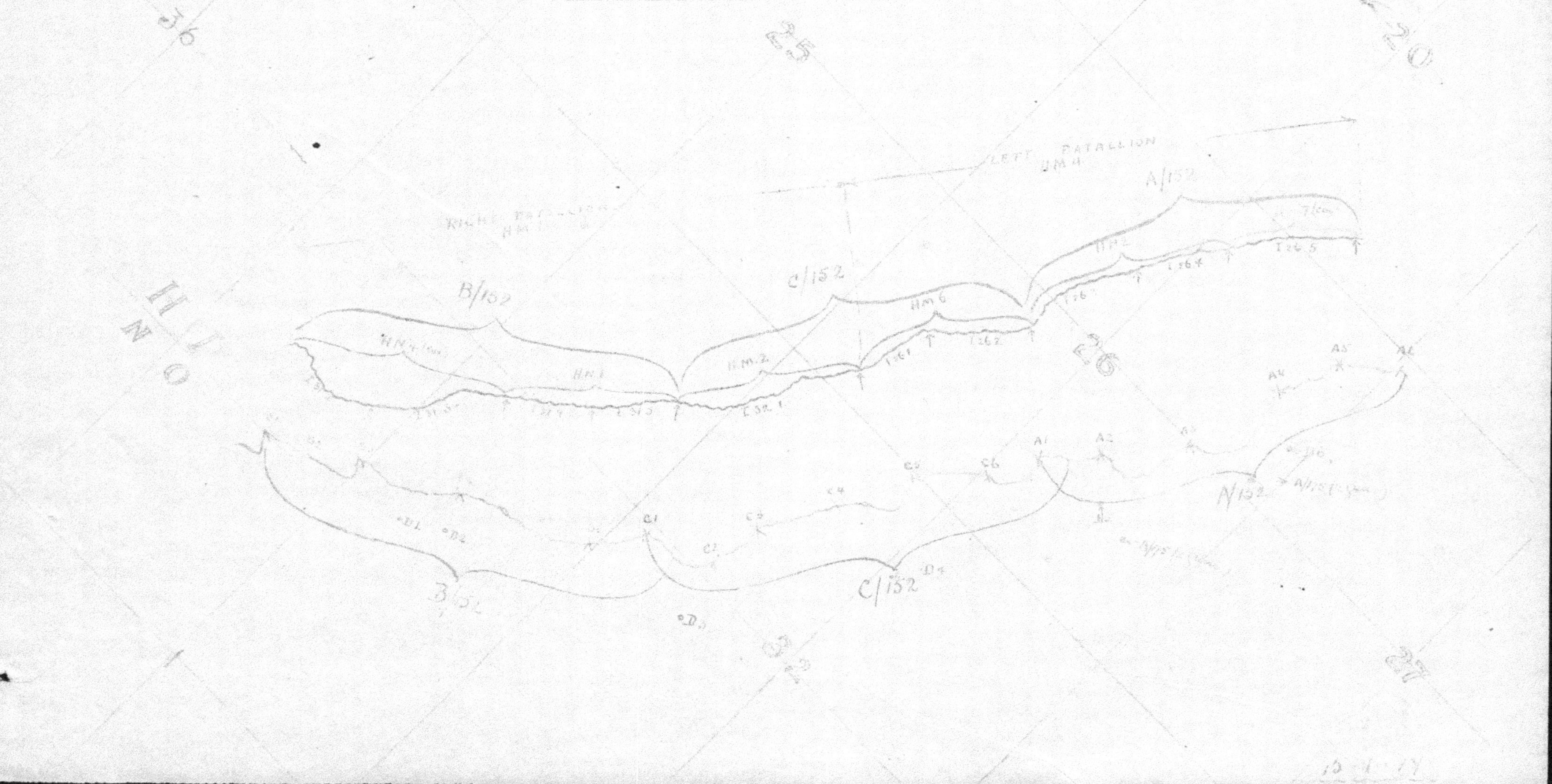

— SECRET —

34TH DIVISIONAL ARTILLERY

Return of Positions, Zones, Night Lines &c.

RIGHT GROUP R.A.

BATTERY	POSITION	ZONE COVERING TRENCHES (TRUE)	NIGHT LINES	MAXIMUM ARC ON ENEMY TRENCHES	ZONES FOR WOR WITH AEROPLANE
A/152	H18 b 48.63 (4 Guns)	I26.3, I26.4, I26.5	1. I26 d 15.48 2. I26 d 32.68 3. I26 a 6.0 4. I26 c 43.43 5. I26 b 82.72 6. I24 a 1.9	I32 c 40.95 to I21 d 1.8	NIL
B/152	H29 b 40.55 (2 Guns)	I31.2, I31.3, I31.4, I31.5	1. O1 a 6.9 2. I31 c 55.10 3. I31 c 98.23 4. I31 d 43.44 5. I31 d 82.60 6. I32 c 00.92	O1 a 40.45 to I32 a 45.45	NIL
	H23 a 7.5 (2 Guns)	O1 a 6.9 to I32 e 30.95		N 6 d 6.2 to I 26 d 2.6	
C/152	H24 a 9.7 (2 Guns)	I32.1, I26.1, I26.2	1. I32 c 15.93 2. I32 a 45.05 3. I32 a 47.30 4. I32 w 68.64 5. I32 b 8.0 6. I26 d 0.2	O1 a 40.45 to I32 a 45.45	NIL
	H24 b 25.95 (4 Guns)	I32 c 15.93 to I26 d 28.57		N 6 d 8.9-6 to I 26 d 8.6	
A/145	H24 c 69.15 (4 Guns)	NIL	1. } 2. } I 26 d 68.49 3. } I 26 d 9.1 4. } 5. I 21 c 15.00 6. I 21 c 50.05	I26 c 85.00 to I K d 2.0	NIL
	H 30 a 00.23 (2 Guns ENFILADE)			RIGHT: I 26 b 60. LEFT: ANY PART OF GERMAN FRONT TRENCHES WITHIN RANGE	
		WHOLE FRONT	1. I 31 d 2.2 2. I 31 d 3.3 3. I 32 c 5.9 4. I 32 c 1.6 5. I 26 d 30.55 6. I 26 d 9.3	N 6 b 4.2 to I 21 b 0.7 N 6 c 0.1 to I 21 d 0.7 N 6 y 3 to I 26 b 3 N 6 d 0.55 to I 26 b 6.0 I 31 d 4.4 to I 32 a 0.3	O1, O2, O3, O4, O5
D/152	H24 a 1.1	O1 a 6.9 to I24 w 1.9			1st In., 132, In.

Observation Position	Alternative Position	Reinforcing Battery Position	Wagon Lines	Remarks
Peach Barn. Apple House			A.19 6 6.5	
Beacon. Crump House			A.21 6.2.4.	
Rendezvous Spencer.			A.21 n.4.4	
Convent Rookery Chatville				
Convent			A.19 4 6.5	
2nd Army 18 Pdr O.P.				

COPY NO 10   SECRET

RIGHT GROUP R.A.
OPERATION ORDER No 38.

Ref Maps 36 NW.4 & 36.SW.2

1. The 34 R.G.A. Arty will fire on enemy communication trenches, transport routes & tram lines on the night of 24th/25th inst. Two salvoes per battery will be fired on each occasion. Batteries will distribute their fire as much as possible over the objectives allotted to them.

2. Batteries will register objectives as far as possible beforehand.

3. All guns are to be relaid on night lines after each period of fire.

4. Objectives of RIGHT GROUP RA are allotted as follows:—

SHOOT A.   A/152   Tram Line I.26.d.1.2 to I.32.b.65.20
                              I.32.b.65 to I.32.d.70.90
           B/152   Tram line along road I.31.d.10 to O.1.b.65.50
                   Comm'n Trench O.1.b.65.25 to O.1.b.60.45
           C/152   Tram Line I.31.d.60.45 to O.2.a.20.45
           A/190 (4 guns) Tram Line I.29.a.05 to I.29.a.02
           B/190 (6 yd'ds. Screens) Tram Line I.29.a.05 to I.29.d.70.45
           D/152   Trench Junct'n O.2.b.15.40
                        do   O.1.b.85.40
                        do   I.2.b.1.6
                   Hostel   O.1.b.85.40
                   Trench Junct'n O.1.b.90.40
                        do   I.32.b.65.20

SHOOT B   A/152   Road T.14 c.9.4 to T.20 d.6.1
           B/152   Road O.2 d.0.95 to O.2 b.85.80
           C/152   Road O.2 b.80.30 B O.9 c.35.10
           A/170 (2 guns)   Road T.34 d.6.1 to T.30 c.2.10
           B/170 (Enflade Section) Support line T.12 d.35.20 to T.2 d.3.0
           D/152   X roads   O.9 d.10.65
                              do   O.9 c.30.10
                              do   O.9 c.30.85
                              do   O.2 a.2.4
                              do   T.34 d.9.1
                              do   T.34 c.9.4

SHOOT C   A/152   Road T.33 a.90.55 to O.3 b.40.50
           B/152   Firm line T.32 d.p.55 to T.33 c.90.55
           C/152   Road   O.3 d.9.4 to O.6a.c.9
           A/170 (4 guns)   Road T.33 b.35.20 to T.33 b.90.15
           B/170 (Enflade Section) Support line about T.32 b.1.6
           D/152   LE GRAND MAISNIL pres
                              LE BAY CHANCE ring
                              X roads   O.9 c.25.10
                              Riv Crossing O.9 d.8.10
                              Road & Trench Junc. T.33 c.70.55
                              LP   T.33 d.10.32

SHOOT D   A/152   Roads T.33 c.1.6 & 2.3 c.6.3
                              Trans line T.33 b.35.00 to T.34 c.1.3
           B/152   Train line O.2 a.y.0 to O.2 d.55.00
           C/152   Tran line O.6a.9.4 to O.6 c.9.8
           A/170   Road T.2 c.0.6 to T.24 c.9.5 Thence along
                              track N. T.28 d.30.55
           B/170 (Enf Sect)   Support line BLANCO HOUSE to OYSTER R.
           D/152   GRAND MAISNIL ,, MONT TINDO
                              T.28 c.40.45 T.34 a 8.3, O.2 d.10.65
                              O.2 a.15.40

5. The above shoots will take place at the following times
   SHOOT A.   1.25 am,   3.40 am,   5.5 am
   SHOOT B.   1.55 am,   3.15 am,   4.25 am
   SHOOT C.   2.20 am,   5.30 am
   SHOOT D.   2.45 am,   4 am

6. Ammunition
   1st day. For registration 25% A, 75% AX.
   2nd   "   Shoot percentage A to AX notified later

7. Watches will be synchronized with Group HQ at 1.10 am 23-1-17.

8. Acknowledge

F. Vane Lieut & Adjt
Right Group. R.A.

23-1-17

Copies to. 1. HQRA   5. C/102   9. Left Group R.A.
            2. 101 I.[?]Bde   6. D/102   10 to 12 Spare
            3. A/102   7. A/145
            4. B/102   8. B/145

Copy No 8

SECRET

RIGHT GROUP. R.A.
OPERATION ORDER No 40

1. Right Group RA will practise a creeping barrage as follows on a date to be notified later.
   Battery Commanders will register their barrages in co-operation so as to ensure that there are no gaps between Batteries.

2. Frontages (on front line) as follows:—
   C/152 — I.26.d.49.68 to I.26.d.59.89
   A/152 — I.26.d.59.89 to I.26.b.73.04
   A/175 — I.26.b.73.04 to I.26.b.9.2

3. Batteries commence at Zero 100˟ short of front line as above and lift at +1 in lifts of 50˟ every minute until they reach the tramline I.27.a.0.1 to I.26.d.90.58 where they remain until +5½ when all guns cease firing. Battery Commanders must note that all guns will not reach the support line at the same time.

4. Rate of fire   3 rounds per gun per min
                   Ammunition all A.X.

5. D/152 stand by to retaliate.

                           S. Fair Lieut & Adj
25-1-19.   Right Group R.A.

Copies to:—   1 HQ RA   5 C/152
              2 101 Bde   6 D/152
              3 A/152   7 A/175
              4 B/152   8-11 Spare

COPY No 12   SECRET

RIGHT GROUP RA SCHEME for 24-1-17.

The following shoot will be carried out by
RIGHT GROUP RA on 24-1-17.

Time 2pm to 2-30 pm.
V/34 H.T.M.   Trench Junt. O1.e.05.85.
2/34 M.T.M.   Parapet & wire about I.10.d.40.55.
Covering fire
B/152 R.F.A.   6 guns   O1.e.05.85 to O1.e.50.45
                        Ammunition 80 AX.

C/152 R.F.A.   6 guns   Support Line OYSTER Lne to Bianco H.
                        Ammunition 80 AX.

A/152 R.F.A.   4 guns   Support line BIANCO Ho to Trench Junt
                        Ammunition 60 AX.

D/152 R.F.A.   1 gun   The Houseain
               "   Blanco House   } 60 BX.
               "   Trench Junction O1.e.90.40.

2/34 M.T.M. cease firing at 2-15 pm.

                                        S. Van Leur
                                        Right Group

23-1-17.

Copies to :- 1. HQ RA   5. C/152   9. V/34 HTM.
              2. 101 Inf Bde   6. D/152   10 & 12. Spares
              3. A/152   7. A/146.
              4. B/152   8. 2/34 MTM.

Copies 1 to 3 to 9 to be acknowledged by telegram please

COPY No.

SECRET

— RIGHT GROUP. R.A. —

— LIAISON & S.O.S BARRAGES —

	A/152	B/152	C/152	A/173 (4.5 in)	A/170 (2 guns) (ENFILADE)	B/170 (2 guns) ENFILADE	D/152
S.O.S RIGHT SUBSECTOR	STAND BY	NIGHT LINES	NIGHT LINES	1 gun I.26.d.0.2. 1 gun I.26.a.9.1 other guns stand by	STAND BY	NIGHT LINES	1, 2, 3 & 4 NIGHT LINES 5. OYSTER F.M. 6. I.21.d.1.7
S.O.S LEFT SUBSECTOR	NIGHT LINES	STAND BY	Nos 3, 4, 5, 6 on NIGHT LINES Nos 1 & 2 STAND BY	NIGHT LINES	* No 1 I.27.a.0.5 No 2 I.26.b.9.1	NIGHT LINES	3, 4, 5, 6 NIGHT LINES No 1 [illegible] No 2 [illegible]
S.O.S WHOLE FRONT (Rt GROUP)	NIGHT LINES	NIGHT LINES	NIGHT LINES	NIGHT LINES	* No 1 I.27.a.0.5 No 2 I.26.b.9.1	NIGHT LINES	NIGHT LINES
CO-OPERATE "RUE DU BOIS"	STAND BY	—	—	I.21.b.7.2 to I.22.a.0.3	NIGHT LINES	—	—
CO-OPERATE "FLEURBAIX"	—	ⓐ FRONT & SUPPORT LINE OPPOSITE N.6.c & I.31.1	—	—	—	—	ⓐ 2 guns N.12.b.5.2 2 guns O.7.b.0.7

— LIAISON BARRAGES —

If assistance is required from Division on our right they are [illegible] call "Co-operate Bridoux"
[illegible] assistance is required from Left Group Centre Division call "Co-operate [illegible]"
* When not required by Left Group, Centre Division

[illegible] required by Right Group, Centre Division

24-1-17

J. Farr [illegible]
Right Group R.A.

152 BRIGADE.

WAR DIARY or INTELLIGENCE SUMMARY

Army Form C. 2118.

152 Brigade R.F.A.

Place	Date	Hour	Summary of Events and Information	Remarks and references to Appendices
Steenwerck	Feb. 1917 1st & 4th		Battery training comprised of marching orders, Standing Gun Drill, Rifle & foot drill, physical exercises, & gas drill with the small box respirators.	
ditto	4th		Lt.-Col. W. G. Thompson proceeded on leave.	
ditto	4th–11th		152nd Brigade Headquarters moved from Croix-du-Bac to Steenwerck. Battery training.	
ditto	11th		Attached 4 guns of D Battery, 152nd Bde. went into action at Bois Grenier to cover a raid of 11th Suffolks to 3rd	
ditto	12th		Bde NZFA 4 guns each of A/152 and C/152 went into action at Bois Grenier for the same purpose.	
	13th		The Brigade moved to Neuf Berquin.	
Neuf Berquin	14th		Lieut.-Col. W. G. Thompson rejoined from leave.	
	14th & 19th		Capt. P. H. Ferguson rejoined D Battery from H. Qrs. B/152 continued its training.	
	16th		A, C, & D Batteries fired in a dummy raid, moving out of action as soon as the operation was completed, rejoining the Brigade at Neuf Berquin.	
	16th & 19th		A, C, & D Batteries carried out the usual training.	
Steenbecque	19th		The Brigade marched to Steenbecque.	
Molinghem	20th		The Brigade marched to Molinghem.	

WAR DIARY
or
INTELLIGENCE SUMMARY

(Erase heading not required.)

Army Form C. 2118.

Place	Date	Hour	Summary of Events and Information	Remarks and references to Appendices
Cauchy à la Tour	Feb. 1917 21st		The Brigade marched to Cauchy-à-la-Tour.	
Bours	22nd		The Brigade marched to Bours.	
"	22nd & 23rd		Battery training.	
"	24th		A working party of 6 officers & 100 O.R. left the Brigade for the forward area.	
	25th		Major P. Knox-Gore Capt. P.H. Ferguson } visited the forward area; & returned. Capt. B. McCall Smith rejoined from leave. Major W.G. Hull rejoined from sick leave.	
	26th			
	27th		A working party of 50 O.R. proceeded to the forward area.	
	28th		Lieut. Col. to 2/Lt Thompson left the Brigade for the forward area.	

Lieut. Col.
Comdg. 168rd (Northm.) Bde. R.F.A.

152 Bde

WAR DIARY
INTELLIGENCE SUMMARY
(Erase heading not required.)

Army Form C. 2118.

15 2 Bde RFA [?]   Vol 14

Place	Date	Hour	Summary of Events and Information	Remarks and references to Appendices
Bours	March 1st		H.Q. Brigade billeted at Bours with A & D Batteries; C & B Batteries in the next village Monneville.	
	2nd		152 Bde moved from Bours; A, B, & D Batteries proceeded to Bethonsart, C Battery to Guestreville.	
	3rd		Orderly Officer reported to Lt Drake of R.A. Signals in the forward area to arrange communications.	
	4th		2/Lt P.C. Young attached to C Battery. " " C. Wilcox " " B " .	
			A Battery moved from Bethonsart ⎫ to wagon lines at E.17 central. C " " Guestreville ⎭	
	6th		Brigade H.Q. moved from Bethonsart to wagon lines at E.17 central. B Battery " " " " " E.17 " .	
	7th		Adjutant & Doctor proceeded to the forward area. Lt G. Hewitt posted from B Battery to C Battery. 2/Lt G.W. Bruntt " " C Battery to Bde H.Q.	
	8th		Enemy shelled gun positions which were in process of construction. The shell	

WAR DIARY
INTELLIGENCE SUMMARY

Army Form C. 2118.

Place	Date	Hour	Summary of Events and Information	Remarks and references to Appendices
	contd.	The Bluff.	was probably 10.5 cm with a very sensitive fuze as only a very small hole was made in loose earth. The following were casualties from this shelling:-	
			7959 Gnr Hutchison. Y.L. B Battery Killed.	
			8098 " Flinton J. B " "	
			8135 " Pegg. A. B " Wounded.	
			11140 " Wheatcroft J. B " "	
			11#300 Bdr Jarvis. B. A " "	
			34th Divl. R.A. Order No 81 postponed owing to snow.	
			34th Divl. R.A. Operation Order No 81 first part carried out.	
			A/160 & D/160 brought up to 6 guns each into their new positions.	
			A/152 relieved one section A/50 in S. Catterini's.	
	9th		C/152 " " C/52 in S. Catherine - Aleji road.	
			Weather cold, some snow.	
			12 wagons of ammunition for battery for the position under construction L.2.k	
	10th		be dumped in S. Catterine owing to the snow.	
			Very misty.	

Army Form C. 2118.

WAR DIARY
or
INTELLIGENCE SUMMARY.
(Erase heading not required.)

Place	Date	Hour	Summary of Events and Information	Remarks and references to Appendices
	11th	Cont.	Very misty. A/152 & C/152 completed their respective relieve of A/160 and C/152. 34th Divl. R.A. Operation Order No 81, i.e. completion of Group consisting of 152 Bde H.Q. A/152, C/152, A/160, D/160. Took defence over the line at 10 p.m. Lt. Col Thompson is in command of the Group. 12 wagons per battery of ammunition had to be dumped at S. Catherine owing to slack of traffic on the road. These wagons were station for the position under construction. Barometer 29.14 Thermometer 48°Fhr. 10AM. British aeroplane shot down by hostile machine, apparently fell in our lines. 11AM. British aeroplane brought down in air fight, descended out of control in enemy's lines. 1.45pm. Own aircraft brought down a hostile machine. Hostile artillery active this a.m. the day between Roclincourt + Ring Crater.	

WAR DIARY
or
INTELLIGENCE SUMMARY.

(Erase heading not required.)

Army Form C. 2118.

Place	Date	Hour	Summary of Events and Information	Remarks and references to Appendices
	12th		Barometer 29.8" Thermometer 50°. Visibility good. A/152 registered zero on right lines. A/52 cut wire at A30d 1.2. C/152 registered zero on right lines. A/52 fired on wagon steam at B25 d 9.4. had movement observed in H 9. Hostile H.T.Ms very active.	
	13th		Barometer 29.33" Thermometer 46°. Thick mist up to 2 p.m. afterwards slight improvement in visibility. Enemy shelled neighbourhood of KING CRATER with H.T.Ms, 10.5 cm, + 7.7 cm. with about 100 pounds in all. About 10 15cm shells fell in trenches just east of Rochlincourt. Two H.T.Ms were observed firing from A30 b 40.05 + A30 d 45.90. Group retaliation, 4.5" Hows, + 6" Hows enfiged these two emplacements. A/152 registered 3 points A30a 95.60.; A30 d 5.4.; A30 d 45.6a. A/52 dispersed a working party at B25 & 8.9. + co-operated with T.Ms on G6 central. Ammunition expenditure 81 A 3 A.X.	

WAR DIARY
or
INTELLIGENCE SUMMARY

Army Form C. 2118.

Place	Date	Hour	Summary of Events and Information	Remarks and references to Appendices
	14th		Barometer 29.07" Thermometer 48°. 4.30am to 5.15am enemy bombarded our support trenches in A30c & A29d with 7.7cm, 10.5cm & 15cm shells. We retaliated with 240 rounds on the enemy support & front line trenches. Fire in No Man's land. During remainder of day, hostile shelling was normal. 12.30 pm C/152 fired 18 rounds on Counter B on an infantry call for retaliation. D/160 retaliated on A30b 40.0's for T.M. activity - 2 apertures drawn in B19b central. 2 slits drawn in top of middle key-attack at B14d 15.85, 52A 383 AX 85 BX. } probably O.Ps. Ammunition expenditure none to noon	
	15th		Barometer 29.62" Thermometer 43°. Visibility good. Working party of 100 men on crest at B.20 central were dispersed by 60 Pdr Battery on being notified by us. 30 15cm shells fell in A27b.	

Army Form C. 2118.

WAR DIARY
or
INTELLIGENCE SUMMARY.
(Erase heading not required.)

Instructions regarding War Diaries and Intelligence Summaries are contained in F. S. Regs., Part II. and the Staff Manual respectively. Title pages will be prepared in manuscript.

Place	Date	Hour	Summary of Events and Information	Remarks and references to Appendices
in A 27 b.	contd		A/152 fired 250 pounds on the wire from A 30 b 20.22. to A 30 b 25.05.	
			A/160 fired 181 pounds at wire at A 30 c 76.53.	
			Ammunition expenditure noon to noon 60 A 33 A.x. 18 B.x.	
	16th		Barometer 30.11" Thermometer 45°.	
			Visibility low, owing to haze.	
			Hostile shelling normal.	
			A/52 cut wire at A 30 d 4.9. with 200 pounds.	
			A/152 fired 118 pounds on the wire at A 30 b 30.00. causing appreciable damage.	
			C/152 carried out a calibration test at an support trench at A 30 d 5.8.	
			110 pounds were expended.	
			Ammunition expenditure noon to noon 452 A 22 Ax 3 Bx.	
	17th		Barometer 30.03" Thermometer 44°.	
			The following shoot was carried out at 6.15 a.m. in conjunction with a raid from the sector on our left :-	
			zero −1 to zero + 2 A/160 6 guns A 30 c 55.67. to A 30 a 50.35.	
			+2 to +7 A/160 2 guns A 30 c 52.93. to A 30 a 50.05.	

WAR DIARY
or
INTELLIGENCE SUMMARY.

(Erase heading not required.)

Army Form C. 2118.

Place	Date	Hour	Summary of Events and Information	Remarks and references to Appendices
	18th	(cont)	Alt° 2 guns A30c 52.93 to A30a 50.05. A/160 4 guns A30c 78.98. to A30a 70.18. Zero-1 to Zero+7 C/152 6 guns A30b 32.20. to A30d 52.40. D/160 did counter battery work with 100 gas shells on Batteries N°s 125 + 172. Our front line opposite the above zones was cleared during the bombardment, 6-30 a.m. A/52 retaliated on a call from the infantry with 20 rounds on G.6.c.7.0. A/52 dispersed a working party at H.8.d.85.15. with 18 rounds. Enemy shelled CHALK FARM. Support trenches in A.29.b with 40 10.5cm; G.5b with 3 15cm; support trench in A.30c with 15 7.7cm. Ammunition expenditure roun k roun 418A 529 Ax 100 Bx. Barometer 29.20" Thermometer 40° Fair visibility. Enemy shelled Suddy Avenue with 10 77mm; trench 104 + trench about G.6.c.2.5. with 15 cm. At 8 p.m. 25th Batt° Northumberland Fusiliers carried out a raid, the group	

WAR DIARY

Army Form C. 2118.

Place	Date	Hour	Summary of Events and Information	Remarks and references to Appendices
		Cont'd	the Group.	

Commanded by Col Thompson Co-operated as follows:-

Point of entry A 30 c 60.45.

Zero to +2 A/160   A 30 c 55.67. to A 30 a 50.05.
            B/160   A 30 c 60.30. to A 30 c 60.00.

Rate of fire 3 rds per gun per minute.

Stokes mortars are firing on A 30 c 55.67.

+2 to cease fire A/160 { 4 guns A 30 c 55.80. to A 30 a 50.05.
                        { 2 guns A 30 c 80.98. to A 30 c 80.88.

                  B/160 { 4 guns A 30 c 65.12. to G 6 a 65.88.
                        { 2 guns A 30 c 80.10. to A 30 c 95.00.

Rate of fire +2 To +12 2 rds per gun per min.
              +12 to +17 3   "   "   "   "   "
              +17 to cease fire 1 "   "   "   "   "

Zero to +15 D/160 (4.5 Hrs) 1 gun Salient G 6 a 60.60. ⎫ Rate of fire 3 rounds
                               1 gun A 30 c 95.55.   ⎬ per gun per 2 mins.
                               1 gun A 30 d 15.18.   ⎪
                               1 gun A 30 d 05.02.   ⎭

WAR DIARY
or
INTELLIGENCE SUMMARY

Army Form C. 2118.

(Erase heading not required.)

Place	Date	Hour	Summary of Events and Information	Remarks and references to Appendices
	19th	Zero to +15	6" Hows 80 rounds Werk Ulm trench A30b 32.20 to A30? 52.40	A30b 32.20 to A30? 52.40
		At +15	D/160 & 6" Hows cease fire.	
			Cease fire was given at 8·45 p.m.	
			Signal for withdrawal of raiding party – Red Very lights.	
			" artillery cease fire – gold yellow rain rockets.	
			Front line opposite this area was cleared.	
			Ammunition expenditure noon to noon 58 A 12 AX	
			Barometer 29·22" Thermometer 41°	
			Enemy T.T.M's were unusually active during the morning; we retaliated with 2 group retaliations on the right of our zone.	
			160th Bde R.F.A. H.Qtrs took over the command of the group for the defence of the line at 12 noon.	
			B/160 & C/160 relieved A/152 & A/52 respectively.	
			152nd Bde H.Q. moved to G32 2.0. (ref: sheet Arras).	
			Ammunition expenditure noon to noon 276 A 115 AX.	
			2/Lt H.T. Bird posted to B Battery.	
			2/Lt C. Wilcox attached to T.M's from B Battery.	

WAR DIARY

or

INTELLIGENCE SUMMARY

(Erase heading not required.)

Army Form C. 2118.

Place	Date	Hour	Summary of Events and Information	Remarks and references to Appendices
	20th		Barometer 29.10" Thermometer 39°. 4 guns each of A/152 & B/152 went into action in the 'e' position in G.3.1.c. The other section of these batteries went into action in the rally at G.4.c. Ammunition expenditure room to room 215 A 101 AX.	
	21st		Barometer 29.05" Thermometer 40°. A & B Batteries registered in. Ammunition expenditure room to room 108 A 48 A.X.	
	22nd		Barometer 29.30" Thermometer 42°. Ammunition expenditure room to room 210 A 407 AX.	
	23rd		Barometer 29.35" Thermometer 45°. Wire was fired on as follows:— A/152 fired 6,300 rounds at No 101., the wire was badly damaged & a lane cut. (b) 300 rounds at No 108 badly damaging the wire. (c) 200 " " No 109 " " " B/152 damaged the wire at No 109 with 400 rounds, apparently cut a lane at No 107. Ammunition expenditure room to room 476 A 77 AX 4 13 Bx.	

Army Form C. 2118.

WAR DIARY
or
INTELLIGENCE SUMMARY
(Erase heading not required.)

Instructions regarding War Diaries and Intelligence Summaries are contained in F. S. Regs., Part II. and the Staff Manual respectively. Title Pages will be prepared in manuscript.

Place	Date	Hour	Summary of Events and Information	Remarks and references to Appendices
	24th		Barometer 29.25" Thermometer 43°	
			B/152 cut a lane in the wire at No. 44 with 550 rounds.	
			A/152 fired 750 rounds at the wire at Nos. 76 & 77, at the former place it was very thick, but both places were badly damaged.	
			Ammunition expenditure noon to noon 1579 A.	
	25th		Barometer 29.16" Thermometer 39°	
			A/152 cut a lane in the wire at No. 74 with 250 rounds.	
			" " " " " " No. 77 " 421 "	
			" " " " " " No. 108 " 300 "	
			B/152 " " " " " " No. 110 with 234 rds.	
			also made a breach about 30 yds broad at	
			Ammunition expenditure noon to noon 1406 A 25 AX 25 BX.	
	26th		Barometer 29.15" Thermometer 36°	
			1 Officer & 23 O.Rs. per battery of 311th A.F.A Bde were attached to us for return.	
			A/152 fired 600 rounds at wire Nos. 76 & 77 with bad effect owing to gusty wind & bad light.	
			B/152 damaged the wire at No. 111 with 250 rounds.	
			Ammunition expenditure noon to noon 1241 A 63 AX.	

WAR DIARY
or
INTELLIGENCE SUMMARY
(Erase heading not required.)

Army Form C. 2118.

Place	Date	Hour	Summary of Events and Information	Remarks and references to Appendices
	27.		Barometer 29.15" Thermometer 34°. Battery Commanders of 79th Bde. R.F.A. 17th Division arrived at 152nd Bde H.Q. this morning to be shown their battery positions (i.e. the 'e' position). A/152 & B/152 fired at wire. 300 rounds were fired at Nos 77 & 78 damaging the wire & probably making a lane. 450 rounds were fired at Nos 112 & 113 badly damaging the wire. There was still plenty of wire standing 1 foot high. 435 rounds were fired at Nos 109 & 110 badly damaging the wire. Ammunition expenditure 850 A.	
	28.		Barometer 29.36" Thermometer 39°. A+B Batteries A/152 & B/152 handed over 'e' position to 79th Bde respectively. The 4 guns of each were left in position there with a limber gunner per gun. C/79 also went into action at 'e' position. The following ammunition was handed over:— 4247 A 6586 A x. 2 guns of A/79 had S.O.S. lines under 160th Bde H.Q. B/152 fired 300 pts on Nos 43 & 44 causing considerable damage to the wire.	

Place	Date	Hour	Summary of Events and Information	Remarks and references to Appendices
	29th		Barometer 29.30" Thermometer 44°. A/152 fired 145 rounds at Nos 82 + 112 causing damage to the wire. B/152 fired 450 rounds at No 106 damaging the wire & making a breach in the left-hand portion. A/79 cut a lane in the wire at No 76 with 250 rounds. B/79 damaged the wire at No 52 with 250 rounds Ammunition expenditure noon to noon 386 A 240 Ax 24 Bx. Wounded. No 64035 Bdr Micel. A.F.T. D Battery.	
	30th		Barometer 29.25" Thermometer 46°. Lane in wire widened at No 76 with 250 rounds Wire at No 104 badly damaged with 100 rounds. No 52 damaged with 250 rounds, it is impossible to observe if a lane has been cut here. 140 rounds were fired at No 114. A/152 + B/152 each moved 4 guns from 'e' position into the forward position near Rochlincourt. A/79 + B/79 moved their own guns into 'e' position. One gun B/152 gone to I.O.M with shaker spring; one gun A/152 gone to I.O.M with Maker spring case (inner)	

WAR DIARY

Army Form C. 2118.

Place	Date	Hour	Summary of Events and Information	Remarks and references to Appendices
	31st	contd.	Spring case (inner) Ammunition expenditure noon to noon 649A 36 AX 26 BX. Casualties Killed Nº 7817 a/Bdr Baker R.H. Nº 7866 Gnr Tomlinson. Wounded Nº 28122 Bdr Pickles. C. } A Battery. Nº 7868 Gnr Meakin. W. Nº 7857 Dr Morris. A.W. Barometer 29.29" Thermometer 47° The following wire was fired on :- Nº 106 damaged with 100 rounds. Nº 110 " 100 " Nº 80 untouched 125 " Nº 81 " 125 " Nº 77 damaged 30 rounds, bad L/R necessitated cease fire Nº 52 damaged with 200 rounds. Ammunition expenditure noon to noon 317 A.	For Thompson Lt Col

WAR DIARY or INTELLIGENCE SUMMARY

Army Form C. 2118.

3rd Div 152 Bde RA

Place	Date	Hour	Summary of Events and Information	Remarks and references to Appendices
Battlefield of Arras (Rœux/Roclincourt Area)	April 1st		Barometer 29.36" Thermometer 42°. Wire was fired on as follows:- At No 75. 400 rds were fired & a lane was cut & the wire round about badly damaged. At No 110 250 rds fired; wire damaged badly. At B: 52 250 rds " ; " " " At No 111 100 rds were fired damaging the wire. At No 112 100 rds " " " " " Amm. Expenditure 340 A 246 AX 83 BX.	
	2nd		Barometer 29.32" Thermometer 45°. A/79 fired 400 rds at No 75. Good gap cut. B/79 " 250 " No 42. Lane apparently cut. C/79 barraged on Black & Blue Lines. A/152 fired 120 rds on Nos 110, 111, 112 damaging the wire. B/152 fired 455 rds on Nos 102, 103, & 104. No 102 was badly damaged & a lane apparently cut. No 103 & 104 each had a lane cut in them. Casualty No 1660 Bdr Maloney. I. Bde H.Q. Wounded Shell fire. Amm Expenditure 415 A 174 AX.	

WAR DIARY
or
INTELLIGENCE SUMMARY

(Erase heading not required.)

Army Form C. 2118.

Place	Date	Hour	Summary of Events and Information	Remarks and references to Appendices
	April	3rd	Barometer 29.23" Thermometer 43°. 200 rds fired on wire at Nº 74. Good lane cut. 100 rds " " " " Nº 73. Much damage done. 400 rds " " " " Nº 47. Gap cut. C/179 (i) Registered S.O.S. lines. (ii) fired 250 rds at junction of Nºˢ 42 & 43. Lane cut. B/179 Registered night lines. D/152 fired 180 rds on wire at Nºˢ 108 & 109. Light rds not good for observation, but several rounds certainly fell into the Borrow Pit which was the objective. 152 Bde H.Q. moved from G.3.d.2.0. to A.28.z.5.2. (51ˢᵗ Dⁱᵛ France) B/179 Coscio Left Group front. Amm. Expenditure 256 A 40 Bx.	
		4th	Barometer 29.15" Thermometer 47°. C/179 fired 300 rds on wire Nºˢ 45 & 46: 1 gap about 8 yds wide was cut in Nº 45; 2 gaps about 6 yds wide were cut in Nº 46. Enemy shelled Observatory Hill with 10·5 cm. Expended from J.B.C & A. Forms C.2118/1500 French trench junctions were fired on.	

WAR DIARY
or
INTELLIGENCE SUMMARY

Army Form C. 2118.

(Erase heading not required.)

Place	Date	Hour	Summary of Events and Information	Remarks and references to Appendices
		(cont.)	300 rds fired at wire at Nº 42, appeared much damaged. Amn Exp. 415 A 100 Bx.	
	5th	"W" Bay.	Barometer 29.44" Thermometer 54°. 600 rds fired on Nºs 73, 74, 75, & 76. Lanes were widened. Wire very much damaged. 800 rds fired on wire at Nºs 43, 44, 7 45; wire here much damaged. 600 rds at Nºs 45, 46, 7 47. In Nº 45 gap about 5 yds wide made; in Nº 46 two gaps one 10 yds other 4 yds broad; wire very much damaged; in Nº 47 small lane about 3 yds wide, wire very thin here well damaged. D/152 fired 300 rds on Nºs 105 to 111 inclusive: no wire now visible in that area. A practice barrage was carried out at 8 am. Enemy retaliated with barrage on our support line N.E. of Rochlincourt, on Wednesday Avenue, & the eastern portion of trench 40. A "Q" day has been inserted between X & Y days. Amn Exp. 92A 7AX 75 Bx.	

WAR DIARY

Army Form C. 2118.

Place	Date	Hour	Summary of Events and Information	Remarks and references to Appendices
	6th		Barometer 29.31" Thermometer 54° "X" Day. A practice barrage was carried out at 1.30 pm. Enemy retaliated as yesterday. Following wire was fired on:- Nos 49 & 50 lanes cut ⎫ 380 rounds No 48 damaged ⎭ Wire destroyed at A 30 a 75.68. with 470 B x. Nos 73 & 76 damaged with 600 pds. Amm. Expenditure 186 A 423 B x.	
	7th		Barometer 29.42" Thermometer 52° "Q" Day. Hostile fire practically nil. Group barrage in conjunction with centre Group & battery of 51st Division on Group's immediate left. One gap was observed & has been rectified. Enemy barrage in retaliation was feeble. 600 pds were fired on wire Nos 73, 74, 78 & 79. Wire was much damaged. In the former two cases good lanes were cut. 34th Division carried out 3 raids, 1 per infantry brigade. Our own infantry Bde (it covered by us) met with no success & some casualties. Zero hour was 9.30 pm.	

Army Form C. 2118.

WAR DIARY
or
~~INTELLIGENCE SUMMARY~~
(Erase heading not required.)

Instructions regarding War Diaries and Intelligence Summaries are contained in F.S. Regs., Part II. and the Staff Manual respectively. Title Pages will be prepared in manuscript.

Place	Date	Hour	Summary of Events and Information	Remarks and references to Appendices
			Zero hour was 8-30 pm.	
			Point of entry A30c 50.75.	
			Objective to search front support lines.	
			Covering fire 79th Bde R.F.A.	
			C/79 A30a 25.45 along support line & A30a 68.20.	
			B/79 Enfilade communication trench from A30a 70.15. L	
			A30a 95.68. along Werk Wm b A30 b 30.33. and thence down communication	
			trench to A30a 98.15.	
			A/79 Werk Wm from A30b 30.33 & A30d 35.78.	
			Rate of fire Zero to + 10 min 3 rds per gun per min.	
			+10 to +30 min 2 " " " "	
			+30 to +45 " 1 " " " "	
			Ammunition 50% A. 50% AX.	
			Watches synchronised at 7 pm.	
			Amm. Exp. from t noon 140 A 1056 BX.	
			Barometer 29.39" Thermometer 54° Y Day 11.15 am. Corrector was 30(G).	
			Practice barrage carried out at	
			Equipment satisfactory	
			Watches synchronised at midnight	

WAR DIARY
or
INTELLIGENCE SUMMARY

(Erase heading not required.)

Army Form C. 2118.

Place	Date	Hour	Summary of Events and Information	Remarks and references to Appendices
	9th		at midnight.	
			2Lt G.W. Brewitt proceeds to 103rd Infantry Bde H.Q. in Battn's footpaths as liaison officer.	
			2Lt I.A. Radford proceeds to Report Centre of Infantry Bde as F.O.O. on Z day.	
			Amn. Expenditure. BA 1 A × 1021 BX.	
			'Z' Day.	
			Barometer 29.11" Thermometer 48°	
			Battery watches checked at 4-30 am	
			Zero hour 5-30 am	
	6-15am		2Lt Brewitt reports German 2nd line captured, & hostile barrage very feeble.	
	6-20am		1 gun B/152 reports out of action with bent spring. No. 42438 Gnr Wilson. G. wounded.	
	7-15am			
	6-20am		Tank observed stranded in enemy front line just N. of King Crater.	
	6-30am		Large explosion about A 30 a 8.9.	
	7-30am		2Lt Brewitt reports Infantry occupy right & left hand portions of Black line on our front.	
	8-5am		B/152 report 2 more guns out of action, thus only 1 gun left on smoke barrage & 2 guns on communication trenches.	

WAR DIARY or INTELLIGENCE SUMMARY

Army Form C. 2118.

Place	Date	Hour	Summary of Events and Information	Remarks and references to Appendices
Fechin		8.30 am	Reports received from 103rd Infy Bde timed 7.34 am stating main portion of Werk W/m captured & consolidated; 200 prisoners had been captured.	
		8.55 am	At 8.25 am isolated parties of men moving east about B 26 central. Considerable bodies of men lining east side of railway in H 26.	
		9 am	R.A.H.Q. ordered Left Group to supply ammunition to 78th Bde R.F.A. This was supplied from 79th Bde.	
		9.45 am	150 men seen advancing over crest in H 3 central. Red flares sent up at Bois de la Maison Blanche. Two batteries of 311 Bde R.F.A. fired. This our position causing C/152 to cease fire with 4 righthand guns. B/152 also ceased fire with its lefthand guns. A/152 to barrage from B 26 c 5.8. to B 26 c 5.2. C/152 to extend to B 26 c 5.8. to sweep at chicken up rate to 2 rds per gun per min.	
		11 am	Unofficial report received that 103rd Infy Bde hold Blue line. 152 Infy Bde on immediate left held up on Black line by machine gun fire. 103 & 152 Infy Bdes are in communication & trying to connect up at Blue line. 2 Lt I.A. Radford was in communication by telephone from Black line to Left Group H. Qrs.	
		11.15 am		

WAR DIARY
INTELLIGENCE SUMMARY

Army Form C. 2118.

Place	Date	Hour	Summary of Events and Information	Remarks and references to Appendices
Left Group H.Qrs.				
		12.30pm	Left Infy Bde (103rd) report that their front line is just beyond New Black line and they are endeavouring to gain ground by working up PLOT, DEE, USK, & BRAY to Blue line. 152 Infy Bde report that they hold Blue line & are joined up with 103rd Infy Bde.	
		1.15pm	79th Bde R.F.A. cease fires, limbers up, & ceases to be in the Left Group Command.	
		1.35pm	152 Bde R.F.A. extend their zone to cover whole Left Group Front. About 200 men observed to have come out of the cutting about B21c S.O. to have gone into the Brown Line.	
		3.38pm	B.M. R.A. ordered 2nds per gun per min on protective barrage of Brown line. German said to be reinforcing. Later this was reduced to 1rd per gun per 2 mins & continued until 8.30 pm.	
		8.30pm	Cease fire given. S.O.S. arrangements made.	
		9pm	Barrage 1rd per gun per 2 mins continued but now on Brown Line sask'd for by Brig-General of 103 Infy Bde. 103 Infy Bde reported to have its front line from B.20 c.1.o. along trench to cutting in B26c. Battn'is ordered to fire 6 Battery Salvos per hour onto western houses into Bailleul.	
		10.30pm	Barrage Programme as issued by R.A.H.Q. carried out successfully.	

Army Form C.2118/12.

2449 Wt W14957/M50 750,000 1/16 J.B.C. &A. Forms/C.2118/12.
Aum EX/A 2355 A 2505 AX 846 A Smoke 1854 BX 300 BJBR 600 BSK 200 BPS 750 AC

Army Form C. 2118.

WAR DIARY
or
INTELLIGENCE SUMMARY

(Erase heading not required.)

Instructions regarding War Diaries and Intelligence Summaries are contained in F.S. Regs, Part II. and the Staff Manual respectively. Title Pages will be prepared in manuscript.

Place	Date	Hour	Summary of Events and Information	Remarks and references to Appendices
	10th	12.20am	Barometer 29.24" Thermometer 49°. Refilling point 10am at E.29.b.	
		7.25am	R.A. orders that after 8am all fire will be lifted to 300 yds east of Green line. Green line to be taken as 100 metre contour running thro' B.21.c, B.27.a, B.27.b, B.27.d, H.31, H.32.	
		8.15am	As soon as 16th Bde is established in action now Batteries will come under the command of their own Brigade Commanders.	
		9.26am	Brown line from junction with Bear in B.27.c to junction with left Bde in B.20.d reported captured. Certain amount of organised opposition at Maison de la Cote. Some prisoners taken. Troops now pushing out Green line re-establishing it.	
		9.30am	103rd Infantry Bde orders cease fire as patrols are being sent out towards Bailleul.	
		11-35am	34th Divisional directive is to work towards Gavrelle.	
		12-23pm	The S. Nicholas - Bailleul Road is now said to be fit for lightly loaded wheeled traffic as far as the Blue line.	
		6pm	Enemy reported to be massing on road from B.21.b.3.0. to B.27.b.3.1. under the left Group 34th Div. & Right Group 51st Div inverted on that front will 1/2" per gun for run.	
		6-45pm	Cease fire given	

2449 Wt. W14957/M90 250,000 1/16 J.B.C. & A. Forms/C.2118/12.

WAR DIARY
or
INTELLIGENCE SUMMARY

(Erase heading not required.)

Army Form C. 2118.

Place	Date	Hour	Summary of Events and Information	Remarks and references to Appendices
		8·12pm	fire was given. 2/Lt Weir acting F.O.O. in the Brown Line at B27 o.a. reports enemy attacking on Left Group front. S.O.S. barrage opened on this Group & its flank Groups fronts at rate of 3 rds per gun per min.	
		8·35pm	2/Lt Weir orders rate to be slackened to 1 rd per gun per min, as enemy had been forestalled. The situation to be well in hand.	
		8·50pm	Cease fire given as 103rd Bde are sending out patrols. C.R.A. reports that portion of 103rd Bde front is being taken over by 51st Div. at 9pm. 152nd Bde R.F.A. will then cover the following zone for S.O.S. barrage:- B27/3.8. to B27a 55.95. 2/Lt Young B Battery liaison officer with 27th Batt N.Fs. 2/Lt Finnie relieved 2/Lt G.N. Brewitt at 103rd Infy Bde H.Q. at 8·30pm O.C. 311 Bde R.F.A. took over support of 102 Infy Bde in the line. Amn. Expenditure 5221 A 4251 AX 2046 Bx. Barometer 29.23" Thermometer 48° Fine morning, cold wind. Snowstorm in afternoon evening.	
	11th	12·30am	Patrols reported to have returned to our line. 152 Bde R.F.A. barrage enemy lines on S.O.S. barrage from 12·45am to dawn. Rate of fire 20 Rds per battery per hour.	
		1am	F.O.O. (2/Lt H.D. Weir) reports a 15cm battery shelling our front line trench about 50 Rds, but causing no damage.	

Army Form C. 2118.

WAR DIARY
or
INTELLIGENCE SUMMARY

(Erase heading not required.)

Instructions regarding War Diaries and Intelligence Summaries are contained in F. S. Regs., Part II. and the Staff Manual respectively. Title Pages will be prepared in manuscript.

Place	Date	Hour	Summary of Events and Information	Remarks and references to Appendices
			No damage	
		2 pm	86th Bde R.F.A. relieves 152 Bde R.F.A. Work over the defence of the line	
		2.30pm	A/152 advanced to forward position at B.25.d.83.85. follows at short intervals by B/152 to A/152 immediate left. followed by C/152 to B.25.d.60.60. followed by D/152 to H.11.b.30.40.	
		6 pm	A & B Batteries reported in position & prepared to shoot by map. C & D Batteries were not in position until 8 pm owing to traffic blockage. 103rd. Infy Bde relieved in the line. Amm. Expenditure 2210 A 2069 AX 1163 BX	
	12th		Barometer 29.17" Thermometer 45°. Bde H.Q. moved up to H.12.d.3.0.	
		11 am	The front line held by the infantry on this front runs from B.27.a.85.85. to B.27.d.35.00. 23rd Batt. H.Q 65 N.Fs is at B.27.d.25.85. Patrols have been sent out further than this but it is impossible to gather how far. Batt- H.Q. is in communication by Telephone with Infantry Bde H.Q. The infantry have suffered a good many casualties from shelling & sniping, also from our own artillery especially the Heavies. Enemy appears to be digging himself in strongly in trenches running the side of Oppy-Gavrelle line B.18.b. - B.30.a.	

WAR DIARY
or
INTELLIGENCE SUMMARY

Army Form C. 2118.

Place	Date	Hour	Summary of Events and Information	Remarks and references to Appendices
B18f - B30a			Small parties of the enemy can be seen walking about in the valley between Bailleul & Gavrelle. Hostile shelling was severe in the neighbourhood of the railway bridge at B.27.a.o.a. along the communication trench from B.27.a.10.15 to B.21.c.85.00.	
			Batteries located:-	
			10.5 cm 4 or 6 gun Battery on or just behind road at B 6 c 75.00.	
			10.5 cm Battery just behind road about B.12.b.45.00.	
			15 cm 2 guns among houses on outskirts of Oppy at B.13.a.4.0. & B.13.a.40.22.	
		1pm.	Situation:- 2nd K.R.R.s 2nd Div. hold line from B.20.d.85.15 to B.27.a.38.80. Thence south 2 posts held by 22nd N.F.s at B.27.a.55.80. and B.27.b.15.35. 24th N.F.s hold the line from B.27.d.30.98. to B.27.b.33.00. Considerable enemy movement about roads in B.28.b yd. Infantry apparently preparing a counter attack; They are in a very bad way, many are dying from exposure. S.O.S. barrage tonight is B.21.d.3.4. to B.27.b.86 to B.28.c.0.8. to B.28.d.0.5. to B.29.c.0.2. to B.29.c.5.0. Dividing point between Brigades of Left Group A.27.b.70.72. Dividing point between Brigades of Left Group B.28.c.0.8. Dividing line eastern position approaching to Gavrelle.	
		10pm to 6am	Harassing fire was carried out on the eastern position approaching to Gavrelle. Rate of fire 50 lbs per Brigade per hour. Ammn. Exp. room N.L.	

Army Form C. 2118.

WAR DIARY
or
INTELLIGENCE SUMMARY
(Erase heading not required.)

Instructions regarding War Diaries and Intelligence Summaries are contained in F. S. Regs., Part II. and the Staff Manual respectively. Title Pages will be prepared in manuscript.

Place	Date	Hour	Summary of Events and Information	Remarks and references to Appendices
	13th		Barometer 29.13" Thermometer 47°. Batteries registering.	
		3pm	2nd Div. patrols have reached B.21.c & found it unoccupied; now moving forward to Bailleul & Sugar factory N. of Bailleul's patrols going to road running from H.4 + B.5.c to S. end of Bailleul.	
		6.15pm	2nd Div. reports patrols in Bailleul. They have secured the crucifix N. of Bailleul. Enemy are shelling N.E. exits of Bailleul. S.O.S. barrage tonight is 100 yds west of Opfy Gavrelle line. 86th Bde from B.30.c.6.0. to B.30.a.4.2. 152nd Bde from B.30.a.4.2. to B.24.d.a.2. Rate of fire 2 rds per gun per min. Left Group to fire intermittent fire day & night on approaches leading from & east of the line I.17.a to Gavrelle. 18 Pdrs 50 rds per Bde during darkness. During the day concealed approaches will be similarly fired at, at intervals. 4.5 Hows on cross roads & road junctions 50 rds per battery per 24 hours. Amm. Expenditure 255 A. 203 AX.	
	14th		Barometer 29.08" Thermometer 46°. 3rd (R.N.) Div. Infantry relieved early this morning by 63rd (R.N.) Division	
		1am	Report that left Batts, Rt Bde, 2nd Div. reaches B.23.b rare consolidating patrols pushing forward to Opfy line B.24.b & d.	

WAR DIARY
or
INTELLIGENCE SUMMARY

(Erase heading not required.)

Army Form C. 2118.

Place	Date	Hour	Summary of Events and Information	Remarks and references to Appendices
B29 b + d		8.45am	2nd Div report patrols going out to examine Oppy line in B30 a + c. Patrol at B29 + 9.9. reports sniping apparently from Windmill C19 c 2.4. & ridge close to Gavrelle.	
		2pm	Arleux en Gohelle - Oppy. Fampoux line reported held as far south as H6 a central. 4th Div hold the line from Hilly Trench H5 d 5.1. to on foot at H4 b 8.5. Continual stream of enemy G.S. wagons coming from I 11 a. 0. 8. dumping wire at I 4 c 3.4. Enemy appear to be digging in this. This point behind Square Wood. Much movement of large parties N. & S along this line. Small parties seen up to Windmill N.E of Gavrelle. Batteries located:- Mmm Hedge C 15 a.1.6. I 15 c 30.90. Gun pits plainly visible. Flashes also observed from behind ridge due E. of this point. 10.5 pm C 8 d 8 5.15. 15 cm C 29 a 8.6. S.O.S. barrage 300x in front of line H4 b 8.5. to B29 a 2.7 Dividing point between Groups B29 c 0.8. A Battery gone to a new position in B26 d 4.0. Capt Thorpe A Battery wounded whilst observing. Amm. Exp. 182 A 100 A X.	

WAR DIARY
or
INTELLIGENCE SUMMARY

(Erase heading not required.)

Army Form C. 2118.

Place	Date	Hour	Summary of Events and Information	Remarks and references to Appendices
		10 am	Batteries active in I.5.a & I.4.d; there is a lot of movement in I.4.d there about 20 parties of 10 men each can be seen advancing from N.W. to S.E.	
		10.50 am	Battery active at C.21.d.20.12.	
		10.55 am	Enemy advancing on Gavrelle.	
		11 am	Large No. of Germans lined up in I.3.a & I.3.a.	
		11.8 am	Germans advancing I.4.a & d	
		11.13 am	2 waves of Germans advancing west gave passing house in I.4.b.95.30. This marks their N.W. flank extends to the South.	
		11.24 am	Enemy in rear in rear I.4.c.00.58. to I.4.d.50.	
		11.35 am	Enemy in force in C.27.c between Square Wood & Hollow Copse. 12 limbers observed at the following two battery positions - (c) I.4.c.8.4. & I.5.a.2.0. Both these batteries are very active.	
		11.45 am	Enemy digging just E. of Square Wood. Germans in C.27.c & d have swung South & reinforced are now in line Square Wood - I.27.c.1.0. due South.	
		12.20 pm	Aeroplane attacks gun in action I.4.a.7.3.	
		12.40 pm	Enemy holds a line from Square Wood to Brickfields to I.10.a in strength	

Date	Hour	Summary of Events and Information
15th	5.30am	Barometer 29.11" Thermometer 47°. A,B,& C Batteries moved into new positions in a line at B.26.79.4.
	3 pm	Rt Battr. held up 300x W. of Gavrelle Trench by rifle & machine gun fire; it could neither advance nor retreat, asked for covering fire. Covering fire was given by Left Group on western houses of Gavrelle & 400x to right of Gavrelle. Infantry ask for intermittent fire on Oppy-Gavrelle line during the night, & for the howitzers to fire on Windmill in C.19.c & house at B.30.a.6.4. & all suspected machine gun emplacements. Left Group ordered to be prepared to cut wire from B.24.c.8.0. to B.30.c.4.7. 152 Bde were shelled in their new positions with about 200 77mm & 10.5 cms. Amm. Expenditure 26A. 60BX.
16th		Barometer 29.41" Thermometer 50°. Batteries reported in & cut wire in the Oppy-Gavrelle line from B.30.a.3.0. to B.30.c.4.8. C Battery cut a lane at the latter place. B Battery badly damaged the wire just N. of this point. Enemy reported to be in strength in Oppy Wood. 100 A9s fired in good effect reported. Amm. Expenditure noon to noon NIL.

Army Form C. 2118.

WAR DIARY
or
INTELLIGENCE SUMMARY
(Erase heading not required.)

Instructions regarding War Diaries and Intelligence Summaries are contained in F. S. Regs, Part II and the Staff Manual respectively. Title Pages will be prepared in manuscript.

Place	Date	Hour	Summary of Events and Information	Remarks and references to Appendices
	17th		Barometer 29.43" Thermometer 52°. Batteries continued to cut wire on the Oppy Gavrelle line, weather not at all favourable owing to wind & indifferent light. 317th Bde R.F.A. took over from this Bde. Guns & rifles were handed over by XIII Corps order. 152 Bde R.F.A. moved about 500 yds further south into XVII Corps. Batteries dug in at the following places. A/152 H26.6.6. B/152 H8b 65.90. C/152 H2b 37.15. D/152 H2c 4.1. Amm. Expenditure 917 A 79 A.X.	
	18th		Barometer 29.64" Thermometer 51°. Batteries continued to make their positions. Amm. Exp. NIL.	
	19th		Barometer 29.92" Thermometer 53°. Batteries registered in & calibrated. The guns received from 317 Bde responsible from defence of the line from H5b 95.15. to H5b 80.80. Night firing ordered on new trench running from H6c 40.35. to H12b 70.55.; roads in T1a 15.15: horse tracks in I2c. 50 rds per hour 18 Pdr: 25 rds per night 4.5 How. The same to be carried on during the day when observation is impossible. Amm. Exp. NIL.	

Army Form C. 2118.

WAR DIARY
or
INTELLIGENCE SUMMARY
(Erase heading not required.)

Instructions regarding War Diaries and Intelligence Summaries are contained in F. S. Regs., Part II. and the Staff Manual respectively. Title Pages will be prepared in manuscript.

Place	Date	Hour	Summary of Events and Information	Remarks and references to Appendices
	20th		Barometer 29.81" Thermometer 53° Batteries were concerned with getting ammunition up to the guns. 9 pm 4th Div R.A. order No 61 received dealing with the attack on April 23rd. Amm. Exp. 122 A. 32 Ax. 61 Bx.	
	21st		Barometer 29.83" Thermometer 53° Batteries cut wire on the Brigade Frome. Hostile batteries active especially on the Amas - Point du Jour Road. These batteries plainly visible in many cases the pits making an excellent target, especially at the following places:— I 5 c. 30.90. I 4 b 95.25. I 4 b 75.50. Amm. Exp. 289 A. 243 Ax 25 Bx.	
	22nd		Barometer 29.83" Thermometer 55° Batteries continued the night firing as usual. Gradually hostile shelling in H8 b & c. cutting during the day. 9th Div: Operation Order No 120 received in lieu of 4th Div... R.A. Operation Order No. 61. 4.40 pm. Amendment No B2/429/172 to 9th Div R.A. O.O. No 120 received. Amm. Exp. 1252 A. 331 Ax 395 Bx.	

Army Form C. 2118.

WAR DIARY
or
INTELLIGENCE SUMMARY
(Erase heading not required.)

Instructions regarding War Diaries and Intelligence Summaries are contained in F. S. Regs., Part II. and the Staff Manual respectively. Title Pages will be prepared in manuscript.

Place	Date	Hour	Summary of Events and Information	Remarks and references to Appendices
	23rd		Barometer 29.83" Thermometer 52°. An operation was carried out with the intention of capturing Gavrelle making a line thro' C.25.c, I.1.b, I.2.c, across the top of Greenland Hill & I.9.c. Zero hour was 4.45 a.m. Artillery barrage will lift of 100 yds from enemy front line (opp. Gavrelle) to a final barrage about 300 yds E of final objective.	
		6.35am	O.P. reports observation very difficult owing to amount of smoke; that there is a heavy hostile barrage on our front line. About 70 prisoners have passed on their way to the rear thro' B.27.d.	
		6.53am	Hostile batteries observed active at I.5.a.3.2 and I.4.b.9.a. Our infantry seen from C.25.c central to I.11.d.9.8. Smoke barrage now fairly thin.	
		7.35am	Batteries very active in C.15.a.a.c.; Counter battery work nil. Urgently required. Red flares still this side of Windmill in C.19. Heavy hostile barrage just west of Gavrelle.	
		7.45am	Batteries in C.16.a. & c. still active.	
		8.5am	B.M.R.A. reports concentration of enemy in Square Wood. Batteries warned to be in readiness for a counter attack from there.	
		8.15am	B.M.R.A. reports S.O.S. from Greenland Hill.	
		8.55am	6 wagons of ammunition per battery ordered up to the guns.	
		9.10am	B.M.R.A. reports that aeroplane flying 500 ft up over C.15.c could see no support of batteries there	

WAR DIARY or INTELLIGENCE SUMMARY

(Erase heading not required.)

Army Form C. 2118.

Place	Date	Hour	Summary of Events and Information	Remarks and references to Appendices
		12.50pm	Aeroplane Signals guns in action C22d 1.4.	
		1.20pm	Enemy reported in mass, estimated at about 3 battalions, from C16 central to C22 central.	
		1.37pm	Large masses of Germans advancing behind Windmill N. of Gavrelle.	
		2pm	6in O.P. controls a 60 Pdr Battery on enemy from C16 central to C22 central.	
		2.15pm	6" How Bty own direction, fires 26 Rounds on Brickworks in I.10a. Good effect reported, enemy running in all directions from there, 60 Pdr fires on I.3 a 3.3. Observation strong of our O.P.	
		2.21pm	2/Lt Peakin (F.O.O) reports he reached Sunken road in H6b; he has seen the Battalion Commander who said our infantry had attained all their objectives, as also had the infantry on our immediate left. The situation on our left is obscure.	
		2.22pm	BM RA warns the Brigade that it may be called during the afternoon to fire a creeping barrage on the 2.9.P.Bde Zone commencing at line 84 trace diff from there to final protective barrage in 100 yard leaps. Then return to our own Protective Barrage.	
		2.25pm	6" How firing on Brickworks in I.10a are falling close to two batteries there - causing the enemy to evacuate.	

Army Form C. 2118.

WAR DIARY
or
INTELLIGENCE SUMMARY

(Erase heading not required.)

Instructions regarding War Diaries and Intelligence Summaries are contained in F.S. Regs., Part II. and the Staff Manual respectively. Title Pages will be prepared in manuscript.

Place	Date	Hour	Summary of Events and Information	Remarks and references to Appendices
		2.51pm	O.P. reports 2 waves of Germans advancing from direction of Fresnes to Gavrelle at about Hollow Copse.	
		3pm	6" Hows again firing on Brickworks in I 10 a by request of O.P.	
		3.15pm	O.P. reports many of the enemy in C 19 1+2 & I C 20. Fire has been directed at them by our batteries, but cannot be continued as our own guns require attention.	
			O.P. directs 60 Pdr battery onto ammunition teams at I 26.9.3.	
		3.20pm	Enemy reported in mass in I 21 b central.	
		4pm	Brigade fires Gun fire at enemy behind Windmill in C 19 c: Observation was direct reverse casualties are believed to have been inflicted.	
			Our infantry seen advancing in I 7 a & I 8 a.	
		4.39pm	Our infantry appear to be advancing towards Greenland Hill from I 1 d 9.1. to I 7 d in skirmishing order. Enemy not evacuated Brickworks have returned. Large party of enemy in I 14 a & b south of railway advancing in direction of Chemical Works.	
		6.10pm	Aeroplane reports guns in action C 27 d 55.75.	
		6.25pm	" " " " " C 22 d 35.20.	
		6.30pm	2 waves of Germans lying down at I 5 a 9.0. reported from O.P.	

WAR DIARY
or
INTELLIGENCE SUMMARY

Army Form C. 2118.

Place	Date	Hour	Summary of Events and Information	Remarks and references to Appendices
		6.50 pm	Aeroplane reports Guns in action I.10.a.1.7.	
		7 pm	O.P. reports enemy retreated as soon as our barrage commenced until they were out of range at about I.2 central, I.3c central, I.9a central. They then watched the operations. Our infantry not following up very fast, appear to be about I.1 central & I.7 central.	
		7.10 pm	O.P. reports Germans advancing in large numbers up N.W. slope of Greenland Hill. Advancing from I.2d & I.8a.	
		7.39 pm	O.P. reports very big counter attack coming from I.10c.9.0. & I.13c.5.5. Batteries firing S.O.S.	
		8.5 pm	B.M. R.A. orders rate of fire to be slackened to 1 rd per battery per min.	
		8.11 pm	O.P. reports enemy track on Greenland Hill. Our infantry appear to be in same position as at 6.30 pm. are sending up Very lights from I.7 a & c.	
		9.16 pm	O.P. reports S.O.S.	Each S.O.S. lasted from 5 to 10 minutes.
		9.30 pm	" " "	
		9.45 pm	" " "	

Amm. Exp. 492 A Smoke 1985 A 4189 AX 2247 BX.

Army Form C. 2118.

WAR DIARY
or
INTELLIGENCE SUMMARY

(Erase heading not required.)

Place	Date	Hour	Summary of Events and Information	Remarks and references to Appendices
	24-		Barometer 29.87" Thermometer 53°.	
		1.45am	S.O.S. fired for 5 mins	
		4.25am	S.O.S.	
		10.25am	F.O.O. reports from Batt's H.Q. that our front line runs I16a.9. I1a.8.0. I1c3.1. He reports that our infantry did not send up S.O.S. rockets during the night that they were not attacked. Thus H.E. rockets must have been sent up by the enemy. The infantry appear happy & confident. Batt's H.Q. (13th Royal Fusiliers) is at H5d7.7.	
		10.37am	2 15 cm Hows firing on B.26 with an angle of 2½° left of centre of farm in C.10a.75.20. Time from flash to report 15 3/5 secs (observed 9 times) from B.27d.4.9.	
		11.35am	500 to 600 Germans observed advancing in line towards Greenland Hill in I.2c. Line extends from I4a.5.9. to Brickworks I10a.	
		11.49am	Present situation of above line is I3b.9. to I9b central. They are stationary now & are sending forward small parties of 2 & 3 men each.	

WAR DIARY
INTELLIGENCE SUMMARY

Hour	Summary of Events and Information
	2 & 3 men each.
12.7 pm	15 cm Hows reported active at 10.37 am, still firing but being engaged. Reports to B.M.R.A. who is applying for counter battery work.
12.15 pm	O.P. reports small parties of 5 & 10 men coming from crossroads at I.2.e & going towards our line from H.6.a.9.0. to H.6.b.0.3.
12.20 pm	O.P. reports 60 Pdr battery firing at gun position at crossroads in C.15.d. This position was evacuated after being shelled by 60 Pdr battery yesterday, & the battery has moved further up the road at about C.15.c.7.85. 60 Pdr Battery informed.
12.40 pm	B.M.R.A. reports 6" MK VII going to fire on 15 cm Hows reported active at 10.37 am.
2.38 pm	Our 500 Germans observed in C.20.
3.7 pm	O.P. reports enemy attacking N. of Gavrelle. Our 18 Pdrs are firing on the enemy & causing great damage.
3.15 pm	Enemy still advancing but is receiving a rough handling. Appears to have got into a small trench by windmill in C.19.c. to the left. Enemy appears to be 500ᵡ from Oppy-Gavrelle line.
3.20 pm	B.M.R.A. reports enemy counter attack repulsed.

WAR DIARY or INTELLIGENCE SUMMARY

Army Form C. 2118.

Place	Date	Hour	Summary of Events and Information	Remarks and references to Appendices
			repulsed	
		3-37pm	O.P. reports enemy advancing in B18d & B24b 9's close to 6pp'y Gavrelle line. Enemy receiving a very hot time & only 15 to 20% getting through our barrage. Heavy enemy barrage on West side of Opp'y-Gavrelle line. Enemy appears to be held up S. of Windmill in C19c on a line parallel to the road. Enemy still advancing up valley in C19c.	
		3-54pm	B.M.R.A. orders S.O.S. on Bde front. Batteries already firing S.O.S.	
		3-55pm	O.P. reports enemy counter attack N. of Gavrelle entirely repulsed with sanguinary losses to the enemy.	
		4pm	B.M.R.A. orders cease fire.	
		4.5pm	O.P. reports enemy on line C25c 9.0. C25a 9.9. to Windmill C19c. 317 Bde R.F.A. informed.	
		4.36pm	O.P. reports enemy advancing in C25b & d behind Windmill. Our batteries appear to be the only ones firing on them. Reported to B.M.R.A. He is informing Bde on left. B/152 reports to have been knocked.	
		4.53pm	3 waves of enemy advancing west between C16c & C23a.	
		7-40pm	F.O.O. with Inf'y Bde H.Q. reports:- Enemy attack on our lines this afternoon was successfully repulsed, a number of the enemy got through the 18 Pdr barrage but were successfully disposed of. — our batch of 80 prisoners remaining in our hands	

WAR DIARY or INTELLIGENCE SUMMARY

Army Form C. 2118.

Place	Date	Hour	Summary of Events and Information	Remarks and references to Appendices
In our hands		8.51 pm	S.O.S. reported by O.P.	
		9.16 pm	S.O.S. from O.P. on our front. O.P. communicating with Batt^s H.Q. to find out whether S.O.S. required.	
		10.22 pm	Brigade put out a new barrage line from I.17.d.90.60. to T.2.a.20.15.	
		8.30 am	Hostile counter battery work very hvy. A Battery had two guns put out of action, C Battery were also shelled but received no casualties either in personnel or in materiel. D Battery had one gun put out of action, 1 man killed & 1 man wounded both.	
			Casualties Killed Bomb^r A. Heward N° 29031 } D Battery	
			Wounded Gn^r T. Ashwell N° 144801 }	
			Amm. Expenditure 2806 A 2492 AX 351 BX.	
	25th		Barometer 29.92" Thermometer 53°.	
		4.10 am	Red Rockets reported from O.P. } reported to B.M.R.A.	
		5.20 am	Hostile barrage reported from O.P. } & 317 Bde.	
		10.40 am	13th Royal Fusilier patrols report enemy working on trench wire from I.2.c.2.7. to I.2.c.3.5. about road to I.2.c.5.2.	
			During the day there was considerable movement work in valley in C.19.a.t., C.20.a.d., C.14.c.d. & in C.15.a	

Army Form C. 2118.

WAR DIARY
or
INTELLIGENCE SUMMARY

(Erase heading not required.)

Instructions regarding War Diaries and Intelligence Summaries are contained in F. S. Regs., Part II and the Staff Manual respectively. Title Pages will be prepared in manuscript.

Place	Date	Hour	Summary of Events and Information	Remarks and references to Appendices
			in C.15.a.	
			The enemy has dug a new trench in this area bearing from C.14 central to C.21 central. Work was distinctly here during the day by our 18 Pdrs.	
			Hostile artillery comparatively quiet today. Hostile batteries seemed active at C.15.d.o.4. C.28.b.2.8. C.28.b.2.5. C.28.c.3.2. & C.10.a.27.	
	5 am		Enemy shells neighbourhood of wagon lines in H.7 with about 20 15cm. 2 casualties were suffered in the Brigade as under. Casualties	
			Killed Bdr Greenfield. T. No 129280.	
			Wounded Farrier Sgt Rankin. J. No 640382. (did since)	
			Amm. Expenditure 279 A 1710 AX 688 BX.	
	8pm		152 Bde R.F.A. allotted a new protective barrage from I.2.c 15.35 to I.7.b.50.70.	

WAR DIARY
or
INTELLIGENCE SUMMARY

Army Form C. 2118.

Place	Date	Hour	Summary of Events and Information	Remarks and references to Appendices
	26th		Barometer 29.91" Thermometer 52°	
			O.P. reports 4 heavy howitzers firing at 12·45 pm from S.W. of Izel les Esquerchin: The flashes & smoke distinctly seen from the freshly ground about of Izel: The left hand howitzer is 2°20' right of the right hand howitzer 3°10' Right of centre of farm C10a 8020. These positions are suspected to be about C 11 b 6.7. (observed from B27 d 4.9) This was reported to B.M. R.A., 6" Hows, & 2 batteries 60 Pdrs.	
		1·45pm	O.P. reports anti-aircraft battery active about C22 c 05.85., also a battery in C 15 c active.	
		2·56pm	Aeroplane reports Anti aircraft guns active in action C22 d 2.1. 2 Hostile batteries active in I 29 c & d. Bearing N & Wthand gun 35'L of Vitry Church, lefthand gun 10'Right of Vitry Church, lefthand gun 35'L of Vitry Church, firing on Scarpe Valley. Reports by O.P.	
		5·30pm		
		7·45pm	O.P. reports - Very large flashes probably 8" Hows 2° & 2°20' Right of Vitry Church. Suspected position I 6 b 90.30. Enemy apparently satisfactorily same protective barrage as last night. A battery moved into a new position at B 27 b 3.5. Ammn. Exp. 444 A. 458 AX 7463 X	

WAR DIARY or INTELLIGENCE SUMMARY

Army Form C. 2118.

Place	Date	Hour	Summary of Events and Information	Remarks and references to Appendices
	27th		Barometer 29.71" Thermometer 55°. A,C,9th Batteries each followed a gun from 293rd Bde near Anzin. Operation order No 122 received from 9th Div. R.A. dealing with an attack on Greenland Hill to take place tomorrow. Barrage Zone from I.1.d.50.80. to I.1.d.5.5. Shoot two lifts of barrage 50x leaps, after by 100x leaps until final protective barrage is reached from I.2.c.98.80. to I.2.d.05.50. Infantry objective on Brigade zone is Black line running from I.2.c.no.82 to I.2.c.+.5. Night firing same as last night. Enemy shelled B.27.c & B.26.d searching sweeping from II crest; this continued intermittently throughout the day chiefly with 15 cm shells. Enemy shelled Point du Jour Rd, spent shrapnel on bridge at H.13.b.o. Visibility bad. In the evening O.P. reported Vickers Fighter brought down in air duel in H.12.a. Infantry got the men out but it was impossible to see in what condition.	

WAR DIARY or INTELLIGENCE SUMMARY

Army Form C. 2118.

Place	Date	Hour	Summary of Events and Information	Remarks and references to Appendices
	28/II		What condition: Another Nielm Fighter landed in C22 after an airfight with level into flames. Killed N° 10106q Dr. Craig. T. A Battery. Amm. Exp. 410 A 259 AX 37 BX. Barometer 29.62" Thermometer 52° Zero hour 4.25 am.	
		7·10am	B.m.R.A. reports considerable machine gunfire on our right. It orders one battery 18 Pdr 91 section 4·5 Hows. to search L8b south of roads I8d, q I14h N of railway. Rate of fire 3 rds per battery per minute 18 Pdrs, q 1 rd per section per min 4·5 Hows.	
		7·12am	B.m.R.A. reports a flare has been seen at I2d.o.8. Barrage is to be lifted 200 yds E of that point.	
		7·45am	B.m.R.A. reports that our infantry are believed to be in I3c: protective barrage therefore to be altered to I3d 1·6. to I3a 25·40.	
		8·8am	18 Pdr taken off their target of 7·10am q1 section put onto L9c N. of railway qa line junction E q W through L9a 0·5. inuitur. Rate of fire 1 rd per section per minute.	

Army Form C. 2118.

WAR DIARY
or
INTELLIGENCE SUMMARY
(Erase heading not required.)

Instructions regarding War Diaries and Intelligence Summaries are contained in F. S. Regs., Part II. and the Staff Manual respectively. Title Pages will be prepared in manuscript.

Place	Date	Hour	Summary of Events and Information	Remarks and references to Appendices
		8.50am	Aeroplane reports 75 infantry at I.10.d.6.5.	
		9.50am	" Guns in action at C.27.d.5.6.	
		10 am	Sections of D & B Batteries ordered to cease fire by B.M. R.A.	
		10.47am	S.O.S. from B.M. R.A.	
		10.52am	B.M. R.A. orders cease fire as S.O.S. is on the 63rd Div. front.	
		10.58am	B.M. R.A. orders us to open fire on S.O.S. lines as large parties of the enemy are reported to be advancing from the N.W. on I.3.d.I.I.	
		11.16am	O.P. reports parties of enemy advancing westwards of Fresnes - Gavrelle Road.	
		11.17am	B.M. R.A. orders cease S.O.S. fire, & to continue at 1 Rd per battery per min on Protective Barrage.	
		11.33am	317 Bde R.F.A. now report they are firing on the German front line of this morning.	
		11.51am	O.P. reports batteries firing S.O.S.	
		12.8pm	D Battery orders to drop 100 yds & to fire 3 Rds per gun per min.	
		12.10pm	O.P. reports enemy still advancing up Greenland Hill	

Army Form C. 2118.

WAR DIARY
or
INTELLIGENCE SUMMARY

(Erase heading not required.)

Place	Date	Hour	Summary of Events and Information	Remarks and references to Appendices
		12.27 pm	O.P. reports column of infantry in C.20 & C.21.	
		12.33 pm	Brigade slackened to 1 Rd per gun per min; 2 guns have been turned onto the infantry in C.20 & C.21.	
		12.34 pm	A Battery position being shelled.	
		12.50 pm	F.O.O. at Battalion H.Qrs. reports cross roads in I.2.c were heavily shelled. Infantry have gone forward 200 yds further east. As far as can be gathered 111th Infy Bde & Bde on its right have taken & are holding their objectives.	
		1.35 pm	Bm. R.A. reports enemy attacking from Square Wood.	
		2 pm	Large numbers of enemy observed in C.12 & C.18 advancing in direction of C.20 & C.21.	
		2.40 pm	Bm.R.A. orders – All guns on barrage lines at 2 rds per gun per min (100ˣ in 2 mins) at 2 rds per gun for 2 mins; then creep forward 400ˣ (100ˣ in 2 mins) at 2 rds per gun per min; then drop back onto barrage lines afire 2 rds per gun.	
		3.21 pm	O.P. reports continuous stream of ammunition teams to I.16.d.	
		4.4 pm	O.P. reports enemy massing East of Manville Farm in C.16.d.	
		4.15 pm	Bm.R.A. orders D Battery to fire 55 Rounds into trench W. little South of road in I.2.a.	I.46.90.30.

WAR DIARY
INTELLIGENCE SUMMARY

Army Form C. 2118.

Place	Date	Hour	Summary of Events and Information	Remarks and references to Appendices
		7.45pm	O.P. reports guns in action in C.5.d. Constant stream of vehicles on roads running through C.16 central from Neuvireuil & Mauville Farm in C.16.d. Batteries in C.15.c firing gunfire into Gavrelle. S.O.S. lines for tonight I.12.c.60.90. to I.12.a.00.60. #1 gun at I.2.d.4.9. Amm. Expenditure 26 A Smoke 882 A 2033 AX 792 BX.	
	29th		Barometer 29.75" Thermometer 52°. Hostile shelling normal; hostile guns observed active in C.29.c.ord. Centre of battery in line C.20.c.0.1. to C.30.c.00.05. S.O.S. barrage for tonight from I.8.a.2.6. to I.2.c.80.45. & I.2.d.5.7. to I.2.b.3.1. Night firing will consist of searching 400x east of the above lines at 1rd per brigade per minute. D Battery will fire 20 rds per hour as follows — 2 guns on trench about I.2.b.2.5.; 2 guns on S.Shere Wood; other targets cross roads in I.2.c presently Trenches in I.2.b. Amm. Exp. 1297 A 209 A Smoke 1397 AX 726 BX.	

WAR DIARY

Place	Date	Hour	Summary of Events and Information	Remarks and references to Appendices
	30th		Barometer 29.73" Thermometer 52° C/152 moved forward to a new position on A/152 immediate right in B.27.b. Wagon lines moved back to Rocklincourt Valley in G.5.a. Hostile shelling normal. Situation Quiet.	
		9.30pm	B.M. R.A. orders S.O.S. to be fired. Amm. Exp. 317 A. 362 AX. 535 BX.	

E. Thompson
Lt.
152 B. RFA
152 B. RFA

Army Form C. 2118.

WAR DIARY
or
INTELLIGENCE SUMMARY.
(Erase heading not required.)

152nd Bde RFA
Vol XVII
Jan to Feb 17

Place	Date	Hour	Summary of Events and Information	Remarks and references to Appendices
H.Qtrs H.173.0. Ref Sheet 51B N.W France	May 1st		Barometer 29.82" Thermometer 56°	
		4 am	Brigade fired on their S.O.S barrage lines.	
		4.3 am	All guns lifted 100 yds east.	
		4.6 am	" " returned to barrage lines.	
		4.8 am	Ceased fire.	
			Rate of fire 3 rds per gun per min. 100% A.	
			Hostile aeroplane fell about L.2.d 6.6. early in the morning; later a hostile party collected there were dispersed by two salvos; aeroplane then engaged with H.E. then direct hits obtained.	
			B 28 c heavily shelled with 15 cm from direction of Izel.	
			B 27 shelled by 15 cm battery situated at C.11.b.6.6.	
			Night firing as usual.	
			Amm. Exp. 586 A 8 A(S) 568 AX 170 Bx.	
	2nd		Barometer 29.72" Thermometer 66°	
			51st Divl. R.A. O.O. No 123 received.	
			Situation normal.	
			State of equipment satisfactory	

Army Form C. 2118.

152ⁿᵈ Bde RTT

WAR DIARY
or
INTELLIGENCE SUMMARY
(Erase heading not required.)

Place	Date	Hour	Summary of Events and Information	Remarks and references to Appendices
	3ʳᵈ		Hostile batteries observed at the following bearings:— (i) 11°30′ L of Mauville F⁻ᵐ probably at C.5.d.6.4. (ii) 9° L " " " in C.107. (iii) 1° L of farm at I.4.b.95.30. in I.1.a. (iv) 30′ R " " " " in I.1.c.a.d. Night firing was on Wobble Trench in Brigade zone, searching 300° east. Amendments Nºˢ 19.2 to 9ᵗʰ D.A.O.O. 123 and P.22 acknowledged Casualty Wounded Nº 8022 Gnr Allen F. B. Battery. Amm. Exp. 3 A Smoke 512 A 1156 AX 208 Bx. Barometer 29.71″ Thermometer 68°. Zero hour 3-45 a.m. 5.11am F.O.O. reports infantry have taken WIT, but not WOBBLE. 7.55am B.M.R.A. orders WIT to be bombarded at a steady rate from 8.5am to 8.35am 8.30am B.M.R.A. orders a salvo to be fired on WIT at 8.40am & 8.45am 9.50am F.O.O. reports a large Coy of 9ᵗʰ Div digging in 200ˣ east of CORK 31ˢᵗ Div. appear to be back in their own Trenches.	

34 152nd Bde: R.F.A.
Vol: 2

Army Form C. 2118.

152" Bde OR777

WAR DIARY
or
INTELLIGENCE SUMMARY.
(Erase heading not required.)

Place	Date	Hour	Summary of Events and Information	Remarks and references to Appendices
	4th	10·37am	B.m.R.A. orders Brigade to register W/T from I 1 b 6.7 to I 1 b 9.0.	
		10·50am	B.m.R.A. allows Brigade to cease fire as that O.P. may observe the situation.	
		3pm	Enemy reports massing in I 2 b and I 3 a. 2nd in.	
		5·25pm	O.P. reports hostile battery active 1"45' R of FRESNES Church from B 27 d 9.4. Annoyed horses probably at C 28 b 4.5.	
		7·15pm	Orders received from B.m.R.A. — 152, 52, 160 Brigades will fire on W/T from I 1 b 6.8 to I 2 a 1.0 from zero to zero + 1 minute. Rate of fire 4 rds per gun per min. At zero + 1' 152 Bde lifts to C 25 d 56m to C 25 d 50.35. and fires on this until zero + 45 minutes. Rate of fire 1·2 per gun per min. No night firing unless called on to fire an S.O.S. S.O.S. lines from I 2 a 3.2 to C 26 c 3.0. Batteries will cover their own zones allotted in today's operation orders, the flank batteries extending to cover the above limits.	
			Ann. Exp. 16 A (s) 1037 A 3851 AX 838 Bx. Barometer 29.72" Thermometer 69°. Hostile shelling normal.	

WAR DIARY
or
~~INTELLIGENCE SUMMARY~~

Army Form C. 2118.

1st Bde RFA

Place	Date	Hour	Summary of Events and Information	Remarks
	5th		Situation quiet throughout the day. Gun liaison officers were relieved at 7pm. Brigade relieved of the defence of the line at 8pm & proceed to the wagon lines in ROCKLINCOURT VALLEY (G5a) for a rest. Casualties accidentally received through kicking up an OD partially buried fuze:- N° 8172 Sergt. ORME. T. Wounded, since died of wounds. N° 8306 Dr MOODY. J. " 28904 " FREER. J. " 95029 " HARE. T. W. } Wounded " 131864 " DRIVER. A. N° 44051 Gnr ADKIN. W. Died of wounds received on April 29th. Amm. Exp. 6 A(s) 460 A 843 AX 277 BX. Barometer 29.70 Thermometer 68°.	
	6th		Brigade in rest. 2nd Li. P.S. RAWSON evacuated with measles. Amm. Exp. 347 AX 150 BX. Barometer 29.68 Thermometer 73°. Majors KNOX GORE, MYBURGH, HULL, & Capt JOHNSTONE proceed to Paris on 48 hours leave.	

WAR DIARY
or
INTELLIGENCE SUMMARY.
(Erase heading not required.)

Army Form C. 2118.

152ⁿᵈ Bde RFA

Place	Date	Hour	Summary of Events and Information	Remarks and references to Appendices
	7ᵗʰ		Barometer 29.68" Thermometer 73°. Brigade still in rest.	
	8ᵗʰ		Barometer 29.65" Thermometer 70°. Rain during the morning.	
	9ᵗʰ		Barometer 29.67" Thermometer 74°.	
	10ᵗʰ		Barometer 29.67" Thermometer 61°.	
	11ᵗʰ		Barometer 29.67" Thermometer 72°. Lt G. Hewitt proceeded to 52ⁿᵈ A.F.A. Brigade as 2ⁿᵈ in command of a battery. B.S.M. BIDDLECOMBE. S.C. proceeded to 252 F.A. Bde as 2ⁿᵈ Lt. Brigade took over defense of the line at 10 a.m. 17ᵗʰ Div. R.A. O.O. Nº 77 & 78 & the continuation of these instructions received. 7-30pm O.O. Nº 77 will amendment to barrage table carried out. All objectives taken. Amm. Expⁿ. none to noon NIL.	
			2ⁿᵈ Lt Thomas. A attd C Battⁿ. posted A Battery. " Young. P.C. from D.A.C. " B " . " Hackett L. attd A Battery " DAC. " Bird H.T. " B " " DAC. " Brewitt H.G.W. A.D.S. For Sec. Offr. " H. Qʳᵗʳˢ. Lt Farr. S. " C Battery.	

Army Form C. 2118.

WAR DIARY
or
INTELLIGENCE SUMMARY.
(Erase heading not required.)

1st Bde R.F.A.

Place	Date	Hour	Summary of Events and Information	Remarks and references to Appendices
	12th		Barometer 29.55" Thermometer 65°	
		6.30am	Lt S. FARR gave up the Adjutancy & proceeded to C Battery. 2Lt G.W. BREWITT took over the duties of Adjutant.	
			17th D.A.O.O. No 78. The continuation thereof carried out.	
		10am	B.M.R.A. reports situation as far as known. We hold CUPID and CURLY & are in touch with the 4th Division on our right. No news of the attack on CHARLIE except that the left company was bombed out. 4th Division report they have all objectives.	
		10.5am	Heavy hostile barrage for 3 or 4 minutes about on CYDER.	
		12.25pm	Counter attack reported advancing over GREENLAND HILL. All batteries warned.	
		12.58pm	Enemy reported to be shelling heavily on our own zone front system. to have a good barrage on GREEN LAND HILL.	
		5.27pm	4 parties of about 30 men each were observed walking from I 9 a 5.0. to I 9 c 0.3. They were dispersed by our howers. 6 Teams of grafers were observed proceeding along road at I 4.8 7.5. They were scattered by our howers, & some made for GLOSTER WOOD.	

Army Form C. 2118.

152" Bde R777

WAR DIARY
or
INTELLIGENCE SUMMARY.
(Erase heading not required.)

Place	Date	Hour	Summary of Events and Information	Remarks and references to Appendices
	13th	6pm	Teams carrying ammunition were strained supply a battery zone number 1 to 6. This battery fired a good deal during the day, was reported to A. B.M.R.A. Heavies fired on it, caused it to cease fire, but it came into action again later. Night firing 18 Pdrs 6 salvos per hour – S.O.S. lines. Further east of this Battery on CHARLIE to pay particular attention to this Trench. Midnight to 1-30 am 4·5 Hrs fired a chemical shell bombardment on SQUARE WOOD Expenditure 100 rounds; BCBR was fired in bursts of 5 minutes each. BSK was fired slowly. Amm. Exp. 56 A(s) 1755A 3402 AX 928 BX. Barometer 29·57" Thermometer 66° Situation normal. Our O.P. at B.27.d 9.7. was heavily shelled. 1 casualty received in the personnel of this brigade. 17 D.A.O.O. No 79 received. Harassing fire carried out throughout the night. C Battery Gnr E. STRETTON No 11334 reported missing, now found killed. Amm. Exp. 4 A(s) 243A 427 AX 167 BX 100 BCBR.	

WAR DIARY
or
INTELLIGENCE SUMMARY

Army Form C. 2118.

151" Bde RFA

Place	Date	Hour	Summary of Events and Information	Remarks and references to Appendices
	14th		Barometer 29.49" Thermometer 75°. Situation normal. Night firing as normal. ²Lt Wilcock F.C. from DAC posted B Battery. Amm. Exp. 244 A 992 AX 113 BX.	²Lt Wilcock. F.C. from DAC posted B Battery.
	15th		Barometer 29.55" Thermometer 78°. Situation normal. About 5 pm enemy put up a heavy barrage in front of GAVRELLE and ROEUX during a Thunderstorm. As observation was impossible, batteries were ordered to fire one salvo per gun per hour on their S.O.S. lines until observation again became possible. I.1.b 62.88. I.2.d.0.7. A & C Batteries share the zone dividing point I.1.b 90.22. B Battery covers the whole zone. This half to be switched off onto other targets. Amm. Exp. 16 A(s) 533 A 362 AX 80 BX. N°11334 Gnr STRETTON. E. C Battery found killed.	
	16th	3·40 am	Barometer 29.60" Thermometer 55°. Enemy began to shell B & D/152 & the other batteries in their neighbourhood. They continued with a slow rate of fire until 5 pm with 10·5 cm instantaneous fuze. D Battery had 2 men killed; B Battery 1 man killed.	

WAR DIARY
INTELLIGENCE SUMMARY

Army Form C. 2118.

1st Bde R.F.A

Place	Date	Hour	Summary of Events and Information	Remarks
		10·15 am	F.O.O. reports situation normal.	
		11·45 am	F.O.O. reports Battalion (right) of Left Brigade requires a close patt of fire on CHARLIE from I.7.d.6.0. to I.7.d.4.3. as it is full of the enemy. Reported to 160 Bde R.F.A. We fire on it until they get on.	
		12·5 pm	O.P. report two batteries firing gunfire; batteries at a bearing of 20°L of VITRY Church from B.27.d.9.4. probably in I.5.a. Reported to Bde R.A.	
		1·30 pm	O.P. reports two batteries observed from 30°R to 30°L of VITRY Church from B.27.d.9.4. probably in I.1.a. Reported to Bde R.A.	
		3·10 pm	B.M.R.A. reports we hold CUPID are tanding up CURLY. Night firing as usual. 80 rds per battery per hour.	
		7·30 pm	Our infantry advanced to retake CUPID and CURLY. 152 Bde R.F.A. assists. Starting barrage on CURLY I.7.d.90.05. I.7.d.50.55. A 100×left due east was made at 7·34 pm, again at 7·38 pm, at 7·40 pm Brigade returned to our normal zone continuous with the usual night firing. Rate of fire 7·30 pm to 7·40 pm 4 rds per gun per min 100% A. 2 hours gunfire was fired by the Brigade at the following times on WOBBLE and WIBBLE – 9·35 pm 10·55 pm midnight 12·15 am 1·45 am 3·50 am.	

WAR DIARY or INTELLIGENCE SUMMARY

Army Form C. 2118.

152ⁿᵈ Bde

Place	Date	Hour	Summary of Events and Information	Remarks and references to Appendices
	17th		Gun flashes were reported by E. O.P. at the following bearings:—	

2° 20' L
30' L } of VITRY Church
1°20' L } probably 2 batteries
3°30' R
4° L (15 cm battery)

Killed Nº 8106 Gnr DUDLEY. B. } B Battery.
Nº 32239 Sergt DOODY. G. } D Battery.
Nº 32322 Gnr BEAUMAN. W.H. }

Amm. Exp. 767 A 774 Ax 9 A(3) 120 Bx.

Barometer 29.40". Thermometer 54°

Situation normal. D/152 moved into a new position just N. of A/152 at B27c2.9. but still keeping 1 section at H3a 45.65. B.m.R.A's G227 received. At 6pm new Brigade zone I1b64.78 I 12c0.7

Amm. Exp. 558 A 1000 AX 640 Bx.

2ⁿᵈ Lt R.W. ANGELL from DAC posted to A Battery.
" J. WILLIAMSON " DAC " C " "

Army Form C. 2118.

1st Bde RFA

WAR DIARY
INTELLIGENCE SUMMARY
(Erase heading not required.)

Place	Date	Hour	Summary of Events and Information	Remarks and references to Appendices
	18th		Barometer 29.23" Thermometer 69°. 2nd Lt J.G.R. Fison wounded in head & leg whilst F.O.O. Night firing as usual - 40 rds per battery per hour. During the movement on our front, a barrage was fired on S.O.S. lines from 2.50am to 3.5am. Rate of fire 1 rd per gun per min. Amm Exp 1139 A 1110 Ax 7 A(s) 226 Bx.	
	19th		Barometer 29.21" Thermometer 69°. Man observed climbing tree at C.18.d.8.5. Tenth man apalling with a lamp from the foot of the tree to some place in a W.N.W. direction. Situation quiet. Amm Exp 466 A 26 A(s) 416 Ax 99 Bx.	
	20th		Barometer 29.33" Thermometer 63°. Situation normal: batteries in C.15.a & active rest of the day. Night firing as usual. Capt H.A. JOHNSTONE proceeded on a fortnight's course for likely battery commanders at HAUTECLOQUE. 2nd Lt G.W. MEAKIN proceeded on a month's gunnery course at HAUTECLOQUE. Amm Exp 412 A 2 A(s) 488 Ax 96 Bx.	

Army Form C. 2118.

151st Bde R.F.A.

WAR DIARY
or
INTELLIGENCE SUMMARY.
(Erase heading not required.)

Place	Date	Hour	Summary of Events and Information	Remarks and references to Appendices
	21st		Barometer 29.52" Thermometer 68°. Situation normal. Enemy artillery chiefly active in the GAVRELLE neighbourhood, in B.26, & in B.27d & H.3b. Amm. Exp. 154A 152 Ax 2 A(s) 93 Bx.	
	22nd		Barometer 29.76" Thermometer 72°. Quiet during the day. Points of importance in the firing to do with the raid on the night 22/23 were registered. 17th Divl. Arty. O.O. No. 156 dealing with the above raid, received. Our front & support trenches were shelled at intervals from 11 am till 4 pm mostly by 105 & 77 mm. Hostile aeroplanes & balloons much in evidence after 4 pm. A battery in C16a particularly active. Chimneys in BIACHE disappeared last night. Amm. Exp. 162 A 157 Ax 80 Bx.	
	23rd		Barometer 29.73" Thermometer 71°. Orders received that no rifle firing is to take place between 9 pm & 1 am. Situation normal. Battery zone number 164 particularly active. Amm. Exp. 427A 411 Ax 10 A(s) 255 Bx. 2nd Lt Jones. H. from D.A.C. posted C Battery.	

Army Form C. 2118.

152- Bde RFA

WAR DIARY

or

INTELLIGENCE SUMMARY

(Erase heading not required.)

Place	Date	Hour	Summary of Events and Information	Remarks and references to Appendices
	24th		Barometer 29.73 "Thermometer 71°. Situation normal. Considerable movement about the battery in C17a & The suspected O.P. in C.19. Battery at C.15.6.5.9. particularly active (4.2 H.V.) Hostile aircraft very active. No 60649 Gnr VYNER. A. Killed. B Battery. 2/Lt H.W. PALFREYMAN proceeded to BOULOGNE for 2 weeks rest. Amm. Exp. 213 A 44 AX 4 A(s) 26 BX.	
	25th		Barometer 29.80 "Thermometer 75°. Two 15cm batteries shelled A & C batteries also 28cm battery C Battery had two guns practically buried. Shells from 7am to 5pm. No casualties to personnel. Batteries were firing from C5c.10.25 & C5d.55.22. Our teams eventually got onto these batteries. A 10.5cm H.V. Battery situated from C15b.42.07 to C15d.52.80. shelled the Bridge over railway cutting at H.11.3.0. from 9am to 10am. Amm. Exp. 158 A 109 AX 3 A(s) 25 BX.	
	26th		Barometer 29.39 "Thermometer 68°. Situation normal. 9.56pm Infantry repulse retaliation on T.M. at I.2.a.57. Amm Exp. 165 A 113 AX 40 BX.	

2353 Wt. W2544/1454 700,000 5/15 D.D.&L. A.D.S.S. Forms/C. 2118.

WAR DIARY
INTELLIGENCE SUMMARY

Army Form C. 2118.

1st Bn RTR

Place	Date	Hour	Summary of Events and Information	Remarks
	27th		Barometer 29.43" Thermometer 69°. Situation normal. A/152, under direction of C.R.A, carried out a test shoot with No. 106 fuze in 18 Pdr H.E. shell. The effect was good. He fired bursts of fire at about ½ hour intervals with C27 & I2a. Wounded No. Gnr Worthington. G. H. { No. Gnr Thorpe. W. { No. Wkr Pearce E. A. Wounded, still at duty. Amm. Exp. 74 A 107 AX 60 BX.	
	28th		Barometer 29.32" Thermometer 65°. 10.5 cm H.V. Battery at C15 & 6.9. very active. 15 cm " " C11a " " 28 cm " " C5 " " Amm. Exp. 66 A 254 AX 74 BX.	
	29th		Barometer 29.41" Thermometer 69°. C.O. & Adjt chose new brigade position in H5d, in case enemy retires to FRESNES. LINE. B27a & c, H7b & H2c shelled with about 100 15cm shells. 103rd Infy Bde same with the left Bde sector. Amm. Exp. 160 A 133 AX 15 BX.	

WAR DIARY
or
INTELLIGENCE SUMMARY
(Erase heading not required.)

Army Form C. 2118.

152nd Bde R.F.A.

Place	Date	Hour	Summary of Events and Information	Remarks and references to Appendices
	30th		Barometer 29.47 "Thermometer 69°. Situation normal. Hostile shelling 7am to 7.30am 12 rds 15 cm on B 27 a. 9am to 9.15am 20 rds 10.5 cm on B 27 d. noon to 12.30pm 12 rds 21 cm on H1 b. Gun fire 160 rds 18 Pdr & 4.5 How on S.O.S. lines during the night; 10am 10 rds checking registration: 6 rds 4.5 How registering WAIT. Amn. Exp. 52 A 54 AX 48 BX.	
	31st		Barometer 29.45" Thermometer 68°. Hostile shelling 12-15pm to 12-30pm 8 rds in H1 a. Gun fire registration. Amn. Exp. 203 A 140 AX 22 BX.	

[signature]
Lt. Col.
152 Bde R.F.A.

WAR DIARY or INTELLIGENCE SUMMARY

Army Form C. 2118.

152nd Bde R.F.A.

Place	Date	Hour	Summary of Events and Information	Remarks and references to Appendices
Area GIVENCHY	June 1st		Bar. 29.63. Ther. 73. 7.40 A.M. to 9.30 A.M. 15 cm Battery at C.5.d.2.1. shelled B.27. Requested at Noon to 12.40 P.M. 1-5 P.M. to 1.10 P.M. A begn battery engaged this battery with good effect. Hostile served to R.1.2.v.1.4.5. E. F.2 P.M. From B.27.d.9.+ Night firing 12 pr. 500 Rds on rifle and foot of that trench. 100 Rds H.S. How on selected points. Ammn. Exp. 1.2.5.3., 1.2.42., 1.X.113, B.I.40	
do	2nd		Bar. 29.68. Ther. 74. 5.50 A.M. A few trench mortar shells fell in B.27-6. 8.7 A.M. Hostile aircraft active & balloon up. 7.35 A.M. to 8 A.M. 3.6d. shelled with 20 rds. 15 cm. Registration of all Batteries carried out during day. Hostile aircraft on lookout was at 11 P.M. Ammn. Exp. 1.2.35, 1.X.95, B.I.173	
do	3rd		Bar. 29.71. Ther. 74. 3.30 A.M. 12-10.5 cm shells in B.27.c. 12-15 P.M. Trench in front of SAILLEE v on the night r. Fd. were shelled. 1 P.M. 4 fine trench mortar on the course of Ther. REV.1.4. 10.45 P.M. Hostile air raid on Wagon lines area & round Battery positions. 12.10 A.M. do. 12.30 A.M. D/152 carried out a Gas Shell bombardment on Northern half of SOUCHEZ wood and trench running N & S far as C.27.e.03.33. Burst of 50 JCBR to be fired by the Battery in 3 minutes, followed along by 150 BSK at 1.3 rd per gun per minute, followed by another burst of 50 JCBR in 3 minutes. 8 P.M. to 8.8 P.M. Chinese Attack in accordance with H.4. 7.12	

T2134. Wt. W708-776. 500000. 4/15. Sir J.C. & B.

WAR DIARY
or
INTELLIGENCE SUMMARY.
(Erase heading not required.)

Army Form C. 2118.

Page 2

Place	Date	Hour	Summary of Events and Information	Remarks and references to Appendices
Area	3rd	9pm	Ammn Expd. A15 by A43, AX1, BX29. 2/1EV.T. Vickers posted to D/152. 2/Lieut	
FAVREUIL	4th		Clark posted to D/152.	
-do-	4th		Bar 29.82. Ther 66. Quiet day. 7.30AM to 7.38AM. A Chinese attack was carried out in accordance with 5th Div. No 992 Ammn Exp A480, AL526, BX205.	
-do-	5th		Bar 29.63. Ther 69. Quiet during the day. 8PM 3rd K.L.R. C.O.'s 92 was carried out successfully. During the attack one red hostile aeroplane was brought down by our aircraft. Ammn Exp. A258, A49, AX107, BX90.	
-do-	6th		Bar 29.66. Ther 70. 11.55AM 3rd XLR No 96 op(?) was carried out. Hostile Ballons, Aeroplanes & Artillery unusually inactive. Infantry asked for fire in Wit & Whp cross roads to keep down rifle fire from 10.30 AM to 3AM. Sunny town 70. No Cm is extended until 29th Inst. Ammn Exp A510, A1064, AX1503, BX357.	
-do-	7th		Bar 29.64. Ther 70. Very quiet day. Ammn Exp A258, A1256, AX1480, BX380.	
-do-	8th		29.66 Ther 74. The 1nd Canadian Corps carried out operations co-operated by firing a creeping barrage on our front at 8.30 PM and again at 11.45 PM & 12.25 AM (9th Inst.) Hostile Artillery very active from 3.45AM to 5.30 AM and again from 3.30 PM to 5.30 PM. Ammn Exp A541, A37, AX85, BX85. 2/Lieut M.J. Bentley went on leave.	

WAR DIARY or INTELLIGENCE SUMMARY

Army Form C. 2118.

(Erase heading not required.)

Place	Date	Hour	Summary of Events and Information	Remarks and references to Appendices

Page 3

FAVREUIL — 9 — Bar 29.66. Ther 77. 2° Very quiet day. Enemy O.P. reported at 6 P.M. working party observed in Guards W/f 7RU5.2. WOOD. They were fired at and dispersed.
Ammo Exp. L210, 2X 893, 3X 368.

— 10 — Bar 29.64. Ther 70. 6.1. and Major L. Shaw Tore went to look over forward position. 2nd Lt Cradley Junr. Enemy Aeroplane flying very low over trenches on our front.
2/Lieut Harris returned from leave. Ammo Exp 3.I.H.

— 11 — Bar 29.5. Ther 70. Quiet day. Shots reported from O.P. by Capt Keane at 12 Noon "620". S.of Windmill. M.S. Cubs 6.2. 42 firing on FAVREUIL also 59 firing over of FRESNES firing on Lendrecoun. 2.Mexfound Tere was slight shelling of our front system but the road & trenches in H.10.d during the day. On the whole the enemy rather quiet on our line. Col W.B. Thompson DSO went on leave. 2/Lieut Williamson posted to I.M.B. Ammo Exp A21, 3X 27.

— 12 — Bar 29.52. Ther 66. 12 Noon to 12.10 P.M. 3rd Sentry OO 11.98 carried out. The enemy retaliation expended 8.55 A.M. 6.A. brought down in neighbourhood of St Nicholas from H.L fire. 8.30 A.M. 7R.R.23 was shelled by a 15" Gun. Our fire Nil. H.A. below normal. Major Hulls went from leave. 2/Lt Willis went on leave.
Ammo Exp A57, 2.882, 2X 297, 3X 100.

Army Form C. 2118. Instructions regarding War Diaries and Intelligence Summaries are contained in F.S. Regs., Part II. and the Staff Manual respectively. Title pages will be prepared in manuscript.

WAR DIARY or INTELLIGENCE SUMMARY

Army Form C. 2118.

Page 4

Place	Date	Hour	Summary of Events and Information	Remarks and references to Appendices
Area FoRFELLE	13th		Jan 29.59 The 72 Quiet day. Aer. Fire. Nil. Hostile Shelling Nil. 1 H.S. Howr out of action. Lieut Farr M.C. proceeded from France. Ammn Expe c.2H. B.X. 20.	
-do-	14th		Jan 29.43 The 74 FARRELLE + ROEUX front line trenches were shelled intermittently from 7.30 a.m. ROEUX X70N8. The trenches on the Right caused not a successful operation at 7.30 A.M. 2.15 p.m Out of Action 1.45 Hrs. Trenches were captured. 3 Off +172 O.R made prisoners Captn Johnstone went on leave. Ammr Exp Nil	
-do-	15th		Jan 29.62 The 74. 12 Noon O.O. T°97 commenced to be continued over 24 hours. 6 P.M. New gone taken over again. D.2 O.O T°95. Situation normal. Hostile fire moderate. Nil. 2.12pm Out of action. S.C. Pearson reported Battery. Casualties. Ammr n= Exp. Nil A.G.15.2.49. Lieut Rodgers returned from leave.	
-do-	16th		Jan 29.40 The 68. O.O T°97 is Noon conducted. Gen Shell bombardment by D/152. 12 M. II.4H.12.25 + 2.12 Situation Normal. Clearweather poor Hostile shelling slightly Nil. 2.12 pm Out of Action. 2/Lieut By the reported to D/152, 2/Lieut Bell reported to 152 Ber. attached to C/152 Ammn Exp. L218, A.X.349, J.X.160, C.37.130, S.Y.125.	
-do-	17th		Jan 29.43 The 70° Hostile Shelling B.27 A. cup shelled with 15 cm. How. The How. was firing from C.56.45.10. 4°55' + 4°35'. Test of Quincy Church. The following of our	

WAR DIARY or INTELLIGENCE SUMMARY

Army Form C. 2118.

Page 5

Place	Date	Hour	Summary of Events and Information	Remarks and references to Appendices
Area LORETTE	17		Trenches were shelled with 4.2, 7.7 Cuthbert, Charlie, Curly, Rupert, Ethel, Cadiz, Carol + Lena. The fire on Cuba being very at times. Kiwi Gun 72 left for dump at Fontelogue. Ammn Exp. 2X 65.	
do	18		Jan. 29.13 Thu 71. 3.6 3.30 PM O.O. N°98(C) carried out 8-8.15 PM O.O. N°98(C) carried out. No hostile shelling. Ammn Exp. 4.39, 2X3, 3X38 CBP7.	
do	19		Jan 29.29 Thu 71. EO N°98(a) 12 Noon to 12 Noon commenced Mobile Fire 200 10.5cm Howzr B 27A. Our front line was intermittently shelled during the day. During the night Charlie + Cuthbert were shelled at 2.15 PM + the Fond du Tiul + Tank Lump at intervals. Ct 3.40 AM H8d was shelled with 4.2 Fas Shells. Ammn Exp. 2.251, 4X.393, 3X 122, CR 7, SX 10. 1.18 pm out of order.	
do	20		Jan 29.31. Thu 70. 2.30 PM O.O N°98(C) Chemical Shell bombardment carried out. 5.15 PM O.O. N°98(CT) carried out. Mobile fire below normal. Retaliation for Chemical Shell bombardment. Our front line en F was shelled with 15cm + 77mm. Late in the day Tno Shells fell at Tr. 5n. Dual Cavalry returned from leave. Ammn Exp. 2.358, 4X 98.5, 3X 80, CR 100, SX 100.	
do	21		Jan 29.26. Thu 68. O.O. N°98(C) Slow bombardment 4-5 PM carried out	

WAR DIARY or INTELLIGENCE SUMMARY

Place	Date	Hour	Summary of Events and Information	Remarks and references to Appendices
Ave LA RETE	21		page 6 Mobile Artillery nil. 2/Lieut Wise MC departed on leave. Amm. Exp. 17.2 PR, AX 222, BX 80	
-do-	22		Bar 29.28, Ther 68. 2 P.R. Report from F.O.O. that a M.Gun active in I2c 7075 was being for Trench Offensive, 20 rds were fired with good effect. 12 Noon C.O. 11/98 (SII) 12 Noon to 12 Noon commenced. 10.20 PM OC 119 carried out. Gas Shell bombardment cancelled. Mobile Shelling nil. B.P.R. Tooted over horsecard of Lieut Burrowal Artillery 211th Coys to B.P.R. 17th Divn. Lieut. Col Thompson D.S.O. returned from leave. Capt Laurie departed on leave. Amm. Exp. 266, AX 33, BX 220.	
-do-	23		Bar 29.30, Ther 71. Orders received that Brigade will move to relieve 30 th Bde commencing on the night of 25 th / 26 th. Quiet day. Amm. Exp. AX 3, AX 67, AX 29, BX 90	
-do-	24		Bar 29.49, Ther 63. 17 th D.A. O.O. Nº 12 Noon to 12 Noon carried out. 11 PR F.O.O. at request of Infantry that Bar. should cease firing until after 10PM, the remainder of B.P. was obtained for this. EZ very active. But more active than L.H. B.C.'s reconnoitred new positions to be taken over from 57th Bde. Amm. Exp. 251, AX 52, AX 29, BX nil.	
-do-	25		Bar 30.03, Ther 60. 3 PR 46 310 PR 17 4 R.A. Operation para 2 carried out. E.O. met Brig. Gen. Seller H. Liverholy @ 10.30 PR, then crossed new positions to be handed over.	

WAR DIARY or INTELLIGENCE SUMMARY.

Army Form C. 2118.

Place	Date	Hour	Summary of Events and Information	Remarks and references to Appendices
Area CURRAGHS	25		Page 7	
		10 P.M.	1st Section each Battery moved to new positions:- B/152 H.27d 6.52, D/152 H.27d H.27d, C/152 27d 40, D/152 22 b 6.0. Ammn Exp 25 -, A.262, A.X.228, B.X.23	
-do-	26	8 a.m. 30.00 Ther. 63.	Hostile fire Nil. Own fire Nil. Sections at new positions registered 8 P.M. Bde Office opened at H.27 b.c. e.g. 8.45 PM Bde Office at H.27 b.4.9 closed. Our two 500° relieved by the 78th & 180 Bdes. 10 P.M. Batteries moved their remaining sections getting into action & reporting all ready at 11.30 P.M. 2/Lt R.S. departed on leave. Lieut. Col. Thompson D.S.O. to command 3rd R.d during his absence. 2/Lieut. Radford went on leave, 2/Lieut W. Clare returned from leave. Ammn Exp. 25 -, A.244, A.L.212, B.X.100.	
YPRES	27	8 a.m. 29.67 Ther. 62	All Batteries registered. From 10 A.M. to 12.45 P.M. enemy H. Batteries shelled 6.2 over Battery positions. Bignacul French (I.25c H.3 & 6) was shelled at about 8 A.M. & from 11am to 2.30 P.M. Our support line was intermittently fired on. A large fire was seen burning in Ypres on the 26th last. Ammn Exp 25 -, A.168, A.L.2, B.X.25.	
-do-	28	8 a.m. 30.02 Ther. 67.	C.O. visited Inf. Bde H.Q. Orders received that Brigade would be responsible for the defence of the line more or less than on the 30th those closing to be responsible for the defence of the time. 6 P.M.	

WAR DIARY
or
INTELLIGENCE SUMMARY.
(Erase heading not required.)

Army Form C. 2118.

Place	Date	Hour	Summary of Events and Information	Remarks and references to Appendices
Area TAMBOUX	28		page 8 3h + D/152 to concentrate in Savage Valley on the 1-7-17. Ammn Exp A.5. A113. B.X. 32.	
-do-	29		Bar. 29.67. Thr. 64. Quiet day. Between 2+10 P.M owing to our Wires being cut we were out of communication with the O.P. Infy for about 1 hour. Two Sections of D/152 relieved by 32nd Bde. C.O visited Wagon Line. Lieut Farr + 2/Lt Meeker returned from Course at Houdelaincourt. Capt Johnstone returned from leave. Ammn Exp A.5.16, A.90, A.X -, B.X 25.	
-do-	30		Bar. 29.73. Thr 68. 8PM Saw over defence of the line to 4th Line of Infy. 10PM Batteries moved to Wagon line. Ammn Exp A.165, A.X 134, B.X.	

J Frankom Lt Col
Cmg 2nd R.F.A.
15 th B.

WAR DIARY or INTELLIGENCE SUMMARY.

Army Form C. 2118.

152 Bde R.F.A

Month of July 1917

Place	Date	Hour	Summary of Events and Information	Remarks and references to Appendices
ARRAS Sector	1st		Bar 29 A/B Nov 71. 9 a.m. Brigade moved from Wagon Lines at ROLLINCOURT to Savage Lines. T.C.C. Batteries moved out at 5.00 Wagon Lines C.D. leading followed by C.D.A and H.A. S.C.C. 3/4 Div inspected Brigade en route at Cross Roads ETRUN. 172 Coy of Brigade arrived. Manoeuvres. Stables + general cleaning up. LIEUT ROBERTSON returned from leave, having been extended by War Office Authority on Medical Grounds	
	2nd		Bar 29 A/B Nov 72. Not Drivers Riding Drill, Gunners Gun Drill, Signals + Fuze Setting.	
	3rd		Bar 29 A/B Nov 70. O.C. proceeded to PERONNE soon to look over new positions etc. Drivers Riding Drill, Gunners Gun Drill, Signals + Fuze Setting.	
	4th		Bar 29 A/B Nov 73. 7.30 a.m. Billeting party left to meet Staff Capt at MONCHIET. 11 a.m. Brigade marched out of Camp at 2.C.B. to MONCHIET via HAUTE AVESNES, IZNES-le-BULLIANS, BERNAVILLE. Last of Brigade arrived at 2.15 p.m. Distance of march about 12 miles. L.O.C. inspected Brigade en route. Head were watered from Horse	
	5th		Bar 29 A/B Nov 71. 7 a.m. Billeting party left to meet Staff Capt at EURETTES at 10 a.m. Brigade marched out of MONCHIET @ 9 a.m. B/152 leading, marched to BERTETZ via BENNAVILLE to LUCES, BEUSARD, ADUIFER Waville, C in FORICOURT via	

WAR DIARY or INTELLIGENCE SUMMARY

Page 2

Place	Date	Hour	Summary of Events and Information	Remarks and references to Appendices
	5th		DOUCHY-lez-AYETTE, COURCELLES to CORBIE. Brigade arrived between 2 + 3 P.M. & Billeted in lines of 58th D.I.2. Distance of march about 12 miles.	
	6th	Jan 29.42	Adv. 71. 8 A.M. Billeting party left to meet body at PERONNE. 8 A.M. Brigade marched from CORBIE via BEAUCOURT + BUSCOURT arriving between 2 + 4 P.M. Brigade bivouacked in field at T29 B22. Distance of march about 30 miles.	
PERONNE district	7th	Jan 29.50	Adv. 74. Capt. McFall Smith proceeded on leave. Capt W. David Ross attached during his absence. F.O. Adjutant + 2 Scout Sergts went to Courcy reconnaissance. St Eur Band played in Square from 2-5 PM.	
		6 P.M.	"Shirkers" concert party performed for the troops. Entally + many of the personnel of the Div Staff were away. I Sense from T152 Burking. The performance of the Hon MAES was lively sung and several others being loud cheered + shaken hands with.	
	8th	Jan 29.52	Adv. 75. Brigade Church Parade attended by the Divisional Band.	
do	9th	Jan 29.46	Adv. 71 Adjutant left at 7 A.M. for new Brigade H.Q. at K35d. 6.0 visited Brig. Gen. Fane, re Liaison. 8 PM Bde HQ Office closed at PERONNE + opened at K35d. 9 PM Bde marched out of camp at T29 a 86 at 500 yds interval as follows:-	

WAR DIARY or INTELLIGENCE SUMMARY

Army Form C. 2118.

Page 3

Place	Date	Hour	Summary of Events and Information	Remarks and references to Appendices
HARRICOURT Section	9th		1/152 H.33.a.6.8. 3/152 Q.34.C.5.3. C/152 W.4.L.5.8. D/152 W.5.a.8.8. Bar. 29.49. Ther. 74. Capt Lowrie returned from leave. 10 P.M. 1 Section of each Battery moved into action, 1/1/152 relieving 1/295 at Z.21.C.n.8. B/152 relieving V/RHA at R.y.C. 33. C/152 relieving L/RHA at Z.33.d.8.3. D/152 relieving D/295 & B/RCHA at R.4.d.7.0. R.11.d.2.7.	
do	11th		Bar 29.48 Ther 72. Remaining Sections of Batteries went into action, relief being reported complete at 12 Midnight. C.O. visited French for Liaison.	
do	12th		Bar. 29.51. Ther. 75. L.O. visited B.-c.-D/152 L.V/RHA All Batteries registered. Hostile Artillery & T.M. very active. From 10.25 PM to 7 AM the enemy shelled our trenches in F.5 & 6 intermittently with 15c/m shells & Bombs. 1 Trench Mor Exp L 81 Z.I 4. Z.I. 24.	
do	13th		Bar 29.53. Ther 75. Situation Normal 9.45 A.M 12 Pdrs 10.5 How on ZOLE TREE Sect. 12 P.N to 2 P.M. 10.5 How shelled TURZGUS Farm. Our fire Nil. E.A flew over our lines & brought down Observation Balloon @ 4.30 P.M. 2 P.M. Enemy attacked UNNAMED FARM & INDIAN TRENCH. The Enemy succeeded in entering trench about F.5 & 6 & 6 Men & a Lewis Gun were missing. Trench Mor Exp L 86. Z.I.6. Z.I. 21.	

WAR DIARY or INTELLIGENCE SUMMARY

Page 4

Place	Date	Hour	Summary of Events and Information	Remarks and references to Appendices
HARGICOURT Sector	14		Bar. 29.49. Ther. 73. Situation Normal. Our fire registrations 8.30 to 10.30 A.M. Hostile Artillery shelled T.23.d. & T.29.d. with 10.5 c/m & 77 m/m 10.30 A.M. to Noon T.14.d. & T.20.b. shelled by 10.5 c/m from direction of N.2.V ROY, 3 guns firing about 100 Rds. 9.50 P.M. Hostile M.G. at B.27.b.7.7. & 2.c.c.i.R.I. shelled with 5.9. Rate of fire 6 Rds every 15 minutes. Firing ceased at 10.40 P.M. 2/Lieut. RAWSON returned from leave. Lamps. Exp. L.52, 2X.53, BX.72.	
-do-	15		Bar. 29.52. Ther. 74. 9 A.M. 20 Rds. 10.5 c/m fell on the T.14.U.2.u.5. N.1.d.82. 9.5 A.M. 7 Rds 10.5 c/m fired along the road from T.34.a.5.3 to T.34.b.00.7.5. 9.10 A.M. to 9.50 A.M. 6.10.5 c/m along road from T.34.a.5.3 to T.34.b.00.7.5. 12.30 P.M. to 5.30 P.M. T.21 bombed 300 rds. 10.5 c/m or 15 c/m from direction of N.2.V ROY. 3 P.M. 50 Men seen drilling in H.Q. Major MYBURGH M.C. 4/1 S.2. wounded during the shelling from 12.30 P.M. to 5.30 P.M. Lamps. Exp. L.101 2X.86 BX.8.	
-do-	16		Bar. 29.49. Ther. 72. Registration carried out. 4.30 A.M. Enemy signalling with Lamps at H.31.a.55.95. 4.40 A.M. Freight train seen on railway at L.30.c.11. 9.45 A.M. Unlimbered teams observed on Road at H.2.d.54. Considerable movement seen in and round B.14.a.4.R.D. c.2.B.S.4. in C.23. 2/Lieut. T. Maduff (S.R.) R.F.A. proceed to the Brigade and attached to C.1/1.52. Lamps. Exp. L.110 2X.111 BX.9.	
-do-	17		Bar. 29.45. Ther. 72. A/152 & V/R.H.A. put down a Barrage on N.E. & S.E. sides of	

WAR DIARY or INTELLIGENCE SUMMARY

Army Form C. 2118.

Page 5

Place	Date	Hour	Summary of Events and Information	Remarks and references to Appendices
HARBICOURT SECTOR	17		ASCENSION WOOD on a Scarf of Suffolks & N.F. were out patrolling & encountered a hostile patrol at S.25.b.9.6. Barrage fired from 11.35 to 11.40 P.M. at request of Infantry. 3.35 P.M. Large enemy patrol reported at about S.26.a.20.65. A/152 & L/RHA were asked to fire 3 rounds Gun fire along the N.E & S.E edges of ASCENSION WOOD & dropped 200× from their previous range) 4 A.M. Range increased 100 × 2 Rds Gun fire from the above Batteries were fired. Hostile Artillery quiet. Enemy registered 105 q.m. How on TITULUS Capt W. Baxter B/152 temporarily attached to A/152 as O.C. W.S. Farr. C/152 temporarily to B/152 as 2ⁿᵈ in command. Ammo Exp A.19 A.X. & B.X.2	
-do-	18		Bar 29.48 How 72 145 S.A.A & Rds 10.5 q.m fell in Decan Copse. "D.4".7. Considerable movement observed throughout the day N of BEFFI N.S.4.15E. Lorries running to Fn. BARQUE. Battery commanders meeting held at Bde H.Q in BERNES WOOD 4 P.M. Ammo Exp A.34. A.X. 22 B.X. -	
-do-	19		Bar 29.36 How 73 Rds P.W.Z. A.W.R.E. temporarily attached to D/29.8 as O.C. W.S.Farr temporarily attached to D/152 as 2ⁿᵈ in command. Situation Normal. Registration carried out on HEAVEN, XERXES & SQUARE COPSE 10-152 A 2 Salvos & register after of trench junction S.33.d.4.0 every several Germans were looking over the parapet	

WAR DIARY
or
INTELLIGENCE SUMMARY.
(Erase heading not required.)

Page 6

Place	Date	Hour	Summary of Events and Information	Remarks and references to Appendices
HARICOURT Sector	19	4.15	3 German Officers wearing telescope & looking SE from S.33.d.6.3. were fired at they got into trench. 2.45 P.M. Hay making party observed at H.3.6. Amn Exp 218 2 X 3	
-do-	20		Jan 29.41 Ther 90. Our Fire. 3.15 P.M. 20 Rds 18 pr in M1d. M2c. M8. 4.30 PM 12 Rds 4.5 How. B.E.F.H. F.X.F.U.S.E., counter offensive to hostile shelling of RED WOOD 4.5 How also fired on newscreen in S.33.a. past Horn avery Hostile Fire 2 A.M. Enemy bombarded S.17d.88. 2.30 A.M. Enemy put down a heavy barrage on the above point, our artillery reply was very weak. This brigade about two not our immediate left with about 40 Rds. our Artillery reply was very weak, considerable movement around Billiard copse & S.17d.88 ready to open fire. Considerable movement around Billiard copse & S.17d.88 F.I. Nil Amm Exp. at 47 1 X 15 BX 102. Capt B. McColl Smith returned from leave. Capt Rose R.A.M.C. returned to 10th F.A.	
-do-	21		Jan 29.42 Ther 68. Situation Normal. Our fire 10.45 A.M. 5 Rds on SQUARE WOOD 4.5 P.M. 13 Rds fired checking registrations. About 150 men observed in lorries & chars a banc S.31.d. 8.8. dispersed by 13 Rds. Hostile fire Normal. 10.50 P.M. Enemy raided FORCE TREE POST with no success. Amm Exp. 2.34 A X 22 BX Nil	
-do-	22		Jan 29.36 Ther 69. Capt Pw Source returned to D/298. Lieut Fair r'd to C/152 Situation Normal 9.15 P.M. Heavy gun firing from behind FORCE R.P. into HOUSE 74	

Army Form C. 2118.

WAR DIARY
or
INTELLIGENCE SUMMARY.
(Erase heading not required.)

Place	Date	Hour	Summary of Events and Information	Remarks and references to Appendices
HEBUTERNE Sector	22		Page 7	
		12.30 P.M. to 2.30 P.M.	Harassing fire with 77 m/m by the enemy in area from K.34.a.6.2 to K.34.c.6.7. 4.15 P.M. Big Van into VIN-DETTES from direction of PUISIEUX. 4.57 P.P.M. 5.7 P.M. to 12.15 P.M. 12 F.I. over our lines. Ammn. Exp. K.1.119 K.I.93 B.I. 120	
-do-	23		Jan 29.38 Ther 70. Situation Normal. Hostile Artillery below normal. Considerable movement around FORT FIZGON. REDOUBT. Ammn. Exp. K.I.24 K.I. 36 B.I. 98.	
-do-	24		Jan 29.52. Ther 68. Our Fire registration. E.I. very active. Ammn. Exp. K.55 K.I.7 B.I.13. Interpreter Lt. Ployhet proceeded on leave.	
-do-	25		Jan 29.53. Ther 70. Situation Normal visibility poor. Hostile artillery Normal. E.I. over our lines at 3 P.M. Ammn. Exp. K Nil A.I.12 B.I. Nil	
-do-	26		Jan 29.55. Ther 71. A/152 forward gun re-registered 6/152 12 Pds at SWAN Redoubt + 8 rds registration. 2/Lieut Young proceeded on leave. 7.55 P.M. 6 E.I. on our lines. Ammn. Exp. K.37 K.I.57 B.I. 9	
-do-	27		Jan 29.A3 Ther 79. Situation Normal. Our fire 30 Pds into BETTI IN ST. IST + 20 neutralization. 1.45 P.M. 20 Pds into VAU ROY for same purpose. Hostile fire 8.30 A.M. to 2.15 P.M. enemy shelled K.24 L + K.27 A intermittently with 10.5 c/m + 15 c/m. 5.30 P.M. Dense cloud of smoke was observed to the right of St. GUEN FIX Cathedral	

T2134. Wt. W708—776. 500000. 4/15. Sir J. C. & S.

Army Form C. 2118.

WAR DIARY
or
INTELLIGENCE SUMMARY.
(Erase heading not required.)

Page 8

Place	Date	Hour	Summary of Events and Information	Remarks and references to Appendices
HARBICOURT Sector	27		E.A. activity above normal. Ammn Exp H.E. 39, 2.X. — B.X. 27.	
	28		Bn. 29.65 Shr. 81. Situation Normal. Our fire 10.35 AM 10 rds 18 pr into S.27.c.9.5.30 neutralization for shelling of S.9.d.5.4. + S.9.d.0. S.27.d.23 for same reason. Hostile Artillery normal. E.A. Normal. Ammn Exp H.E. 37, 2.X. 57, B.X. 9	
	29		Bn. 29.24 Shr. 61. Our fire 11 rds on S.27.d.05.75. + 13 pr fired on Sentry at S.34.d.2.0. Hostile fire Enemy shelled ASCENSION N. FARM with 8 77 m/m. T.34a shelled with 10.5 cm at odd intervals. 2/Lt Rev Argyll + H Lalley wounded pm came. Right Group carried out Burst of fire as per Sec duty O/147/3. Ammn Exp H.E. 6, 2.X. 6 A.X. 93 B.X. 70	
	-do-	30		Bn. 29.24 Shr. 60. Capt Fen Baxter proceeded on leave. Hostile Artillery Normal. Our fire 7 2.R. Smoke observed from St. H.E.E.N.E. which 2/R.H.A fired at 6 2.R. Several Germans seen on road B.22.1 N.E. 4 IS.E. which 2/R.H.A fired at 2 every seen to fall. E.A. Nil. Ammn Exp H.E. 60 A.X. 71. B.X. 48	
	-do-	31		Bn. 29.26 Shr. 60. Hostile Artillery Normal. Our fire Nil. E.A. Nil. C.O. attended conference at R.A. H.Q. 12 Noon. Ammn Exp Nil.	

WAR DIARY
or
INTELLIGENCE SUMMARY.
(Erase heading not required.)

Army Form C. 2118.

152 Bde R.F.A. Vol 19

Place	Date	Hour	Summary of Events and Information	Remarks and references to Appendices
HARGICOURT SECTOR	Aug 1st		Bar. 29.26. Ther. 60. Our Fire 12.45.A.M. Div Arty O.O. 0/167/3 carried out in conjunction with 103 Inf. Bde. 10.2 P.M. 27 Rounds on trench at F.34. & 10.20. 12 Noon 32 Rounds on trench at F.33.d.5.0. 10.30 P.M. to 12 P.M. Bursts of Fire by 71 RHA on 3 bridges over Canal W of BELLENGLISE. 10.30 P.M. w/ RHA 50 Rounds per hour on tracks leading West from those bridges & main Road to ST HELENE. Hostile Artillery 2.30 to 3.30 P.M. 16 Rounds 10.54 P.M. Gun fell in LE VERGUIER 6.2 N.W. Ammn. Expd. 17.252 17 X 190 3 X 19.5	
	2nd		Bar 29.30. Ther 58. Our Fire 1.15 to 1.48 A.M. O.O. 119 0/167/3 carried out. 10.30 A.M. 20 rounds on screen at F.35.c 8.A.M. 10 rounds at movement in SQUARE WOOD Hostile Fire Below normal. Movement 4.45 a.m. Large working party at F.35 F.17 all day. Wiral Reg. making in progress. Ammn Exp 1X 30	
	3rd		Bar 29.26. Ther 63. Our Fire 1.15 to 3.A.M O.O. 0/167/3 carried out 1.30 P.M. 17 rounds 15 Pdr on M.3.C. 87 where stop trench core observing. 3.4 P.M. 22 rounds 13 Pdr on M.3.L.28 Lemons seen working open. Observation during the day practically impossible. Hostile Fire Nil. 6.2 Nil Ammn Exp. 23 2I 2	
	4th		Bar 29.31 Ther 63 Our Fire 20 rounds registration. Hostile Fire Normal.	

Army Form C. 2118.

WAR DIARY
or
INTELLIGENCE SUMMARY.
(Erase heading not required.)

Instructions regarding War Diaries and Intelligence Summaries are contained in F. S. Regs., Part II. and the Staff Manual respectively. Title pages will be prepared in manuscript.

Place	Date	Hour	Summary of Events and Information	Remarks and references to Appendices
HERPICOURT SECTOR	4th		Page 2. Movement considerable activity during the afternoon about the trenches in S.20.c.d. others were seen to be working. E.A. Nil. Ammn Expd $\underline{A.42}$ $\underline{R.I.29}$ $\underline{B.I.23}$	
	5th		Bar. 29.33. Ther. 62. F.O. left on tour for Camouflage Inspection. Our fire 10.30 am. 16 rounds checking registration. 11.20am. 36 rounds 13 pdrs on working party in M.3.b. & 8.2.40 pm. 10 rounds on FILLER REDOUBT. 6.2 PM. 20 rounds registration on church at BELLEU FUSE. Hostile Artillery 15 rounds during the afternoon on M05.9.4 Post & ASCENSION FARM. E.A at 2.25, 3.55, 7.45 high right hand. Ammn Expd $\underline{A.59}$ $\underline{R.X.50}$ $\underline{B.X.61}$	
	6th		Bar. 29.31. Ther. 64. Our Fire 12.40 PM 15 rounds on SWAN & FILLER REDOUBT. Hostile fire 9.15 am 6. 10.59pm shells on DEAN COPSE. 12.30 pm to 1pm. 20. 10.59 pm on REDWOOD and FORT GARRY. Movement Nil. E.A on our lines at 9.30, 9.45, 10.15, 10.25 PM. Our F.W. Back attacked to T.5.3.B.C.a. I.Ammn Exp. $\underline{A.27}$ $\underline{R.X.37}$	
	7th		Bar. 29.37. Ther. 65. 2/Lieut. H. Howes departed on leave. Our Fire 3 PM. 38 rounds 13 pdrs on T.33d. 4.10 PM. 36 rounds 13 pdrs on F.3r. E.O.B. Hostile fire Nil. Movement 5.25 to 6.15 PM. considerable movement on BELLEN FUSE-AH BARRAGE road E.A at 8.30 PM. I crossed our line high Ammn Exp. $\underline{A.210}$ $\underline{R.X.36}$ $\underline{B.I.20}$	
	8th		Bar. 29.29. Ther. 42. Our Fire C.O. M°.16 carried out 9.45 AM to 10.30 am 50 rounds on Wire	

WAR DIARY or INTELLIGENCE SUMMARY

Army Form C. 2118.

(Erase heading not required.)

Page 3

Place	Date	Hour	Summary of Events and Information	Remarks and references to Appendices
HARGICOURT SECTOR	8th		Opposite ST. HELENE TRENCH at M.33.B.2. Hostile Fire 9.30am to 9.40am & 11.59pm Shells then ASCENSION FARM. Movement. Early morning parties between BELLE EGLISE & F.R. BARIQUE E.A. over our lines 5.20 P.M. F.O. returned from Camouflage Tour	
	9th		2/Lieut Young returned from leave. Ammo Exp. L16 A.X 35 B.X 37 Bar. 29.29 Thr. 67 Our Fire O.O. 7147 carried out at 10.20 P.M. 12.50-1.15 am g.a.m. 42 rounds engaging by 13th on B.5.a.5.5. 3 P.M. 12 rounds 12 pdr on Trench S27d 02.02 Hostile Fire 18 rounds on ASCENSION & SOMERVILLE between 7.40 & 11.2 am 12 Noon 7.10.5 pm Hos in Rw.d Movement 2.30 & 7.30 P.M. 1 Man seen looking over parapet at S27.d. Usual by making parties during afternoon E.A over our lines from 7.30 to 7.50 P.M. 7.45 P.M. 5 E.A flew over our lines. Ammo Exp. L.X. 12	
	10		Bar 29.33 Thr 69 Major S.C. Loy. Tho. Gre. R.C & Capt Baxter returned from leave Our Fire 9.30am 10 rounds registration of LITTLE BIVY 2.30 PM 50 rounds on West approach ST. HELENE M.3A.20. 9.55 PM 59 rounds on ST. HELENE TRENCH to CROSS ROADS Hostile Fire 11.2 am 14 rounds 4.2 In- fell about R18.C 11.45 am 5.15 pm How fell about L.94 C.8.8. Movement. Normal. E.A very active. 7.30 PM Several attempts made to cross our lines but ours Aeroplanes & good A.A Shooting those were stopped F.O.C 34 N Div raided L/152 Ammo Exp. L.X. 16 A.X. 23	

WAR DIARY or INTELLIGENCE SUMMARY

Army Form C. 2118.

Place	Date	Hour	Summary of Events and Information	Remarks and references to Appendices
			Page 4	
HARGICOURT SECTOR	Aug 11		Bon 29.47 Shr 71. 2/Lieut Wilcox proceeded on leave. Our Fire 9.30 AM all 7 P.M. 85-13pdr rounds fired on various movements. 10.15 P.M. to 11.30 P.M. O.O. Nº19 carried out Hostile FIRE 9.2M to 11.30 A.M. 46 rounds in an Area. 7.20 P.M. 24 rounds 5.9 How fell at irregular intervals about R.16.c. Movements from/notable recent BIZIARD COPSE FARMONZA unsatisfactory. moves all day on the ridge between FONCOURT and FOSSEWOOD E.17 71L T+T observed 3.c.D/152. Z.U/18H.A. Annus Exp L105 R.L 92 BX 48	
	12		Bon 29.44 Shr 68. Major D Ferguson M.C. + Capt J.W. Brecht went on leave. Our Fire 11A.M. 9 rounds 13pdr on + then observing from parapet §90-650. 12.30 P.M. 11 rounds 10pdr registration. Hostile Fire 18 rounds between 8.10 A.M. in ASCENSION FARM 7.15 P.M. 2 Shells sounding like Tao Shells fell about 12.9.22.9. Movement Hand movements of individuals in vicinity of screen. §35-F.06 E.17 very active 7.45 P.M to 8.10 P.M. 6 even our line. Lieut. Robertson D/152 returned from 10 days funny leave at HOUTECROURE. Ammo Exp L149 BX 44 BX 48	
	13		Bon 29.46 Shr 68. Our Fire O.O. Nº 20 carried out 13pdr fired on movement in BELLENGLISE-LE GARAQUE ROAD 6.29 Central L24a88. 18pdr fired on 4 men standing in trench parapet behind Eleven Trees. Hostile Fire. Enemy bombarded trench line near	

Army Form C. 2118.

WAR DIARY
or
INTELLIGENCE SUMMARY.
(Erase heading not required.)

Instructions regarding War Diaries and Intelligence Summaries are contained in F.S. Regs., Part II. and the Staff Manual respectively. Title pages will be prepared in manuscript.

Place	Date	Hour	Summary of Events and Information	Remarks and references to Appendices
			Page 5.	
HERBICOURT SECTOR	13th		St QUENTIN with 60 shells in early morning. During the day ASCENSION FARM, 5 EVERBIER v. MAISSNET were shelled. TURBULUS & ASCENSION POSTS Nos 1-5 were also registered. Movement Hay making parties observed at Sq. 7 central & Sq.a 88. Ex enemy slow. Normal. Today 34th Divisional Horse Show. Army Commander visited the Divisional Area. Ammn Exp. Z10.	
	14th		Bar 29.44 Ther 66. 2nd Lieut H. Jones proceeded on leave. 2nd day 34th Div. Horse Show. Our fire consisted entirely of shooting targets, in one case casualties were obtained amongst a working party. Hostile fire. Normal, chiefly into ASCENSION FARM & PoSTs & LEVERGIER. Movement Hay making & Harvesting in neighbourhood of LE TRONQOY. Working parties at F.3b.a. 31. F.3.b.c 5.3. v 12.5.c.a.8. Amm Exp AX 66	
	15th		Bar 29.41 Ther 67. Our fire 13 pdr did a considerable amount of sniping. Hostile Artillery practically NIL. Ex activity Normal. 14 R.H.A. moved out leaving to some under command of the Right Group. v 7 mm Exp 64 AX 35	
	16		Bar 29.42 Ther 69. Scout of Enquiry held at 152 Bde. H.Q. Lieut Col W.B. Hayson E.S.O. President Major G.C. Perry Kn.ca the M.O. a Member. 11.30 a.m. Conference of Group Commanders at R.A. H.Q. 4.30 p.m. Battery Commanders meeting at 152 Bde R.F.A. H.Q.	

Army Form C. 2118.

WAR DIARY
or
INTELLIGENCE SUMMARY.
(Erase heading not required.)

Instructions regarding War Diaries and Intelligence Summaries are contained in F. S. Regs., Part II. and the Staff Manual respectively. Title pages will be prepared in manuscript.

Place	Date	Hour	Summary of Events and Information	Remarks and references to Appendices
			Page 6	
HARGICOURT	16th		St Quentin In bed out front down during night 15/16 "Aug" Hostile Artillery Silent	
SECTOR	17th		Normal. E.A. Normal Movement. H.E. Ammo Exp. L216 AX50 BX35 BPS200	
			Bar.29.40 Ther.58 Our Fire Right Grop. No.23 carried out 1.32PM Hostile Artillery	
			more active than usual. E.A. 13cm on lines. Right Grop. OP. Nº 25 signed In Fire	
			volume of HF called on the assistance of the Artillery with a Green Light.	
			Ammo Exp. L19 AX62	
	18th		Bar.29.32 Ther.65 Our Fire Right Grop. No.26 carried out at 12.30 PM. Situation Normal	
			Ammo Exp. L48 AX48 BX40	
	19th		Bar. 29.47. Ther.71 Our Fire ActiveA. C.O. Nº 110 carried out 4.5 How. BPS Hostile Fire	
			11.2AM to 11.30AM & large How. Shells from direction NAUROY. Moment Nomal. Ry. on Reg.	
			fired. E.A. very active from 6.3AM to 2.35AM + 4.40PM to 7.50PM. 2/LIEUT Shears	
			returned from leave. Ammo Exp. L37 AX40 BX40.	
	20th		Bar.29.46 Ther.72. Our Fire Movement fired on during the day + suspected OP	
			at F.33.d.7.2. Hostile Artillery Very slight wandering shelling of no Rounds 10.5cm.	
			How. into the Northern part of JEANCOURT. E.A. 6 over our lines during the day.	
			Ammo Exp. L12 A87 BX5.	

Army Form C. 2118.

WAR DIARY
or
INTELLIGENCE SUMMARY.
(Erase heading not required.)

Place	Date	Hour	Summary of Events and Information	Remarks and references to Appendices
			Page 7	
HARBICOURT SECTOR	21st		Bar. 29.49 Ther 76. Civ. Fire. 50 rounds 13 pdr fired during the day on movement and a 77 m/m Battery in H25a. Hostile Artillery shelled LE VERGUIER BERTHAUCOURT T421. R17c. Movement vy little seen. E.A. 13 up during the day. Ammo Exp. 7il. D/152 moved to L21d 4550. 1 Section G/152 moved to L27d.	
	22nd		Bar. 29.47 Ther 81. Quiet day. Civ Fire 45 rounds on Wire at M2d 35. E.A. above normal. Ammo Exp 219.	
	23rd		Bar. 29.51 Ther 83. Civ Fire. Naval sniping by A/Rbde. Hostile Artillery below normal. E.A. above. Ammo Exp L35 L2X7 BX328. 2 Sections C/152 moved to L27d.	
	24th		Bar. 29.48 Ther 22. Capt. F.W. Brewitt returned from leave. 2/Lieut Wilson. Civ Fire 50 rounds 13pdr. Wire cutting. Usual amount of sniping. Hostile Fire Nil. E.A. 1 crossed our line 7.45 PM Major F. Hull to 101st Bde as Liaison Officer. Ammo Exp 7 113 LX 13 BX 909	
	25th		Bar. 29.44 Ther 82. Capt F. Ferne returned from short leave. Mirage at HAUTEELOGUE. Civ Fire Naval sniping by 13 pdr. B/152 registered Hostile Artillery 3.45 AM. Enemy opened fire on our left until 5.30 AM. Movement below normal except in vicinity of LA BARAQUE. E.A. Nil. Ammo Exp L 2674 LX 700 BX 3057	

WAR DIARY or INTELLIGENCE SUMMARY

Page 8

Place	Date	Hour	Summary of Events and Information	Remarks and references to Appendices
HAUTECLOQUE SECTOR R	26		Jan 29.57 Hos. 61. Our Fire 16 Rounds during the day on movement in BELLEN ELISE. 2 rounds on Battery Zone number SD 8 which was in action 10.45 P.M. & 11.23 A.M. Bursts of fire on tracks & approaches to front line. 10 PM to 10.15 PM 35 rounds 18 pdr. on LITTLE BILL in conjunction with Infantry scheme. Ammo Exp. B 1021 & X 1358 BX 992	
	27		Jan 29.32/Hos. 62. Our Fire. 15/18pdr 13 2pdr on movement S.S.S. a.12 + BELLEN ELISE. Hostile Fire 10.15 to 10.30 A.M. Enemy shelled Fort FRENCH + trenches round COLOGNE FARM with 15 cm & 10.5 cm. 6.2. I cm over our lines but was driven off. Ammo Exp. B 193 & X 162 BX 672 25.6. 2/Lieut JONES returned from leave.	
	28		Jan 28.87/Hos. 62. Our Fire 9.15 to 10.5 A.M. 22 rounds 13 pdr on working party BELLEN ELISE. 3.5 PM 15 rounds 13 pdr advancing party WEST of MASNY WOOD 9 PM 7 rounds 18 pdr on LITTLE BILL at request of infantry. Hostile Artillery. Nil. Movement 0.6.1 of movement observed which appears to be a duty cart in F.18d central. Hay making in progress at 4rd TRONQUOY. E.A. Nil. Ammo Exp. L 48 BX 49 BX 112 Major B. Hill returned from 101 Bde as Liaison Officer.	
	29		Jan 29.15/Hos. 61. Our Fire Sniping by 13pdr 40 rounds Hostile Fire Nil. Movement Nil. E.A. Nil. Very rough day. Ammo Exp. L 247 & X 168 By 118	
	30.		Jan 29.58/Hos. 66. Major D.S. Nybergh & Y.C. returned from leave. Enemy aeroplane having been	

WAR DIARY
or
INTELLIGENCE SUMMARY.

Army Form C. 2118.

(Erase heading not required.)

Instructions regarding War Diaries and Intelligence Summaries are contained in F.S. Regs., Part II. and the Staff Manual respectively. Title pages will be prepared in manuscript.

Page 9

Place	Date	Hour	Summary of Events and Information	Remarks and references to Appendices
HARGICOURT	30		evacuated wounded. Our fire usual ongoing during day. 7.50 P.M. 10 rounds 18 pdr on	
SECTOR			target 908 from Aeroplane call 9.20 P.M. 30 rounds into BELLENGLISE on sounds of heavy traffic being reported. Hostile Artillery 5.30 A.M. Several 77 m/m Shells were fired in direction FRESNOY. 7.30 P.M. 4.2 Gun fired several rounds into LONTRE. Aviation 2 of our planes crossed the German line at 5.30 A.M. They were heavily shelled. 2 P.M. 8 of our planes over our lines. Ammo Exp. B 247 L 168 Bx 112	
	31		3 A.M. 29.3? L 66. Our fire 3 P.M. 60 rounds into 11 Sens. 8.10 P.M. 13 pdr registered Seven Les 29.8 11.30 & 12.45 A.M. Bursts of fire as relief of 176 by 1/ Rxx. B.C/152. Hostile Fire 6 P.M. 4 rounds 77 m/m at ASCENSION Fm 6.15 P.M. Enemy shelled M9 d 1.8 with heavy HE about 20 rounds in all 7.15 P.M. 4. 4.2 Shells fell 200 yds South of EPEREGLIER. Ex. N.L. Ammo Exp. L 141 L 95 Bx 24	

Asr Thompson
J.C. Moore
152 Bde RFA

WAR DIARY or INTELLIGENCE SUMMARY.
(Erase heading not required.)

Army Form C. 2118.

Instructions regarding War Diaries and Intelligence Summaries are contained in F. S. Regs., Part II. and the Staff Manual respectively. Title pages will be prepared in manuscript.

Vol 20

Place	Date	Hour	Summary of Events and Information	Remarks and references to Appendices
HARGICOURT SECTOR	1917 Sept 1		Bar. 29.61. Ther. 60. Weather Stormy with heavy showers. Ammo. Exp. 4 rn. AX 93 BX 24	
	2nd		Bar. 29.42. Ther. 52. Weather Showery. Our Fire Normal. 8.30 + 9.15 P.M. Bursts of Fire on Company HQ at Sept 25.57. Hostile Fire 9.5 A.M. FEVERSIVER enshelled with 5.9. 8 P.M. 60 to 70 rds 10.5 9/m How West of FEVERSIVER. 25% were duds. 6.2 sessed our lines between 6 + 7 P.M. were driven off by A.A. fire. Ammo. Exp. 4 72 AX 87 BX 91. Capt. S.W. Baxter returned from Sea fame at ALBERT.	
	3rd		Bar. 29.41. Ther. 58. Weather Fine + dry. Our Fire 12 Noon 20 rds 13 pdr on SWISS REDOUBT at request of Infantry. 8.15 P.M. 45 rds 13 pdr at Machine Gun Fd at 35.30 which was silenced. Hostile Fire 11.45 A.M. to 12.10 P.M. 65 rds in ASCENSION FARM + FEVERSIVER 3.30 P.M. 80 rds 4.2 fell behind FEVERSIVER. Movement 7 to 7.20 P.M. 6 party of 30 each about a Bn strong seen on road in R.14 d moving towards M.A.5.27.	
	4th		Bar. 29.43. Ther. 59. Weather Fine + dry. 50 rds engaging by 4/RHA throughout the day. Hostile Artillery 9.30 A.M. 9 rds 10.5 9/m How on TUMULUS 12 Noon to 10.59m FURCOSSE. 2 P.M. 9 10.59m on K.36.L. partially registering MORTIER. Enemy Aeroplane active 9.15 P.M. 1 Hostile plane descended at R.16 owing to engine trouble. Observer Pilot were made prisoners by 4/RHA. Ammo. Exp. 4 21.	

WAR DIARY or INTELLIGENCE SUMMARY

Page 2

Place	Date	Hour	Summary of Events and Information	Remarks and references to Appendices
HARICOURT SECTOR	5th		Bar. 29.51. Ther. 62. Weather fine & dry. Capt A. Ramsden proceeded to join 8th Div. 2/Lieut A. Bell proceeded on leave. Monsieur Loridis Eastern attached as Interpreter. Our Fire Nil. Sniping by 13pdr. Hostile Fire 3.15PM 4.2 Battery shelled vicinity of MAISSMET 5.15PM shelled neighbourhood of COOKERS QUARRY 9.10PM a few shells in vicinity of N° 9 Post. Aviator much activity throughout the day. Ammunition Expended 24 AX, 3X50	
	6th		Bar. 29.53. Ther. 63. Weather fine & dry. On Fire 70 rds sniping by A/RHA. Hostile Fire 24.5AM to 10.15AM 4.2 Battery was shelling R.H.A. central 10.15AM to 12.30PM 4.2 & 5.9 shelled VADENCOURT from direction of MASNY. Movement seen round SWAN REDOUBT nearly all afternoon. Major I.C.Sey Lowe proceeded on Two horses at ALBERT. Ammn. Exp. 3X 57	
	7th		Bar. 29.57. Ther. 67. Weather fine & dry. Our Fire continual sniping by A/RHA from 8.30AM to 6.10PM 50 rds in all 10.40, 11.30 & 12.10AM O.O N°36 carried out Hostile Fire. German Heavy Battery fired in direction of RUD at a slow rate for 2 hours Enemy Aeroplane several tried to cross our line during afternoon & were driven off by A.A. Fire. Ammn Exp A 5, 3X 50	

WAR DIARY or INTELLIGENCE SUMMARY

Army Form C. 2118.

Place	Date	Hour	Summary of Events and Information	Remarks and references to Appendices
HARGICOURT SECTOR	Sept 8		Page 3	
			Bar. 29.59. Ther. 68. Weather Fine & dry. Capt. L. Ferrie. M.C. proceeded on leave. 2/Lieut. P.W. Milligan proceeded on leave at HAUTECLOQUE (7days). Our Fire 1.A.M, 1.30 A.M. 2y rds each time into LITTLE BILL at request of Infantry. 8 A.M. to 7.50 P.M. 15M rds Sniping by 4/RFA. Hostile Fire 5.10 P.M. 20 rds into ASCENSION FARM 6.30 P.M. 12 rds 5.9 How at LEFT BATT. H.Q. I hit registered Aviation E/A crossed over line & was engaged by A.A. Ammu Exp A17 B.X 235	
	9th		Bar. 29.57. Ther. 69. Weather Fine & dry. Major I.C. Perry Knox Gore. M.C. returned from leave. ALBERT. Our Fire 10 A.M. 12.10 & 3 P.M. Sniping by 4/RFA 10.45, 11.30 P.M. + 12.5 AM. Bursts of Fire by 2/RFA on suspected reliefs of 11 L + R. Hostile Fire 10.30 A.M. 10.15 p.m. on FEVERSUIER 11.15 to 12.30 P.M. Left Front heavily shelled 4 to 5.30 P.M. Intermittent shelling on our Left front 5 to 5 P.M. 30 rds 7.7 9cm on FEVERSUIER Aviation 6.10 P.M. 1 E/A over our lines.	
	10th		Bar. 29.55. Ther. 64. Weather Fine & dry. Our Fire 21 rds to 13pdr Sniping Hostile Artillery 11-12 Noon 50 rds 4.2 on SAND PRIEL FARM 11.20 P.M. 4 rds 77m/m fell between PONTRUET & BERTHACOURT. 4.15 P.M. Enemy heavy Battery shelled vicinity of MAISSEMY. Aviation Several over our lines. 2/Lieut Vickers returned from leave. Ammu Exp A625 + X 217. B.K 630	

WAR DIARY or INTELLIGENCE SUMMARY

Army Form C. 2118.

Place	Date	Hour	Summary of Events and Information	Remarks and references to Appendices
HARGICOURT SECTOR	Sept 11th		Bar. 29.38. Ther. 66. Weather fine & dry. Our fire 9.35 A.M. to 6.25 P.M. 47 rds. Sniping 14. A/RFA. Hostile fire Nil. Movement Nil. Aviation 1.62 own own fires. Ammn Exp 1.824 AX 513 BX 448	
	12th		Bar. 29.71. Ther. 65. Weather fine & dry. 2/Lieut Mackie proceeded on leave. Our fire 60 rds. Sniping. Hostile fire Intermittent fire of P.R.B.D. BRIEL F.d P.M during the afternoon 5.45 P.M. 6 rds. fired at TUMULUS 7.30 P.M. 6.59 fell then 2 own fire just South of FEVERFEIER. Ammn Exp Z 383 AX 504 BX 226.	
	13th		Bar. 29.70. Ther. 63. Weather. Dull & cloudy. Slight Shower. Our fire 27 rds. 13 rds. sniping during day. Hostile fire 30. 7.7 m/m fell in FEVERFEIER. 2/Lieut A.J. Fowley transferred from 3 R.B. to 3/1 S.B. Lieut P.S. Howson from 3/1 S.B. to 3 R.B. Ammn Exp BX 16.	
	14th		Bar. 29.66. Ther. 61. Weather. Dull & cloudy. Our fire 9.15 to 7.15 P.M. 39 rds. 13 rds. by A/RFA. Sniping 10.30 P.M. 11.15 P.M. 12.5 A.M. Bursts of fire on suspected relief of 196 I.R. opposite Left Bat. Hostile fire 11.55 A.M. 3 7.7 m/m Shells know in direction of MAISSEMY. 2.50 P.M. Y 4.2 fell in BERTHECOURT. 7.15 P.M. 10. 4.2 Shells fell in vicinity of TUMULUS. Ammn Exp Z 40 AX 48 BX 26.	
	15th		Bar. 29.66. Ther. 62. Weather fine. Major W.F. Hall proceeded on 1 months leave.	

Army Form C. 2118.

WAR DIARY
or
INTELLIGENCE SUMMARY.
(Erase heading not required.)

page 4

Place	Date	Hour	Summary of Events and Information	Remarks and references to Appendices
HARBICOURT SECTOR	15th		Major L. Ferguson MC returned from Leave. Our Fire Naval comprising by 4/RHA. Hostile Fire. 35 rds fell in VAUCOURT during the afternoon. Aviation 1 E.A. over our lines. Ammt Exp Z 73 B.I. 150 B.I. 250	
	16		Jan 29.62 Ther 61 Weather Fine 1 Section D/152 returned to original position at 9h. Our Fire Naval comprising by 4/RHA 10.30 4.45, 11.50 & 2.30 A.M. Bursts of fire by C/RHA on Hostile Fire Tel. 6.12 Tel. Ammt Exp Z 18 B.I. 62. Inspected relief of W.I.R. by 60 pdrs co-operated. Hostile Fire Nil. 6.12 Tel. Ammt Exp Z 18 B.I. 62.	
	17		Jan 29.76 Ther 72 Weather Fine Strong S.W. Wind Our Fire 22 rds Sniping by C/RHA Hostile Fire 8.30 AM 12 10.59pm fell about Rg 2.35 AM & 9.17pm fell about Rg 10.10 AM 4-10.59pm fell about TERNUS 3.55 PM 2 10.59pm fell N.W of FEUERSIER. Aviation 6 E.A. crossed our lines at 6.30, 8.5, 8.40 A.M. 2 Lieut L. Bell. returned from leave. Ammt Exp B.I. 120	
	18		Jan 29.79 Ther 80 Weather Fine Strong S.W. Wind 2 Lieut A.S. Bell M.C. posted to 153 Bde. Our Fire 8.20 AM to 7PM 50 rds Sniping by C/RHA 10.25 PM 10.9 to 4.5 How on B 20 d. 88 & 3 by reques of Infantry as retaliation for shelling of Mg Post 10.3 to 13 pdr on B 20 d. 25.35 same hour. Hostile Fire 9.30 AM 6.47 mym in direction of MAISSNEY 12.30 PM 6.47 mym in direction BERTHACCOURT 10.10 to 11.35 AM 30 rds 10.5.9pm in LITTLE FILL vicinity from direction ETRICOURT 11.15 AM 14 pds 10.59pm in FEUERSIER from direction of N-F-V ROY 2.35 to 5.30 P.M 1.59 pds 1.59pm fell	

T2134. Wt. W708—776. 500000. 4/15. Sir J. C. & S.

Army Form C. 2118.

WAR DIARY
or
INTELLIGENCE SUMMARY.
(Erase heading not required.)

Instructions regarding War Diaries and Intelligence Summaries are contained in F.S. Regs., Part II. and the Staff Manual respectively. Title pages will be prepared in manuscript.

Place	Date	Hour	Summary of Events and Information	Remarks and references to Appendices
HARICOURT SECTOR	Sept 18		Fieces in TEARCOURT from direction of N.20.R0 x WOOD Direction 11.25 P.M. 3 G.12 crossed our lines. Aimes Exp. 2.I.21.	
	19		Bar. 29.75. Ther. 77. Weather Fine. Strong S.W. wind. Gun fire 2.30 A.M. to 7.28 P.M. 50 rds. Enemy by 4/R.H.A. Hostile fire. During whole day Heavy Battery of 3 fire from direction N.21 & fired a slow rate of fire at S.N.28.A40 to 7 P.M. a Heavy Battery from N.E. of N.20.R0 fired towards R.b.c. 6.45 to 7.30 P.M. 13 rds 10.5 cm. on HUDSONS POST Direction 2.10 P.M. G.12 crossed French lines & was driven back by A.A. fire. Ammn Exp. 2.I.27 A.X. 67 B.I. 31	
	20		Bar. 29.91. Ther. 81. Weather Dull. Slow rain fell early morning. Kept E. Ferrie N.C. returned from Cave. Gun fire 23 rds. Sniping by 4/R.H.A. 4.5 P.M. 20 rds. 13 pdr. 1.4.3 How. at B3e to & F.2 C. as retaliation for shelling of GRAHAM POST. 3.30 A.M. Slow rate of fire by D/152 on HINDENBURG LINE until 5 A.M. Hostile fire 2.1.2 & 10 A.M. BERTHAUCOURT vic. shelled with 97 rds 10.5 + 150 mpm. 10.30 A.M. to 12.30 P.M. 100 150 mpm. Shells were fused R.2 a.N.7.E. 4 P.M. & 10.5 cm. on GRAHAM POST Direction N.L. Ammn Exp. 2.I.53	
	21		Bar. 29.78 Ther. 70. Weather. Fire + dry. Stray sharp N.W. wind. Gun fire 11.30 A.M. 6 rds 4.5 How on F3d 8575 11.40 to 12.30 P.M. 30 rds. Suppression of BUISSON RAVAINE F2.R.4. x F2.d.19 x TA.BERTE. 6.P.M. 6 rds 13 rds a.12.P.M. observing from French F.O.G. 10.5.11.15-11.55 P.M. 1.10 A.M. Bursts of fire E.9 1/4 P.K.a	

Army Form C. 2118.

WAR DIARY
or
INTELLIGENCE SUMMARY.
(Erase heading not required.)

Instructions regarding War Diaries and Intelligence Summaries are contained in F. S. Regs., Part II. and the Staff Manual respectively. Title pages will be prepared in manuscript.

Place	Date	Hour	Summary of Events and Information	Remarks and references to Appendices
HARGICOURT Sector	Sept 21		Page 6 2nd B/152 in support Relief of 176 IR Hostile Fire A/152 was shelled from 2 a.m. to 10.30 a.m. 1 Gun damaged. Hostility 77th H.E. POS. B. L. Saunt 9.15 a.m. & 10.15 p.m. into 17 RDESCOURT 9.30 a.m. 3 rds. 10.5 gm. into 28 T.R.U. 10.15 p.m. 6 rds. 10.5 gm. near TOMBUS. 11.30 A.M. 6 rds. 4.2 pm fell in FEVER RUE R. Movement Party of Men excavating Screens at F19 a. 5.0 Aeroes were informed + fired. Aviation 4.4.30 & 6 P.M. 6.2 flew on our lines & were driven off by A.A. fire. Lieut. L. Post Meara proceeded to P.A.S m.a. 6 weeks course. Ammn Exp. 289 AX 159 BX 116.	
	22		Jan 29.78 Ken. 78 Weather Fine & dry. 2/Lieut A. London posted to 2/152. Cas Fire 6.2.2 Co 6.55 A.M. 9 rds. 18 rds on M.G. emplacements in SWITN. FILLER REDOUBT 6.5 A.M. 2 rds on SWAX REDOUBT et. aque. of Infantry. 6.30 P.M. 4 rds 13 rds on Movement on Road in E33 a.10. 10 40, 11.20 11.50 P.M. Right Jamp. O.O. 714 received and (Relief of 141 IR) Hostile Fire. 5.30 A.M. 77 r/m. Shells on RAILWAY BEN POSTS. 3 P.M. Enemy fired 10 r/ds into M.2a. Junction. 3 p.m. 1. 6.4 on our lines 2/LIET F. Milligan & 2/Lieut L. Macduff returned from Artillery School HAUTELOO OF. Ammn. Exp. A52 LX 64 BX 118.	
	23		Jan 29.80 Ken. 80 Ken. 81 Weather Fine & dry. 2/Lieut L.Lourie 2/Lieut L.Lourie to D/160. Cas Fire 5.2.12 Ale Ken. put down a heavy Barage on the Right Centre Coys Front. Right Comp. replaced	

WAR DIARY
or
INTELLIGENCE SUMMARY.
(Erase heading not required.)

Army Form C. 2118.

Place	Date	Hour	Summary of Events and Information	Remarks and references to Appendices
HARBICOURT SECTOR	23rd		page 7	
		3.1152	DEFEND PRIEL DISR. & 2nd Quarry Fire. Trench Artillery DEFEND BUISSON BAULAINE. The bombardment was replied to with great force. About 5.15 A.M. S.O.S. was composed to a red star shell. Bombardment which continued for 10 minutes. The S.O.S. was fired with Box Respirators on, only one man reported to the M.O. feeling the effects of Gas. Our Lewis Gun company did not fire throughout the day. Hostile Fire 6.55 A.M. about 50 rds. 10.5 g.m. into R10-11. 11.45 A.M. 12 rds. on ASCENSION FARM. Aviation 10.12. 1 Observation lines at work, being AA much driven back by A.A. 6.15 P.M. 1 E.A. chased by 2 English & Sent back to his own lines. Ammo Exp. I.T. 910 A.X. 220. J.X. 325.	
	24		Jan. 24. 16. Ther. 76. Winter fine & dry. 2/Lieut W.L. Lewis & F.J. Milligan proceeded on leave. CRZ 2A 4/34 " Learning Gun Positions. Our fire 4.15 A.M. 3rds 18rds at 2 Men starving in F20 B who dispersed. 12.53 P.M. 3rds 18 pdr at Man walking in F20 B with good effect	
		6 P.M.	11 rds. 18 pdr. Registration. Hostile Fire 9.15 to 10 P.M. 20 to 10.5 g.m. fell in rear of TEMULUS	
		10.12	5 m. 5 g.m. ASCENSION FARM from direction ETRICOURT 10.15 A.M. 12 10.5 g.m. near DRAGOON POST. Movement 1.20 P.M. 2 Waggoneers in rear of Aviation 11.20 & 1.30 P.M. E.A. over our lines. Ammo Exp. I.T. 43 A.X. 140.	
	25		Jan. 25. 16. Ther. 76. Weather fine & dry. Lieut. Col. W.T. Thompson D.S.O. proceeded on leave	

WAR DIARY
or
INTELLIGENCE SUMMARY
(Erase heading not required.)

Army Form C. 2118.

Place	Date	Hour	Summary of Events and Information	Remarks and references to Appendices
HARGICOURT SECTOR	25		Page 8	
			Our Fire 11.15 A.M. 8rds. 13rds on Road E.29.d 22 6 P.M. 15rds on Movement M & a.14. 2 P.M. 9rds. 13rds on Road E.29.d 22 6 P.M. 15rds	
			13rds on Movement M & a.14. 2 P.M. 9rds. 8rds on Movement on Road E.29.d 25rds 13rds	
			7 P.M. 20 rds 13 rds on 2 Men observing over Trench at E.29 c.14 Hostile Fire 10.20 A.M. 3.10-5 P.M.	
			on TM Post 11.2 A.M. & 10.50 P.M. on GRAND PRIEL FARM 11.30 onwards 12.15 P.M. How Battery fired on E.21 c	
			11.15 A.M. 2.10.5 P.M. on PRIEL Int. HAUTE Road 4.30 to 5 P.M. 30.77 M/m in TEVERGNIER Farm dweller	
			of MALFAIT-LA-FOSSE Aviator E.1 over our lines at 10.10.10, 11.30 P.M. 2 Lieut I.W. M? Ken	
			returned from leave. Hostile Cop Z.14 X X 102	
	26		Bar. 29.60 Ther. 68. Weather Dull & Windy Stormy S.W. Capt. I.S. Farr M.C. & Capt. H.L. Thorber	
			proceeded on leave. Our Fire 12 Noon 12 rds 18rds on Trenches E.20 6 bombs Offensive at request	
			of Infantry 12.30 P.M. to 3.45 P.M. 56 rds Sniping by A. P Bd. 4-6 P.M. 20.7rds 10 P.M. at Men	
			carrying E.29 d + E.29 a Hostile Fire 10.45 P.M. 9 rds 10.5 P.M. on ASCENSION FARM from dweller	
			of E.TRICOURT 10.30 to 11.30 A.M. 20 rds 10.5 P.M. on LITTLE Biel. + TM 9 Post 10.30 to 11.10 A.M. 22 rds on	
			GOAT TREE POST from direction of ETRICOURT Battery Commanding Colonel & Adjutant	
			106 Bde visited Batteries HQ etc. 6 P.M. S.O.S. 2.134 + S.W. Garrisons evaded Alarm Lines	
			Amm & Eqp.	
	27		Bar. 29.82 Ther. 73. Weather Early morning Wet then Dull & Close Our Fire 9.25 A.M. 6	

WAR DIARY
or
INTELLIGENCE SUMMARY.
(Erase heading not required.)

Army Form C. 2118.

Place	Date	Hour	Summary of Events and Information	Remarks and references to Appendices
	Sept		page 9	
HARICOURT	27	6.7.15 P.M.	132rd Seige Bty H/RHA 9.A 10.15 A.M. 10 rds by B/152 Hostile Fire 10.55 A.M. 9rds	
SECTOR		7.7 m/m 72g Pod M. 12.30 P.M. 10 rds on GRAND PRIEL FARM 4.20 P.M. 14 rds. 7.7 m/m 77.2g Pod. 5.10.6		
		5.15 P.M. 6 rds 10.5 g/m fired on SILVER BOIS R 5.40 & 6.7.2 10 rds 10.5 g/m fired on SILVER BOIS R		
		Position Nil. 9.30 P.M. 1 Section 106 Bty Ammn Exp Att AX 104		
	28	Bar. 29.88 Ther. 62 Weather Fine. Our fire 26 rds Bty 2/RHA Sniping 10.30, 11-10 11.15 P.M.		
		Bursts of fire by B. D/152 afon OC. D/152 Hostile Fire 10.50 A.M. 15 10.5 g/m fired behind		
		USSE RIVOIR FARM With 7000 Stewrands of fire on 27 from Enemy Gun appeared to be		
		MISTY. 3.10 P.M. Heavy Bombardment at TATROO 27 fired several rounds on 4, 9, 6		
		101 Hamelon + Adjutant arrived at 1.30 3rd H.B. Ammn Exp. LX 184 BX 30		
	29	Bar. 29.85 Ther. 61 Weather fine. 106 Bde H.Q. moved to relieve 152 Bde H.Q. e H.A.H.		
		2.30 P.M. Batteries + 9a H.Q. moved from HARICOURT + HINTZBURY to Camp at ST DENIS		
		PERONNE arriving at 5.30 P.M. Remaining Sections arrived at 11-12 P.M. 3rd H.Q. returned		
		at FLAMICOURT 10 P.M. Relief of 106 Bde completed at 10 P.M. Ammn Exp. LX 118 LX 29 BX 125		
PERONNE	30.	Bar. 29.96 Ther. 62 Weather Fine. Major P.H. Furgusson H.C. assumed command of 152 Bde RFA		
		Usual Routine for first day out of action.		

Weymer Major 152 B^{de}

Army Form C. 2118.

WAR DIARY
or
INTELLIGENCE SUMMARY.
(Erase heading not required.)

152 Brigade R.F.A.
Vol 22

152 Bde W.D.

Instructions regarding War Diaries and Intelligence Summaries are contained in F. S. Regs., Part II and the Staff Manual respectively. Title pages will be prepared in manuscript.

Place	Date	Hour	Summary of Events and Information	Remarks and references to Appendices
PERONNE	1917 Oct 1st		Weather Very Fine. 2/Lieut L. Harland and R. Lickess transferred to 59th Division. 2nd day at Rest.	
--	2nd		Weather Very Fine. 3rd day at rest.	
--	3rd		Weather Dull. Rain early morning 4 day at rest. S.O.C. Rest. III Corps awaited Brigade.	
--	4th		Weather Mild & very stormy 5th day of Rest. A & B/152 exhibited their turn.	
--	5th		Weather Cold & wet 6th day of Rest. C/152 exhibited their turn.	
--	6th		Weather Cold & wet 7th day of Rest. Entrainment postponed.	
		24 hours.		
--	7th		Weather Cold, wet & windy. 8th day of Rest. 1244 Revert to Summer Time.	
--	8th		Weather Cold, cold & windy. Brigade entraining for PROVEN.	
		A/152	Arrival at CHAPELETTE 7.15. Train departs 10.10	
		B/152	" " " 10.15 13.10	
		B/152	" " " 13.15 16.10	
		C/152	" " " 16.15 19.10	
		D/152	" " " 19.15 22.10	

WAR DIARY or INTELLIGENCE SUMMARY

Army Form C. 2118.

(Erase heading not required.)

Page 2

Place	Date	Hour	Summary of Events and Information	Remarks and references to Appendices
PROVEN A REA	1917 Oct 9	3am	Weather fair. Brigade detrained at PESELHOEK. B/152 – 3am	
		3am – 7am.	B/152 – 10am. C/152 – 1pm. D/152 – 4pm. Brigade went into Camp in neighbourhood of 1st SIXTHE. Lieut. Col. W.F. Thompson met Brigade on arrival. Having returned from leave direct to ROPERINGHE. Capt H.Z. Tonstone	
			Capt St Fair & Lieut. G.J. Milligan returned from leave.	
-do-	10th		Weather fair. Weather cold, wet & windy. B.O. visited Wagon Lines	
-do-	11th		fair. Weather cold, wet & windy. B.O. Adjutant & B.C. visited H.Q. & Gun Position of 295 Bde. South of WIDEN DRIFT Road	
-do-	12th		fair. Weather cold, wet & windy. The 14th Bde attacked at 5.25 A.M. & the Brigade were in readiness to move forward to support the Infantry. This order cancelled at 11 A.M.	
-do-	13th		fair. Weather cold & wet. Advanced parties to take over 295 Bde. 1 hour whilst being taken into position was subjected by a direct hit causing 2 casualties. The Knight & Lt of wounds. Br. S. Smith.	
-do-	14th		fair. Weather cold & wet. 152 Bde completed relief with 295 Bde by 10 P.M. Lieut. Col. Thompson & Capt Brush proceeded to MARIE TEANER Rn. to relieve	

WAR DIARY
or
INTELLIGENCE SUMMARY
(Erase heading not required.)

Army Form C. 2118.

Place	Date	Hour	Summary of Events and Information	Remarks and references to Appendices
	1917 Oct		page 3	
	14th		Brig. Gen. Sterling to take command of Right Group. Reft. Ord. Clays. 1-18 pdrs Siem. 3/152 knocked out. Ammo. Exp. ÷ 30. Bon. Weather Fine.	
WIEL TJEDRIFT	15th		Weather Fine with Occ. Hostile Fire. Normal. Our Fire. Normal. Horse supply attached to D.A.C. for Ammo. supply. Hostile Fire Normal. 50 Horses per Battery with 1 Officer from the Bde. Ammo. Exp. A 37. A X 55. 3 X 38. Bon. Weather Fine with Good Wind. Our Fire. Registration only.	
do	16th		Casualties Nº A2931 Dr Flack Killed, Nº 11170 Dr Crosby Wounded both 6/1/52. Nº Ammo. Exp. A 11. 3 X 52. B A N. 3 x 91 leave to Comet started. Bon. Weather Fine with Good Wind.	
do	17th		152 Bde. Right Group taken over by 29th Cir. Arty Charge of SOS Lines. Our Fire. Registrations only. Ammo. Exp. ÷ 90. Bon. Weather Rain early morning Fine clays. Our Fire. SAR + 5.35AR	
do	18th		All 18pdrs + 4.5 How start on SOS Line for 1 minute then Lift at 100 pr. made for 3 minutes. Rate of Fire 18pdrs-2 +4.5 How-1 rd.pr.m. E.O. met. 6 Rt. Right Group. Wind Force 12 Noon. Bde. ordered to start moving forward to the BRAMBECK. Major P.H. FERGUSON returned to D/152. Capt Myball Smith M.O. proceeded to ENGLAND. Lieut. N.R. Lawrence attached as M.O. from 103rd F.A. Ammo. Exp. ÷ 117. A X 97. 3 X 40.	

Army Form C. 2118.

WAR DIARY
or
INTELLIGENCE SUMMARY.
(Erase heading not required.)

Instructions regarding War Diaries and Intelligence Summaries are contained in F.S. Regs., Part II. and the Staff Manual respectively. Title pages will be prepared in manuscript.

Place	Date	Hour	Summary of Events and Information	Remarks and references to Appendices
	1917 Oct		page 4	
WD DRIFT 2nd DRIFT AREA	18th		Casualties. Sgt Southern killed 2/152. Staff Sergt Com. Cond. Teggero H.Q. wounded. Fire. Weather fine.	
AREA	19th		5 A.M. 2 & 3/152 moved to new position on the BROMBECK. 9 Guns were got into action by Noon. The remaining 3 Guns of 3/152 were caught on the Road in the neighbourhood of Captains Farm by Bosche shells causing great damage to number of casualties to Men & Horses. Major Pr Hill returned from month's leave. Casualties. Wounded. Lieut A.J. Sowley, Lieut F.C. Wilcox, Dr. Cocker & Wilkins, Btn Weiner. Sent to Hospital suffering from Gas. Capt. S. Farm. Ammunt. Exp. A 30. A X 20. B X 10. Fire. Weather fine.	
-do-	20th		C+D Moved to rear position on the BROMBECK getting 9 Guns into action by 2 P.M. Brigade H.Q. moved from F.A.P.I.N.E. F.2.R.M. to Mon T.7.B.1 R.E.L.E. FARM closing the former at 5 A.M. & opening the latter at 6 A.M. Brigade completed registration. Major Hill & Lieut Lewis returned from leave having been delayed en route. Ammunt. Exp. Nil. Weather fine.	
-do-	21		Weather fine. One Gun Each Battery on duty for 4 hours at a time with harassing fire. 3/152 Wire cutting at 11. 6. t. 20.75 to t.t. 6.55.75. Machine Gun target at V.12. 01.04 engaged by Hows. & 12 pdr. Bros Rd W.8. r. Cross Rds COLOMBO.	

T2134. Wt. W708-776. 500000. 4/15. Sir J. C. & S.

WAR DIARY or INTELLIGENCE SUMMARY

Army Form C. 2118.

page 5

Place	Date	Hour	Summary of Events and Information	Remarks and references to Appendices
	Oct 21		Horse engaged during day. Practice Barrage carried out at 12 Noon & 4.30 P.M. Final preparations made for forthcoming operations. Ammn Exp. 1/460 L×450 BX 30. Casualties 7820 Sergt Shaw J, 1130 Corpl Wilkes J, 176121 L Sear J, 42209 L Jarvis L, 29041 L Machin J.G, 32198 L Lewis T. all wounded. Weather Fine.	
WIDENDRAFT	22		Bar. Ther. Weather Fine. Zero Hour 5.35 A.M. S.O.O. No. 7. Hunt. London. 4/152 as F.O.O. 2/Lieut Franklin in charge of forward Signal Station. 4.47 P.M. S.O.S. was continued until 5.30 P.M. Batteries were shelled whilst on his way to the Dressing Station. Major P.H. Ferguson was fatal and died whilst on his way to the Dressing Station. Casualties Killed Major P.H. Ferguson M.C. Wounded Lieut. J. Walker, 2079 Bdr. Hughes T.H. 8204 Gr. T. Roper, 9265 Gr. T.C. Smith, 8147 Gr. E. Bolton, 2320 Dr. A. Elmes, 39,250 Dr. T.E. Hinckcliffe, Gr. Champeney, Gr. Campbell, Gr. Harper, Gr. Sargent, 40415 R.W. Fieldbury accidental.	
" 2 F.A.			64.0421. Dr. W. Klein Missing. Ammn Exp. L5 122 L+AX 6050 L×1310 BZ596. 7858 Bar. Ther. Weather cool. On Fire 12.10 A.M. 30 minutes searching Erie Island Pier.	
"	23		On Zone 5.20 A.M. S.O.S. Kill 5.57 4.10 P.M. Counter Preparation for 30 minutes 5.20 P.M. S.O.S 5.35 P.M. Counter Preparation for 10 minutes. During the day Harassing fire on points as ordered. Ammn Exp. L+AX 2640. BX 330.	

WAR DIARY or INTELLIGENCE SUMMARY

Army Form C. 2118.

Page 6.

Place	Date	Hour	Summary of Events and Information	Remarks and references to Appendices
HIDDEN DRIFT AREA	24th	8am	Ther. Weather Wet. 10 A.M. Funeral of Major D.K. Ferguson M.C. at EXED 2 F6 PM 2180 Shelled New Peasant Brig. Hon. Br. Walthall. Lieut Col. Thompson Major Myhough, Mr. Makin. Our Sie Harassing Fire & reveling line behind our S.O.S. lines. 5·5 & 5·20 PM fired on S.O.S. signal both times phoned Hostile Fire. The BROMBECK VALLEY over Shelled at 11 AM for 45 minutes. Ammn Exp. 12·7·5 1890. 3×350.	
do	25	8am	Ther. Weather Wet. Our line fine Night firing as per Regt Coop Instructions 7pm - 9pm Practice Barrage Ed Mil Ammn Exp 4·7·5 1916. 3×550.	
do	26	8am	Ther. Weather Wet. Zero Hour for OO 7PM 5·10 AM Our Fire as per O.O 7N continued throughout the day BRSZ fired 100 Rds on Pill Box 27 a 4·2 at required of BHQ Commander. Hostile Fire Normal. Casualties Capt Geo. Baden wounded 7PR·17·9 903. R. Roadman (inoculated) CHS2. Ammn Exp 17·5 300 4·2×500 3×848	
do	27	8am	Ther. Weather Fine Major IC. Lay Crie attd to Div arty to act as 2nd Major vice Major Moen to 19th Bgde. Our Fire Harassing fire as ordered 5PM to 3AM 70·4·16 Fire 5PM to 6 PM BROMBECK VALLEY heavily shelled by 105 & 115 c.m. How. E.I active "flying very low". Lieut Stewart & King reported 3pm 160 Ste	

WAR DIARY
or
INTELLIGENCE SUMMARY.
(Erase heading not required.)

Army Form C. 2118.

Instructions regarding War Diaries and Intelligence Summaries are contained in F. S. Regs., Part II. and the Staff Manual respectively. Title pages will be prepared in manuscript.

Place	Date	Hour	Summary of Events and Information	Remarks and references to Appendices
	1917 Oct			
Knovallis	27th		Knovallis 117995 Bdr Monkee C.T, 134519 L. Kingston Pvy 104092 L. Fordyce J. 252882 L. Charlesworth R.W. 23376 L. Smith J. 10153 L. Bishop R. all wounded. Ammn. Exp. 12+7 X 3535. BX 600. Ben. Fen. Weather Fine. Our fire usual harassing fire. Hostile fire normal.	
Witendrift	28th		Knovallis 137787 Dr Boon H. killed 31/52, 4267 Dr. Elliott wounded 31/52. 11225 Dr Shaw J.T. Died of wounds 5/52. Ammn. Exp. 12+7 X 350 BX 217 Ben. Fen. Weather Wet. Our fire 3pm to 9am Cen. Shooting 10AM to 5Pm Harassing fire. Hostile fire. Normal all day 4.30 to 5.30 pm. The Hun dropped 61 SRSR sh from BROMBECK to 101 DENDRIFT until 97 pm. 10.5, 16.5 21 pm.	
-do-	29th		Knovallis 79143 Bdr Wild H, 23421 L. Hazel R. wounded Ammn. Exp. A.+A.X 2078 BX 350 Ben. Fen. Weather Still wet + rough. Our fire Area shooting + harassing fire Hostile fire Normal. Ammn. Exp. 12+AS 554. BX 225	
-do-	30th		Ben. Weather Fine + mild. Our fire 6.2 pm to 6.4 pm Night firing on Shock. Orders received to only run up 2 guns 12pm in the 3rd sec + 3 it's then remainder to proceed to Waqon Line. Ammn. Exp. 12+AX 142 BX 15.	
-do-	31st			Per Thurston Lt Col RFA Bde RFA 152. Bde RFA

WAR DIARY
or
INTELLIGENCE SUMMARY.
(Erase heading not required.)

Army Form C. 2118.

152 B⁴ R.F.A.

VII 22

Place	Date	Hour	Summary of Events and Information	Remarks and references to Appendices
BROEMBEEK	1/11/17	Bar 29.33 Ther 53	Our Fire Night firing only as per P.8.	
	2	Bar 29.44 Ther 48	Our Fire Night firing only as per P.8. Hostile fire Very active Brombeck Valley & Wijdendrift. Shelled very heavily all day. Great damage to Guns, ammunition & roads	
	3	Bar 29.50 Ther 59	Brigade relieved by 242 A.F.A Brigade	
	4	Bar 28.50 Ther 44	Brigade at rest at Sataway Camp	
	5	Bar 29.63 Ther 47	Brigade marched to vicinity of Godewsvelde. Received good en route from I.O.M. 9th Corps.	
	6	Bar 29.32 Ther 50	Brigade moved to Calonne sur la Lys.	
	7	Bar 29.35 Ther 51	Brigade moved to Marles Les Mines	

Army Form C. 2118.

WAR DIARY
or
INTELLIGENCE SUMMARY.
(Erase heading not required.)

Instructions regarding War Diaries and Intelligence Summaries are contained in F. S. Regs., Part II. and the Staff Manual respectively. Title pages will be prepared in manuscript.

Place	Date	Hour	Summary of Events and Information	Remarks and references to Appendices
	8/11/17		Bar 28.51 Ther 44 Brigade moved to MINGOVAL area	
	9		Bar 29.39 Ther 49 Brigade moved to BOIRY ST MARTIN. G.O.C. 34th Div inspected the Brigade en route.	
	10		Bar 28.74 Ther 43 Brigade + Battery Commanders reconnoitred gun positions of A/By 312 Bde RFA. One section for battery relieved one section per battery of the 312 Bde RFA.	
HENINEL	11	Bar 29.18 Ther 51	Remaining sections relieved 312 Bde. Responsibility for the defence of the line was taken over by the 152nd Bde RFA and 312 Bde RFA. Brigade took over 312nd Bde Waggon Lines at X6c	
	12	9/m Bar 29.23 Ther 53	Batteries registered during the day.	
		6pm to 6am	Gas Hose Neighbouring as W 3ff DA N2 Horrible type. Very quiet throughout the day	
	13	Bar 29.25 Ther 53	Visibility poor	

Army Form C. 2118.

WAR DIARY
or
INTELLIGENCE SUMMARY.
(Erase heading not required.)

Place	Date	Hour	Summary of Events and Information	Remarks and references to Appendices
HENINEL	13/11/17		Gunfire. Registration & Calibration	
		6am to 6am	Night firing as per 34th D.A. O/N/2	
		3 pm	Hostile fire sketch No 6. 10.5 cm.Hows on O.31.3	
			Flashes of 15 cm how. observed M. Bearing 6th Army WEST O.P.	
			Feuy on an enemy observer on "the Park area".	
	14	Bur. 29.25 Ther. 51 Visibility low		
		5.6.5.15 pm	Our fire. Bd. oper. 34th D.G. O/B/2	
			Tracks etc. in back areas fired on throughout the day	
			Hostile fire No 1	
			The C.O. + B.C's of A, C + D/152 + B/160 reconnoitred	
			trenches in 16th Div area for forthcoming operations	
	15	Bur. 29.30 Ther. 50 Visibility from 11 am good		
		11 am to 11.30 pm	Our fire. 300 R + A.X. 60 Bx as per 34 D.A. O/B/2	
		3.30 pm	Brigade fired 6 rounds per gun on "Many Fortain Two" in Retaliation for enemy T.M activity, in reprisal from 101st Inf. Bde	

WAR DIARY
or
INTELLIGENCE SUMMARY.
(Erase heading not required.)

Army Form C. 2118.

Place	Date	Hour	Summary of Events and Information	Remarks and references to Appendices
HENINEL	15/10/17	6 am to 6 am	Night firing ad. per. for 34th D.A. O/N/2 Hostile fire J2 T.M's fell in O31.7.	
		11.15 am	20 77 m/m shells in O31.7 + O25.c	
		12.30 to 2.45 pm	6 T.M's fell in O25d + O31.7.	
		3.15 pm	3 10.5 c/m shells fell in O25d.	
		3.30		
	16	Bar 29.44 Ther 48	Hostile gas. Battery registered + calibrated. Our fire.	
		11 am	15 rounds 18 pdr. fired on movement in O.10.c.	
		6 am to 6 am	Night firing as per 34th D.A. O/N/2	
		2 am to 2.30 pm	20 10.5 c/m Brown Lyddite about T16 a 85.90	
		Bar 29.50 Ther 57	Our fire Calibration + registering	
	17	5 pm	A.C + D/152 + B/160 with above Group positions as Reg H Group, 34th D.A. + moved into positions at circles as below Left Group, 16th D.A. A/152 (5 guns) T22 a 35.95, B/160 (5 guns) T16 c 33.36, C/152 (5 guns) T10 c 28.02, D/152 (6 How) T16 a 60.25, Left Group HQ at T14 7 40.00	

WAR DIARY
or
INTELLIGENCE SUMMARY.
(Erase heading not required.)

Army Form C. 2118.

Place	Date	Hour	Summary of Events and Information	Remarks and references to Appendices
16 Div Area	17/11/17		O.C. Left Group, Lt. Col. W.J. Thompson D.S.O.	
		5 pm	B/151 came under orders of O.C. Left Group 34th D.A.	
	18.		Bar 29.64. Thr 47. Bars fire. Registering Zero line by all batteries. Left Group not in defence of the zone.	
	19		Bar 29.65 Thr 49. Batteries continued registration & checked flank of barrage.	
	20	6.20 am	Bar 29.45 Thr 48. Zero hour for 16th Div of Advance. Left Group under Lt. Col. W.J. Thompson D.S.O. became responsible for the front of the 49th Inf Bde (6th Div) Bat this hour Left Group (B,C,D/152 & B/150) opened as per 16th Div offensive orders on enemy front line creeping forward by lifts of 100x every 4 minutes until reaching Bretledge Barrage at +20. Enemy sent up single red, rows of green, double red & double Green rockets shortly after our attack was launched. No apparent action to Manuel	

Army Form C. 2118.

WAR DIARY
or
INTELLIGENCE SUMMARY.
(Erase heading not required.)

Place	Date	Hour	Summary of Events and Information	Remarks and references to Appendices
16 Div area	20/11/17	7.2 am	Right Bath. (K.O. 2/Lt. E.C. Lemon) reported all three objectives taken & at least 50 prisoners	
		7.18 am	Left Bath. (K.O. 2/Lt O.L. Bell) reported enemy front line in Bath. front in our hands, but worse details of at U9.75.2 (same trench) This not confirmed by Capt J. Fowie M.C. (K.O. 2/9th Inf Bde.)	
		7.20 am	C/152 ordered to fire on protective barrage at rate of 1 R.P.G.M.	
		7.50 am	Reported from 16th D.A. that 47th & 48th Inf Bdes had taken their objectives & many prisoners	
		7.5.3	Left Bath. (2/Lt O.L. Bell) reported enemy bombing his own Prince trench U9f & requested artillery support. D/15 opened fire on following points at the rate of 1 R.P.G. 9.6.m. U9.73.70, U8a.03.47, U8a.20.65, U8a.37.33 & U8a.55.23.	
		8.5	C/152 quickened fire to 4 R.p.G to 9 p.m. on protective barrage at request of Left Bath. while infantry bombed way up Prince trench	
		8.15	Left Bath. reported all objectives taken, 20 prisoners &	

WAR DIARY or INTELLIGENCE SUMMARY

Army Form C. 2118.

Place	Date	Hour	Summary of Events and Information	Remarks and references to Appendices
16 Div Area	20/11/17		4 machine guns and wire establishing blocks & wiring new line C/152 slackened off to 1 Rd pg p.gm.	
		8.20 a.m.	Right Battn reported all well & about 200 prisoners taken	
		8.22	C + D/152 ceased fire	
		8.37	O.C. Centre Group reported that Right Group had received S.O.S. Left Group then opened on S.O.S. lines. 18 pdr 2 Rds 9 p.m, 4.5 How 1 Rd Left Group ceased fire after conducting Barrage	
		8.47	Patrol of enemy reported in U8 central & sunken road U147	
		8.55	A/152 fired Thicks of 2 Rds gun fire every ten minutes from S.O.S. lines to 500 x fast (searching & sweeping)	
		8.56	49th Inf Bde report enemy hurrying up on FONTAINE – BULLECOURT road also about 200 men massing at sunken road U15a. B/160 fired on FONTAINE – BULLECOURT road, 3 Rds pg pm for 10 minutes	
		9.35	A/152 ceased fire	
		10.25	Snipers reported active on HANDY trench. D/152 3 How fired on this trench 1 Rd pg pm every 2 minutes for 15 minutes	

Army Form C. 2118.

WAR DIARY
or
INTELLIGENCE SUMMARY.
(Erase heading not required.)

Instructions regarding War Diaries and Intelligence Summaries are contained in F. S. Regs., Part II. and the Staff Manual respectively. Title pages will be prepared in manuscript.

Place	Date	Hour	Summary of Events and Information	Remarks and references to Appendices
16 Div Area	29/11/7	10.45 a.m.	Snipers in KANDY trench reported silenced. D/152 continued slow fire	
		10.50	1 Rd to 9 P. 20 minutes on this trench. A large number of enemy reported in CEYLON trench from U8a 40.00 to OLDENBURG Lane. B/166 concentrated on this trench. 3 Rds P. 9. P. m. for 5 minutes & repeated 20 minutes later.	
		10.10	C/152 fired 9 salvos on trench U7b 95.40 to 80.80 on enemy bombing party attempting to force a way to PRINCE trench	
		2.20 p.m.	Reg'l. Batn. reported enemy T.M.s. active on trench O7d 75 to 8.2. D/152 fired on them on each of the following emplacements O2d 45.45, U8a 42.52, U8a 80.90, U8c 40.98, U8d 64.81 & U9a 19.57. 2 Rds to 9. P. m. for 10 minutes & 1 Rd P. 9. P. m. for 5 minutes	
		2.29	Enemy bombing parties reported in PRINCE trench as far as U7 9.4. C/152 on section searched this trench for 10 minutes. 3 Rds P. 9. P. m.	
		2.40	Patrol reported bombing down PRINCE trench & OLDENBURG Lane. C/152 one section Prince trench & one section Oldenburg Lane, 3 Rds to 9. P. m. for 10 minutes	

WAR DIARY
or
INTELLIGENCE SUMMARY

Army Form C. 2118.

Place	Date	Hour	Summary of Events and Information	Remarks and references to Appendices
Divl Area	16/11/17	2.45 pm	Left Batth. asked for Protective Barrage so he fire down on the +12 +16 line (creeping barrage map) B/160 3 Rds p.g. f.m. for 10 minutes + 1 Rd p.g.f.m. for 10 minutes + search as far as the FONTAINE - BULLECOURT road.	
		2.55	D/152 2 Guns on U8a 20.65 + U8a 35.30. 2 Rds p.g.f.m. for 10 minutes	
		3.6	C/152 reopened on PRINCE + OLDENBURG lane 1 Rd p.g.f.m. two minutes	
		3.8	D/152 complete battery section opened on UB5 with Lethal shell as ordered by B.M. C.R.A.	
		3.13	Inf Bde requested barrage down from U.7.75.40 to 80.80 to be shelled, as bombing party was attempting to push down the trench	
			B/160 lifted on above 3 Rds p.g.f.m. for 10 minutes + 1 Rd p.g.f.m for 5 minutes	
			Left Batth. reported enemy rally and safe in PRINCE trench + OLDENBURG lane + had retired on the Garrisons of FONTAINE	
		3.35		
		3.55	Enemy sent up single red, single green, double red + double green rockets from behind his front system. No apparent action followed.	
			Enemy again requested Bde. be brought down PRINCE trench + OLDENBURG lane	
		4.10	C/152 1 Section on each of the above 3 Rds p.g.f.m for 10 minutes + 1 Rd p.g.f.m	

Army Form C. 2118.

WAR DIARY
or
INTELLIGENCE SUMMARY.
(Erase heading not required.)

Instructions regarding War Diaries and Intelligence Summaries are contained in F. S. Regs., Part II. and the Staff Manual respectively. Title pages will be prepared in manuscript.

Place	Date	Hour	Summary of Events and Information	Remarks and references to Appendices
16 Div Area	20/11/17		for 15 minutes. B/160 5 3 gard on the +12 to +16 Barrage line on Left Battn Front only 2 Rds t 2 p.m. for 25 minutes	
		4.15 p.m.	S.O.S. received from L.O. (Capt J. Fanos M.C.) at 49 4 Inf Bde A/152 dropped 200* on S.O.S. lines, C/152 & B/160 continued as above (4.10) D/152 S.O.S. fronts	
		4.30	A/152 ceased fire on report from Right Battn that S.O.S. was not required	
		4.45	C & D/152 & B/160 slowed down rate of fire. Left Battn specially requested Barrage to be continued at a slow rate, as they noted very short in Personnel & had no rly on Enemy barrage 46 a great extent	
		5.45	Ceased fire on report from Left Battn that all was quiet	
		5.45 & onwards very quiet		
		6.50	Our trenches and just 16 D m orders	
		9.30		

Army Form C. 2118.

WAR DIARY
or
INTELLIGENCE SUMMARY.
(Erase heading not required.)

Instructions regarding War Diaries and Intelligence Summaries are contained in F.S. Regs., Part II. and the Staff Manual respectively. Title pages will be prepared in manuscript.

Place	Date	Hour	Summary of Events and Information	Remarks and references to Appendices
16 Dn Area	29/4/17		Bar 29.36 Ther 50. Visibility bad all day	
		4.15 am	Barking opened fire on S.O.S. lines at request of Left Battn. who started S.O.S. signal had been sent up	
		4.20	Left Battn reported that S.O.S was a mistake, but wanted a slow barrage on PRINCE trench & OLDENBURG Lane. C/152, 2 guns PRINCE, 2 guns OLDENBURG Lane. B/160 4 guns on S.O.S. line on Left Battn front searching back for 500ˣ. D/102, 1 How V8a20.65 + 1 How V8a 35.30. Burst of 2 pdr gun fire every 10 minutes for an hour.	
		3 am	French Wyl 8.2. heavily shelled by 77mm & 10.5cm How. B.M., R.A. informed & Counter Barking work got on.	
		5.7	Left Battn requested Arty to stand to at 6am	
		6.5	Hostile arty very active on new front & support lines & old front & support lines. C & D/152 & B/160 opened fire as at 1 pdr to 9 am for 15 minutes	
		6.25	Left Battn reported all quiet	

Army Form C. 2118.

WAR DIARY
or
INTELLIGENCE SUMMARY.
(Erase heading not required.)

Instructions regarding War Diaries and Intelligence Summaries are contained in F. S. Regs., Part II. and the Staff Manual respectively. Title pages will be prepared in manuscript.

Place	Date	Hour	Summary of Events and Information	Remarks and references to Appendices
16 Div Area	21/4/17	6.45 a.m.	S.O.S signals sent up all along the front A.C + D/152 + B/160 opened fire on S.O.S lines at rate laid down.	
		7.2	Right Battn reported very heavy barrage on our front system. Nothing definite known. Had enemy refused to be attempting to counter attack. The quick rate of fire was resumed.	
		7.10	Right Battn reported much quieter, but still wanted the Barrage at a slow rate kept up.	
		7.16	Left Battn reported no enemy infantry action had materialised on D Battn front + batteries on the Efront could "cease fire" A.C + D/152 ceased fire	
		7.21	Right Battn reported "all quiet" + no enemy infantry action had taken place. B/160 ceased fire.	
		2 pm to 6.6 pm	D/152 fired 1 Rd to 9 to hour on S.O.S. front + also on sus T.M emplacements (from captured German map) 18 Rds searching east of S.O.S lines on Grouse zone 2 bursts per hour of 3 Rds gun fire	

T2134. Wt. W708-776. 500000. 4/15. Sir J. C. & S.

WAR DIARY
or
INTELLIGENCE SUMMARY.
(Erase heading not required.)

Army Form C. 2118.

Place	Date	Hour	Summary of Events and Information	Remarks and references to Appendices
16 Dn Area	21/4/17	3.30 p.m.	D/152 Sunken road U.8.a.9.2.20 to U.6.c.10.4.7, burst of fire as ordered by B.M., R.A.	
		4	180 Bde. R.F.A. hook over Left Group front & 180 R.F.A. A, C + D/152 + B/160 became superimposed on the front covered by 180 & 23rd R.F.A. (Left Group) S.O.S. lines from 4 p.m. became - 18 pdr U.14.7.20.40 to U.7.8.50.40. D/152 S.O.S. points remained the same.	
		6 p.m. onwards	Night firing as ordered in 16th D.A., R.H./215.	
	22/4/17	Bas.29.35 Thus 51	Verdelly hrs.	
		5.20 a.m.	S.O.S. Batteries fired on S.O.S. lines. Enemy put down a heavy barrage on our front system.	
		5.40	Scotch fire. Right + Left Infty Battns reported that the Boche had not attempted to attack on their front but believed they had on the right. Cdr Grant.	
		12 a.m. 1.6 p.m.	Harassing fire as ordered in B.M. D194.	
		12.30 p.m.	Right Battn (2/4th Lemon) reported much movement in trench.	

WAR DIARY
or
INTELLIGENCE SUMMARY.
(Erase heading not required.)

Army Form C. 2118.

Place	Date	Hour	Summary of Events and Information	Remarks and references to Appendices
16 Dec Area	22/11/17		running through U.8 central & O.9a. 18 fds. howitzers enclosed thus	
			trench on 5th. harassing fire	
		6 p.m to 6 a.m	Ng. hd. firing as ordered by B.M., R.A.	
	23/11/17		Bar 29.33 Ther 53 Visibility Excellent	
		8 a.m	Low flying enemy plane flew over our trench	
			Day firing. In following shoots were carried out	
		3 p.m	D/152 CRUX trench from O.9.a.90.25 to U.9d.0.0. 3 fds gun fired B.x.	
		4.30	D/152 OUSE lane O.3.c.6.63 to 50.40 50 fds what as squd at Juderle	
		5	A/152 OUNCE trench in U.2d. C/152 Roads east of FONTAINE, in U.2d. and	
			trenches north of OUNCE trench. B/160 UNA lane in U.2d. & trenches N. of OUNCE trench	
			3 fds 9 a.m fire	
			Ng hd firing was carried out as follows	
		6 p.m to 8 a.m	18 fds howitzers on huns searched U.2.c & d. 45° fds per hour	
		9 - 10 a.m	D/152 OUNCE trench & OUSE lane 40 fds B.x.	
		5 a.m to 6.30 a.m	" " 60 " "	

Army Form C. 2118.

WAR DIARY
or
INTELLIGENCE SUMMARY.
(Erase heading not required.)

Place	Date	Hour	Summary of Events and Information	Remarks and references to Appendices
16 Div Area	25/11/17	6.45 p.m	Left Battn reported enemy shelling front system heavily & asked for retaliation. D/152 on T.M. emplacements at U.26.d.45.45.etc. 3 Rds per How per minute for 5 minutes & 1 Rd. p.h. p.m for 15 minutes B/152 by permission of O.C. Right Group, 34th D.A. Fired 2 guns on KANDY trench 3 Rds p.h.p.m. for 3 minutes & 1 Rd p.g. p.m for 15 minutes. L.O. (180th Bde R.F.A.)	
		7.5	S.O.S. signal went up on Left Group front. Batteries opened immediately also Bestified at	
		7.15	No defensive were available from L.O., so a slow trade (1 Rd. p.h 9 p.m) was kept up on S.O.S. lines	
		7.20	Enemy T.M's again active D/152 2 Rds per How per minute on T.M. emplacements	
		7.33	Situation still obscure, reduced rate of fire to 1 Rd. p.h g.to. 2 minutes.	
		7.37	L.O. Left Battn. reported all quiet. Batteries ceased fire	
		8.25	Lamp signalling seen at U.67.9.6.	

Army Form C. 2118.

WAR DIARY
or
INTELLIGENCE SUMMARY.
(Erase heading not required.)

Instructions regarding War Diaries and Intelligence Summaries are contained in F.S. Regs., Part II. and the Staff Manual respectively. Title pages will be prepared in manuscript.

Place	Date	Hour	Summary of Events and Information	Remarks and references to Appendices
16 Div Area	24/4/16		Bar 29.12 Ther 60 Visibility good	
		10 am to 6 pm	Day firing A/152 USHER trench from U9c.15.20 → Eastward	
			B/160 OLDENBURG Lane " U8a.36.36 → N. Eastward	
			C/152 OUNCE trench " U2d.20.35 + N. Eastwards	
			100 Rounds per battery fired on any & sundry throughout the day	
			D/152 COPSE trench from U8c.35.35 to U8d.70.70. 200 Rds Bx during the day	
		7pm to 7am	Night firing Searched OUNCE, USHER & CROFT trenches	
			& tracks in U2d & U9c. 40 Rounds per hour	
		10 am	Intermixed movement in U4, chiefly down ULSTER trench	
			Engaged by A/152 & heaved also dispersed	
		12 noon	R. Party of 20 men seen at U4a.9.3. A/152 fired on & dispersed it	
		1.5 pm	Party of 50 men in U5a, fired on & dispersed	
		3 to 4 pm	Considerable movement seen on road running N.E. out of FONTAINE	
			C/152 observed many parties on this road	

WAR DIARY or INTELLIGENCE SUMMARY

Army Form C. 2118.

Place	Date	Hour	Summary of Events and Information	Remarks and references to Appendices
In Sun Area	25/10/17		Bar 28.51 Ther 44 Visibility excellent	
		5.20 am	Opened on S.O.S lines just east of Left Battery	
		5.40	Ceased fire on S.O.S lines. No enemy infantry attack launched	
		9 am	Numerous small parties in U3 & U9. Engaged by C/152 with good effect	
		2 pm	Movement seen in front of CROWS NEST & CHATEIRN WOOD engaged by A/152	
			Considerable movement throughout the day on HENDECOURT - DURY Road, also in U3, U4, U9	
			Dumps observed at 05c 60 50.	
	26/10/17		Bar 29.24 Ther 40 Visibility poor.	
		6 am to 6 pm	Day firing. Batteries searching east of CRUX trench, 100 Rds per battery.	
		12.30	Movement in U8c fired on by C/152	
		2.30 pm	Party observed by C/152 in U8c. Small parties seen in U3 & U3 during the day. Lamp signalling again seen at U.1639.6	

Army Form C. 2118.

WAR DIARY
or
INTELLIGENCE SUMMARY.
(Erase heading not required.)

Instructions regarding War Diaries and Intelligence Summaries are contained in F.S. Regs., Part II. and the Staff Manual respectively. Title pages will be prepared in manuscript.

Place	Date	Hour	Summary of Events and Information	Remarks and references to Appendices
16 Div Area	26/11/17	10.30 am	Hostile fire 6. 10.5 c/m Howt on U14c	
		1.50 pm	6. 10.5 c/m - T117	
		2 to 2.12 pm	U3d + U30a heavily shelled with 10.5c/m Howrs	
		9 pm to 9 am	Night firing as ordered on R1/222 40 Fold fus Rds	
	27/11/17		Bar 28.84 Ther 48 Weather fine.	
		9 am to 6 pm	Day firing as ordered	
		6 pm to 6 am	Night firing as ordered on tracks on U9a + U3c 300 Rounds	
		11 am	Movement Van U3d fired on by C/152 + dispersed	
		11.45	" " - U9a " " " "	
		12.12 pm	" " - U9b " " " "	
		12.25	" " - U9c " " " "	
		1 pm	The HENDECOURT - DURY Road was much used during the day. A horse + cart on this road was engaged by 18 Pdr + knocked out. Hostile fire 15" Rounds 10.5c/m Howt on trenches on U1a.	

T2134. Wt. W708-776. 500000. 4/15. Sir J.C. & S.

Army Form C. 2118.

WAR DIARY
or
INTELLIGENCE SUMMARY.
(Erase heading not required.)

Instructions regarding War Diaries and Intelligence Summaries are contained in F.S. Regs., Part II. and the Staff Manual respectively. Title pages will be prepared in manuscript.

Place	Date	Hour	Summary of Events and Information	Remarks and references to Appendices
16 Div Area	28/11/17		Bar. 29.20 Ther. 51. Visibility poor.	
		4.30 pm	Day firing as ordered. A. & C/152 + B/160 + 152 Bde H.Q. moved from 16th Div Area to trenches in 34th Div Area. A/152 to new position T.4.b.7.0. C/152 were prepared to fire on S.O.S. but not called on.	
HENINEL	29		Bar. 29.36 Ther. 51. Visibility good.	
		4 pm	Day firing. A & C/152 Registered Zone front & S.O.S. line. 152nd Bde R.F.A. became Right Group. 34th D.A. under Lt Col Thompson D.S.O. & became responsible for the defence of the Right Inf Bde Front.	
		6 am to 11 am	Neg Ll firing A/152 H.Q. at U.T.a.5.0 - 11.7.1.3.	
			B/152 - 03.c.8.3. - 03.c.9.6.	
		3 am to 6 am	C/152 - 02.b.8.63 - 02.b.9.85.	
			45 rounds per battery.	
		11 pm to 3 am	Fired on supposed relief of enemy Support Batts.	

Army Form C. 2118.

WAR DIARY
or
INTELLIGENCE SUMMARY.
(Erase heading not required.)

Instructions regarding War Diaries and Intelligence Summaries are contained in F.S. Regs., Part II. and the Staff Manual respectively. Title pages will be prepared in manuscript.

Place	Date	Hour	Summary of Events and Information	Remarks and references to Appendices
HENINEL	29/11/17	9.30 am to 1 pm	Hostile fire. 400 15cm Hows on B/152 howitzers (N.29 d.45.65) Z.A. opened to regisger just two rounds Walford carried on. 2 Gun pits, mess cook house & Disainville line hit & destroyed. Gun No 1036 knocked but not damaged in action again same day. Gun No 5531 badly damaged & sent to I.O.M.	
		7.30 pm	D/152 left 16th Div Area & returned to Peronne (N.28 B.65.50) reported O.K.	
	30/11/17	Bar 29.32 Ther 51	Visibility fair. Day firing. D/152 registered Dashen front & S.O.S lines L.O. reported Right Company, Right Battn front line heavy shelled. A/152 ordered to open fire on enemy front system at 1 pm F.G. to m.	
		5.45 am		
		6.10	A/152 ceased fire	
		10.45	Right Group ordered to "stand by" on Adeed Jacob 16"NW front being heavily shelled	

Army Form C. 2118.

WAR DIARY
or
INTELLIGENCE SUMMARY.
(Erase heading not required.)

Place	Date	Hour	Summary of Events and Information	Remarks and references to Appendices
HENINEL	30/11/17	10.58 to 10.58 am.	At request of 180 Bde R.F.A. A, B + D/152 fired on target "Aunt Sarah".	
		11.13 to 11.22 am	9.13" dispersed 5" Gds on small party at 7327	
		10 am	Night firing 18 fph on following bridges over the	
		6 pm to 6 am	SENSEE in trenches O32 d 80.25, O32 d 60.45, O32 d 96.45 O29 c 45 40, 500 Rounds	
		8 pm to 10.10 pm	D/152 on selected H.Q.s at V 2a 5.0 + O 32 c 8.3 109 Rounds Hostile fire above normal, intermittent shelling strong point the day chiefly on C.T.s	

Lt. Thorpe
J. Selecta
R.F.A.

WAR DIARY or INTELLIGENCE SUMMARY

Army Form C. 2118.

157 Bde RFA VA 23

Place	Date	Hour	Summary of Events and Information	Remarks and references to Appendices
HEBUTERNE	Dec 1		Bar 29.94 Ther 42° Visibility fair. Our fire. Registrations & calibrations. Night firing 6PM to 6AM 279 Rds 18 pdrs & 120 Rds 4.5" How on roads from CHERISY Cross Rds along CHERISY VIS Rds to maximum range & harassing between above road & SENSEE River. Hostile fire. Normal 6.t 7.30 AM one machine. 8AM 4 over own lines. Movement Nil. Ammo exp A241 2X 332 BX 124	
	2nd		Bar 29.94 Ther 40° Visibility good. Our fire. Registration by Batteries during day. 9.45AM 2.10PM 2.30PM Small working parties dispersed. 6PM to 6AM Night firing 10pdr Troops C.O. 79M. Hostile fire. 10.30AM 20 Rds 10.59m How on Trench in O.25d. 11.25AM 14yds 10.59m How in vicinity West O.P. 3PM 10Rds 10.59m How on Trench O.25.E. Movement 9AM 2 Men carrying shutters disappeared in UPTON QUARRY 10.20AM 2 Trollies on Light Railway at 17E 14.5AM 7 Men seen carrying water in O.29.c.d. Considerable movement seen on HENDECOURT DRURY Rd during the day. Ammo Exp A2125 AX155 BX140. Leave. 2/Lieut D. Thomas proceeded on 10 days leave 9 — F. Ward proceed to fee & attached to D/152	
	3rd		Bar 29.92 Ther 41° Visibility good. Our fire. 2PM to 3.30PM D/152 70 Rds Calibrated on O.32 a.6.9. 3PM B/152 Registered enemy frontline W.1.b 6PM to 6AM Night firing as per R.S.O.O. 7N13. Hostile fire 9.30PM to 11PM 50 Rds. 10.59m How in vicinity HENIN E school. 11.30PM 15Rds 10.59m How in ERRECOURT Sugft. Trench. Movement 7.30PM Several Bosche carrying stretchers seen about O.9a. Usual movement on HENDECOURT-DRURY Rd.	

Army Form C. 2118.

WAR DIARY
or
INTELLIGENCE SUMMARY.
(Erase heading not required.)

Page 8.

Place	Date	Hour	Summary of Events and Information	Remarks and references to Appendices
HENINEL	3rd		E.A. 9 A.M. Flew over our lines at low altitude for 15 minutes. 10.11.15 P.M. 2 E.A. over our lines. 11.20 A.M. & 1.45 Miscellaneous 10.55 A.M. & 11.15 A.M. 2 Enemy dumps exploded in FEAUCOURT Area. Ammn Exp. A 301, I.X 315, B x 13h.	
do	4th		Bar. 29.44. Ther 39°. Visibility Fair. Our Fire. Registrations carried out during the day. 12.53 P.M. Working party at WESTER TRENCH U.3.C.d. dispersed by 3/1152. Night. 1.20 P.M. Working party at WESTER TRENCH U.6.B.9.1. dispersed by 3/1152 M.P.B. Night Firing as per R.F.O.O. 70 M. Hostile Fire. 11.40 A.M. 10.5 pm How. shelled PELICAN Dug't TRENCHES 1.50 P.M. 10.5 pm How. shelled 7.6A. M.7.5. Movement 2.50 P.M. Horse & Red Cross Wagon on HENDECOURT, DRURY Road + usual movement at all. Much movement observed in O.29 b. during afternoon. Miscellaneous 2.30 2.A. Enemy Dump Blown up in UPTON Quarry. Ammn Expt. A 362, I X 344, B X 209. Capt. H.J. WISE M.C. returned from leave after extension to Dec'r 2/Lieut. L.C. Young 3/1152 proceeded to England on 14 day's leave.	
do	5th		Bar. 29.30. Ther 38. Visibility poor. Our Fire. Bays opened fire as per 3H.Dot no 0307. Scarcd fire at 10.40 P.M. Raiders failed to get on enemy lines owing to Machine Gun fire. Heavy Trench Howithers 4 P.M. to 8 A.M. Night firing as per R.F.O.O. 70 M. Hostile Fire. 10.30 to 2.30 P.M. Shrapnel at 2 minute intervals fired on & around Dominicle line in HENINEL, 9.21 M. to N.2 M. 10.5 pm How shelled C.25 C.15 3.15 P.M. 15.20. 10.5 pm How in N.35.6. Movement Individual movement in O.34.6. O.35 a. throughout the day. 5 P.M. Lamp Signalling from house in FEAUCOURT at O.23 a. 8.8. Ammn Expt A 226, I X 204, B x 171.	

Army Form C. 2118.

Instructions regarding War Diaries and Intelligence Summaries are contained in F.S. Regs., Part II. and the Staff Manual respectively. Title pages will be prepared in manuscript.

WAR DIARY or INTELLIGENCE SUMMARY

Army Form C. 2118.

Instructions regarding War Diaries and Intelligence Summaries are contained in F. S. Regs., Part II. and the Staff Manual respectively. Title pages will be prepared in manuscript.

(Erase heading not required.)

Place	Date	Hour	Summary of Events and Information	Remarks and references to Appendices
HENINEL	6th		Bar 29.42. Ther 40. Visibility fair. **Gun Fire** 1 PM Working party at function ULSTER. OK. Trenches disposed by 4/1152. 4 PM Working party O33.6.3.5. dispersed by 4/1152. Night Firing 7 PM to 9 PM & 11 PM As per Night Group G.O. No 16. **Hostile Fire** Normal. **Movement** 10. 11 AM Small parties seen on HENDECOURT - DURY Road proceeding in direction DURY. E.A. fairly active. 2/12 Pte Angell returned from 10 days leave. Ammo Exp Z 1356. AX 680. BX 1126	
-do-	7th		Bar 29.25. Ther 40. Visibility good. **Gun Fire** Registration. Night Firing as per Night Group O.O. No 17. **Hostile Fire** Normal throughout night 4/8th Inns about 60 77 NM & 10.5 PM. Hostile Etc fairly active in HENINEL. **Movement** Usual movement on HENDECOURT Dury Road. Etc. Ammo Exp Z 136. AX 150. BX 130	
-do-	8th		Bar 29.20. Ther 47. Visibility Low. **Gun Fire** 1 PM 4:30 PM 4:45 PM Night Group fired as per A.H.D.A. O/3/4. 2.10 PM 4/1152 fired on men working round a Brazier at CROWS NEST. Night Firing as per Night Group O.O. No 18 (night 8/9). **Hostile Fire** Normal. 6 AM. 20. 10.5 PM. How on A.A. Battery in O.29.c. During night 8/9th about 25. 10.5 PM into HENINEL. **Movement** 11.15 AM flash signalling at 22a.R.2 from DEXTER. E.2 No. 6. 2/Lieuts A.E. Lowter (B/152) & W.S. Dyer (B/152) proceeded to ABBEVILLE for Section Commanders Course assembling 9th Inst. Ammo Exp Z 260. AX 209. BX 72.	
-do-	9th		Bar 29.10. Ther 47. Visibility Low. **Gun Fire** About 200 men seen in O10. c & d. 4/1152 fired 40 rds in three squares. LightWar Regt result unknown 9.2 M. 2.7 M seen working on parapet at U.1.67.2 3/1152 fired 5 rds 9.2 M. Working party in	

WAR DIARY or INTELLIGENCE SUMMARY

Army Form C. 2118.

Page 4

Place	Date	Hour	Summary of Events and Information	Remarks and references to Appendices
HENINEL	9th	Contd	ULSTER trench at U.8.b.0.3. fired on & dispersed by B/152. 3.20 P.M. A/152 fired 20 rds on enemy dumps at C.23.c.3.8. doing considerable damage to material. Night firing as per R.F. OO 7820 (night 9/10). *Hostile Fire* Normal. *Movement* No fixed on in our line'. *Ammo Exp.* A.291. A.X.276. B.X.114. 2/Lieut H.S. Bell M.C. (D/152) returned from Hospital was posted to B/152. Lieut Col W.F. Thompson D.S.O. R.A. at 9 A.M. & proceeded to R.E.H.Q. Major P.S. MyBurgh took over Right Group at 9 A.M.	
-do-	10th		Bar. 22.34. Ther. 39. Visibility good. *Air Fire* 7.30 A.M. 12 Noon 4.15 P.M. as per 3d. L.D.A. 7 PM 0/315. 11.30 to 12 P.M. D/152 engaged M.B.V. at 0.32.b 0.2.50 with aerial observation. 12.10 Fired only 1 observed 12 Noon C/152 30 rds. registration. 2.30 P.M. C/152 10.2.16 on movement in 0.28 c.7.0. Night firing as per R.F. 00. 7.821. *Hostile Fire* Normal. 12 P.M. A few 10.5.9.m How. in HENINEL. During night 10/11 about 200 10.5% So. HE into HENINEL. *Movement* Much above normal. *E.A.* above normal. *Ammo Exp* A.207. A.X. 218. B.X. 115. A/26 & 117 Batteries 26 Bde A.F.A. joined Right Group. Lt. Col. J.B. Kenton C.M.G. became O.C. Right Group at 9 P.M.	
-do-	11th		Bar. — Ther. — Visibility indifferent. *Air Fire* 6.40 A.M. A.B.D/152 fired on 488187 "JACOSE" at request of "JACOSE". N.E.N. C/152 fired 2.165 on movement in 0.296.85. Night firing 480 rds on CHERISY. V.15. road from 0.32.c.7.0. to C.23.a.0.7. *Hostile Fire* Normal. 2.A.17. to 3.30 A.M. 10 10.5.9.m Gas on these H.Q. *Movement* Normal. *E.A.* 6.30 A.M. Low flying planes flew over our front line during. *Ammo Exp.* A.391. A.X. 560. B.X.205.	

WAR DIARY
or
INTELLIGENCE SUMMARY

Army Form C. 2118.

page 5.

Place	Date	Hour	Summary of Events and Information	Remarks and references to Appendices
HENINEL	12		Bar. 29.20. Ther. 34. Visibility Poor. Our Fire. 2.30 PM 6/152 fired 37 Rds. movement at C.21.a.7.5. Night Firing 4.90 Rds on CHERISY & vis. ROADS from C.32.c.7.0. to C.58.c.6.7. C.24.a.8.2.2. Enemy fired as per 8th D.A. 0/13/15. Hostile Fire. Above normal 4.24 to 8.24 N.28. N.34. N.35. Heavily shelled with 77 m/m, 10.5 + 15 c/m Pro-Stoll Between 2000/3000 rds and continued on & off throughout the night. 12.30 P.M. to 2.30 P.M. Heavy T.M. active on our front and also T.M's were observed firing from FONTAINE WOOD. Movement. Nil. E.A. Nil. Ammn Exp. 2400. LX.500. BX.205.	
do	13		Bar. 29.40. Ther. 26. Visibility Bad. Our Fire. 2.24 to 2 P.M. 90/m 34 K.D.it 0/13/15. 4.2 P.M. fired m 10.5 m orders from R.t. H.a. False Alarm. Night Firing 290 rds on CHERISY v/s Road from 0.32.c.7.0. to 0.28.a.0.7. Hostile Fire 12.30 PM to 2.30 P.M. Heavy T.M. × very active on our front trenches. 12 P.M. 30.15 c/m How in N.34. o.v.c. During night HENINEL shelled by 77 m/m v 10.5 c/m gas-sell. Movement. Nil E.A. Nil. Ammn Exp. A.323 A.X.229. B.X.140.	
do	14		Bar. 29.35. Ther. 46. Visibility Poor. Our Fire. Night Firing × on 13th. Hostile Fire. Normal. 3 A.M. 20. 10.5 c/m How in FOSTER AVENUE. Movement Nil Ammn Exp. A.173. A.X.268 BX.165.	
do	15		Bar. 29.35. Ther. 53. Visibility good. Our Fire. 12.15 P.M. A/152 fired on movement on ULSTER TRENCH. 1.30 P.M. 6/152 fired m 4 7 m at STAR CORNER. 2.45 P.M. B/152 Regiment movement in 0.35.6. 6.24 to 8.24. 4.80 rds 18 rds 4.5 How on trucks in V.28.a.6. Hostile Fire 5 P.M. 10.5 c/m How on BROWN. SU.22. P.T. Movement Normal. E.A. 10.4 A.M. 40. 11 am 12. 6.P.M. crossed our lines engaged by A.A. Ammn Exp. A.195 A.X.258 B.X.120.	
do	16		Bar. 28.72. Ther. 35. Visibility Poor. Our Fire. Night Firing 4.90 Rds 1 P.M. + 4.5 How a.m. 15 " Hostile Fire. Normal. J.15 A.M. 20. 77 m/m on cemetery A/152. M.&M. few light 7.77 on FOSTER AVENUE	

WAR DIARY
or
INTELLIGENCE SUMMARY.

Army Form C. 2118.

Page 6.

Place	Date	Hour	Summary of Events and Information	Remarks and references to Appendices
HENINEL	16	10am	Movement Nil. E.A. Above normal. Ammn Exp A 283 AX 369 BX 152.	
do	17		Casualties Wounded 77052440 Pte Ward E T. 3/452. Jan. 28.71. Sha. 35. Visibility very bad. Cur Fire 7.30AM 8AM 2.45AM & PM 4.30. 4.35 PM no. per 34 & D.2 OB/6. Night Firing a/c on night 16/17 Hostile Fire below normal. During night a few 77 m/m + 10.5 g/m gas & HE into HENINEL Movement Nil. E.A. Nil. Ammn Exp. A 296. CX 400. BX 150.	
do	18		Jan. 29.27. Sha. 31. Visibility very bad Cur Fire 3.30 PM troop concentration on "SUN QUARRY. 3.45 PM troop concentration 18 pdrs SUN. QUARRY 4.15 How. MOON QUARRY 6 PM 6. 6.12 Night Firing a/c 17/18 Hostile Fire. 4.30. 6 PM 40 77 m/m EARLSCOURT TRENCH E.A. Nil. Movement Nil. Ammn Exp. A 334. CX 413 BX 156. 2/Lieut D. Thomas returned from 14 days leave.	
do	19		Jan. 29.26. Sha. 34. Visibility Very bad Cur Fire. Night Firing 4.20 4.50 12.pds. 4.55 am on tracks W.20. O27. O32. O33 Hostile Fire. 12.30 PM. 8.15 PM. 3.50 PM 3.50 PR Area Shoots on WANCOURT - HENINEL Movement Nil E.A. Nil. Ammn Exp. v2 433 AX 822 BX 148. 2/Lieut P.C. Young returned from 14 days leave. Casualties Wounded 77042678 E. Lowrie.	
do	20		Jan. 29.17. Sha. 29. Visibility very bad Cur Fire 9.2AM 12.7AM troop fired as per D.L.O. 13/6. Night Firing a/c night 19/20 & Movement Nil. E.A. Nil. Ammn Exp. A 357. AX 699. BX 128.	
do	21		Jan. 29.09. Sha 27. Visibility bad Cur Fire Night Firing a/c for 20/21 Hostile Fire 9 pm into N 28. Movement + E.A. Nil. No 6 Anz. (22nd) About 200 77m/m + 10.5 Shr. + HE into N.28. 2/Lieut P.L. Bell (9/152) proceeded on 14 day leave. Ammn Exp A 155 AX 773 BX 146	
do	22		Jan. 29.33. Sha. 32. Visibility Improved Cur Fire night firing a/c for 21st Hostile Fire E.A. 10.30 AM 2 planes over our lines. Engaged by A.A. Capt Geo Brunt (Capt.) handed over to Capt Belmont (Capt) 26 Bde & proceeded to take up the Normal Movement Nil E.A. his residence with D.T.M.O.	

WAR DIARY or INTELLIGENCE SUMMARY

Army Form C. 2118.

page 7.

Place	Date	Hour	Summary of Events and Information	Remarks and references to Appendices
HENINEL	23		Bde H.Q. out of action. Nothing of interest. Lieut E.C. Robertson D/153 returned from Holly's leave.	
	24		do	
	25		do	
	26		do Lieut-Col. W.G. Thompson D.S.O. became O.R.A. in Bdier. Lieut Col. Kinloo. C.M.G. 26th Bde. F.F.A. became O/c R.A. in Bdier. Major Rt. Lovell M.C. became Right Group Commander (temporary)	
	27		Jan 27.4.2. Ther 33 Visibility Poor. Our Fire 6 P.M. to 6 A.M. Road C.9.e. 80.95- C.9.a 85.20. CHERISY-HENDECOURT Road. Double track O.32 & 9540. Hostile Fire. Normal. Movement 1 P.M. 2 parties of men carrying full sacks moving HENDECOURT Rest, 10 men in each party. 2 P.M. 3 Wagons on DRORF LANE stopped at CROWS NEST men got out of each. E.Z. fairly active. A 32 A X 88.	
			Jan 27.9.0. Ther 37 Visibility fair. Our Fire. Night Firing as night 26th Hostile Fire. Normal. Movement 7.30 A.M. 6 S.E. Wagons on DERY-HENDECOURT Road appeared to offload at U.6.d.50. Engaged by 60 pdrs. E.Z. Normal. Annie Coy A 152 A X 36 B X 20	
	28		Jan 28.36 Ther 35 Visibility Poor. Our Fire 9 P.M. to 5 P.M. open 7 H D.2 O/13/17 N X 20 6 P.M. to 6 A.M. Night Firing as 27th Hostile Fire 11.30 A.M. & 9 P.M. Hows. wrecked WANCOURT about 50 rds. Movement R.L. very active. 12 Noon 1.6.E. through dozen in vicinity O/13/17 Night Group Enemy Amm? Expd. A 232 R.E. 60 B X 02 Movement 10 A.M. Right Group became Enemy Amm? Expd. A 232 R.E. 60 B X 02 Miscellaneous.	
	29		Jan 29.10 Ther 37 Visibility Poor. Our Fire as per O/13/17 Night Enemy Road O.27.e 52.92 6.0.27.n 80.20. CHERRY FRYSE Road along SEMSEE. Hostile Fire 3.15 P.M. 7 B 4 Shelled 4.15 P.M. How E.Z. 11 A.M. 2 planes over our lines 11.30 A.M. 1 plane over our lines. Not engaged by Anti Movement N.E. Amm? Expd A 259. A X 256. B X 128.	

Army Form C. 2118.

WAR DIARY
or
INTELLIGENCE SUMMARY.
(Erase heading not required.)

page 8

Place	Date	Hour	Summary of Events and Information	Remarks and references to Appendices
HENINEL	30		Bar 29.32 Ther 36. Visibility bad. Our Fire Counter Battery Night firing as for 29th 1.20 PM we fired "COUNTER CHERISY" Several Hostile Fire. normal 5.10 PM to 10.55 159m into HENINEL 1.45 PM HENINEL again shelled. Movement Nil. Casualties Died of wounds 7113489 Acgl H.T. Engine, killed 610352 L.R. McFarlane, Wounded 23954 L.R. Jacom, Ammo Exp.d A/152 A.X. 210 B.X 80. Lieut Sev Maclean proceeded on leave	
do	31		Bar 29.30 Ther 35. Visibility good. Our Fire. Night firing same as for 30th Lent 1.24 A/152. 12.5 to m Hostile Battery OD 15. 2 P.M 117. 12.5 to m Hostile Battery OD 65. 4.30 PM COUNTER CHERISY NORTH 20 rds per Battery. A.B.D/152. 4/26. 117. Hostile Fire. HENINEL & vicinity was shelled during morning. Movement Nil. E.L. Nil. Casualties killed N° 109571 L. Ward. Wounded 9229 F. Holton F. 29922 Bn. Parktone J. Ammo exp A/152. A.X. 253. B X 80. Lieut H.S. Bell proceeded on leave. Lieut T. Laing proceeded on Signalling Course at D.A.C.	

[152nd BRIGADE, R.F.A.]

Army Form C. 2118.

WAR DIARY
or
INTELLIGENCE SUMMARY.
(Erase heading not required.)

Month of January 1918

Army _____ R Brigade _____

Place	Date	Hour	Summary of Events and Information	Remarks and references to Appendices
HENINEL	Jan 1st		Ser 29.38 Ther 30. Weather Cold + Dull. Wind NE. Visibility Poor. Car fire 9.5 11.20 AM 2.40 PM Concentration Shoots as per Appendix. This AM Enemy Trench Morters CHERISY-VIS. Road. ENERGETIC. Main Road U.26. 69.95. W.26. 25.85. Hostile fire. Follow morning 10.2.24 -29 x ret -2 New fell on N.3rd. Movement. Must endeavor l movement seen around SENGUINTRY + UPTON WOOD. E.17. 11.25.x.13. 12.30 - 12.50 PM one in line. All engaged by 24 miscellaneous 3.50 - 24 on Road Crossroad at I.11.6.60.20. Pilot unmentioned. Count. Cap 4.172. 7.X.397. B.X.102.	
	2nd		Ser 29.53 Ther 34. Weather Cold + Fine. Visibility Good. Car Fire Nightfiring CHERISY VIS.Road. MICHEELS Road. CHERISY. HAM. STREET - Bridge. HENDECOURT Rd. 4/150 feet 10 AD 9 per hour throughout the night on U.16. 60-20 astrue the PLP fell. Hostile fire Enemy during night. 10-A.M, 10.30 - 11.15 x 2+4 Enemy First Series under HENIN at about 80.100. each burst. Eit. Normal. Movement. Wil. Miscellaneous. The P.P. Halfrecat Unlined was considerably damaged by our fire throughout the night. Court. Cap 4178. 7.X.400. B.X.92 Car fire 7.29.10 Enemy as per Appendix 2. Hostile fire Normal Ct. Entire Rescue throughout.	
	3rd		Ser 29.38 Ther 34. Weather Cold + Fine. Visibility Good. Normal C. HENINEL + enemy walked throughout the night. Movement Nil. Et. Nil. Rescue throughout morning reported by 12 Corps Cap 4178. 7.x.402. B.x.40	
	4th		Ser 29.69 Ther 31. Weather Cold + Fine. Visibility Good. Car fire Night firing ENERGY VIS Road. St. MICHAELS STATUE. 2.15-2.9 Ends at Men seen to man SEN. G.X.AP.Y. Hostile fire Below Normal C. 2.15.24. 7.4.8 active on SPORT. ST.STRRT at C.9.a.6. Rl Corp active Down x Cap I.Z 30 12X x 99 BX.93. Honors + Curtains New Jersey Homeward Reserve Mile C M.11.27.B. R.5.4. A. Wingfield L.25.244 Bond J.K. Munk from the London Regiment abed 11-1-9. Military hours 7 Cpls (Ryl Py) W. S. Heal. L.8114 Cpl B.T.Burton	
			Wastinoved T. Copl R.A. Johnstone. M7497. Br W. Jackson.	

WAR DIARY or INTELLIGENCE SUMMARY.

Army Form C. 2118.

(Erase heading not required.)

Instructions regarding War Diaries and Intelligence Summaries are contained in F. S. Regs. Part II. and the Staff Manual respectively. Title pages will be prepared in manuscript.

Page 2.

Place	Date 1918	Hour	Summary of Events and Information	Remarks and references to Appendices
HENINEL	Jan 5th		Bar. 29.60. Ther. 37. Weather Cold + Fine. Visibility Poor. Our Fire. Night Firing Bursts on Railway Crossing. O.32.d.42.00 - O.26.p.90. 50 rds per Battery; 20 rds 4'5"How. 11.15 P.M, 12.20 P.M. Engaged working party at O.28.c.25. 8.30, 10.2 P.M. Concentration shoots as per Appendix 1. Hostile Fire. Below normal on our front 10.15 P.M. Vickers Barrage on our Left stopped at 10.25 P.M. 6.25 P.M. Enemy Barrage at our right for 18 minutes. E.Z. 2 P.M. own aero lines. Ammn. Exp. 2.44. 4X. 244. BX. 20.	
	6th		Bar. 29.06. Ther. 36. Weather Cold + Fine. Visibility Bad. Our Fire. Night Firing 6 P.M. to 8 P.M. Bridge over SENSEE O.32.d.92.46. CHERRY BRIDGE. BOTTOM BRIDGE. 150 rds 18 pdr. Hostile Fire Normal. Movement much above normal in back areas. E.Z. Normal. Ammn. Exp. 175. 4X.437. BX.20. Course 2/Lieuts A.B.Porter + W.S. Dyer returned from 1 month's Gunnery Course at ABBEVILLE.	
	7th		Bar. 28.48. Ther. 38. Weather. Rain early morning, misty later. Visibility Bad. Our Fire Night Firing 6 to 9 P.M. O.32.d.92.46. O.33.a.03.10. CHERRY BRIDGE. Hostile Fire. HENINEL shelled slightly throughout the night. Course Major W.S. Pitt proceeded to 2/LEVEL on a 5 day - Fr. Course Leave. 2/Lieut. P.B. Bell returned from leave. April 4.P. Lawrence proceeded on leave. Ammn Exp. +Y.O. +X.209 BX.20.	
	8th		Bar. 28.68. Ther. 33. Weather Snow + Frost. Visibility Bad. Our Fire Night Firing 8.10 P.M. SUN QUARRY. N. edge of FONTAINE. 11.30 P.M. CHERRY (WOOD). St MICHAELS STATUE. 150 rds. 18 pdr. 20 rds 4'5" BX. Hostile Fire. Below Normal. E.Z. Nil. Course Major R.N. Shall returned from Sen Bourn + 2/LEVEL. Ammn Exp. 141. 4X 130. BX 20.	
	9th		Bar. 28.82. Ther. 35. Weather. Snow + Frost. Visibility Bad until Noon. Fine afterwards. Our Fire Night Firing Targets D + E of Appendix 3. 7.25. P.M. 12.05 P.M. 3.5 + 4.20 P.M as per Appendix 3. Hostile Fire. Nil. E.Z. Normal. Leave Capt F.B. Milligan proceeded on 14 day Leave. Ammn Exp. 2.124. 4X 239 BX 38.	

A 5834 Wt. W 4973 M 687 750,000 8/16 D.D. & L. Ltd. Forms/C.2118/13

WAR DIARY or INTELLIGENCE SUMMARY

Army Form C. 2118.

Page 3

Place	Date Jan 1918	Hour	Summary of Events and Information	Remarks and references to Appendices
HENINEL	10th		Bar. 29.34. Ther. 40. Weather. Thawing. Line + middle. Wind SW. Visibility Fair. Gun fire. Night firing 5.30 to 7.30 P.M. 50 rds 18 pdr on targets D + E of Appendix 3. 11.35 A.M. Working party dispersed at 11.0 C.T. 9. 80 rds on T+2 target. 0.5.C 70-23. O.5ds + 5. Fire opened from 11 EST O.P. Hostile fire. 5.30 to 7.30 P.M. 50 15 pm on N+C rd. Gtz. Mod? Own artillery engaged by Hos. Ammo Exp. 12 pdr. 190. 2X 326. 3X 18.	
	11th		Bar. 29.20. Ther. 43. Weather. Thawing Wet + Mild. Visibility Poor. Gun fire. Night firing 8.30 to 10 P.M. Targets CHERRY WOOD. Northern edge of FONTAINE WOOD. 50 rds 18 pdr. 10 rds + 3 yprs. 11 P.M. 12 noon Working party. 10 rds 0.5.C. 30.80. Hostile fire. Nil. Gtz. Nil. Ammo Exp. A.243. 2X 157. 3X 89.	
	12th		Bar. 28.94. Ther. 37. Weather. Fair. Wind NW. Visibility Fair. Gun fire. 1.30 rds B.C.B.R. on pack at D.2. 0.3/6 on Hostile Barrels. 13.21-22. Fire from 10 P.M. 10.7 P.M. Hostile fire. 10 P.M. to 6 A.M. 1 Ides 18 pdr fired 480 rds in cooperation with D/153. Movement 3.20 PM Ext. Below Normal. No retaliation on this point to our fire. Enemy parties in full marching order seen entering D.O.P. followed by Horse transport. Ammo Exp. 2 240. 2X 402. 3X4. BCBR 1300.	
	13th		Bar. 28.91. Ther. 35. Weather. Fine. Visibility Good. Gun fire. Night firing 8. 10.10 P.M. 150 rds on OTTER LANE + OBUS AVENUE. 25 + 8.30 x 9 A.9 pdr Appendix 3. 10.30 + 10.15 A.M. Working parties dispersed. 127. 335 + 4.41. 10 rds per Appendix 3. Hostile fire. Normal. 6.5.1. much above normal. Gas. 2 plant a London returned from leave. Ammo Exp. 2 84. 2X 280. 3 X Nil.	
	14th		Bar. 29.06. Ther. 35. Weather. Fine. Visibility Fair. Gun fire. Night firing. 5.15 to 7.15 P.M. C.32.c. O.32.d. O.2.c. 150 rds 18 pdr. 20 200 BX. Hostile fire. Below normal.	

WAR DIARY or INTELLIGENCE SUMMARY

Army Form C. 2118.

Page 4

Place	Date 1918	Hour	Summary of Events and Information	Remarks and references to Appendices
HENINEL	14th Jan		Contd E.Z. Below normal. Conference B.C. at 2.15. Inspection S.O.C. Division inspected Brigade Wagon Lines. Ammn Exp. 2161 A x 38, B x 20. Bar 28.72 Ther 48 Weather Wet Wind SW. Visibility Poor. Our Line. Night Enemy	
	15th		8.2 P.M 180 rds SOS QUARRY DAWN LANE. CHERISY BRIDGE + CHURCH PS0-9. S.P.M firds fire in and one Angle to 10-11 P.M 50 rds per battery on COUNTER CHERISY. 5.45-6 P.M 5 rds OF met same by all Batteries on SUPPORT LINE in rear over Zones 7/152 on O.26.C.60.40 + O.32.A.40.60. Hostile Fire. 6 AM 48.212 6.21 PM on FIRST AVENUE 9.30 AM after 77x 10.59 pm on N28d 4.212 to 5.15 AM 50 105 9m onto HENINEL E.Z. Nil. Leave. Capt. L. Esame proceeded on leave. Ammn Exp 2191 Ax 214 Bx 32	
	16th		Bar. 29.78 Ther 43. Weather Wet Wind SW Visibility Poor for Observation Good. Our fire. Night Enemy as per Appendix 4. Hostile Fire. None seen than during the next week. E.Z. nil Ammn Exp. 2140. Ax 85, Bx nil	
	17th		Bar. 29.03 Ther 40 Weather Icex Visibility Poor. Our fire. Night Enemy as per Appendix 4. 9.45 P.M SOS fire fire all Batteries COUNTER CHERISY NORTH Hostile Fire. 2.40 AM 12 ph 15 ph BROWN SUPPORT 5.12 M to 10 PM 10 xds 10.59 PM HENINEL + vicinity. The road between DEXTER R. HENINEL was shelled thorough the night. Movement considerable during afternoon on tracks near E.Z Nil. Lead. Lieut 4.S. McAllister proceeded on leave. Lieut G.W. Mather returned from leave. Ammn Exp. A51. 2 x 60. Bx 68	
	18th		Bar. 29.97. Ther 45. Weather Fair. Visibility Poor. Our Fire. Night Enemy as per Appendix 4. Working parties dispersed at 10.50, 11.20 A.M 3.15 P.M. M. 57.2 A + 3.15 P.M. 103 rds Bx at occupied Till improvement Dugouts sandbags	

Army Form C. 2118.

WAR DIARY
or
INTELLIGENCE SUMMARY.
(Erase heading not required.)

Page 5

Place	Date	Hour	Summary of Events and Information	Remarks and references to Appendices
HENNEL	18		Hostile fire. 2.30 & 5 AM. 10.30 pm. Hour on SUNKEN Road DEXTER & HENNEL. 9.30 to 9.50 AM BROWN SUPPORT CONCRETE + TANK Fenced. Shelled with 10.5 pm. 25 Kill. 4.40 PM 30 roads + 2 yd SHELLS in FONTAINE CROISSEUR 5. 2.30 PM 15.59 onto HENNEL. 6.9 PM 30 rds 15 pm in vicinity of DEXTER R. B.Z. N.C. Pivot Exp. A 85, 2 × 60 J × 20.	
	19th		Bar. 28/94. Ther 47. Weather Fair. Our Fire. Night Firing as per Appendix + 10.50 PM 20 rds on proposed T.M. Emplacements at C 26 d 95.57. Compliance observed. Hostile Fire 3.15 PM 20 mo rounds 2 PM + 4.30 PM. Working parties dispersed. Normal Movement Individual movement in back area out of range Normal. B.Z Active. Ammn Exp A 86 A× 62 J× 100	
	20th		Bar 28.78 Ther 54. Weather Fine Wind S.W. Visibility Good Our Fire Night Firing as per Appendix + Working parties fired at throughout the morning. 8.10 PM 20 rds. N.Z Battery COUNTER CB RISV SEC TH. Hostile Fire. Normal. Hennel was shelled intermittently with 4.2 + 5.9 till Noon afterwards HENNEL FRONT. B.Z Normal. Ammn. Exp. A 51 A× 104 J× 160.	
	21st		Bar. 29.11 Ther 43. Weather Fair with rain Wind S.W. Visibility Fair. Our Fire Harassing fire on tracks etc O.07, O.32 U.d, P.33. Working parties placed at throughout the day 4.45 to 5.45 + 6.15 PM 20 pm Yendica 4. Hostile Fire. 2.50 PM BROWN SUPPORT + CONCRETE shelled with 10.5 pm. B.Z Active Ammn Exp A 152. A× 201 J× 20. Fire Kind P's Reserve powered on leave	

WAR DIARY or INTELLIGENCE SUMMARY

Army Form C. 2118.

Page 6.

Place	Date 1918	Hour	Summary of Events and Information	Remarks and references to Appendices
KEMMEL	Mar 22nd		Bar. 28.92. Ther. 51. Weather Fine wind S.W. Visibility Good. Night firing as per Appendix 5. 1.30 A.M. Hostile T.M. engaged by 3/152 (B's A.9.5) Aeroplane observation 100 rds fired 12 hits scored. Considerable movement fired at during the day. Hostile fire normal. E.Z. very active. Amm. Exp. 1500 x 4.5" BX 40.	
	23rd		Bar. 29.22. Ther. 51. Weather Fair wind most. Visibility Fair. Our fire. Night firing as per Appendix 5. 10 PM 30 rds 4.5 How. + 20 rds 18 pdr at hostile T.M. O pd.S.5. Rg. 30 rds of infantry. Movement + working parties fired on throughout the day. Hostile fire below normal. 7.15 PM 13 rds 10.5 PM into PELICAN DUMP. EZ N.R. as per Appendix 5. 2.10 AM - 2.40 PM Green Rockets fired from CHERISY. No german movement observed. Amm Exp. 4123. 4 X 106. BX 101.	
	24th		Bar. 29.86. Ther. 62. Weather Fair. Visibility Good. Our fire. Night firing as per Appendix 5. 11.20 AM, 11.30 AM, 2.45-2.50 PM Working parties + movement dispersed. Hostile fire Normal. 10.55 AM till 3 PM constant shelling of H/152 certo 1590. Then about 300 rds in all. Damage 1 pistol + rod sight damaged. E.Z. Constant planes over during the day. Command Major PS Myburg M.C. assumed command of 152 Bty + Centre Group once Major R. Powell MC on leave. Amm Exp. 4163. 4 X 120. BX 61.	
	25th		Bar. 29.97. Ther. 47. Weather Fine Visibility Fair. Our fire. Night firing as per Appendix 5. 10.15 AM, 10 rds 13 rds + 10 rds 4.5 How on T.M. Opd D.2. retaliation for T.M. shelling of trenches in C.25. Hostile fire. 9.10.30 AM 30 rds H.M. on Co.5d + O.31.6.9.45 AM 30 rds 10.5 PM in N.35. E.Z. very active. Leave. Capt S.J. Milligan returned from leave. Amm Exp. 2110. 4 X 90. 3 X 50.	

Army Form C. 2118.

WAR DIARY
or
INTELLIGENCE SUMMARY.
(Erase heading not required.)

Instructions regarding War Diaries and Intelligence Summaries are contained in F.S. Regs., Part II. and the Staff Manual respectively. Title pages will be prepared in manuscript.

Page 1

Place	Date Jan 1918	Hour	Summary of Events and Information	Remarks and references to Appendices
HENINEL	26th		Bar. 29.93. Ther. 45. Weather Fine & Misty Visibility Bat. Our fire Night firing as per Appendix 5, 9.10 A.M. Enemy concentration 30 yds 18 pdr & 10 yds 8" on H.E. at O.26.d.83.63 as retaliation for T.M. shelling on O.25.d. Hostile fire Normal E.2. Nil. Ammn. Expr. A.91. A.70. B.X.95.	
	27th		Bar. 29.96 Ther. 41. Weather Fine & Misty. Our fire. Night firing as per Appendix 6. Hostile Fire Nil. E.2. Nil. Ammn. Expr. A.35 A.X.39 B.X.20	
	28th		Bar. 29.83 Ther. 39 Weather Fine & Misty. Our fire. Night firing as per Appendix 6. 3-29 P.M. 2p/sq. 100 yds on Hostile T.M. O.26.d.2.0. First 29 yds Aeroplane observation. 4 P.H 5 7 yds on Hostile T.M. O.26.d 96.15 Aeroplane registration. Hostile fire. Nil E.2 Cefino Ammn. Expr. A.70. A.X. 60 B.X. 20	
	29th		Bar. 9.83 Ther. 37 Weather Fine & Misty Visibility Poor. Our fire. Night firing as per Appendix 6. 2 P.M. 16 yds 4.5 How on T.M. Emplacement O.26.d 95.16. Aeroplane observation but the light was bad. Hostile fire. 10-12 P.M. A/per Batts in HENINEL & vicinity & Reserve all quiet on our front. E.2. Very active all day Ammn. Expr. A.156 A X 104 B X 96.	
	30th		Bar. 29.68. Ther. 34. Weather Fine & Misty. Visibility Poor. Our fire Night firing as per Appendix 6. 10.35 to 11.24 24 yds. 8"on T.H. Emplacement at O.26.d. 96.15. Aeroplane observation. 11.842 to 11.45. 29 yds 8" on T.M. Emplacement O.26 b.2. by Aeroplane observation 12 Noon & further 71 yds on this target. Hostile Fire. 7 P.M. 9 rounds during night about 60 yds 77 m/m & 10.3 pm into HENINEL 60% for. 5.5 P.M. Heavy bombardment on the Post Post on our left lasting about 30 minutes at intense rate & finally ceasing at 6 P.M. 1.5 P.M. 10 yds. H.2 How on evento. RESERVE E.2 Very active all day. Ammn. Expr. A.75 A.X. 60 B.X.16	

Army Form C. 2118.

WAR DIARY
or
INTELLIGENCE SUMMARY.
(Erase heading not required.)

Page 8

Place	Date 1918	Hour	Summary of Events and Information	Remarks and references to Appendices
HENINEL	31		Par 29th Mar 33 Weather Dull & misty. Visibility Bad. Gun Fire Night Firing as per Appendix 6. 2.30 P.M. Enemy concentration onto CHERISY. Hostile Fire 11 P.M. 12 rds SG into HENINEL. 5 Z.O.Z 29 rds 10.5 p.m. into HENINEL 7.35 Z.O.Z 12 rds 10.5 p.m. onto N36B. P.A. Tel. Comm. & Exp. A.126. AX130 BX151. Course 2/Lieut P. Young returned from Lewis Gun Course.	[signature] Myburgh Maj 152 Brigade RFA

Copy No. War Diary Appendix 1.   SECRET.

Right Group Operation Order No 28.
Reference 34th D.A. No O/B/8.

1. Targets are allotted batteries as under:—

SERIAL No 1.

    A/152   O.32.b.05.05. — O.32.a.88.13.
    A/26   O.32.a.88.13. — O.32.a.72.26.
    117   O.32.a.72.26. — O.32.a.59.38.
    B/152   O.32.a.59.38. — O.32.a.43.51.
    C/152   O.32.a.43.51. — O.32.a.32.65.

SERIAL Nos 3 & 10.

    A/26   O.26.d.30.92. — O.26.d.34.89.
    117   O.26.d.34.89. — O.26.d.47.88.
    B/152   O.26.d.47.88. — O.26.d.59.92.
    C/152   O.26.d.59.92. — O.26.d.75.90.

SERIAL Nos 11 & 14.

    A/152   O.32.c.85.40. — O.32.d.10.56.
    A/26   O.32.d.10.56. — O.32.d.28.60.
    117   O.32.d.28.60. — O.32.d.48.60.
    B/152   O.32.d.48.60. — O.32.d.73.52.
    C/152   O.32.d.73.52. — O.32.d.92.45.

SERIAL No 13.

    A/26   O.26.c.50.32. — O.26.c.58.28.
    117   O.26.c.58.28. — O.26.c.62.18.
    B/152   O.26.c.62.18. — O.26.c.70.10.
    C/152   O.26.c.70.10. — O.26.c.75.05.

2. Acknowledge, please.

                                          G.W. Brewitt Capt.
27/12/17.   Adjt. Right Group

Copies 8.   Nos 1/6 To Batteries
                    7 This office
                    8 War Diary.

Copy No 11 *War Diary Appendix 2* SECRET.

Centre Group Operation Order No 29.

1. Night firing orders for night Jan 2/3.

"A"
A/152	2 Guns.	OTTER Lane O.32.d.00.53.–62.64.	"AX"
B/26	1 "	O.32.c.83.41. and O.32.c.87.52.	"AX"
	1 "	Searching & sweeping from OTTER Lane to 200x South between road in O.32.c. & railway in O.32.d.	"A"
117	1 "	O.32.d.92.48.	"AX"
	1 "	O.32.d.94.59.	"
B/152	1 "	O.32.d.15.90. and O.32.b.05.05.	"
	1 "	Search & sweep between CHERISY Lane & CHERRY Wood.	"A"
C/152	2 "	CHERISY Lane O.32.d.10.90.–65.75.	"AX"
D/152	2 Hows.	Road O.32.c.77.20.–O.32.b.05.05.	

Times: 5.30 p.m. to 9 p.m.
Expenditure: 18 pdrs. 10 Rounds per hour per battery.
           4.5 Hows. 15   "   "   "   "   "

"B"
A/152	2 Guns	Track U.2.b.38.85.–U.3.a.28.88.
A/26	2 "	O.32.d.55.32.–U.3.a.34.95.
117	2 "	O.32.b.22.42.–O.32.b.50.95.
B/152	2 "	O.32.b.05.05.–O.32.b.22.42.
C/152	2 "	O.32.b.50.95.–O.26.d.84.67.
D/152	2 "	CHERRY & BOTTOM Bridges.

Times: 9.10 p.m. 5 Rds gun fire. all AX.
       9.10 p.m. to 10.20 p.m.
Expenditure: 18 pdrs. 30 Rds per battery per hour. all "AX".
           4.5 Hows. 50 "   "   "   "   "

"C" 10.27 p.m. Targets "A" 5 Rds gun fire.
    10.50 p.m.   "   "B" 5 "   "   "

G.W. Brewitt Capt.
Adjt. Centre Group.

1/1/18.

Nos 1/6 To batteries.
    7 BM, R.A.
    8 BM, Centre Inf. Bde.
    9 This office
   10 War Diary.
   11 Spare.

Army Form C. 2118.

WAR DIARY
or
INTELLIGENCE SUMMARY.
(Erase heading not required.)

Instructions regarding War Diaries and Intelligence Summaries are contained in F. S. Regs., Part II. and the Staff Manual respectively. Title pages will be prepared in manuscript.

152nd BRIGADE, R.F.A.

Place	Date	Hour	Summary of Events and Information	Remarks and references to Appendices
HENINEL	Feb 1st 1918		Bar. 29.76. Ther. 31. Weather. Foggy cold. Visibility Bad. Gun Fire. Night Firing as per Appendix 1. 2.45 PM 20 rds on Hostile TM Emplacement C21d.4.5 by request of Infantry. F.A. Nil Attachment. 1st Lieut W.S. Wachner 150 Bridge F.A. 67 Bde. Ammo Exp. 2.95 AX.105 3X.30.	
"	2nd		Bar. 29.77. Ther. 36. Weather. Fair cold. Visibility fair. Gun Fire. Night Firing as per Appendix 1. 11AM to 11.05 PM 60 rds BX on TM C32 b.2.2. by Request of Infantry. Observation by SO on own target 4.05 PM 20 rds on Hostile TM C20d.5.5 Hostile Fire Nil. G.A. Normal. Ammo Exp. 1.89. AX.99 3X.147.	
"	3rd		Bar. 29.68 Ther. 41. Weather fine + cold. Visibility Poor. Gun Fire. Night Firing as per Appendix 1. 11AM 30 rds at TM Emplacement C32a.70.52 at request of Infantry. 2.30 PM 20 rds movement in W32g.5 Hostile Fire. Much above normal. HENINEL (WOOD) TRENCH front line Osd POST NEAR G.A. Very active over our lines at 6.45 AM, 10.15 PM, 10.45 AM + 2.15 PM. Ammo Expended. A 94 AX.117 3X.40. 2nd Lieut. Hanly attached to A/152. Lieut N.S. MacAlister resigned from case Posted to Brigade. Ammo Exp. 217 AX.112 3X.40.	
"	4th		Bar. 29.62. Ther. 47. Weather. Dull + Mild. Wind SW. Visibility fair. Gun Fire. Night Firing as per Appendix 2. Considerable movement during day which was fired on. Hostile Fire. Normal. G.A. Own gun fired 12.30 + 1 PM. Lieut Lieut A. Wright proceed on leave. Ammo Exp. 217 AX.112 3X.40.	
"	5th		Bar. 29.55. Ther. 46. Weather. Very fine. Visibility Poor fast day. Gun Fire. Night Firing as per Appendix 2. Much movement during day which was fired at Hostile Fire. Normal. G.A. Very active. Leave. Major W.W. Wilmot K.C. returned from Sunday leave at Steenbecque + 14 day's leave. Ammo Exp. A.147 AX.202 3X.50.	
"	6th		Bar. 29.53. Ther. 50. Weather. Very fine. Visibility Good. Gun Fire. Night firing as per Appendix 2. Much movement fired at during the whole day. Hostile Fire. Normal. G.A. Normal. Ammo Exp. A.74 AX.101 3X.30. Leave. Major W.S. Hull KC. proceed on leave. Firing Gun A. Wright posted to K.R. Battery.	

WAR DIARY or INTELLIGENCE SUMMARY

Army Form C. 2118.

Page 2

Place	Date Feb 1918	Hour	Summary of Events and Information	Remarks and references to Appendices
KEMMEL	7th		Bar 2940 Ther 49 Weather Misty Visibility Good until Then then mod to Air Line. Night Firing to an Opportunity 2 Manoeuvre fired at during day. Hostile Visit. During night Enemy Shelling was active on our front spasm chiefly 10.5 9.2 How. CB Ntl. Relief 2 Sections per Battery relieved by 26 H.A.F.R. Bde A/152 by 116 B/152 by 117. C/152 by D/138. D/152 by Sgt Jur HisTory Battery. Relief completed by 9.45 P.M. Armour Capt Agg, A.K. Cpl O'Keefe, Lieut. Pot Parson returned from fatigue base.	
—	8th		Bar 29.36 Ther 50 Weather Misty Visibility Poor. Neil Cos. Fire 1.30 A.M. SOS sent up from left of Ferme Brigade. Batteries started firing at 6.30 A.M ceased fire at 7.5 A.M all being reported quiet. Night firing as per Operation 2. 9.2H remaining Sections per Battery relieved 10.2PM 26th Bde HQ mounted command of Ferme Group, Ammn Exp 2.393, A×540, Bx 39. Returned from Field Ambulance. Capt L.J O'Brien Sloane Capt WBruce proceed on Leave. Attachment. 1st Lieut W.C. Koehner left for from his Unit. (USA)	
FICHEUX	9th		Bar 29.42 Ther 47 Weather Misty. Brigade out of Action at Wagon Lines	
On the March.	10th		Bar 29.46 Ther 43 Weather Fine. Brigade marched from Wagon Lines to BIENVILLERS via ADINFER. LONCHY-aux-BOIS. Started at 9AM arriving at 12.15 PM. 76 Brigaded Brigade en Route.	
—	11th		Bar 29.57 Ther 46 Weather Fine. Brigade marched from BIENVILLERS to WAMIN via POMMIER. SAULTY, SOMBRIN, GRAND RULLECOURT Started at 9AM arriving 9.30 PM. HQ A/152 at WAMIN. B. C/152 ROZIERE. D/152 BROUILLY.	
WAMIN	12th		Bar 29.41 Ther 48 Weather Fine Brigade at Rest. Training carried out	
—	13th		Bar 29.43 Ther 51 Weather Wet Brigade at Rest " " "	2nd Lieut Legroy proceeded on leave
—	14th		Bar 29.51 Ther 52 Weather Wet Brigade at Rest " " "	"
—	15th		Bar 29.32 Ther 44 Weather Fair " " " "	2nd Lieut. Jarvis (promoted to Brigade Lewisgun School)

Army Form C. 2118.

WAR DIARY
or
INTELLIGENCE SUMMARY.
(Erase heading not required.)

Instructions regarding War Diaries and Intelligence Summaries are contained in F. S. Regs., Part II. and the Staff Manual respectively. Title pages will be prepared in manuscript.

Page 3

Place	Date Feb 1918	Hour	Summary of Events and Information	Remarks and references to Appendices
WARMIN	16th		Bar 29.72 Ther 41 Weather Fine & cold. Brigade at Rest. Training carried out. Capt. L.C. Brown proceeded to join R.F.A.	
"	17th		Bar 29.58 Ther 39 Weather Fair & cold. Brigade at Rest. Training carried out.	
"	18th		Bar 29.86 Ther 37 Weather Fine & cold. Brigade at Rest. 6 R.A. Sergeant Bombs. Have leave ex. Lieut. W.H. Lewis returned from leave.	
"	19th		Bar 9.55 Ther 37 Weather Fine & cold. Brigade at Rest. Training carried out.	
"	20		Bar 29.52 Ther 41 Weather Wet. Brigade at Rest. Training carried out. 2nd Lieut F. Price returned from T.M. Course. Lieut. E.G. Roberson returned from leave in France. Lieut. A. Wright returned from leave. proceeded to join R.A. 4th Battery.	
"	21st		Bar 29.57 Ther 45 Weather Finer Mild. Brigade paraded in F.S. Marching Order. 2nd Lieut D Coborn + A. Freemount joined the Brigade + posted to D & C/152 Batteries.	
"	22nd		Bar 29.41 Ther 43 Weather Fair but stormy S.W. Gale. Brigade at Rest. Training carried out. Major W.S. Roll R.E. returned from leave ? Post to Emergency Brigade attached to W&D	
"	23rd		Bar 29.95 Ther 53 Weather Fair & Mild. Brigade at Rest. Training carried out.	
"	24th		Bar 29.92 Ther 50 Weather Fair. Brigade at Rest. Mare's Parade. Kit Inspection	
"	25th		Bar 29.70 Ther 47 Weather Brigade at Rest. Training carried out. Kits ? Brunsyhurst fine	
"	26th		Bar 30.10 Ther 40 Weather Fine & cold. Brigade at Rest. 11AM Brigade Inspected in F.S. Marching Order by G.O.C. III Corps. 3 P.M. Lecture by C.R.A. to all Officers.	
"	27th		Bar 29.70 Ther 50 Weather Fine. Brigade at Rest. Training carried out.	
"	28th		Bar 29.9 Ther 49 Weather Fair. Brigade at Rest. Last H.D. War R.C. ordered T.A.? proceeds on 10 days leave.	

R.A. Harman Lt Col
Comdg 152 Bde R.F.A. 1/3/18

2.

7. Night Feb. 1st/2nd.

A/152	Dump, junction of rail-
B/152	way and tracks at
C/152	O.27.d.10.80.
II/152	

Rate of fire 6 p.m.-6.45 a.m., 7.15 p.m.-10 p.m., 10.10 p.m., 11 p.m.
18 plus 55 Rounds per battery, 50% A.
II/152 20 Rounds.

8. Acknowledge.

26/1/18.

G.H. Brewitt Capt.
Adjt. Centre Group.

11 Copies. Nos 1/4 To batteries.
5   B.M., R.A.
6   B.M., Centre Inf. Bde.
7   This office.
8/9 War Diary.
10/11 Spare.

2.

7. Night Feb. 1st/2nd.

A/152	Dump, junction of rail-
B/152	way and tracks at
C/152	O.27.d.10.80.
II/152	

8. Acknowledge.

Rate of fired
6 p.m. 6.45 p.m. 7.15 p.m.
10 p.m. 10.10 p.m. 11 p.m.
18 pdrs. 55 Rounds
per battery. 50% A.
II/152 20 Rounds.

G.H. Brewitt Capt.
Adjt. Centre Group.

26/1/18.

11 Copies. Nos. 1/4 To batteries.
5 B.M., R.A.
6 B.M., Centre Inf. Bde.
7 This office.
8/9 War Diary.
10/11 Spare.

Copy No 10   War Diary Appendix 3.   SECRET.

Centre Group Operation Order No 30.
Reference 34th D.A. 1st O/B/9

1. **Targets**

   A.
   - D/152   O32 b 25.38 – 30.50 – 25.45.
   - A/152.   O32 b 05.05 – 22.41.
   - A/26.   O32 b 22.41 – 39.69.
   - 117.   O32 b. 39.69 – O26 d 52.00
   - B/152.   O26 d 52.00 – 68.32
   - C/152   O26 d 68.32 – 85.60.

   B   as per O/B/9.

   C   B & C/152 Northern Area. CHERRY WOOD.
   - A/152. A/26. 117. Southern   do
   - D/152.   O32 d 48.96.

   D.
   - A/152.   O32 c 90.50 – O32 d. 13.56.
   - A/26.   O32 d. 13.56 –   31.59
   - 117.   O32 d. 31.59 –   51.60.
   - B/152.   O32 d. 51.60 –   74.52.
   - C/152.   O32 d 74.52 –   92.45.

   E.
   - A/152.   O27 d 98.68 – O27 d 63.53.
   - A/26.   O27 d 63.53 –   26.39.
   - 117   O27 d 26.39 – O27 c 95.25.
   - B/152   O27 c 95.25 –   60.08.
   - C/152   O27 c 60.08 –   28.20.

   F.
   - A/152.   U2 a 55.65 – U2 a 68.92.
   - A/26.   U2 a. 68.92 – O32 c 79.21.
   - 117   O32 c. 79.21 –   90.52.
   - B/152.   O32 c 90.52 –   95.77.
   - C/152.   O32 c 95.77 – O32 b 05.05.
   - D/152.   O32 c 81.30.

8-1-18.   R.W. Angell

Nos 1–6. Batteries   for O.C. Centre Group.
7. B.M. R.A
8. B.M. Centre Inf. Bde
9. This Office
10. War Diary.
11. Spare.

Copy No. *War Diary Appendix 4.* SECRET.

Centre Group Operation Order No 34.

Night firing orders for week ending Jan 19/20.

1. **Jan. 15/16.**

Unit	Target	Time/Rounds
A/152	Track O.32.c.91.42. – O.32.d.53.35.	8 p.m. to 8.30 p.m.
C/152	O.32.d.53.35. – O.32.d.85.20.	20 Rounds per
117	O.32.d.85.20. – U.3.a.33.97.	battery.
A/152	O.32.c.90.50. – O.32.d.48.60.	8.35 p.m.
C/152	O.32.d.48.60. – O.32.d.93.46.	5 Rounds
117	O.32.d.93.46. – Sun Quarry.	Gun fire.

(Otter Lane)

Jan. 16/17.

Unit	Target	Time/Rounds
A/26	O.27.b.15.50. – O.28.a.05.70.	2.45 a.m., 2.55 a.m.,
B/152	St. Michael's Statue. – O.27.b.15.50.	3.5 a.m., 3.10 a.m.
117	O.26.b.35.00. – St. Michael's Statue.	5 Rounds gun fire.
II/152	O.26.d.78.68.	at each time.

Jan. 17/18.

Unit	Target	Time/Rounds
A,B,C/152	O.27.b.79.23.	5 p.m. to 6 p.m.
		1 Rd per gun per 6 minutes.
A/152	O.27.c.75.60. – O.27.d.20.81.	6.35 p.m.
B/ "	O.27.d.20.81. – O.27.b.50.05.	10 Rounds
C/ "	O.27.d.20.81. – O.27.a.75.20.	gun fire.
II/ "	O.27.d.20.81.	

Jan. 18/19.

Unit	Target	Time/Rounds
A/26	O.32.c.90.48.	5.15 p.m., 6 p.m.,
B/152	Cherry Wood.	6.20 p.m., 8.0 p.m.
117	O.26.d.70.35.	5 Rds gun fire ea. time.

Jan. 19/20.

Unit	Target	Time/Rounds
A/152	Obus Avenue.	6 p.m. to 7 p.m.
C/152	Dawn Lane.	
117	Otter Lane.	40 Rds per battery
II/152	Sun Quarry	
	O.27.d.2.8. (ridge).	60 Rounds

2. Acknowledge, please.

15/1/18.

G.W. Brewitt Capt.
Adjt. Centre Group

11 Copies. Nos 1/6 To Batteries
7 BM., R.A.
8 B.M., Centre Inf Bde.
9 This office.
10/11 Spare.

Copy No. 10   SECRET.

Centre Group Operation Order No. 36.

Night firing orders for week-ending Jan. 26/27.

War Diary Appendix 5

1. **Night Jan. 21/22.**

A/, B/ & C/152	O.27.b.79.23.	4.45 p.m. to 5.45 p.m. 1 Rd per gun per 5 mins.
A/152	O.27.c.75.60. – O.27.d.20.81.	6.15 p.m.
B/152	O.27.d.20.81. – O.27.b.50.05.	10 Rounds gun-
C/152	O.27.d.20.81. – O.27.a.75.20.	fire.
D/152	O.27.d.20.81.	18 pdrs 30% A.

Night Jan. 22/23.

A, B & C/152	Sun Quarry.	10 p.m.
"	S. & W. sides Cherry Wood.	10.10 p.m.
"	O.26.d.85.63.	10.55 p.m.	5 Rounds gun-fire each time.
D/152	Dug-outs in railway cutting between Otter lane – O.32.c.55.40	10 p.m. 10.10 10.55 p.m. 5 Rounds gun fire each time.

Night Jan. 23/24.

B/152	Track U.2.a.7.9 – U.2.b.56.86.	
A/152	Search & sweep O.32.d.55.90.	4.30 p.m. to 6 p.m.
C/152	1 Gun O.32.d.60.58. 1 " O.32.b.05.05.	40 Rounds per battery.
D/152	1 How. O.32.c.90.68. 1 " Cherry bridge.	
A/152	O.32.d.30.32. – O.32.d.54.33.	6.5 p.m.
B/152	O.32.c.85.45. – O.32.d.30.32.	5 Rounds gun fire.
C/152	O.32.d.54.33. – O.32.d.85.20.	
D/152	St. Michael's Statue. Bottom Bridge.	

Jan. 24/25.

A/152	Any targets in O.27.	5 a.m. to 7 a.m.
B/152	" " . O.33.	60 Rounds per battery.
C/152	" " . O.26.d, O.32.b & d.	

2.

Night Jan. 25/26.

A/152	U.3.a.32.97.	
B/152	O.32.b.50.93.	
C/152	Trench in CHERRY WOOD.	7.15 p.m. 5 Rounds gun-fire.
D/152	CHERRY WOOD BRIDGE.	
A/152	Search & sweep CHERISY SOUTH.	
B/152	" " " CENTRAL.	7.45 p.m. 5 Rounds gun-fire.
C/152	" " " NORTH.	
D/152	O.32.b.05.05.	
	O.26.d.85.63.	

2. Batteries acknowledge, please.

G.W. Brewitt Capt.
Adjt. Centre Group.

21/1/18.

11 Copies. Nos 1/4 To Batteries.
            5   B.M., R.A.
            6   B.M., Centre Inf. Bde.
            7/8 War Diary.
            9   This office.
            10/11 Spare.

Copy No 8   War Diary Appendix 6   SECRET.

Centre Group Operation Order No 37.
Night firing orders from Jan.26/27 to Feb.1/2.

1. Night Jan.26/27th

Battery	Target	
A/152	O.32.c.28.00. – O.32.c.54.35.	4 a.m. to 4.50 a.m.
B/152	O.32.c.54.35. – O.32.c.47.75.	25 Rds per battery
C/152	O.32.c.47.75. – O.32.c.50.95.	(18 pdrs).
II/152	O.32.c.58.50.	20 Rds II/152.
	O.32.c.50.95.	(i.e. 10 Rds ea. target)

2. Night Jan.27/28th

Battery	Target	
A/152	O.32.c.90.55. – O.32.d.60.60.	Bursts of fire at
B/152	O.32.a.70.75. – O.32.b.20.40.	11p.m., 11.15p.m., 2a.m.
C/152	O.26.c.75.05. – O.32.b.50.95.	2.10a.m. & 2.30a.m.
II/152	O.26.18363. (Dug-outs, trench & road crossing.)	18 pdrs 50 Rds per battery. 50% A. II/152 20 Rounds.

3. Night Jan.28/29th

Battery	Target	
A/152, B/152, II/152	Bridge, tracks & railway junction in area U.2.b.05.40 – 05.10. U.2.b.30.40. – 30.10.	Bursts of fire at 5p.m., 5.45p.m., 6p.m., 7p.m., 7.20p.m., 9p.m.
C/152	O.26.d.83.63. (Road & trench junction.)	18 pdrs 60Rds per battery. 50% A. II/152 20 Rounds.

4. Night Jan.29/30th

Battery	Target	
A/152, B/152, C/152	STAR Corner & tracks leading to it.	Bursts of fire at irregular intervals between 6p.m. & 12 m.n. 30 Rounds per battery. 50% A.

5. Night Jan.30/31st

Battery	Target	
A/152, B/152, C/152	Tracks leading into sunken road between O.32.c.82.30. & O.32.c.95.75.	Bursts of fire at 6p.m., 6.30p.m., 7p.m., 10p.m., 10.15p.m., 11p.m. 60 Rounds per battery.
II/152	Dug-outs in sunken road between above points.	18 pdrs. 50% A. II/152 40 Rounds.

6. Night Jan.31/Feb.1st.

Battery	Target	
A/152	UPTON QUARRY & dump O.35.c.10.35.	Bursts of fire between 5 p.m. & 11 p.m.
B/152, C/152, II/152	BOTTOM bridge & tracks leading into it.	18 pdrs 50 Rds per battery 55% A. II/152 20 Rds.

COPY No 10   *War Diary Appendix 1*   SECRET

Centre Group Operation Order No 37.
Night firing orders from Jan. 26/27 to Feb. 1/2.

1. Night Jan. 26/27th

A/152	O.32.c.28.00. – O.32.c.54.35.	4 a.m. to 4.50 a.m.
B/152	O.32.c.54.35. – O.32.c.47.75.	25 Rds per battery
C/152	O.32.c.47.75. – O.32.c.50.95.	(18 pdrs).
II/152	O.32.c.58.50.	20 Rds II/152.
	O.32.c.50.95.	(i.e. 10 Rds ea. target)

2. Night. Jan. 27/28th

A/152	O.32.a.90.55. – O.32.d.60.60.	Bursts of fire at 11 p.m., 11.15 p.m., 2 a.m., 2.10 a.m. & 2.30 a.m.
B/152	O.32.a.70.75. – O.32.b.20.40.	18 pdrs. 50 Rds per battery. 50% A.
C/152	O.26.c.75.05. – O.32.b.50.95.	II/152 20 Rounds.
II/152	O.26.1.83.63. (Dug-outs, trench & road crossing.)	

3. Night Jan. 28/29th

A/152 }	Bridge, tracks & railway junction in area U.2.b.05.40 – 05.10.	Bursts of fire at 5 p.m., 5.45 p.m., 6 p.m., 7 p.m., 7.20 p.m., 9 p.m.
B/152 }	U.2.b.30.40. – 30.10.	18 pdrs 50 Rds per battery. 50% A.
II/152 }		II/152 20 Rounds.
C/152	O.26.d.63.63. (Road & trench junction.)	

4. Night Jan. 29/30th

A/152 }	STAR Corner & tracks leading to it.	Bursts of fire at irregular intervals between 5 p.m. & 12 m.n. 50 Rounds per battery. 50% A.
B/152 }		
C/152. }		

5. Night Jan 30/31st

A/152 }	Tracks leading into sunken road between O.32.c.82.30. & O.32.c.95.75.	Bursts of fire at 6 p.m., 6.30 p.m., 7 p.m., 10 p.m., 10.15 p.m., 11 p.m.
B/152 }		60 Rounds per battery.
C/152 }		18 pdrs. 50% A.
II/152	Dug-outs in sunken road between above points.	II/152 40 Rounds.

6. Night. Jan. 31/Feb 1st

A/152	UPTON QUARRY & dump O.35.c.10.35.	Bursts of fire between 5 p.m. & 11 p.m.
B/152 }	BOTTOM bridge & tracks leading into it.	18 pdrs. 50 Rds per battery. 50% A.
C/152 }		II/152 20 Rds.
II/152 }		

COPY No 8 War Diary - Appendix 2 SECRET

Centre Group Operation Order No 38
Night firing orders from Feb 2nd/3rd to Feb 9th/10th

1. Night Feb 2/3rd

A/152	Track U 3d 40.85 - U 3c 8.4	Bursts of fire at 5 P.M. 6 P.M. 8.30 P.M. 6.30 P.M. 11 P.M. 10 pdrs 50 Rds per Battery 50 % A D/152. 20 rds.
B/152	Tracks between U 3c 8.4 & U 3c 2.7	
C/152	Tramway Junction O 28 6. 3.5.	
D/152	Dugouts at U 3c 8.4 + U 3c 2.7	

2. Night Feb 3/4th

A/152	CHERISY-VIS en ARTOIS Road in O 27a.	Bursts of fire at 5 P.M. 5.30 P.M. 6 P.M. 6.15 P.M. 7.15 P.M. 8 P.M. 10 P.M. 10.10 P.M. 4.30 A.M. 5 A.M. 10 pdrs 50 Rds per Battery 50 % A. D/152. 20 rds between 5 P.M. & 11 P.M.
B/152	-do- O 27 b.	
C/152	-do- O 28 a.	
D/152	Dug outs on Track at O 28c 32.82 + O 28c 40.60.	

3. Night Feb 4/5th

A/152	CHERISY-VIS en ARTOIS Road in O 27a.	Bursts of Fire at 4.45 P.M. 5.15 P.M. 5.20 P.M. 6.15 P.M. 6.30 P.M. 7 P.M. 7.30 P.M. 9.30 P.M. 10 P.M. 4.45 A.M. 10 pdrs 50 Rds per Battery 50 % A. D/152. 20 rds between 5 P.M. & 11 P.M. each night.
B/152	-do- O 27 b.	
C/152	-do- O 28 a.	
D/152	Dugouts in SUNKEN ROAD from BOTTOM BRIDGE to O 28 c 00.45.	

4. Night Feb 5/6th

A/152 } B/152 }	Tracks leading from U 3a 30.45 to U 2b 3.3.	Bursts of fire at irregular intervals between 5 P.M. & 2 A.M. 10 pdrs 50 Rds per Battery 50 % A. D/152 20 Rds.
C/152	Junction of SUNKEN ROADS O 28 b. 9.9.	
D/152	Dugouts U 3a 1.3 + SUNKEN ROAD U 2 b 90.45.	

5th Night Feb 6/7th

A/152	Track U 2 b 30.80 - U 2a 65.85.	Bursts of fire at irregular intervals between 5 P.M. & 2 A.M. 10 pdrs 50 Rds per Battery 50 % A. D/152. 20 rds.
B/152	Junction of tracks & roads in N.W. corner of U 3a	
C/152	Same as for 5/6th	
D/152	O 32 d 10.15 + U 3 a 48.90.	

2.

6. Night Feb 7/8th

A/152	Tramway from	O27b 45.00 – O27d 20.60
B/152	" "	O27d 20.60 – O27c 70.60
C/152	" "	O27c 70.60 – O27c 30.35
D/152		O27d 20.60 + O27c 45.45

Bursts of fire at 5 P.M. 6.15 P.M. 6.15 P.M. 6.30 P.M. 7 P.M. 7.40 P.M. 7.50 P.M. 8 P.M. 9.05 P.M. 9.00 P.M. 10 pdrs 60 Rds per Battery 18 P.A. 4.5" How. 40 Rds. D/152

7. Night Feb 8/9th

A/152 ⎫	Tracks leading on to SUNKEN
B/152 ⎬	ROAD between O32c 82.30 +
C/152 ⎭	O32c 95.75
D/152.	Dugouts in SUNKEN Road between above points

Bursts of fire at irregular intervals between 7 P.M. and 11 P.M. 18 pdrs 60 Rds per Battery 4.5" How. 40 Rds. D/152

8. Night Feb 9/10th

	Tracks	
A/152	O32d 55.40	– O32d 1.4
B/152	O32c 30.00	– O32d 86.20
C/152.	O32d 65.20	– O32c 55.40
D/152	O32d 10.36	– O32d 65.20

Bursts of fire at irregular intervals between 5 P.M. & 2 A.M. 18 pdrs 60 Rds per Battery 4.5" How. 20 Rds. D/152

Photos referring to above Targets Nos 3050 (copy sent to B-C+D) 3111 (copy to all Batteries) 3079 (copy to C+D)

9. Acknowledge.

R.W. Angell, A/Lieut.
for O.C. Centre Group

2-2-18

11 Copies Nos 1-4 Batteries
           5.   B.M. R.A
           6.   B.M. Centre Inf Bde
           7.   this Office
           8-9.   War Diary.
           10-11. Spare.

34th Divisional Artillery

WAR DIARY

152nd BRIGADE

ROYAL FIELD ARTILLERY

MARCH 1918

WAR DIARY or INTELLIGENCE SUMMARY

Army Form C. 2118.

15-2 B/4 7 F

(Erase heading not required.)

Place	Date	Hour	Summary of Events and Information	Remarks and references to Appendices
WAMIN	March 1918 1st		Brigade having been ordered to relieve the 90th Bde at Westby Barracks. killed in RUYENFIRE.	
On the March	2nd		Brigade marched to Major Lines near BOISLEUX St MARC, 1 section per Battery proceeded into action, relieving 119th Brigade	
St LEDGER	3rd		Major A. T. Mcr. DSO temporarily acting O.C. 152 Bde left to resume station over command of Major. DS.O. "A.F.A. Bde making promoted Lieut Col. Lt. Col. "A.F.A Bde making promoted Lieut Col. Major D S.M. Kerd took over temporarily command of 152 Bde. Lieutenant J.G. Bellamy wounded: no other casualties. Complete relief of the 119th Brigade of the Line Group at 5 PM Command of the Line Group at 5PM.	
-do-	4 & 5 10 mb		Enemy shot on her infrequent happening to the Brigade Diary. Got Post No 10 was summary, and effort to be completed as desired. From the 15 the Enemy put down heavy Expectation A.R. during all nights put down very intense harassing fire. Lieut Col W.R. Thompson DSO recalled from England took over command of the 152 Brigade on about the 8th of Post	
-do-	21st		After having two awful fire from Trenches at 4.30 am the Enemy attacked the Barrage became at from the line to the Battery position and continued with them intensive from 11 Noon. By this time the enemy was near back but fell a forced to send to line 12 Noon. By this time the enemy was near Back and our infantry were running confusion, anxiety support. The Enemy were and out in and out of the Brigade Lines in Hd. Prom two Batteries. B/M Crain a line of Division Service to emboldened line in their position. D/M 23nd Batty pulled off late in this Group. 10 PM Crain given for A.C.D. + 23 Batty's to retire to selected positions near BOYELLES. Wounded: Captain R. J. Crowley + A. Lagny. Major. H.Q. Washington Road.	
-do-	22nd		2 am Bde moved from St LEDGER to HENIN with 103rd Bd/ Bde. The night & early morning duly passed. The Barrage attacked HENIN HILL about 7 AM	

WAR DIARY or INTELLIGENCE SUMMARY

Army Form C. 2118.

Place	Date	Hour	Summary of Events and Information	Remarks and references to Appendices
HENIN	22nd March 1918		11AM B.H.Q. & 109th Inf Bde retired to BOYELLES 12 Noon 3/152 retired to position South of Road HAMLINCOURT–MOYENVILLE. 12.30 2PM A.C+D retired to same posn. 1PM 1 Secton C/152 returned to engage position near BOYELLES. 2PM A.B.D returned to same position manned to fire on all kinds of observed movement. 6PM 23rd Battery & C/152 retired to HAMLINCOURT–MOYENVILLE. Shed on the enemy approaching ST LEGER R.WOOD. 8PM B.H.Q. & B.D Batteries retired to positions alongside 9/152. C/152 governed their own Group. Casualties 2nd Lieut. A. Fisher evacuated gassed.	
MOYENVILLE	23rd		Weather fine. Heavy firing all morning on observed movement. 2PM Our front attacked back from T.29d to T.29b. 6PM J.H.Q. retired to MOYENVILLE.	
do	24th		Weather fine. Heavy firing all morning both on our front & the right. Several S.O.S showing the dept. 10.20PM SOS on our Right which we continued repeated finally ceasing at 11.50PM 23rd Battery rejoined their own Division. Casualties Killed 2nd Lieut R.J. McLean. Wounded 2nd Lieut W. Thompson D.S.O. Bde reported to take over Command 297th R.H. Trench Fol. F. Olived took over command 152 Bde RFA.	
do	25th		Weather fine. In the early hours of the morning the enemy entered EPINLLERS & was later driven back about 100 yds. 1.30 PM A. Hussars to B.H.Q. Ordered 62N Bde HQ retired to AYETTE & Batteries to position in S.26 & 27 May Start 5PM. During the night Batteries again redrew to position in X.22.23. 9PM Sheet 51B S.E.	
do	26th		Weather fine 9AM B.H.Q withdrew to ADINFER. 6AM No pos. Gms withdrew to FONCAS. No Bois Fairly quiet day.	
do	27th		Weather fine v cold. 3.6AM Lights 17pdr per hour on MOYENVILLE. 9.50AM All Batteries 25 rds.	

Army Form C. 2118.

WAR DIARY
or
INTELLIGENCE SUMMARY.
(Erase heading not required.)

Instructions regarding War Diaries and Intelligence Summaries are contained in F.S. Regs., Part II. and the Staff Manual respectively. Title pages will be prepared in manuscript.

page 9.

Place	Date	Hour	Summary of Events and Information	Remarks and references to Appendices
ADINFER	March 1918 27th		on MOYENVILLE disposal of Infantry. 11.35AM. SOS on Right Batts front. Responded for 5 minutes with 12 d. g.f. m. 11.30 PM Slow rate of fire on SOS continued, Wagon Lines moved to BELLACOURT. 4.30 PM BHQ withdrew to RANSART Batteries withdrew to X15 a.6	
RANSART	28th		Weather Cold-Wet 5.30AM Opened on SOS at 12pm & 12.19pm responded SOS for 30 minutes. 9.50 AM Opened SOS at 1 pm in on orders from D.A. Earlier part of the day quiet. Wagon Lines moved to GAUDIEMPRE	
-do-	29th		Weather Very Cold NE Wind. Quiet day. Hostile shelling generally nil.	
-do-	30th		Weather Wet 4.30 AM 5.30, & 6.30 AM opened on SOS for 3 minutes at 2.30 PM. Hostile Shelling Normal.	
-do-	31st		Weather Fine and Cold. Very quiet day.	

Y. Newport R.F.A.
152 Bde. R.F.A.

34th Divisional Artillery

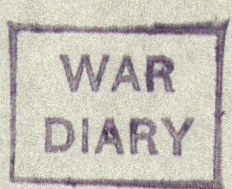

152nd BRIGADE

ROYAL FIELD ARTILLERY

APRIL 1918

Army Form C. 2118.

WAR DIARY
or
INTELLIGENCE SUMMARY.
(Erase heading not required.)

152 Bde RFA VOL 27

Page 1

Place	Date	Hour	Summary of Events and Information	Remarks and references to Appendices
RANSART	April 1st 1918	—	Ther. — Visibility fair. Weather wet. Quiet day.	Amm. Exp.
	2nd	—	Ther. — Visibility fair. Weather wet. Quiet day.	Amm. Exp.
	3rd	—	Ther. — 1 Section of each Battery relieved by Batteries of 161 Bde 32nd Div. Weather fair. Quiet day	Amm. Exp.
		—	Ther. — Visibility fair. Weather fair. Quiet day.	Amm. Exp.
		8 PM	2 Sections per Battery relieved by Batteries of 161 Bde & Bde HQ relieved	
		10 AM	Wagon Lines moved from CAUDIEMPRE to SOUASTRIONS	
BOC.Y.	4th	—	Ther. — Weather fair. Brigade out of action	
On the March	5th	—	Ther. — Weather wet. 9 AM Brigade marched to St Bar arriving 2.30 PM	
—	6th	—	Ther. — Weather fine. 8 AM advance Partyunder Capt Bacaet left to take	
			over from 122nd Bde 38th Div. 9 AM Brigade marched to ECOIVE DEQUES arriving 3 PM.	
—	7th	—	Ther. — Weather fine. 9 AM Brigade marched to HAVERSKIRKE arriving 12.30 PM	
		10 AM	inspected all Guns.	
—	8th	—	Ther. — Weather fine. 1 Section each Battery proceeded into action relieving	
			Brigade numbers of 122 Bde.	
—	9th	—	Ther. — Weather fine. 5 AM there was a heavy Bombardment and ...	
			appeared to be due East from HAVERSKIRKE. 9.15 AM orders received for the remainder	
			of the Brigade to report with Ammunition expended to LE SART CHURCH & there await	
			Further orders, & to be prepared to proceed into action to reinforce the 57th Div on the Lys river.	
		12 Noon	Orders received to proceed to Pte PNS BOIS L7d in a place of security	
			Brigade arrived at 2 PM. 3.15 PM Brigade went into action at L16 c.17 c. 6 in support	
			of the 151 Inf. Bde. 50 Div. Our line was as follows :- PIETENS BRIDGE Nr Klemen the	
			Railway & River to the central. During the night Brigade carried out harassing fire.	
			Capt Ferrie M.C. & Lieut H Torres returned from leave having been detained at the Base owing to Smallpox. Capt W. Bacaet & Lieut D.L. Bell Joined. 6 PM	Amm. Exp.

Army Form C. 2118.

WAR DIARY
or
INTELLIGENCE SUMMARY.

(Erase heading not required.)

Place	Date	Hour	Summary of Events and Information	Remarks and references to Appendices
	April 1918		Page 2.	
On the Move	10th		Fair. — Sher — Weather fine. 2AM. A/152 moved position to L10c29. 6AM. 8 & 9AM. remaining Batteries moved. 7AM Bde HQrs moved to L9d6000. 12 Noon Infantry Line remained as before 3PM Hand reload factory reported in ESTAIRES. 52M Enemy reported holding the Town on far North on the ESTAIRES. The 151 Inf Bde then counter attacked. 8PM. Enemy main body reported to be in the neighbourhood of STEENWERCK. The night was quiet. Casualties OR. Animals Eqp. A293 AX 893 BX 175	
-do-	11th		Fair — Sher — . Weather fine. 6AM Heavy Machine Gun Barrage constant on our Right after which our line fell back to BEAUPRE & LESTREM 11AM. the 151 Inf Bde fell back & were holding the line L'EPINETTE DE SELOBESE. 1.30 PM Batteries retired to positions K12+18. 3.2M Bde HQ moved to K10d52 5.PM Batteries retired to positions in K4+10. 8PM Bde HQ moved to E39d52. Quiet night. Casualty Lieut E.J. Lane Wounded. 1 OR Animal Eqp A790. AX 827. BX 94	
-do-	12th		Fair 29°3 Sher — . Weather fine. During the early hours B.C. "G" Div circus to positions in SE side of NIEPPE FOREST. The 4th Guards Bde came into the line during the early morning took up position from FORT ROUDIN VIEUXHOUCK to MERVILLE 4PM Bde HQ moved to E22a. 8PM JHR moved to D17a. Batteries received to positions in E19+20. During the night the 29th Inf Bde (5th Div) relieved the 150 Bde. Animal Eqp. A795 AX1497 BX115	
LE TIR ANGLAIS	13th		Fair. 29°7 Sher — . Weather fine. Saw our line re-established as follows:- Rise to Kst'd. 10AM Enemy evidently intended to attack Epl 3950 evident caught by our Artillery & rifle fire, some parties of the enemy 'bit reported to have been entirely annihilated 5PM A+B Batteries moved to fresh positions in J29. 6.30 PM C+D to. 7.30 PM our line established as follows:- K10 E30 K9d46. K10c99. Houre. Hashworthy road to K9a2.c6 to E28c2 B. E22 c2 2 6 Ref. 2a Polis'. Casualties Killed OR 1. Wounded OR 4 Animal Eqp A823 AX791 BX 243 Lieut Torrie & Unsell attached from SR & TM O to D/152.	

Army Form C. 2118.

WAR DIARY
or
INTELLIGENCE SUMMARY.
(Erase heading not required.)

Instructions regarding War Diaries and Intelligence Summaries are contained in F. S. Regs., Part II. and the Staff Manual respectively. Title pages will be prepared in manuscript.

Place	Date	Hour	Summary of Events and Information	Remarks and references to Appendices
		1918	Page 3	
LE TIR ANGLAIS	April 14th		Bar. 29.85 Ther. — Weather Wet Visibility Bad. Enemy Infantry went attacked at 10 AM. We put down a successful Barrage & congratulatory message from G.O.C. 5th Div. Many targets successfully engaged during the day. Fight very quiet. Ammn Exp. A1789 AX1973 BX226	
-do-	15th		Bar. 29.85 Ther. — Weather Wet. Visibility Poor. Fairly Quiet throughout the day. 6 PM. We carried to cover part of B.C. coopered in ?? of ?? engaged during the day. Ammn Expended A979 AX1056 BX190	
-do-	16th		Bar. 30.02 Ther. — Weather Fair Visibility Fair. Fairly Quiet throughout the day. 8.20 PM fired on SOS for 20 minutes. Harassing fire carried on throughout the night. 11.30 AM Enemy fired on 290 rds per Battery. Ammn Exp. A235 AX897 BX382	
-do-	17th		Bar. 30.01 Ther. — Weather Fair Visibility Fair. Our Fire 4.30 to 5 AM Harassing fire on LA COURONNE. Targets fired on during the day included LA COURONNE carried out 200 rds per Battery. Ammn Exp. A284 AX1574 BX528 Posn RONDIN Road FM5 COMBERT Road Exp. H5 + d Harassing fire by night used 75's Needle posted to Brigade + attacks to B152	
-do-	18th		Bar. 29.97 Ther. — Weather Fair. Visibility Fair. Our fire 9.15 AM to 5.15 AM Preparation 200 rds per Battery. 12.55 PM, 100 rds on GAS PREARNE Road Exp c. Road E9c 5.10 PM 20 rds on NF cold 672M 300 rds per Battery N5 + d 9.2M 6 AM 180 rds per Battery by night Harassing Fire. N55 PM, SQ5M, N5 L+d. Hostile fire Normal. Ammn Exp. A038 AX1065 BX256	
-do-	19th		Bar. 29.94 Ther. — Weather Fine + cold. Visibility Fair. Our fire 4.30 to 5 AM 20 M 9 pm Battery 5.15 PM 100 rds on E.30 a g.3 7.20 d 7.20 PM 100 rds by all Batteries Engage. 9a 8 a 9 PM 100 rds to all Batteries N.5 L + d. 9.2M 6 AM Usual night Harassing Fire. Hostile Fire Normal Ammn Exp. A225 AX1684 BX694	
-do-	20th		Bar. 29.97 Ther. — Weather Fine + cold. Visibility Fair. Our fire. 4.15 to 4.45 AM 300 Rds per Battery November Preparation 200 to 4.30 PM 3 minute concentration on LA COURONNE from R2a, "E2a" c5-9, 9 PM 6 AM Usual night Harassing Fire. Hostile Fire Normal. Ammn Exp. A218 AX1065 BX522	

A5834 Wt. W4973 M687 750,000 8/16 D.D. & L., Ltd. Forms/C.2118/13.

Army Form C. 2118.

WAR DIARY
or
INTELLIGENCE SUMMARY.
(Erase heading not required.)

Instructions regarding War Diaries and Intelligence Summaries are contained in F.S. Regs., Part II. and the Staff Manual respectively. Title pages will be prepared in manuscript.

Place	Date	Hour	Summary of Events and Information	Remarks and references to Appendices
LE TIR ANGLAIS	April 21st		Page 4. Par. 29.72 Wea — Weather fine Visibility good Air Fire 9AM to 6PM & from 3AM to 9PM Hostile Fire Operation. 9.30AM D/152 on 2nd Corps BROOCHE. 9.2M to 6PM Usual night harrassing fire. Mobile Fire 10.50PM to 3AM Hostile Bn Shell Bombardment, mustard + others. Engineer followers fires 7PM found. Enemy Egn A206 AX 137 BX 528.	
do	22nd		Par. 29.97 Wea — Weather fair Visibility fair Air Fire 9AM to 9.25 & 11.15 to 5.15PM Hostile fire Operation. 10PM D/152 40 rds W Shell on K.10, K.30. LE COOMET 2FRDV 9.2PM to 1AM Usual night harrassing fire. Mobile fire Normal Enemy Egn A260 AX 747 BX 496.	
do	23rd		Par. 30.04 Wea — Weather fair Visibility fair Air Fire 9.10 to 10.30AM & 2PM to 9PM Hostile Operation. 9.40PM Operation Order No 72 carried out as per Appendix 1. The Raid was successful, resulting in prisoners. 9.2PM to 11AM Usual harassing fire. Mobile fire 2AM to 5AM No Shell bombardment in D34-30, 77PM + 10:59PM Mustard 10AM Prepared on D24. E.A. Active. Enemy Egn A278 AX 890 BX 194 Bn 396.	
do	24th		Par. 29.96 Wea — Weather fair Visibility fair Air Fire 3PM to 4.55PM Counter Bombardment 9.2M 6.6AM Usual night harrassing fire. Mobile fire Normal E.A. Nil Ideal A + Adams — reported from 2nd?? A Enemy Egn A156. AX 1391 BX 528.	
do	25th		Par. 29.95 Wea — Weather Dull Visibility Fair Counter Gun Fire 5.10 5.15AM Counter Preparation 11AM D/152 20rds on Bridge E.30a. 2.00PM A/152 30 rds on Hostile Battery Md.70 Road Fur? as per Appendix 2 attacked. Mobile Fire Normal Enemy Egn A224 AX 4AM BX 236.	
do	26th		Par. 30.14 Wea — Weather Dull Visibility Bad Air Fire 4.45 & 5AM Operation Order N° 4 as per Appendix 3. 10AM A/152 Reduced Rounds at E.28.D.5.0, 6.2.P.13.5 Burnt Bivouac FME enemy Shernike H.E. Hostile fire Normal Enemy Egn. A 486 AX 461 BX 231.	
do	27th		Par. 30.12 Wea — Weather Dull Visibility Bad Gun fire 3.30AM Operation Order N° 6 as per Appendix to correct an error 9.2M to 6PM Usual night harassing fire. Hostile fire 12PM to 2.30AM WIEPEE FOREST SHELLED 12.7PM to 3PM 60 rds C	

WAR DIARY or INTELLIGENCE SUMMARY

Army Form C. 2118.

Place	Date	Hour	Summary of Events and Information	Remarks and references to Appendices
LETTR ANGLAIS	April 1918 27th		15 gun in E.W.C central 12.7 om so Pdr Sn SW. 21 E & remainder E.S. Tell Ammn Exp. A.1125 AX.1171 BX.935 Warmels 29 pdr 120.	
do	28th		Weather Fine - DCC viited by Bat. Con Fire a.1 m & 9 pm 70 Rieger Battery which E.O.O. 4.10 PM 100 Rds old Battries found Buganian trajectories. Bn 3 minute concentration at request of Infantry on Exy Z.02 NKC no.65 NKC.22 Noth Evning from 10.215 to 2 am on Cyanide & Mobile Fire 2.30 to 4.30 Harry Barrage 4.2 on our Front Line. E.A. Nel Ammn Exp. A118. AX.105 BX.140	
do	29th		Weather Dull. Visibility Fair. Con Fire 5.20 to 6 am Never rapt. Harassing Fire Mobile Fire Buri movement. Throughout the night a long bombardment was kept. E.A. Sevral German airo dropped bombs at 7 pm 10.15, 11.10 PM, 1.40, 3.20 2.3 PM Ammn Exp. A603 AX.890 BX.287.	
do	30th		Weather Dull - Visibility Dull. Con Fire Routine Barrage fired at 3.30 to 3.50 AM 4.10 to 4.29 AM 11.5 PM Gun to Area 7PM as per Operation Order 9 PM to 6 AM Night Firing Varying Rates. 2 1/2 to 10 rds of 9 pdr, 4-100 rds of 5 How 9 ER. Nel Ammn Exp A. 795. AX 362 BX 266. 9 final At. Adamo sent to Field Ambulance	

J. Wanford
Lt. 152 Bde. R.F.A.

SECRET.   Ypendoos 1   Copy No 17

152nd BRIGADE R.F.A. ORDER No 2

1. **Raid.**

   Irish Guards Battalion (4th Guards Bde) propose carrying out a raid in E.28.d.& K.4.a. tonight April 23/24.

2. The Artillery arrangements will be as follows:-

   18 pdr. Creeping Barrage from E.28.c.85.85. to K.4.b.58.30 to Protective Barrage E.29.a.03.13. - K.5.b.7.5.

   4.5 Hows. Creeping Barrage from E.28.d.16.93. - K.4.b.80.73. to Protective Barrage E.29.a.8.0. - E.29.c.8.2.

1 18 pdr batty 286th Bde R.F.A.	E.28.c.85.85 – E.28.d.0.5.	
C/152	E.28.d.0.5. – E.28.d.14.23.	
B/152	E.28.d.14.23. – K.4.b.25.95.	
A/152	K.4.b.25.95. – K.4.b.4.7.	
1 18 pdr. batty 286th Bde R.F.A.	K.4.b.4.7. – K.4.b.58.30.	
D/152		} E.28.d.4.6. – K.4.b.80.73.
D/286 on the left		

   The Creeping Barrage will open on above lines at Zero Hour & will remain on them for 3 minutes. The Barrage will then lift by 100 yards lifts per 3 minutes until the Protective Barrage is reached.

3. **Rates of fire.**

18 pdrs.	Zero to Protective Barrage	4 Rounds p.g.p.m.
	Protective Barrage to Zero + 50'	2 " " "
	Zero + 50' to Zero + 60'	½ " " "

   4.5 Hows. ½ 18 pdr Rates.

4. **S.O.S. Lines.**

   S.O.S. lines will remain on Protective Barrage until notification has been received from 4th Guards Brigade that all the infantry are in.

5. **Heavy Artillery.**

   6" Hows will put down a Standing Barrage as follows:-

1	6" How	L'Epinette.	
1	"	Le Cornet Perdu.	} Zero to
2	"	Gars Brugghe.	} Zero + 60'
1	"	E.29.a.3.9.	
1	"	E.23.c.2.9.	

6" How   Rue Goulbert E.29.c.8.2
         & Roads E.29.c.8.7.

Zero to Zero + 30' then lift to LA COURONNE E.30.a.
+ remain until Zero + 60'.

6. Zero hour will be 8.40 p.m. April 23rd

7. Watches will be synchronised at 4th Guards Bde HQ. at 3 p.m. Batteries 152nd Bde R.F.A. will each detail an officer to attend.

8. Acknowledge.

                                 G.W. Brewitt Capt.
                                 for O.C. 152 Bde. R.F.A.

23/4/18.

18 Copies   Nos 1/4 Batteries 152 Bde.
                 5/8   286 Bde. R.F.A.
                 9   B.M. 4th Guards Bde.
                 10   B.M., 57th D.A.
                 11   B.M., 34th D.A.
                 12/14 Heavy Group
                 15   Liaison Officer 4th Guards Bde.
                 16   This office.
                 17/18 Spare

SECRET.   *Appendix No. 6.*   COPY No. 8

152 Brigade R.F.A. Order No. 11.

1. At 11 p.m. Stokes Mortars will bombard FME BEAULIEU.

2. At 11-1 p.m. to 11-9 p.m. A. and B. Batteries will fire on hedge E.28.d.4.5. to E.4.b.7.7.

   C. and D. Batteries will search houses and enclosures in E.29.c.

3. Rate of fire:-

   18 pdrs. 3 rounds per gun per minute.

   4.5" hows. Half of the above rate.

4. Watches will be synchronized with this Office at 10 p.m.

30-4-18.

R.W. Angell.
2nd./Lieut,
for O.C. 152nd. Brigade, R.F.A.

Copies to :-

1/4 Batteries.
5. B.M. Infny. Bde.
6. B.M. 34th. R.A.
7. This Office.
8/9. War Diary.

SECRET. Copy No. 13

Amendment to 152 Brigade, R.F.A. Order No. 2.

1. Ref. para 2 delete line 3 and substitute as follows:-
Protective Barrage will be
1 Battery 286 Bde E 29.a. 05.13 to E. 29 c 2.8.
152 Bde   E 29.c. 2.8 to K.5.a. 5.9.
1 Battery 286 Bde K 5.a. 5.9 to K.5.a. 7.5.

2. Ammunition to be used
   50% A and AX. 50% on Graze.

R. W. Angell
2/Lieut. for
O.C. 152nd Brigade, R.F.A.

23-4-18

To all recipients of Order No. 2.

SECRET *Appendix 2* 152nd. Bde. No. NF/1.

Harassing fire tonight April 25/26 will be carried out as under :-

TARGETS.
18 pdrs. Hedge behind BEAULIEU FARM K.4.b.70.65 - E.28.d.42.52.
Infantry report that enemy brings up light field guns at dusk, puts them in this hedge and removes them be--fore dawn.

4.5.Hows. Road and houses E.30. central.

TIMES.
    A/152. 9.p.m. to 12.mn.
    B/152. 12.mn. to 3.a.m.
    C/152. 3.a.m. to 6.a.m.
    D/152. 9.p.m. to 6.a.m.

AMMUNITION.
    120 rounds per 18 pdr battery.
    90 " " 4.5.How " .

25-4-18.

G.W. Brewitt Capt.
for O.C. 152nd. Brigade. R.F.A.

SECRET   COPY No. 8

Appendix 9.

152nd. Bde. R.F.A. Order No. 4.
Reference 57th. D.A. No. X/58.

1. On the morning of the 28th April, at an hour to be notified later a barrage will be put down on the following line :-

    E.11.b.6.6. – E.11.d.7.9. – E.11.d.7.0. – E.17.b.4.0.

    The 152nd. Bde. R.F.A. is allotted the following line :-
    E.11.d.75.30. – E.17.b.50.65.

    Batteries are allotted the following :-
    A/152.   E.17.b.50.65. – E.17.b.60.87.
    B/152.   E.17.b.60.87. – E.11.d.68.10.
    C/152.   E.11.d.68.10. – E.11.d.75.30.

2. PHASES.

    Zero to Zero plus 5 on above line.
    Zero plus 5 Lift 200 yards.
    Zero plus 10 Lift 200 yards.
    Zero plus 15 Cease fire.

3. RATES OF FIRE.

    Zero to Zero plus 5.   4 rds per gun per minute.
    Zero plus 5 to Zero plus 8.   3 "   "   "   "   "
    Zero plus 8 to Zero plus 12.   2 "   "   "   "   "
    Zero plus 12 to Zero plus 15.   4 "   "   "   "   "

4. AMMUNITION.

    50% A and AX. A to be 50% on graze.

5. 4.5. Hows will fire in their own Brigade Zones on Counter-Preparation targets.

6. Acknowledge.

25-4-18.
                                            G.W. Brewitt Capt.   for
                                            O.C. 152nd. Brigade. R.F.A.

Copies to :-
    1/4.   Batteries.
    5.   B.M. 34th D.A.
    6.   B.M. 4th Guards Bde.
    7.   This office.
    8/9.   War Diary.
    10/11. Spare.

Appendix 4

SECRET   COPY No. 7

152nd. Bde. R.F.A. Order No. 8.
Reference 0700 L.A. 3.C. No. 20. attached
and 298th Bde. R.F.A. C.S.1/05.

1. Reference attached, batteries are allotted tasks as under :-
Zero to Zero plus 40'.
18 PRs.
    A/152. 3 guns E.29.a.40.50.

Zero to Zero plus 8'.
    A/152. 6 guns E.23.a.25.45. — E.23.a.30.52.
    B/152. 6 guns E.23.c.25.52. — E.23.c.22.70.
    C/152. 6 guns E.23.c.22.70. — E.23.c.20.83.

Zero Plus 8' to Zero plus 11'.
    A/152. 3 guns E.23.c.55.45. — E.23.c.50.57.
    B/152. 6 guns E.23.c.53.57. — E.23.c.52.70.
    C/152. 6 guns E.23.c.52.70. — E.23.c.50.83.

Zero plus 11' to Zero plus 14'.
    A/152. 3 guns E.23.c.77.50. — E.23.c.73.62.
    B/152. 6 guns E.23.c.73.62. — E.23.c.73.75.
    C/152. 6 guns E.23.c.73.75. — E.23.c.72.87.

Zero plus 14' to Zero plus 17'.
    A/152. 3 guns E.23.c.95.95. — E.23.a.93.93.
    B/152. 6 guns E.23.c.95.95. — E.23.a.90.10.
    C/152. 6 guns E.23.a.90.10. — E.23.a.90.20.

Zero plus 17' to Zero plus 20'.
    A/152. 3 guns E.23.d.15.95. — E.23.d.15.97.
    B/152. 6 guns E.23.d.15.97. — E.23.b.15.08. —
    E.23.b.05.15.
    C/152. 6 guns E.23.b.05.15. — E.23.a.90.33.

Zero plus 20' to Zero plus 40'.
    A/152. 3 guns E.23.b.15.08. — E.23.b.05.12.
    B/152. 6 guns E.23.b.05.12. — E.23.a.80.37.
    C/152. 6 guns E.23.a.80.37. — E.23.a.60.53.

4.5. Howitzers.
Zero to Zero plus 7'.
    B/152. Enclosures and farm buildings in LA BECQUE.

Zero plus 7' to Zero plus 40'.
    Road from E.23.b.7.0. to Main VIEUX BERQUIN road.

2. Zero hour will be 3.30 a.m. April 27th

3. Watches will be synchronized by phone at 3.15 a.m.

4. Acknowledge by wire.

                                                                G.W. Brewitt Capt.
20-4-18.   O.C. 152nd. Brigade. R.F.A.

Copies to :-
    1/4   Batteries.
    5.   B.M.R.A. 34th. D.A.
    6.   B.M. 4th Guards Bde.
    7/8.   War Diary.
    9.   This office.
    10.   Spare.

SECRET   Appendix 5.   COPY No 7

152nd Bde. R.F.A. Order No. 9.

1. **Harassing Fire and Neutralization of Hostile Batteries Zone.**

   Harassing fire and Neutralization of Hostile Batteries zone from now onwards will be :-

   E.28.b.9.7. - F.26.a.0.5. - L.1.c.5.4. - K.4.d.7.4.

2. **Harassing fire.**

   An enemy relief opposite this Bde front is suspected between 11.p.m and 1.a.m. Harassing fire will be increased, attention will be paid to roads and houses in Bde Zone and will be carried out as follows :-

   A/152. 10.p.m. to 11.p.m. 40 rounds. Not West of line E.23.d.1.4. - K.5.d.5.5.

   A/152. 11.p.m. to 12.m.n. 130 rounds. In Brigade Zone.
   B/152. 11.p.m. to 1.a.m. 170 " " " " "
   D/152. 11.p.m. to 1.a.m. 120 " " " " "
   C/152. 1.a.m. to 3.a.m. 170 " " " " "

3. **Test of S.O.S. Signal.**

   Following tests will be carried out this evening for purpose of seeing if S.O.S. Signal can be seen from Battery positions :-

   9.30.p.m. 1 salvo of 3 White Very lights.
   9.35.p.m. 1 salvo of 3 " " "

   Position from which these lights will be sent up is not very definite. Infantry say on the left portion of Brigade Zone.

   Batteries will look out for same and report on same to this office.

4. Acknowledge by wire.

28-4-18.

G.W. Brewitt Capt. for
O.C. 152nd. Brigade R.F.A.

Copies to :-
    1/4.   Batteries.
    5.   B.M. 86th Infy Bde.
    6.   This office.
    7/8.   War Diary.

WAR DIARY or INTELLIGENCE SUMMARY

Army Form C. 2118.

152 Bde R.F.A.
SS 28

Place	Date 1918	Hour	Summary of Events and Information	Remarks and references to Appendices
LE TOR ANGLAIS	May 1st		Bar. 29.80. Ther.— Weather Dull & cold. Visibility Bad. Our Line. During day registration only. 9.2M to 6AM. Usual night harassing fire. Hostile Fire. Below normal. E.A. Nil. Ammn. Exp. A 110. Ax 343. Bx 189.	
	2nd		Bar. 29.80. Ther.— Weather Fine. Visibility Fair. Our Fire. 9.2M to 6AM. Usual night harassing fire. Hostile Fire Normal. E.A. Nil. Ammn. Exp. A 198. Ax 186. Bx 132.	
	3rd		Bar. 29.76. Ther.— Weather Fine. Visibility fair. Our Fire. Registration & calibration on 2M. B/152 50 rds on Hostile Battery E50c 43.90. 9.2M to 6AM Night harassing fire. Hostile Fire Normal. E.A. Active. Casualties Wounded. Capt T.A. Rufford & Hav. Laker. Killed. O.P.1. Wounded. O.R.1. Ammn. Exp. A 818. Ax 220. Bx 103.	
	4th		Bar. 29.72. Ther.— Weather Fine. Visibility Fair. Our Fire. 3.30 to 3.45 AM. Events Zigzagation 24 rds per Battery. B/152 engaged Hostile Battery K21.B. 9.2M to 6AM Night harassing fire. Hostile Fire. 9.45AM 50 15cm shells in E19a. E13d. 22M 10.17pm shells in D2d. E.A. Normal. Ammn. Exp. A 905. Ax 397. Bx 139.	
	5th		Bar. 29.68. Ther.— Weather. Rain. Visibility Fair. Our Fire. CO No 21 as per Appendix 1. Fire carried out. 11.50 AM 30 rds by A/B/152 on Hostile Battery E25c 35.40. 5.2M 40 rds by D/152 on Stamp Land. N.R.E.20.26. 4.2M 60 rds by C/152 on K.B.21.22. 9.2M to 6AM Night harassing fire. 20 rds per Battery. Hostile Fire. Below Normal. E.A. Normal. Ammn. Exp. A 1874. Ax 601. Bx 264.	
	6th		Bar. 29.70. Ther.— Weather. Rain. Visibility Poor. Our Fire. 2.50 AM. Operation Order No 14 as per Appendix 2. 9.2M to 6AM. Night harassing fire carried out. Hostile Fire Normal. E.A. 10.30 AM. Four our lines. Ammn. Exp. A 916. Ax 510. Bx 101.	
	7th		Bar. 29.64. Ther.— Weather Mist. Visibility Poor. Our Fire. Registration 9.2M to 8AM Usual night harassing fire. Hostile Fire. Normal. E.A. 12.15.2M 3 over our lines. 2.2M 6 over our line.	

WAR DIARY or INTELLIGENCE SUMMARY

Army Form C. 2118.

(Erase heading not required.)

Place	Date	Hour	Summary of Events and Information	Remarks and references to Appendices
	May 1918		Page 2	
LE TIR ANGLAIS	4th		Ammn Exp. A189 A1 210. BX140. Rejoined the Brigade. Capt. L.W. Brooker & Lieut P.G. Bell	
		8PM	1 Section per Battery relieved by 38th AFA Bde	
	8th		12 Noon 2 Section per Battery 4 Brigade HQ relieved by 38th AFA Bde (Head Col. Hood DSO)	
			Ammn Exp. A19. AX115. BX68.	
		2.30 PM	Brigade marched to WITTES.	
WITTES	9th		Par. — Ther. — Weather very fine. Brigade at Rest.	
			I.O.M. inspected all Guns of the Brigade	
	10th		Par. — Ther. — Weather fine. Brigade at Rest	
	11th		Par. — Ther. — Weather fine. Brigade at Rest	
	12th		Par. — Ther. — Weather fair. Brigade at Rest	
	13th		Par. — Ther. — Weather wet. Brigade at Rest	
	14th		Par. — Ther. — Weather fine. Brigade at Rest. 10AM C.R.A inspected Brigade	
			dismounted. 5PM 1 Section per Battery proceeded into action A/152 relieving 119 at 7/30.0.2 B/152 relieving 120 at 75.0.30. C/152 relieving 121 at 7/10 6 6.0. D/152 relieving 97 at J6.0.5.	
	15th		Par. 30.15 Ther. — Weather fine Visibility Good. 6PM 1st Bde HA took over command of Lys Group. Lt.Col. J.M. Dawson Lucas Tooth Berks R.F.A. DSO. 10.2 PM Remaining Sections of Batteries relieved 27th Bde R.F.A.	
	16th		Par. 29.97. Ther. — Weather fine. Gun fire harassing. Fire carried out. 4.30 PM 1 Coop remonstration carried out as per L.S.O.O. N°1 (Appendix 9). Hostile Fire 8.9 PM Burst of fire of about 20 shells per period of Upper yellow line Nº 5 Shells in vicinity of J.10.c.2.3 intermittent Nos shelling in J3.9.d during night E.A very active during night & early morning. Ammn Exp. A411. AK952. BX528.	

Army Form C. 2118.

WAR DIARY
or
INTELLIGENCE SUMMARY.
(Erase heading not required.)

Instructions regarding War Diaries and Intelligence Summaries are contained in F.S. Regs., Part II. and the Staff Manual respectively. Title pages will be prepared in manuscript.

Page 3.

Place	Date	Hour	Summary of Events and Information	Remarks and references to Appendices
LE PARC	May 1918 17th		Per 29.8 Ther. ___ Weather fine. Visibility good. Our fire Harassing fire carried out by day & night. 3.15 AM & 4.5 PM 5 minute concentrations as per L.O.O. N°1 (Appendix 3). Hostile fire. During most night's No shelling on T.S.A. during day 9 AM - 11 AM Enemy shelled KM 6 50 rds 5.9 Hour. E.A. Very active own air force during night & morning Ammn. Exp. A259. AX 406. BX 301.	
do	18th		Per 30.9 Ther. ___ Weather fine. Visibility fair. Our fire Harassing fire carried out 10 PM fired 5.9 Horn. 7.5 L.B. shells sent to T.A. Fired 100 rounds on Tackers. Night Harassing fire carried out. 3.15 AM & 5.30 PM 5 minute concentrations carried out as per L.O.O. N°1 (Appendix 3) 4 PM Round at K21 L2 6 engaged & silenced two retained. Hostile fire 2.30 PM 100 rds A2 & 59 on road in T.S.C. from direction of MERVILLE. 9 to 2.30 PM 50 yds H.2 in T.S.C. E.A very active during night & morning. Ammn. Exp. A492. AX 353. BX 380.	
do	19th		Per 30.32 Ther. ___ Weather fine. Visibility fair. Our fire Harassing fire went out at 10 PM returned 2 AM Having engaged rds & trucks in Brigade zone. 7 PM & 7 AM Night Harassing fire carried out. 3.40 AM & 2 PM 5 minute concentrations as per L.O.O. N°1 (Appendix 3) Hostile fire. Hostile Ho shelling throughout the night. 12 Noon 75 Sho H.E. 10.5 gun. Gun on T.S.C. E.A. Very active during night. Ammn. Exp. A216. AX 240. BX 299.	
do	20th		Per 30.30 Ther. ___ Weather fine. Visibility fair. Our fire. 7 PM to 7 PM Night Harassing fire carried out 8-10 AM Wire cutting by A 7152 at K16 B 80.60 to 90.95 & 15 PM to who THERMITE at House K15 6.2. 4.30 PM C.O. N°5 (Appendix H) Effective taken & 30 prisoners Hostile fire 9.15 to 9.45 PM B/152 shelled with about 8rds H.2 3 groups of AmmnN Dist Tvi. Enemy shelled during the night T.S.C., Tn.6. 7.29d., 7.22B., 7.22C. 4.30 AM about 50 rds H.2 K13 a cent & 10 AM Several bursts of fire on/about LE PARC from Doulieu bridge to T.g. 6. E.A. Normal. Ammn. Exp. A 390 AX 654. BXH 26. The following officers named the MC. Keeles P.S. Tavrant, L.E. Robertson. D.C. Young, & Lieuts. L.C. Beck T. King.	

WAR DIARY or INTELLIGENCE SUMMARY

Army Form C. 2118.

Place	Date May 1918	Hour	Summary of Events and Information	Remarks and references to Appendices
LE PARC			Page 4	
	21st		Ber 29/72 Ther. Weather Fine. Visibility Good. Gun Fire 7 PM to 7 AM Night harassing Fire carried out. Roving Gun went out from 9 PM to 3 AM + fired 100 rds well behind the enemy S.O.S. 10.35 AM. Fired on S.O.S. on our new line also Hostile fire active. EA Normal 2/Lieut H. Gretton + A.V. Oskam returned from LA. 2/Lieut R.F. Bamber joined the Brigade. Amm. Exp A 1639 AX 538 BX	
	22nd		Ber 30.04 Ther. Weather Fine. Visibility Good. Gun Fire 7 PM to 7 AM Night harassing fire. Roving Gun went out + fired and into back area. Hostile fire. Normal EA regular Amm Exp A 660. AX 109 BX 413	
	23rd		Ber 30.20 Ther. Weather Fine Strong NW Wind. Visibility Good Gun Fire Usual night harassing fire 11.15 PM Bde concentration on 77 m.m. Battery at NM.a.30. 120 Rds 18 Pdr + 30 Rds 4.5 How. no 23 to 10.30 AM Roving Gun went out + fired into back area. Hostile fire very active chiefly during night EA very active. Mentioned in despatches from London Gazette dated 20/5/18 Capt W.E. Borden 79135502 Cpl S.M. Lewis M/152. Amm. Exp A 705. AX 214. BX 187	
	24th		Weather. Mist. Visibility Poor. Gun Fire. Usual night harassing fire Roving Gun went out from 9.30 PM to 1 AM + fired 150 rds into NP VILLE 150 rd + 150 rd S.O.S. + NW art retaliation for shelling of front system. Hostile fire. 11 PM Enemy shelled front line. 4 AM to 6 AM Enemy shelled T.S.C. with 150 Rds. 11 m.m. Gas 1A 778 Amm. Exp A 142 AX 153 BX 172	
	25th		Ber 30.18 Ther. Weather Fine. Weather Fine. Visibility Good. Gun Fire 7 PM to 7 AM Night harassing Fire carried out 10.30 PM 16 at intervals to 1.30 AM 17/460 engaged Hostile Battery K.11.c.1.8 50 Rounds in all 11PM Roving Gun went out + fired 150 Rounds. 1.30 AM 200 Rds m.M.G Bat Hostile Fire. Very active EA very active. Amm Exp A 870 AX 5. BX N	
	26th		Ber 30.18 Ther. — Weather. Fine. Visibility. Poor. Gun Fire Very active. Usual night harassing Fire. 9.30 PM + 10.13 PM +3.45 AM Group fired attack period 600 Rds. 500 East of S.O.S. Line. E.A. Normal Hostile Fire. Mme active than usual. Amm Exp. A746 AX 265 BX 157	

Army Form C. 2118.

WAR DIARY
or
INTELLIGENCE SUMMARY.
(Erase heading not required.)

Page 5

Place	Date	Hour	Summary of Events and Information	Remarks and references to Appendices
LE PARC	May 1918 24th		Weather fine. Visibility fair. Our Fire. 9.5 - 10.30 P.M. Rop. Bays. 2 rear Fd. S.O.S. line + 500 yds East thereof. 800 Rds each period. 7 P.M. to 7 A.M. 80 Rounds per gun night harassing fire. 7.9 P.M. J/152 engaged Mobile Battery at N.16.a.75.40 with Aeroplane observation. Hostile fire. Normal. E.A. 10 over during the day. Ammo. Exp. A.1945 AX.440 BX.540	
-do-	28th		Weather fine. Visibility Good. Our fire. 6 P.M. to 9 P.M. J/152 engaged Mobile Battery K.17.a.67.40 with aeroplane observation. 7 P.M. to 7 A.M. Usual night harassing fire. 10.20 P.M. 50 Rds per Battery 1000' East of S.O.S. 10.30 P.M. to 1 A.M. Roving fire went and + fired into back areas. 2.40 P.M. 100 Rds per Battery 500' East of S.O.S. Hostile fire. Very active. E.A. 30 over. No time during the day. Ammo Exp. A.900 AX.67 BX.290. Capt. T.P. Radford M.C. + Lieut. T.S. Rhoades returned from Hospital.	
-do-	29th		Weather fine. Visibility Good. Our Fire. Aeroplane Cooperation with 10.40 Rds per Gun. 9.20 P.M. 50 pdr Battery 100' East of S.O.S. line. 2.40 P.M. 100 Rds per Battery 500' East of S.O.S. Hostile fire. Very active. E.A. 12 over our lines up to midday. Ammo Exp. A.1008. AX.156 BX.281	
-do-	30th		Weather fine. Visibility Good. Our fire. 7 P.M. to 7 A.M. Usual night harassing fire. 4.50 to 5 A.M. Retaliation fired at request of Infantry. 12.30 P.M. 50 Rds on H.B. 1389. 4.15 to 5.40 P.M. 300 Rds distributed shoot on H.B. K.7.10 (K.32.81) Hostile Fire. Normal. E.A. active. Ammo Exp. A.576 AX.35 BX.101	
-do-	31st		Weather fine. Visibility Good. Our fire. 7 P.M. to 7 A.M. Usual night harassing fire. 12.30 P.M. 2/60 supposed a Raid. 10 P.M. to 12 M. Roving gun went out + fired into back areas. Hostile fire. Normal. E.A. 26 over during the day. Ammo. Exp. A.44. AX.155 BX.216	

H. Weare.
Lieut. Col. 152 Bde. R.F.A.

Scale 1/10,000
1 Mile.

Artewage.
Strauing Baymage
C. view
Potchielier Valley

Ref. Left Group 115 & 6th D.A. 11917c.

SECRET.   War Diary Appendix No 4   COPY No. 6

152 Bde Order No. 16.

Ref. 57 D.A. Operation Order No. 21 (attached).

1. Batteries will co-operate as under:-

   18 pdrs.
   Zero to Zero Plus 2'

   A/152.   E.17.b.90.80. - E.11.d.0.0. - E.11.d.30.00.

   B/152.   E.11.d.30.35. - E.11.d.30.80.

   C/152.   E.11.d.30.00. - E.11.d.30.35.

   Zero Plus 2' to Plus 4'.

   A,B & C/152. E.17.b.70.83. - E.11.d.70.10.

   Zero Plus 4' to Plus 40'.

   A/152.   E.17.b.90.78. - E.17.b.36.75.

   C/152.   E.17.b.36.75. - 39.70. - E.17.b.70.80.

   B/152.   E.11.d.70.92. - E.11.b.30.25.

   4.5.Hows.
   Zero to Plus 40'.

   D/152.   E.12.c.05.03. - E.12.c.48.50.

2. **Rates of fire.**
   As per table attached 57th D.A. O.O. No.21.

3. Zero hour will be notified later.

4. **Synchronizing.**
   An Officer from this H.Q. will visit batteries during evening to synchronise watches.

5. Acknowledge.

4/3/18.

G.W. Brewitt. Capt.
for O.C. 152nd. Brigade. R.F.A.

Copies to:-
   1/4.   Batteries.
   5.   This office
   6/7.   War Diary.

SECRET   COPY No. 15

152nd. Bde.R.F.A. Order No.14/1.

Reference 152nd.Bde.R.F.A. Order No 14 attached.

1. The 160th. Bde R.F.A. have been asked to co-operate by putting down a Standing barrage as follows :-

   5 - 18 pr batteries.

   Along hedge and ditch K.10.b.70.95. - K.4.d.85.05. - K.5.c.00.20. K.5.c.40.5. - K.5.a.50.90.

2. Rate of fire.
   Zero to plus 60', half round p.m.p.gun.

3. Zero hour will be notified later.

4. ~~Addition from this H.Q. ....~~ willing to synchronize

5. Please acknowledge.

4.5.18.   G.W.Brewitt Capt.
                                                  O.C. 152nd. Brigade.R.F.A. per

Copies to all recipients of D614.

SECRET   *War Diary. Appendix 2*   COPY No. 15

152nd. Bde. R.F.A. Order No.14.

1. The 86th Infantry Brigade will raid FERME BEAULIEU on the night of May 5/6th. Zero hour will be notified later.

2. The 285th Bde. R.F.A. are placed at our disposal for this minor enterprise.

3. Artillery arrangements are as follows:-

   (a) A/152. Zero to o plus.
      K.4.b.50.60. to K.4.b.30.60. thence by switches of 1° lift every 3 minutes to E.28.d.30.40. to E.28.c.90.50. thence to protective barrage till o plus 60. E.28.d.30.85. to E.28.c.90.9.

   B/152. Zero to o plus 3.
      K.4.b.75.60. to K.4.b.50.90. thence by switches of 1° lift every 3 minutes to E.28.d.50.50. to E.28.d.30.40. thence to protective barrage till o plus 60. E.28.d.9.9. to E.28.d.30.85.

   C/152. Superimpose. Zero to o plus 3.
      Line E.28.d.1.0. - E.28.d.5.0. thence to Protective barrage by switches of 1° lift every 3 minutes.
      E.28.c.9.9. to E.28.d.9.9. till o plus 60.

   (b) 285th Bde. R.F.A. 3 18.pdr batteries.
From Zero to o plus 3. E.29.b.0.3. - K.5.b.7.7. thence to protective barrage E.28.d.9.9. - K.5.a.5.2. by drops of 100 yds every 3 minutes and remain till o plus 60.

   (c) D/152. and D/285. 4.5 Hows. superimpose. From Zero to o plus 3.
      E.28.d.7.7. - K.4.b.9.0. thence to Protective barrage E.29.a.8.3. - E.29.d.4.5. by lifts of 100 yds every 3 minutes and remain on protective till o plus 60.

   (d) 1.6" How.   E.29.c.9.8.
      1 " " . E.29.a.85.95.
      1 " " . K.5.b.30.75.
      1 " " . K.5.d.35.60.
      2 " " . K.11.a.5.5. and vicinity.
   (e) 1 " " . E.29.c.85.65. }
      1 " " . E.29.c.8.2.   } Zero to plus 30.
   then lift to LA COURONNE and vicinity till o Plus 60.

4. **Rates of fire.**
   18 pdrs. Zero to Protective barrage. 4 rounds p.g.p.m.
           Protective to o plus 30.   2 " " " .
           o Plus 30 to o plus 60.   1 " " " .
   4.5.Hows. Half of above rates.

5. **Ammunition.**
   (a) A. 50% graze.
   (b) 50% A. and AX. 101 fuze. 50% graze.
   (c) Zero to protective. 101 fuze.
      Protective till plus 60. 50% 101 and 106 fuze.

6. Watches will be synchronized with this office at 6.30.p.m.

7. Acknowledge.

3rd. May. 1918.

                                             G.W. Brewitt Capt. for
                                             O.C. 152nd. Brigade R.F.A.

Copies to:-   1/4. Batteries 152.   12. B.M. 34th. D.A.
                5/9. 285th. Bde. R.F.A.   13. 57th. D.A. for. S.A.
                10. B.M. Infy. Bde.   14. This office.
                11. B.M. 57th. D.A.   15/16. War Diary.
                    17/18. Spare.

War Diary Appendix 3

COPY No. 12

Left Group Order No. 1.
Reference 5th Divl. Arty. No. HBM/15/24.

1. Concentrations will be carried out as follows :-

   (a) May. 6th. 4.30.p.m.
   2 - 18pdr batteries 160th. Bde. R.F.A.   K.21.b.0.2. to K.21.b.4.4.
   D/152.   K.21.b.0.2. to K.21.b.2.3.
   D/160.   K.21.b.2.3. to K.21.b.4.4.

   (b) May. 17th. 3.5. a.m.
   D/152.   K.26.c.6.3. to K.26.c.9.4.
   D/160.   K.26.c.9.4. to K.26.d.2.5.

   (c) May. 17th. 4.45 p.m.
   A/152.   K.21.b.85.95. to K.16.c.10.13.
   B/152.   K.16.c.10.13. to K.16.c.3.3.
   D/152.   K.21.b.85.95. to K.16.c.10.13.
   D/160.   K.16.c.10.13. to K.16.c.3.3.

   (d) May. 18th. 3.15. a.m.
   2 - 18pdr batteries 160th. Bde. R.F.A.   K.16.a.0.9. to K.15.b.55.75.
   D/152.   K.15.b.55.75. to K.15.b.75.80.
   D/160.   K.15.b.75.80. to K.16.a.0.9.

   (e) May. 18th. 5.30. p.m.
   D/152   }
   D/160.   }   Same as (b)

   (f) May. 19th. 3.40. a.m.
   2 - 18.pdr batteries. 160th. Bde. R.F.A. }
   D/152.   } Same as (d)
   D/160.   }

   (g) May. 19th. 2. p.m.
   A. & D/152.   Area   K.33.a.30.85. - K.33.a.6.9. -
                                            K.33.a.4.4. - K.33.a.67.53.
   B/152 & D/160.   Area. K.33.a.6.9. - K.33.a.9.9. -
                                            K.33.a.67.53. - K.33.b.0.6.

   (h) May. 20th. 3.20. a.m.
   A/152.   K.15.b.55.75. to K.15.b.75.80.
   C/152.   K.15.b.75.80. to K.16.a.0.9.
   D/152.   K.15.b.55.75. to K.15.b.75.80.
   D/160.   K.15.b.75.80. to K.16.a.0.9.

2. 4.5.Howitzers will use 106 fuze for these concentrations.
   18.pdrs will use H.E.

3. Rates of fire.
   18.pdrs.   4 rounds per gun per minute.
   4.5.Hows.   2 rounds per how per minute.

4. Each concentration will last 5 minutes.

5. Time will be sent out from these H.Q. 1½ hours before each concentration by telephone.

- Acknowledge.

16th. May. 1918.   G.W. Brewitt Capt. for
                                          O.C. Left Group. 5th Divl Arty.

Copies to :-
   1/5. 160th Bde. R.F.A.   11. This office.
   6/9. 152. Batteries.   12/13. War Diary.
   10.   B.M. 95th Infy Bde.   14. Spare.

SECRET   War Diary Appendix No 4   COPY No. 15

Left Group Order No. 5.
Reference 55th D.A. Order No. 176.

1. Barrage.
B & C/160. will form a standing barrage as per attached tracing.
A, B & C/152. and A/160. will form a creeping barrage as per attached tracing.

   J. B. Bars.
   Zero Hrs K to Zero.
   B/152. K.15.b.6.35. to K.15.a.75.80.
   A/160. K.15.a.75.80. to K.10.d.4.0.

   Zero to Zero plus 2.
   B/152. 6 Rows. K.15.a.2.1. - K.16.a.75.00.

   Zero plus 2 to Zero plus 25.
   B/152. 6 Rows. K.16.a.45.75. to K.16.a.75.00.
          "   "   Search East from line K.16.a.2.1. - K.16.a.45.75.
                  as far as the RED PUESEHEEQUIN - ARMENTRE Road
                  paying particular attention to Orchards and houses

   Zero to Zero plus 25.
   A/160. K.15.a.75.80. - K.10.d.5.5. - K.10.d.5.7.

   Rates of fire.
   As per 55th D.A. Order No.176

2. A/152. will engage house at K.15.b.8.8.(house latest) with one
   Section from Zero - 18 minutes. to Zero + 5 minutes.

   Ammunition. Thermite. 50 rounds

3. Liaison.
   Captain C.Fennie M.C. B/152 will be Liaison Officer with 1st Battn
   West Surrey Regt at K.9.c.56.30.
   155th Bde R.F.A. Signalling Officer is arranging telephonic
   communication.
   Particulars as to time to Report at Battn H.Q. will be sent to
   O.C. A/152. later.

4. Zero day and hour will be notified later.

5. Acknowledge.

                                      G.W. Brewitt.
10th May 1918.   Capt & Adjt.
                                      Left Group 55th Divisional Arty.

Copies to :-
          1/5. 155th Bde.R.F.A.
          6/9. Batteries.152.
          10.   B.M. 55th D.A.
          11.   B.M. 5th D.A.
          12.   B.M. 55th Infy Bde.
          13.   Capt. C. Fennie.
          14.   This office.
          15/16. War Diary.
          17.   Spare.

Army Form C. 2118.

WAR DIARY
or
INTELLIGENCE SUMMARY.
(Erase heading not required.)

152nd BRIGADE, R.F.A.

Place	Date	Hour	Summary of Events and Information	Remarks and references to Appendices
LE PARC.	June 1st 1918		Page 1.	
			Bar. 30.48. Ther. 58° Weather. Fair. Visibility. Poor. Gun Fire. 12.30 pm Gun Fire. Night. Harassing Fire. During day went no forward positions - Fired 150 Rds. 1.40 AM 2.10 pm Harassing fired 100 Rds. and on S605 + B601. 5.15 am 2.19 pm Batteries fired 100 Rds on S605 + P600 + P600. K18 C. 8.0 PM Wise cutting at T001.B.15. 10.45 AM 50 Rds. 45 Rds on K7910 Hostile Fire. Normal. E.A. 21 over during the day. Ammn. Exp. A791. AX 155. BX 216.	
	2nd		Bar. 30.48. Ther. 60° Weather. Fair. Visibility. Poor. Gun Fire. 7.30 pm 9.0 pm 2.30 pm Gun Fire. Night Harassing Fire. 1 1½ hrs 2 AM Nothing to record - Fired 150 Rds. on hostile area. Hostile Fire. Normal. E.A. 15 over during the day. Ammn. Exp. A692. AX 90. AX 150. BX 156.	
	3rd		Bar. 30.24. Ther. 59° Weather. Fair. Visibility. Fair. Gun Fire. 7.30 pm 9 pm 2.30 pm Gun Fire. Night. Harassing Fire. 1.10 AM 2.18 pm per Batteries fired 120 rounds - variation of situation taken. Hostile Fire. Rent Cave 11.45 PM C.O. No. 13 (Appendix 1) carried out, 2 minutes a station taken. Hostile Fire. Consists the amount of shelling during the night, otherwise normal. Hostile Fire. Harassing fire. E.A. Normal. Ammn. Exp. A283. AX 176. BX 190	
	4th		Bar. 30.16. Ther. 69° Weather. Fair. Visibility. Fair. Gun Fire. 1.30 pm 9 pm 10.30 pm Gun Fire. Night Harassing Fire. 10.30 pm 20.10 19 pm on Hostile Battery K7910 Hostile Fire. Normal. E.A. Normal. Ammn. Exp. A1108. AX 850. BX 990.	
	5th		Bar. 30.24. Ther. 61° Weather. Fair. Visibility. Fair. Gun Fire. 7 pm 9 pm 25 Rds pm Gun Fire. Night. Harassing Fire. 10 PM 1 AM Firing Rounds went out in front 158 Rds Hostile Fire. Wire cut. Harassed up to 4 PM Y/103 shelled between 2 + 3.30 PM very little main Fire. E.A. Calm. Ammn. Exp. R295. AX 157. BX 102.	
	6th		Bar. 30.15. Ther. 59° Weather. Fair. Visibility. Poor. Gun Fire. 7 PM 9 PM 10.30 pm. Gun. Night Harassing Fire. 11.10 AM 12.10 19 pm on Hostile Battery K591 Hostile Fire. Normal. E.A. Normal. Ammn. Exp. A333. AX 52. BX 119.	

Army Form C. 2118.

WAR DIARY
or
INTELLIGENCE SUMMARY.
(Erase heading not required.)

Page 2.

Place	Date	Hour	Summary of Events and Information	Remarks and references to Appendices
LE SARS	June 7th	1918	Bar. 30.2, Ther. 58. Weather fine. Visibility Good. Our Fire. Usual night harassing fire. Barrage fire continued. Fired 150 Rds. Registration & checking of Ammo carried out. 6.30 PM Hostile Bty covering Bty Bde fired 7537 SOS. Hostile Fire. Normal Bee OP succeeded in getting C of E observation during the morning. E.A. Normal revealed hostile aeroplanes seen during the morning. Ammo. Exp. A409 AX80 BX140.	
-do-	8th		Bar. 30.15 Ther. 60. Weather fine. Visibility Poor. Our Fire. 2.30 pm fire. Night harassing fire. 1.30 AM B-C/152 fired as per L.30.79.18 (Appendix 2) Hostile Fire. Normal C. Ogan very active. Fired the OP EA. Seen during the day. Annie Exp. AA16 AX165 BX102	
-do-	9th		Bar. 29.92 Ther 60. Weather fine Visibility Poor. Our Fire. 30 Rds pm fire. Night harassing fire 12.30 AM Operation Order 71-19 carried out as per appendix 2. 11.30 to 2 AM Firing for evacuation party into back area. Hostile Fire. less than normal. E A over our lines. Ammo Exp. A286 AX526 BX216.	
-do-	10th		Bar. 29.96 Ther. 58. Weather fine. Visibility Poor. Our fire. 25 rds pm fire. Night harassing fire. Registration & testing of Ammo carried on. Hostile Fire. Somewhat normal. E.A. Nil. Ammo. Exp. A012 AX40 BX102.	
-do-	11th		Bar. 29.93 Ther. 62 Weather fine Visibility fair. Our Fire. Usual night harassing fire. Barrage fire went out & fired 150 Rds. 6.15PM 30 rds fired on Hostile TM on road. Eerie Setting carried out in front. Hostile Fire. Below normal. E.R. Nil. Saw Hari A. Frazer proceeded on ten day leave. Ammo Exp. A215 AX385 BX116	
-do-	12th		Bar. 29.95 Ther. 62 Weather fine Visibility fair. Our Fire. Normal night harassing fire. 10.30 AM 29 rds on Hostile Battery K1710. 10 rds 4.5 How on ITCHIN FARM. Hostile Fire. Normal. Missile 7143. Inactive than usual. E.A. 11 over during the day. Ammo. Exp. A311 AX129 BX96.	
-do-	13th		Bar. 29.91 Ther. 61 Weather fine Visibility fair. Our Fire. 1.25 Rds pm ten Night harassing fire 10 AM 30 Rds 18 pds at House K19a 35.50 retaliations on fire. from LICINETTE + House K11a 23.30 at Hoggs K1lse. Normal. Hostile Fire. Normal. EA 7 over during the day. Ammo Exp. A253 AX100 BX32A	

WAR DIARY
or
INTELLIGENCE SUMMARY.
(Erase heading not required.)

Army Form C. 2118.

Page 3

Place	Date	Hour	Summary of Events and Information	Remarks and references to Appendices
LE PARC	1918 June 12th		Bar. 29.82. Ther. 61. Weather fine. Visibility Poor. Gun Fire 25 Rds per Gun. Night Harassing fire. Roving Gun went out & fired 150 Rds onto Tick area. 4 PM D/152 Rel. T/CXLIII C.R.G.A. Forecup. 20 Rds fired at R.10.d.6.5.45 ret on fire. 8 PM 80 Rds fired at Ridge R.10.C.6.1 + R.10.a made. Hostile fire considerable quantity of Gas shell fired in vicinity of the Reserve between 2 AM - 3 AM. E.A. Nil. Ammo Exp. A.203 AX.194 BX.272 B.7.8	
	13th		Bar. 29.65. Ther. 60. Weather fine. Visibility fair. Gun fire 12AM-9AM usual night harassing fire. Roving Gun went out 10.30 to 11 PM + 1.30 to 2.30 to 3.30 AM. 80 Rds fired. 10 Rds added to roving on fire. 4 PM 40 Rds. 11pm on BOSSUM FARM. Hostile fire Normal. E.A. gas shell burst. Billem + Enemy O.P.s brought down during the day. Ammo Exp. A.252 AX.148 BX.182 B.7.50	
	16th		Bar 29.65. Ther 56. Weather fine. Cool. Some rain. Visibility good. Gun fire 25 Rds per Gun. Fire broken to 6 PM. Night Harassing fire. 31.5AM 15 Rds at New H.7M K.21.d.5.6. Hostile fire 180 Rds 15.5pm on T.29 a.7.6. Otherwise Normal. E.A. 1 overcome Lines. Ammo Exp. A.211 AX.100 BX.105 B.7.94	
	17th		Bar 29.62. Ther 59. Weather fine. Visibility fair. Gun fire 25.50pm Fire. Night harassing fire. 1 PM T/152 set 1 out on fire. K.16. F.40.20. 5.50 PM D/152 fired 90 Rds onto Ridge K.16.C.6.8. Hla 20.90 5.10 PM. 100 BX on wire NSC.13 K.SC.10.55. Hostile fire considerable harassing fire carried out throughout the night + early morning. E.A. 12 on our lines during the day. B + C/152 moved to forward position at M.a.9.8 + M.d.9.3. Major W.B. Neill. M.C. assumed form F M Command. Ammo Exp. A.124 AX.174 BX.188	
	18th		Bar 29.60. Ther 60. Weather fine. Visibility good. Gun fire. 25 Rds per Gun. Night harassing fire. 6 PM 140 Rds + shots fired into angeled Battue fired Observed shorts + checked ammunition. Hostile fire. Very active. Ridges of Visit at L'ERNETTE. Quantity of dead Rds obtained at Trench FIRE very actual E.A. soon harassing fire carried out by the enemy. large quantity of gas shell used on our lines during the day. Ammo Exp. A.294 AX.50 BX.182 B.7.18	
	19th		Bar 29.60. Ther 63. Weather fine with some rain. Visibility fair. Gun fire. 7PM to 9PM 25 Rds per Gun. Night harassing fire in Brigade Zone. Hostile fire. Usual night harassing fire carried out by the enemy. E.A. 1 Aeroplane during the day. 4 PM Hostile Plane brought down in NIEPPE FOREST by one of our squadrons. Ammo Exp. A.202 AX.99 B.X.92	

WAR DIARY or INTELLIGENCE SUMMARY

Army Form C. 2118.

(Erase heading not required.)

Place	Date	Hour	Summary of Events and Information	Remarks and references to Appendices
LE SARS	May 1st 1917		Bar 29.85. Ther 55. Weather Fine. Visibility Fair. Our Fire. Usual night harassing fire on Enemy front line. Hostile Fire 200 rds at intervals 7.7. 4" on RUE DES MORTS chiefly gas & phosgene shells. Normal. E.A. Nil. Ammn Exp. A308 AX128 BX187	
	2nd		Bar 29.55. Ther 62. Weather Fine. Visibility Fair. Our Fire. 7 Fire 7.00 PM 25 rds per gun Night Harassing fire. 3 PM 150 rds on wire at K12.a.90 on KSC003. Hostile Fire Below normal. Fire with special attention paid to R.E. Dump pts MORTS. E.A. Below normal. Ammn Exp. A228 AX124 BX30	
	22nd		Bar 29.88. Ther 60. Weather Fine. Visibility Fair. Our Fire. 2500 pm gun night harassing fire. 8 PM 100 rds BX on wire KSC00.02. 11.30 to 10 AM 35 rds on HMS N10.a.1.2 Hostile Fire. Normal. E.A. Nil. Ammn Exp. A372 AX187 BX90.	
	23rd		Bar 29.61. Ther 58. Weather Fine. Visibility Good. Our Fire. 25 rds pn gun night harassing fire. 4 PM 150 rds on wire K10 C 30.15 to K10 a 40.05 many direct hits obtained. 4.15 PM 12 rds MJ152 on House K17 a 85.50 which burnt to the ground. 5 to 7 PM 25 rds MJ152 on wire & Hilla 10 rds with on infantry. 8-10 PM 30 rds by the Bde in retaliation on shelling of Sept Bars Hqrs. Very quiet throughout the night, normal clearing the day. Hostile Fire. E.A. Nil. Miscellaneous NEUF BERQUIN Church Spire knocked down by an Heavies Ammn Exp. A352 AX139 BX129.	
	24th		Bar 29.65. Ther 60. Weather Fair with Rain. Visibility Poor. Our Fire. Usual night harassing fire. 5PM 130 rds by MJ160 on wire N10 d 15.50 to N10 d 20.70 Hostile Fire. Normal. E.A. 13 mm on lines during the day. Ammn Exp. A292 AX — BX175	
	25th		Bar 29.60. Ther 60. Weather Fair. Visibility Good. Our Fire. Usual night harassing Fire. 12.30 AM 60 rds 18 pdr on HB K3B81. 8.20 AM 39 rds on K3B81. 3 & 4.30 PM 150 B X on HB 12.30 AM 60 rds 18 pdrs on HB 12B 50 rds 18 pdrs. K17c 9532. Hostile Fire. Considerable harassing fire during night with mustard gas. E.A. 2 mm on lines during the day. Ammn Exp. A415 AX 33 BX 28	

WAR DIARY
or
INTELLIGENCE SUMMARY.
(Erase heading not required.)

Page 5

Place	Date	Hour	Summary of Events and Information	Remarks and references to Appendices
LE PARCQ	June 26th 1918		Bar 29.58 Ther 57 Weather fine Visibility Good Gun Fire 8PM to 6AM Normal Night Harassing Fire. 12.10.12.20 209 S.O.S 12.45 to 2. S.O.S. call on VIERHOUCK. 12.40 3PM S.O.S. call on VIERHOUCK. KUO.0002. 5PM 59pdr 4.5.2hr on Wire Nira. Hostile Eie. Very active during the day. E.A. Low machines during the day.	
	27th		Pass "Majors" D.S.O. "M" left me + W.S.Still me proceded to Paris on 10 days leave. 2/Lieut R. Brown returned from leave. Annex Exp A 290 AX230 BX107 B740	
			Bar 29.63 Ther 64 Weather fine Visibility Fair Gun Fire 8 PM to 10 PM by 152d on wire Kroeystr – Kroeas8M to 9.30 M. 4c.3/150 on House KIO6.20. 2 Gun sharpoon 9PM to 1AM Night harassing fire. Hostile Fire. Normal E.A. Normal Annex Exps A372 BX- BX154	
	28th		Bar 29.60 Ther 67 Weather fine. Visibility fair. Gun Fire 8PM to 6AM small mgt of harassing fire. 6PM. Fire Plan for Operation 'BORDERLAND' handed pieces pumpt act objectives paired with very little opposition. 10.30 - 10.35 PM S.O.S. called for but no attack made by the enemy. Hostile Fire. Very feeble enemy put down enemy 9 to our barrage, considerable harassing fire in back area during the day. E.A. Nil. Annex 2/Lieut H. Jones (S.R.) rejoined the M.C. Annex Exp A 563 AX674 BX 293	
	29th		Bar 29.63 Ther 67 Weather fine Visibility Good Gun Fire 8PM to 6AM shorn in Gun Night harassing fire 2.50 to 3.45 AM Counter Preparation. 7/152 fired more to still on the Quarten. Hostile Fire. Nothing to remark concerning our recent operation E.A. In active Miscellaneous Lieut. T.S. Headd painted 6 weeks leave in Canada + made off the adjt K	
	30th		of the Brigade. 2/Lieut S. Argyll + R. Jones rejoined. T.M.R. Annex Exp. A769 AX1392 BX098B31 Bar 29.66 Ther 69 Weather fine Visibility fair. Gun Fire 2050 to 2059M thunder Barration. 3.25 AM SOS fixed fire 3.50 5.55 AM 8gnds 18pdr M03 + N16 d 1565 N16d65 N7240-65. 8PM to 6AM 25rds pr gun Night harassing fire. Hostile fire Normal. E.A. active 2 enemy Kite Balloons brought down by our planes. Annex Exps A862 AX923 BX 615.	

H. Weearfurt
152 Bde R.F.A.

WAR DIARY or INTELLIGENCE SUMMARY

Army Form C. 2118.

152. Bde. DFA

Place	Date 1917	Hour	Summary of Events and Information	Remarks and references to Appendices
LE DRC July	1st		Bar. 29.70. Ther. 70. Weather Fine. Visibility fair. Our line. 3PM to 6PM. Normal. Night harassing fire at Meinight, 50 rds each on Hostile Machine Guns N.7.d.6.5, N.7.d.6.5. Wind 13.65. Hostile line Normal. 8PM to 1PM 1 Section per Battery relieved by 1 Section per Battery of 296 Bde. Divine Exp. A60. N.7.201. B.X.90.	
	2nd		Bar. 29.69. Ther. 71. Weather Fine. Visibility Good. Our line. 8PM to 1PM. 1 Section per Battery of 296 Bde relieved by 1 Section per Battery of 152 Bde. Hostile line Normal. Night harassing fire. Fire relieved by 1 Section per Battery 296 Bde. Divine Exp. A.80. N.X.335. B.X.94.	
	3rd		Bar. 29.69. Ther. 68. Weather Fine. Visibility Good. Our Fire. Usual night harassing fire. Hostile Fire. Very Heavy. No Shell bombardment on 7.a. & b. from 12 PM to 5 PM. Remaining Section per Battery relieved by 296 Bde. Field Col. W. Allard D.S.O. to Hospital (sick). 6PM Command of 152 Bde passed to O.C. 295 Bde. 2PM Command of 152 Bde. Divine Exp. A.M. N.X.22. B.X.178. Major E.W. Willcocks M.C. to Command 152 Bde.	
On the March	4th		Bar. 29.84. Ther. 65. Weather Fine. 8.30 PM Brigade marched from Wagon Lines at REBROUCK AREA via LYNDE, EBBLINGHEM, LE NIEPPE, COIN STEENBECQUE to REBROUCK AREA. Head of Brigade arrived 2.30 PM. PRADELLE MENECHT CROSS ROADS.	
	5th		Bar. 29.63. Ther. 65. Weather Fine. 9.30 PM Brigade marched from REBROUCK AREA to HANDEKOT AREA via WORMHOUDT, HERZEELE, HOUTKERQUE Tail of Brigade arrived 2PM.	
HOUTKERQUE	6th		Bar. 29.63. Ther. 66. Weather Fine. 2 Guns per Battery placed in positions of observation. A/152 at F.19.c.4.5. B/152 F.23.6.5.5. C/152 F.24.d.7.9. D/150 F.17.d.6.5. 10AM Inspected all Guns of the Brigade. MC P. II. Camouflaged 4/152.	
	7th		Bar. 29.08. Ther. 73. Weather Fine. Guns Lines. Brigade at Rest Horse Gunnery Series D/152. L.O. Worth artillery School. TILQUES.	

WAR DIARY or INTELLIGENCE SUMMARY

Army Form C. 2118.

Page 2

Place	Date	Hour	Summary of Events and Information	Remarks and references to Appendices
HOUTKERQUE	July 8th	10:18	Bar 29.86 Ther 71 Weather Fine Brigade at Rest. Major P.S. Mylreigh MC & W.S. Hill MC returned from leave in PARIS. Major W.I. Hill MC to command 1st Bde.	
	9th		Bar 29.86 Ther 73 Weather Showery Brigade at Rest	
	10th		Bar 29.81 Ther 57 Weather Showery Brigade enquired Mounted Drill order by Major Gen. A. Robertson C.B. C.M.G.	
	11th		Bar 29.81 Ther 75 Weather Wet Stong SW Gale Brigade at Rest	
	12th		Bar 29.53 Ther 61 Weather Wet Stong SW Gale Brigade at Rest	
	13th		Bar 29.67 Ther 65 Weather Fine Brigade at Rest	
	14th		Bar 29.68 Ther 65 Weather Fine Brigade Church Parade held.	
			Stong Brigade received orders to be prepared to entrain	
On the March	15th		Bar 29.71 Ther 70 Weather at 8 P.M. orders postponed until 3 A.M. Fruitful trial. Scouts joined the Brigade. Thunderstorm. Brigade entrained as follows:- 5 A.M. AM52, 5 AM AM52	
			Ther ---- Weather HEIDBEEK, 6 A.M. C/52 PROVEN 9 A.M. B/52 HEIDBEEK 9 A.M. D/52 PROVEN 11 A.M. HQ HEIDBEEK.	
	16th		Bar ---- Ther ---- Weather Stong Stony Brigade detrained as follows:- 4 A.M. AM52 ROUSSANVILLE, 8.30 A.M. C/52 LOURPES, 4 A.M. B/52 LOURPES, 12 M D/52 ROUSSANVILLE Brigade after detraining marched to Billeting area as follows:- HQ and C/52	
	17th		VEMARS B.D/52 MOUSSY LE NEUF.	
	18th		Bar ---- Ther ---- Weather Fine Hounds H.B. Peck, T. Edwards & E.W. Kendall C.C. proved to the Brigade.	

Army Form C. 2118.

WAR DIARY
or
INTELLIGENCE SUMMARY.
(Erase heading not required.)

Page 3

Place	Date	Hour	Summary of Events and Information	Remarks and references to Appendices
VEMARS	July 19	Bar - 19.8	Weather fine. 1AM Brigade received orders to the ready to move at 5 AM. Brigade marched to LE BEUVRE near FEIGNEUX via DOUY, FROUVILLE, NANTEUIL, CREPY. Head of Brigade arrived 3 P.M., last of Brigade 5 P.M. Sent LA tanks posted to the Brigade reported B/152.	
On the March	20th	Bar - Ther -	Weather fine. 11.45 P.M. Brigade marched to LONGAVESNES, via EMEVILLE, HARAMONT, VIVIERS arriving 4 A.M.	
"	21st	Bar - Ther -	Weather fine. Brigade moved LONGAVESNE 8 A.M.	
"	22nd	Bar. 2905 Ther -	Weather fine. C.O. "B C" reconnoitred positions in the vicinity of VIERZY.	
VIERZY	23rd	Bar. 2913 Ther -	Weather stormy. Brigade marched at 9.30 P.M. from LONGAVESNES to 11.50 P.M. LEMES S.W. of LONGPONT in the FORET de RETZ arriving 12 Noon. 7 to 8 P.M. Batteries proceeded into action South of VIERZY. Bde bivouaced in the WOOD about 400X North of FMO MORIENROEUF. Exact M.D were Recounted. Weather fine. Map Ref of Brigade HQ 2" Batteries as follows:-	
"	24th	Bar. 2907 Ther -	Map OUCHY-LE-CHATEAU. HQ. 290.52.5, A/152 70.5.59.5, C/152. 70 0.52.5, B/152 67.0. 61.5, B/152 68.54. Funeral Stewarts Quiet. Infantry active. M.G. Hostile Artillery Intermittent shelling of VIERZY + LARCY-TIGNY. 11AM - 2P.M. Large ammo dump seen burning East of Bois d'HARTENNES. E.A. very active before 9 A.M. Enemy A.50. Infantry action nil.	
"	25th	Bar. 29.35 Ther -	Weather fine. Situation Normal Infantry action nil. Hostile fire 6 A.M. to 12 M. VIERZY heavily shelled + LARCY TIGNY E.P. very active. 1.2M Enemy Dump burning 13° West of HARTENNES Church from 8.758. Lancastico 30P faced Enemy Cap. A193, A.X.192 BX142	
"	26th	Bar. Ther -	Weather hot. Situation Normal Infantry action nil. Hostile fire. Very active on VIERZY E.A. Normal. Two Bde reconnoitred enemy lines. Ennefrs A.9.3, A.X.221 BX17 Enemy fire slightly more scattered 11. Morning. 2 killed ammo Cap.	

WAR DIARY or INTELLIGENCE SUMMARY

(Erase heading not required.)

Army Form C. 2118.

Page 4

Place	Date	Hour	Summary of Events and Information	Remarks and references to Appendices
VIERZY	July 27th		Bar — Ther — Weather Wet. General Situation quiet. Infantry quiet up till 1 p.m. Gun fire desultory about on Bois de REUGNY. Hostile fire 12 N to 7 P.M. Enemy shelled VIERZY from 2 to 7 P.M. otherwise none came thro' usual 92nd Brigade intermittent harassing fire concentrated in BUISSON de BRETWISON away to midnight. Casualties 2 O.R. Killed. 1 O.R. wounded. Amm. exp. 9/315 AX.259 BX.182.	
BUISSON de BRETWISON	28th		Bar — Ther — Weather Fine. 92nd Brigade proceeded into action N.W. of OURCQ V.2.A. WILE. Wagon Lines at ROZET ST ALBIN. Map Reference of position 9/152 0678. B/152 0578 9/152 0215 7295 III/152 0473 Brigade HQ. Bois St HILAIRE 9575 0574.	
BOIS ST HILAIRE	29th		Bar — Ther — Weather Fine. 5.10 A.M. Our attacked South of GRAND ROZOY of GRESSAIRE. The enemy being encountered throughout the day. 7 P.M. Our new line gained. B/152 I/152 1st to N. of GRAND ROZOY, to 2/152 128. Harassing of enemy to 10.50 P.M. was a feature. 10 P.M. Wagon Lines moved to MONT CHEVILLON. Amm. exp. A 810 AX 805 BX 180 nothing at 5090 + Sh.92. 95th Battery moved to new position 9/152 0678. Casualties 9 O.R. Infantry action.	
—do—	30th		Bar — Ther — Weather Fine. Quiet day. No Infantry action. Gun line. No following positions 9/152 0251/7. B/152 023,735. C/152 2573 III/152 04.73 92nd Bde. 8/52 027/18. GRAND ROZOY JOURNEUX ROQ occupied on front line. N of B in Beaugnet 15 km to HILL 128. Barrow was A 1157 AX 905 BX 1566.	
—do—	31st		Bar — Ther — Weather Fine. Hostile fire throughout the day. Our own sporadic in retaliation. Infantry action lull 1 O.R. wounded 1 O.R. wounded. Amm exp. 25 AX.87 BX 123.	

W. Sauill Lieut Col
152 Bde RFA

WAR DIARY or INTELLIGENCE SUMMARY

Army Form C. 2118.

152 Bde R?? 9/8/31

Place	Date	Hour	Summary of Events and Information	Remarks and references to Appendices
OULCHY LA VILLE	August 1918 1st		Page 1. Bar 29.7 Ther 66 Weather fine. Operation Order for attack issued on an appendix with 75th French Inf: Objective East of Ridge from ORME du GRAND ROZOY, HILL 205, HILL 190 = Northern slopes of the Ridge. Forming up line BOIS de la TERRE d'en haut WOOD. GRAND ROZOY - BEUGNEUX Road to B in BEUGNEUX - 2 houses in BEUGNEUX - OULCHY LE CHATEAU ROAD. The attack was preceded by a bombardment of 5 hrs. from on the following points - R.11.c.159, BEUGNEUX, Road 6.9.5.50.97.85, VALLEY NORTH of BEUGNEUX. The attack was a complete success on B/152 & 5/152 from finals + Tanks going through. B/152 & 5/152 reached their final objectives, B/152 to 177.9.0.4 & came into line with 5/152 at BO3 (13.7) b.4 3d 9.m B/152 to 23.m.2 & B/152 to 57.35.97.5 7/152 to 18.99.8. 10 am remaining action followed. 10 AM. B/152 returned to 50.85 152 Bde I G moved to BOIS MORICEAU. 11 am B/152 Wagon Lines moved to south of OULCHY LE CHATEAU. 2 pm B/152 Wagon Lines bombed during the following casualties: 1 OR KILLED 3 OR wounded Ammn: Expended.	
BOIS MORICEAU	2nd		Bar 29.8 Ther 73 Weather wet. Batteries did not fire the enemy having retired out of range. 9 PM Brigade concentrated in valley N E of OULCHY-LE-CHATEAU. Ammn: Exp.	
	3rd		Bar 29.93 Ther 68 Weather fine. Brigade marched at 1 PM. to marked in wagon around VICHEL arriving 7 PM. Major W.S. Hall MC returned from Hospital (wounded).	
	4th		Bar 29.79 Ther 71 Weather fine. 2.30 am Brigade marched from VICHEL to COULANGES via NEUILLY-S-FRONT (TOWN WET). MAREUIL SUR OURCQ arriving 2 PM	
	5th		Bar 29.74 Ther 70 Weather wet. Brigade marched to the following places & entrained on Railway transferred to II Corps. A/152. ORMOY-VILLERS 12 Noon. B/152 NANTEUIL 1 PM. B/152 LE PLESSIS 9 PM. HQ LE PLESSIS 9 PM	
	6th		Bar 29.82 Ther 73 Weather cold. Brigade moved. A/152 detrained at BERGUES 4 PM. proceeded to Buvet billeting area. II ROBLAND T. B/152 detrained at ESQUELBECQ 6 PM C/152 at BERGUES 12 Midnight. HQ152 ESQUELBECQ 10 PM	

Army Form C. 2118.

WAR DIARY
or
INTELLIGENCE SUMMARY.
(Erase heading not required.)

Instructions regarding War Diaries and Intelligence Summaries are contained in F.S. Regs., Part II. and the Staff Manual respectively. Title pages will be prepared in manuscript.

Place	Date	Hour	Summary of Events and Information	Remarks and references to Appendices
	Aug. 1918		Page 2.	
IRELAND	7th		Par 29.81 Jun 73 Weather fine. M/152 detrained at BERGUES 4 AM. M/152 & Hq of Battery Battn as follows:- Shed 27 Ed.3 Y9600. Bn Hq K1098. A/152 E5090. M/152 Y9.0560. B/152 T5.8960. C/152 D90.21. D/152 V9.0.63 & J8 D9.0.65.	
do.	8th		Par 29.73. Bn. 69. Weather fine. Brigade at Rest.	
do.	9th		Par 29.95. Bn. 70. Weather fine. The undermentioned officers received French honours at a presentation by G.O.C. 34th Div. (Major Gen L. Nicholson C.B.C.M.G.) held at PROUVENT Cross Roads. Lt. Col. N. Shute. 7.5.0 Croix de Guerre (with palm.) Major H. Whitehead M.C. (infantry) Major D.S. Maturin M.C. Croix de Guerre (with palm.) Major H. Whitehead M.C. Croix de Guerre (with palm.) Capt M. Powle Croix de Guerre (with palm) Lieut N. Inglefield Croix de Guerre (with palm.) 2.O.R Powle rejoined unit Major Maturin & 2.O R Inglefield proceeded to join the Brigade Linge. T.A) visited various of the Brigade from 10.am to 24.pm. Lieut D.S. Moore reported. proceeded on leave to England from 10.9.18 to 24.9.18. Lieut F. Hull M.C. proceeded to England on leave from 11.9.18 to 2.3.9.18.	
do.	10th		Par. 29.94. Bn. 70 Weather fine. Brigade at Rest.	
do.	11th		Par. 29.93 Bn. 71 Weather fine. B.O.R attended a special Parade Service at TERDEGHEM at 10.30 AM at which HIS MAJESTY THE KING attended.	
do.	12th		Par 29.82 Bn. 70 Weather fine. Brigade moved to HANDSCHNOT as arranged Billets as follows :- HQ E.16.a.J.5. M/152 E.10.b.7. B/152 E16.b.76. C/152 E13.1.9.4. D/152 E11.d.6. & J5.2 Essingh. Men proceeded to England. Brigade not 1 Section Four of Lieut in England 12 N.C.O's Men proceeded to England to cover in positions covering the EAST POPERINGHE LINE. Major & 1 Sec & Battery in action in positions covering the EAST POPERINGHE LINE. Major R. of Junction A/152 L.16 a.12.58. B/152 L.2.d.23.42. C/152 L9.a.78.10. D/152 L.15.b.85.66.	
HANDSCHNOT	13th		Bn 29.92 Bn 67 Weather fine. Brigade at rest. Major F. Furnie M.C. proceeded to PARIS on leave.	

Army Form C. 2118.

WAR DIARY
or
INTELLIGENCE SUMMARY.
(Erase heading not required.)

Instructions regarding War Diaries and Intelligence Summaries are contained in F. S. Regs., Part II. and the Staff Manual respectively. Title pages will be prepared in manuscript.

Page 3.

Place	Date	Hour	Summary of Events and Information	Remarks and references to Appendices
	Aug 1918			
HAZIEBROUK	14th		Bar. 29.86 Ther 70 Weather Fine. Brigade at Rest	
do	15th		Bar. 29.86 Ther 71 Weather Fine. Brigade at Rest	
do	16th		Bar. 29.91 Ther 73 Weather Fine. Kent M.G. & 10 Men proceeded to Paris Railway A.O.B. REES E.L.E.S.	
do	17th		Bar. 29.93 Ther 72 Weather Dull from overnight	
do	18th		Bar. 29.86 Ther 74 Weather Fine. Lt. BCP Vigilant + Bdr Signal C Officer arrived	
do	19th		Bar. H.Q. + En. Comms in 29 + 2 + Area	
do	19th		Bar. 29.2 Ther 71 Weather Dull Brigade at Rest	
do	20th		Bar. 29.97 Ther 73 Weather Fair Brigade at Rest. Lieut B Bentley reported from Hospital (wounds). Lieut H Thomas moved to B/152. Lieut M Jones reported from Hospital returned to HAZIE + R.O.H.	
do	21st		Bar. 29.8. Ther 72 Weather Fine Location of Batteries relieved + relieving Battery w.g. Bde A.C. + Following positions:- Stew 28 NW Y60,000 A/152 - 2 Guns I.7a.56 B/152-2 Guns B.17.5.8. C/152 - 2 Guns I.7c.A.5. D/152 - 2 Guns I.7.6 - 4.2.39 X - 7/152 moved up to 215 Bde (AA Div) recognised as B/152 B.22a.18 B/152 A.97a.8.9 B.21a.28 B.40,000.	
do	22nd		Bar. 29.93 Ther 70 Weather Fine. Remnants of BdN moved to 21st Bde Wagon Line Henancy stations relieved. 21S Bde in reserve Bde HQ. H50.9.9. A/152 K50.c.8.2 B/152 B.29.c.00 C/152 H.5b.55.65 D/152 I.6.9.77 H.11.b.90.35	
YPRES	23rd		Bar. 29.94 Ther 69 Weather Fine Hostile Artillery Normal. Gas Respirators carried out during the night. Ammn. Exp. A.346 B.362 B.16	
do	24th		Bar. 29.97 Ther 72 Weather Fine. Hostile Arty Normal. Gas Lie 4010 B.X on H.Cats. Enemy fire & several deluded rifles. Ammn. Exp. A.251 A.342 B.X.99 Lieut K.F. Pollock proceeded to TILQUES on 22 Interior Officer Course. Lieut & R Locke proceeded to England on 10 day Special Leave.	

WAR DIARY or INTELLIGENCE SUMMARY

Army Form C. 2118.

Place	Date	Hour	Summary of Events and Information	Remarks and references to Appendices
YPRES	25th Janry	1918	Page 44	
			Bar. 29.79 Ther. 59. Weather Fine. Our Fire 4.10 P.M. 7/152 carried out harassing Battery shoot on J.24.5 & J.24.53. Harassing Fire continuous during the night. Hostile Artillery Normal. Ammo Exp A.289 A×378 B×16 D.760 B.M.G 144. 16 MGC Hostile M.G. Answered fire in day. alerts.	
-do-	26th		Bar. 29.68 Ther. 68 Weather Showery. Our Fire 11.a.m to 12 pm 11/152 firing Lloyd M.S.G. 8.30 P.M. 16.7a – 4.5 How. C.36.35.10, 9.25 P.M. 11/152 Shot Shell on Angels Tran. E.29 + 57. 18 pdrs carried out harassing fire on roads. MGC Hostile M.G. Answered fire. Ammo Exp. A.260 A×328 B×72. Leave. 4 Other Ranks 1/6 Robertson MC + 1 Early proceeded to England on 14 days leave.	
-do-	27th		Bar. 29.70 Ther. 66 Weather. Fair. Our Fire 7.45 pm in B'on Hostile Battery J.Y.55. 8.30 AM. 10.5 H on H.B. J.Y.53. During Night shrap. fire on special targets. no.160 18 pdr harassing fire. Hostile fire. More active than usual. 5.30 PM 80 to 100 15 pdrs shells near B/152 ? Found garbon 77.d. 50.40. Ammo Exp A.287 A×240	
-do-	28th		Bar. 29.70 Ther. 63. Weather Fair. Our Fire. Usual. Night harassing fire carried out. Hostile Artillery. Normal. Ammo Exp. A.508 A×332. 602 F.R.I. Lsgt. erected B/above.	
-do-	29th		Bar. 29.75 Ther. 63 Weather Fair. Our Fire 600 Rds 18 pdr at Trench etc. Harassing fire. 1.30 a.m 4.5 How (including 6no) Hostile Fire. Normal. Limit Major 2nd W.Yorks ME. proceeded to Paris on 10 days leave. Hospital Lead R.B. 6.002/5 1 F.R. Ammo Exp A.239 A×391.	
-do-	30th		Bar. 29.59 Ther. 65 Weather. Fine. Our Fire. Usual. Ther. 17 pdr. Night Harassing Fire 1/100 Rds 9× + 60s Hostile Fire. Normal. Ammo Exp. A.24/3 A×470. B×20.	
-do-	31st		Bar. 29.71 Ther. 65 Weather Fine. Our Fire 4.28 to 5.30 pm 7th ML Battalion answered SOS calls on B×30 + J.M.B.n. Expenditure Night Harassing Fire 2000 Rds 18 pdrs + 400 Rds + other including 200 J.Y.55 + J.M.B.n. (see appendix) Hostile Fire. Below on 1st off the whole day about Z.11.d B.7. H.7 B.W.D. R.OST.A q. 7.35 enemy airdane to Y.P.RES	

Army Form C. 2118.

WAR DIARY
or
INTELLIGENCE SUMMARY.

(Erase heading not required.)

Page 5

Place	Date	Hour	Summary of Events and Information	Remarks and references to Appendices
YPRES	Sept 7th 1918		Miscellaneous. Patrols sent out by the troops on our Right. Found that the enemy had evacuated MONT KEMMEL 2 PM Infantry on our front went forward 2 patrols were received at 9.2 PM having found the enemy to be in strength.	

J. M. Caule Lieut Col.
Commands 152 Brigade R.F.A.

Appendix I

C.O.P.N. No. 10

Night Artillery Brigade, Operation Order No. 4.

31st August 1918

1. There will be no Harassing Fire West of the following line tonight until further orders are issued :-

   J.23.d.0.7. - J.17.a.45.00. - J.17.b.21.65. - S.E. Corner of "Y" WOOD - ODER HOUSE

2. Zones.
   B/152 Brit(ish) Divisional Boundary to E and W line thro' HELL FIRE Corner.
   C/152 E and W line thro' HELL FIRE Corner to Southern Divisional Boundary.
   Batteries concerned will fire a total of 660 rounds each on as many tracks as possible in these zones and will search and sweep.

   Special targets in lieu of those ordered by D.A.
   A/152.
   A.17.   B.41.   C.34.   D.47.   E.54.   F.58.
   About 110 rounds will be fired on each of these targets during the night.

   D/152 will fire on targets B.79. D.55. and also C.130 instead of C.33. in Gas programme and make up to a total of 600 rounds for the night with Harassing fire on selected targets on the whole Divisional front.

3. Acknowledge by wire.

S.N. Crewitt   Captain
Adjutant, 152nd Brigade, R.F.A.

Issued at B.D.M.

Copies to :-
1/4.   Batteries.
5.   B.M. 34th D.A.
6.   B.M. 43rd Infantry Bde.
7.   B.M. 41st Infantry Bde.
8.   This Office.
9/10. War Diary.
11.   Spare.

Appendix I

Army Form C. 2118.

WAR DIARY
or
INTELLIGENCE SUMMARY.
(Erase heading not required.)

152 Bde
R.F.A.
September 1918

Vol 36

Place	Date	Hour	Summary of Events and Information	Remarks and references to Appendices
Abancourt	1	29.6.0 7pm	Our Arty – 2000 rds 18/pr. 600 rds 4.5" how. Night Harassing Fire. Hostile Fire – Normal. Brigade relieved by 159 Bde (35 Div) + no return to Brigade tonight.	
Montrecourt South	2	29.70 6.2 "	Brigade relieved 2nd Bde R.F.A. (6th Div). Bdr. H.Q. H8C 65.40. (B.H.Q. 28 N.W.) – B & D Battery (11th R.F.A. Bde.) attacked. Relief completed by 6.45pm. Battery positions as per Appendix No 1.	No 1
"	3	29.70 6.3 "	Our Fire – 900 rds 18 /pr. night harassing – 100 rds 4.5" how into 7 Elon Gate (not required by Infantry). Hostile Fire – Active against infantry in our forward area. Brigade warned to be advance N.E. of WALKER FARM, HYBLES.	
"	4	29.70 6.6 6.5	S.O.S. 5.30am 8 Rennie infantry reported attack. Object obtained. " 6.39am Harrassing 100 rds 18/pr + 40 rds this hr. Our Harassing Fire. 100 rds 18/pr + 40 rds this hr. Hostile Fire – heavy barrage all calibres on forward pm. Thence normal. Causes – 1 O.R. killed – 6 O.R. wounded.	
"	5	29.70 6.9 "	Our fire – 800 rds 18/pr night harassing. Hostile fire – very active & will on our left, normal on our front. After exchange gas shells with Alligo as Nieu S.26.6.5.	
"	6	29.60 6.2 "	Our fire – 600 rds 18/pr night harassing. Hostile fire – normal. No change of position – all B/190 at Nieu 1.8.	

Army Form C. 2118.

WAR DIARY
or
INTELLIGENCE SUMMARY.
(Erase heading not required.)

September 1918

Place	Date	Hour	Baro / Ther / Weather	Summary of Events and Information	Remarks and references to Appendices
DICKEBUSCH	7th		29.50 / 59 / Fine	Our fire - 500 rds 18 fdr night harassing. D/152 East Shoot on Pill Boxes & strongpoints. Hostile fire - normal during day. 300 rds fair shells in H38a at 23.00 to 01.00, also 100 rds 10.5 cm how. harassing fire.	Appendix (1)
	8	19.00 23.30	29.70 / 54 / Fair	D/152 exchanged positions with C/190 at N14 a & 30. D/152 moved to position at N33 a 4.8 Our fire - 500 rds 18 fdr night harassing. D/152 Co. Shoot on pill boxes & strongpoints. Hostile fire - normal.	
	9	09.00	29.50 / 58 / "	Bde H.Q. moved to FROWSTY FARM (M 6 c 30.30). Our Operation Order No 12. Our fire - 400 rds 18 fdr night harassing & 400 rds during day into PETIT BOIS and Craters at N34 a 9.7 & N24 a 95 45, also 200 rds 4.5 how. on same targets. Hostile fire - normal.	Appendix (2)
	10		29.50 / 59 / Fair	1 Section D/152 moved to N4 b 77. Our fire - 300 rds night harassing. FO also observed shooting ammn dump 100 rds Gas Shoot by D/152 on O1 d 3.5 Hostile fire - normal.	
	11	23.00	29.90 / 61 / "	Our fire - 500 rds night harassing. FO also observed shooting ammn dump 100 rds Gas Shoot on O20 b 5.5 Hostile fire - normal.	
	12	21.00	29.70 / 58 / Wet	Gun fire - Same as previous day. Hostile fire - normal.	
	13		29.60 / 56 / Fair	Our fire - Same as previous day, also 30 rds to WYTSCHAETE as retaliation for hostile shelling on Road M 6 b 4 d.	

Army Form C. 2118.

WAR DIARY
or
INTELLIGENCE SUMMARY.
(Erase heading not required.)

September 1918 (3)

Place	Date	Hour Barometer	Thermometer	Weather	Summary of Events and Information	Remarks and references to Appendices
DICKEBUSCH	14th	29.50	59	Wet	Our fire - 600 rds 18/pr night harassing - 75 rds 4.5 hows day character shoot. 100 rds 4.5 gas shoot on O1vd.3.4. at 3am	
"	15th	29.90	58	Fine	Hostile fire - normal. Our fire - same as previous day.	
"	16th	29.60	59	"	Hostile fire - normal. Our fire - 500 rds 18/pr engl. harassing, 100 rds gas shoots, 115 shows at 3am 7pm	
"	17th	29.90	60	"	Hostile fire - normal. Our fire - 500 rds 18/pr night harassing, 100 " - transpt harr.	
"	18th	29.90	60	"	Hostile fire - normal. Our fire - 500 rds 18/pr " 100 " - 3.30am r.L	
"	19th	29.00	59	"	Our fire - 500 rds 18/pr " 180 " - 9.45pm r 11.45pm	
"	20th	29.20	58	"	Hostile fire - normal. Our fire - 500 rds 18/pr " 180 " - 2.15am r 3.30am	
"	21st	29.75	58	"	Hostile fire - normal. Our fire - 200 rds 18/pr "	
"	22nd	29.70	59	"	Hostile fire - normal. Our fire - 300 rds 18/pr " Hostile fire - very active during day. Barrage fired on mouth to GRETNA REDOUBT. H.35.c.58	
"	23rd	29.60	61	"	Our fire - 200 rds 18/pr ought harassing, 180 rds gas shoot at 1.30am. Hostile fire - normal.	
"	24th	29.60	59	Showery	Our fire - 600 rds 18/pr night harassing, 115 rds 18/pr day character shooting Hostile fire - normal	

WAR DIARY
or
INTELLIGENCE SUMMARY.
(Erase heading not required.)

Army Form C. 2118.

September 1918

Instructions regarding War Diaries and Intelligence Summaries are contained in F. S. Regs., Part II. and the Staff Manual respectively. Title pages will be prepared in manuscript.

Place	Date	Hour				Summary of Events and Information	Remarks and references to Appendices
DICKEBUSCH	25th	29.65	58	hot		Our fire 600 rds night harassing 18/pdr, 300 rds (375 short) 4·5" how at 10·30pm. Hostile shelling normal.	
	26th	29.72	60	Showery		Our fire 600 rds night harassing, 60 rds day shooting, 18/pdr. Hostile shelling normal.	
					10pm	A/152 and C/152 active sections at N.14.b.9.2 and N.11.b.6.7 (1 regiment. New registrations (silent) for return of N.14.b.4.9, N.14.b.6.1	
	27th	29.70	60	"		Our fire 600 rds night harassing 16/pdr, 150 rds (on short) 4·5" how at 9·10pm	
					3pm	Hostile fire returned Brigade HQ moved up to N.3.a.3.3 (Sheet 28, 1/40000), D/152 near section to advance and position N.4.d.3.a. and B/152 two new sections. Appendix (3) to advance new position No.16.b.5.5 in connection with Operation	Appendix (3)
					10pm	12 mls. Orders N.B.19, 26/9/18. to cover infantry advance on enemy intrenchments from Wytschaete – Messines Ridge.	
	28th	29.70	58	Wet	5·30am	Zero Hour of Operation order No. 19, 26/9/18. Shorts barrage started Artillery until stopping at 7·42am on orders from 3rd Div. Art. HQ.	
					8·10/9·30am	Saw concentrated fire on detailed points as per Op. Ord. No. 19, and during day fire brought to bear on enemy movement on reports from infantry.	
					10pm	Blue Line (1st objective) occupied & consolidated Green Line (2nd objective)	
					9pm/11·30pm	Barrage covering advance of infantry to Green Line which was occupied during the night.	
	29th	29.70	59	Showery Rain	5am	101 Infantry Brigade reported occupy WYTSCHAETE advance to capture Brown Line (Final	
						10·3 " Objective) and on to Ypres-Comines Canal	
					7·30am	B/152 and one section D/152 moved forward to N.12.	

Army Form C. 2118.

WAR DIARY
or
INTELLIGENCE SUMMARY.

(Erase heading not required.)

September 1918

Place	Date	Hour		Summary of Events and Information	Remarks and references to Appendices
DICKEBUSCH HUTS	29th September	29-30	5.8	10.55 Warning Order given for Brigade to concentrate at HALLEBAST, 11.3.a. (Sheet 28-1/40,000) 2pm 34th Div. Squadron out of the line owing to 141st Div. on left advancing S.E. along Ypres Commines Canal and joining 30th Div. + XV Corps at about NOUTHAM on our right. Mobile Striking through this afternoon on our front (practically nil). Warning orders for Brigade to move to following camps ZANDVOORD area (P3 - Sheet 28, 1/40,000).	
	30th	29.30	5.8	10pm	

[signature]
Lieut Col
Comdg 152 Bde RFA

SECRET

Left Artly Brigade Operation Order No. 1.

Appendix No 1

7th Sept. 1918.

1. Locations of Left Artly Bde :-

			Wagon Lines.
Bde H.Q.		H.8.c.65.10.	H.7.a.9.4.
A/190.	2 guns.	H.22.d.7.3.	G.18.b.4.9.
	2 "	H.23.c.2.4.	
	2 "	H.29.a.4.6.	
B/ "	6 "	H.29.c.45.15.	G.10.c.7.9.
C/ "	4 "	H.23.d.30.65.	G.16.d.45.80. (ELGIN FARM)
	2 "	H.23.a.4.6.	
D/ "	6 "	H.29.c.45.30. & 90.55. G.11.a.5.2. (QUERY FARM)	
84th Bty.	6 "	H.29.a.0.7.	

2. Liaison arrangements.
   A senior liaison officer from the Right Group at Infantry Brigade H.Q. (HAGUE FARM H.31.a.60.90.) who should be in communication with both Groups.
   The Right Group will also be responsible for liaison with the Right Front Battalion at N.10.b.2.6.
   The Left Group will be responsible for liaison with the Left Front Battalion at N.4.b.3.3.
   Roster should have been handed over by batteries 152nd Brigade. R.F.A.

3. S.O.S. Lines.
   A/190.   J.7.c.60.75. - O.7.b.3.6.
   C/ "   O.7.b.3.6.   - O.1.d.95.30.
   B/ "   O.1.d.95.30. - O.1.b.95.20.
   84th.   Superimposed on S.O.S. Lines of A, B & C/190.
   D/190.   100 yards East of A, B, & C/190 S.O.S. Lines.
   The above S.O.S. Lines will come into force on receipt of this order.

4. O.P.
   HEADY O.P. (H.35.d.3.3.) is manned as a Brigade O.P. See roster taken over from batteries 152nd Brigade. R.F.A.

5. Ammunition.
   To be maintained at Gun Positions :-
      18.pdrs.   500 rds per gun.
      4.5.How.   400 rds per How.

6. Acknowledge by wire.

G.W. Brewitt.
Captain. R.F.A.
Adjutant, Left Artly Brigade.

Issued at 3.45.p.m.

Copies to :-

1/4.   Batteries, 190th Bde.
5.   84th Battery.
6.   B.M. 34th D.A.
7.   B.M. 123rd Infy Bde.
8.   This Office.
9/10. War Diary.

SECRET   COPY No 9

Left Group Operation Order No.12.

8th September, 1918

1. **Group Boundaries.**
   Northern : N.T.central - N.18.d.0.3. - O.13.d.8.9 - O.13.d.8.1.
   Southern.: BEAVER CORNER (N.15.c.3.3.) - Road Junction N.22.a.0.8.
              - Road Junction N.24.d.0.2.

2. **Battery Dispositions.**

		Position.	Wagon Lines.
Brigade Headquarters.	FROWSTY HOUSE.		
		M.6.c.30.30.	M.6.a.0.8.
A.Battery.	6 guns.	N.14.a.80.60.	M.5.d.30.80.
B. do	do	N.14.c.1.8.	M.3.b.40.90.
C. do	do	N.14.a.60.30.	G.33.d.80.50.
D. do	do	N.33.a.4.8.	M.4.a.20.30. (rear)
			M.6.c.80.10. (for)

3. **Infantry Dispositions.**
   Left Infantry Brigade.   N.20.d.4.7.
   Battalion H.Q.   N.22.d.6.1.

4. **Group O.P. and Roster.**
   Group O.P. is situated at N.22.a.8.8. and will be manned by
   batteries in turn for a period of 24 hours (9.a.m. to 9.a.m.)
   See roster under :-
   B.Battery.   11,15,19,23,27.
   C. do   8,12,16,20,24,28.
   D. do   9,13,17,21,25,29.
   A. do   10,14,18,22,26,30.

5. **Liaison arrangements with Left Infantry Brigade.**
   This Group maintaines a Liaison Officer at Left Infantry Brigade
   and will not be under the rank of Captain, and will be detailed by
   O.C. Group. At present Capt.J.A.Radford,M.C. is performing this duty.
   Capt.G.W.Baxter will relieve him at 4.p.m. 10th instant.

   Liaison with Battalion H.Q. (N.22.d.6.1.)
   This duty will be performed by batteries in turn for a period of
   48 hours. Relieving Officer will relieve at 4.p.m. (see roster under)
   C.Battery.   8/9, 12/13, 16/17, 20/21, 24/25, 28/29.
   D. do   9/10, 13/14, 17/18, 21/22, 25/26, 29/30.
   A. do   10/11, 14/15, 18/19, 22/23, 26/27.
   B. do   11/12, 15/16, 19/20, 23/24, 27/28.

6. **S.O.S.Lines.**
   S.O.S.Lines from 6.p.m.today will be :-
   B/152.   N.24.c.2.3. - N.24.a.55.00.
   A/152.   N.24.a.55.00. - N.24.a.8.4. - N.24.a.75.75.
   C/152.   N.24.a.75.75. - N.18.c.65.60.
   D/152.   1 How. Crater. N.24.a.90.95.
            1 "   "   N.24.a.9.7.
            1 "   "   N.24.c.95.45.
            2 Hows.   PETIT BOIS.
            1 How.   Track N.24.c.85.88.

7. Acknowledge by wire.

G.W. Brewitt.
Captain.
Adjutant, Left Group Artillery.

Issued at 3.50p.m.

Copies to :-
   1/4. Batteries. 152nd Bde.
   5.   B.M. 34th D.A.   7. This office.
   6.   B.M. Infy Bde.   8/9. War Diary.

SECRET   COPY No. (93)

152nd Brigade, R.F.A. Operation Order No.19.

Reference MAP "X" 1/20,000 (Sheet 28.S.W.)
WYTSCHAETE Sheet 1/10,000.

26th September, 1918.

1. It is probable that the enemy may withdraw in the near future beyond the WYTSCHAETE – MESSINES RIDGE, or still further East. The day on which the withdrawal may commence will be known as "J" day.

2. 152nd Brigade, R.F.A. will cover the advance of 103rd Infantry Brigade, following up the withdrawal of the enemy.
Map "X" shows the boundaries and objectives of 103rd Infantry Brigade.

3. Patrols will be sent out during "J" day if the enemy is seen to be withdrawing by day, but if no enemy withdrawal is seen by day patrols will not move out till 7.30.p.m.
The objective of these patrols will be the points marked A.1, A.2, B.1, B.2, etc on map "X".
The patrols will be adequately supported and followed up by the remainder of the Battalions in line, 5th A & S. Highrs on the Right and 8th K.O.S.B.'s on the Left, as soon as they reach the BLUE, GREEN and BROWN lines successively.
No general advance will take place from either of these lines without orders from Divisional H.Q.

4. (1) If the advance is made by day the 152nd Brigade, will cover the advance by keeping under fire known centres of resistance as long as possible. The actual targets to be engaged and guns to engage them are shown in Table "B".
(2) If the advance is made by night the artillery will fire occasional rounds of "AT" in accordance with Table "A", as a guide to the patrols, and will stand by ready to fire on any points where resistance may be met. They will only fire on these points if called upon to do so by the Battalion Commander concerned through Brigade H.Q.

5. The Left Battalion 103rd Infantry Brigade will take advantage of the barrage on our left on the morning of "J" day to push their line forward to PICCADILLY FARM. A & B/152 will co-operate in the barrage in accordance with instructions issued separately to them. (Barrage tracing to 103rd Infantry Brigade herewith).

6. No advance will be made from the GREEN LINE by night. If this line is reached on "J" day the Infantry will not advance beyond it that day unless it is certain that they can establish themselves on the BROWN Line before dusk. If this line is reached by night the advance will not be resumed till the following morning. Patrols, however, will always be pushed out in front of each line as soon as it is established. Patrols advancing from the GREEN and BROWN lines will be liable to come in contact with patrols of 14th Division advancing from N.W. towards HOUTHEM.

7. All shooting beyond the GREEN LINE must be observed, if possible, to avoid any danger of firing on the troops on our left, and battery F.O.O's will be provided with every possible means of communication, lamps, flags etc as well as telephones. Observation from the GREEN line itself may not be easy, and F.O.O's must be prepared to go forward with or behind the patrols.

8. F.O.O's must endeavour to send back reports at least once an hour after the advance begins, and must remember that negative information is often as useful as positive. Anything of importance that they see, and especially any signs of a withdrawal by the enemy on our front, must be transmitted to Brigade H.Q. at once.

9. Batteries will be prepared to move forward at any time after the GREEN Line is reached. B/152 and 1 Section D/152 will move first to a position about the Broad Gauge Railway in N.12.c.
A/152 and 1 Section D/152 will be ready to move forward as soon as the first move is completed, and C/152 and 1 Section D/152 will be prepared to follow A/152.

9. (contd.) The positions to be occupied by A, C and the 2 Sections of D/152 accompanying them will depend on the rapidity of the advance, but the choice will lie between positions near B/152 or in the vicinity of OATEN WOOD.

10. On "J" day H.Q's will be at the following points:-
    103rd Infantry Brigade.   N.10.a.2.7.
    152nd Brigade.R.F.A.   N.3.a.3.1.
    Right Battalion.   HOLLANDSCHESDHUUR Craters.
    Left Battalion.   O.1.c.0.8.
    Reserve Battalion.   N.11.a.8.4.

11. After 14th Division has reached its objective (Northern Divisional Boundary) the 14th D.A. will not be allowed to search and sweep W of a N and S line through C.8.b.2.0.
    After the completion of the barrage tasks of A & B/152 there will be no firing by batteries of this Brigade E of O.9.a.0.0. – O.3.c.0.0. or N of a line running due E from O.9.a.0.0. through O.9, 10 and 11 central.

12. SIGNALS.
    Patrols will signal their arrival on the GREEN Line by means of the following signal Rifle Grenades.
        (a) By day.   "RED Smoke".
        (b) By night.   "WHITE over WHITE over WHITE".
    Patrols will also signal when they are held up by the enemy using "BLUE Smoke" Signal Rifle Grenades.

13. LIAISON and F.O.O's.
    Liaison Officers will be found as follows:-
        A/152. Infantry Brigade H.Q.
        B/152. Left Battalion H.Q.
        C/152. Right Battalion H.Q.
    These officers will report to the Battalion Commanders concerned to-morrow morning for instructions as to joining them.
    D/152 will supply an Officer (Lieut. AIRD) with ALDIS Lamp to act as F.O.O. with a roving commission under orders, issued separately to him.
    Each battery will man an O.P. in addition.

14. ZERO HOUR.
    Zero hour for the operations on our Left will be notified later. This will be known as ZERO HOUR.
    Zero hour for the advance of our patrols from the Front line will be signalled by day by 3 "BLUE smoke" Rifle Grenades fired from HOLLAND SCHESDHUUR Craters and also from PIMPERNEL.
    By night the Zero hour for this move will be 7.30.p.m.
    Zero hour for this move will be known as "RED ZERO".
    Zero hour for the move of patrols forward from the BLUE, GREEN and BROWN Lines will be known as "BLUE ZERO", "GREEN ZERO", and "BROWN ZERO" respectively, and will be notified later.

15. MEDICAL ARRANGEMENTS.
    An Aid Post will be established at N.4.b.3.3, under the Brigade M.O. and all casualties will be attended there.
    In case of very severe wounds, the M.O. will be sent for at once, and each battery will have at least 2 men, who know the location of the Aid Post, ready to take messages there.
    Cases considered very severe will include
        (a) Cases of severe bleeding.
        (b) Wounds in the abdomen.
        (c) Fractured thigh.

16. All arrangements will be completed by the evening of 27th inst. Orders for the moves of detached Sections have been issued to all concerned.

17. Acknowledge by wire.

R.W. Angell

Captain,
Adjutant, 152nd Brigade, R.F.A.

Issued at 7.p.m.
Distribution:- Copy No.1. 103rd Infy Bde.

Issued with 152nd Brigade.O.O.No.18.   TABLE "A".

PROGRAMME OF FIRE WITH INCENDIARY SHELL.

TARGET.	BATTERY.	TIME.	REMARKS.
A.1. A.2. A.3. A.4.	C/152.	7.30.p.m. to 7.45.p.m.	One gun will fire "AT" on each target. Rate of fire 1 round every 3 minutes.
B.1. B.2. B.3. B.4.	B/152.	7.50 to 8.29.p.m. 7.50. to 8.44.p.m. 7.50. to 8.29.p.m. 7.50. to 8.11.p.m.	This programme will only come into effect if no advance takes place by day, in which case patrols will leave our Front line at 7.50.p.m."J" Day.
C.1. C.2. C.3. C.4.	A/152.	BLUE ZERO to + 30 mins.	Guns and Howitzers not firing in this programme will be ready to fire on any points at which the Infantry may be held up
D.5.	C/152.	BLUE ZERO + 60 mins to + 90 mins.	

PROGRAMME OF FIRE IN SUPPORT OF INFANTRY ADVANCE BY DAY

Time from ZERO	BATTERIES & No of GUNS	TARGET.	BATTERIES & No of GUNS.	TARGET.	BATTERIES & No of GUNS.	TARGET.	BATTERIES & No of GUNS	RATE OF FIRE	REMARKS
-10 to +5	A.4. 4.	a/1.	A2, A4, D1.	a/1.	A2, C2, D1.	a/1.	C.4, D.1.	(1)	x. All
+5 to +15						a/2.	C.4.	(2)	
+15 to +30	A2, D1.	a/2.	A.4, D.1.	a/2.	A.4, D1.	a/2.	C.4, D.1.	(2)	
+30 to +45	A4, D1.	a/3.	A.2, D.1.	a/3.	C.4, D.1.	a/3.		(3)	
+45 to +60	B.8, D.1.	a/4.	B.8, D.1.	a/4.	C.4, D.1.			(3)	
+60 to +65	A.2, D.1.	a/5.	A.2, D.1.	a/5.				(3)	
Time from ZERO									
+0 to +5								(3)	x Open on Dugouts &
+5 to +15	A.6, D1, 2.	a/6.	A.6, D1, 2.	a/5.	C.4, D.1.	a/1.		(2)	Creep up Road Shell at rate of 1 per every 5 mls. 5 rds per Gun. Start on C.O.Y. and O.P.

RATES OF FIRE. (1) INTENSE, for 5 mins. RAPID for 2 mins. NORMAL for 3 mins or UNTIL conclusion of shoot.
(2) RAPID for 1 min. before and finish 1 min before the 15 mins. given (2) shoot 1 rd. 10 secs. up to 15"
(3) Faster for 2 mins. NORMAL for 1 min.

NOTES:—

x Line is bent in two about C4, 4, 6, 7. Turn on to Lo... Little
+ Muston fire Start on to so.

SECRET   COPY No 9

ADDENDA to 152nd Brigade.R.F.A., O.O.No.19.

27th September.1918.

1. Add at end of para 8. "F.O.O's sending back information must not omit to time their messages, or state the time at which any movement, etc that they report took place. This is most important, especially in the case of delayed messages"

2. Add at end of para 14. "If the advance takes place by night "BLUE ZERO" will be 9.30.p.m.".

3. As soon as the BLUE Line is reached the Infantry Brigade will establish an Advanced Report Centre at CREONART CHAPEL.

4. Maps "A" and "B" are issued herewith.
   Map "A" shows suitable targets to engage should the necessity arise.
   Map "B" shows barrage lines and Brigade Boundaries for barrage fire.
   Should C/152 not be engaged in firing a Smoke barrage from "ZERO HOUR", this battery will fire the barrage covering the whole Brigade Front in accordance with 34th D.A. O.O.No.23 (issued herewith to C/152 only).
   The actual lines marked for the barrage need not be adhered to, but a searching and sweeping barrage will be put down lifting 100 x every 3 minutes and patrols may advance behind this barrage, so it must continue to move steadily forward at this pace.
   Batteries will keep Map "B" for reference in case an order is issued for a barrage to be put down on any line shewn on the map at any time during the progress of the operations.

5. Ammunition for the barrage covering the junction of 34th and 14th Divisions (fired by A & B/152 from Zero minus 5 mins) will be as follows :-
   In the Left lane (3 guns) All "A".
   In the Right lane (9 guns) All "AX" (106 fuze if available)

6. All firing will begin at H - 5 instead of H, and the first barrage lift will be at H in accordance with 34th.D.A. Amendments issued herewith.

7. N.F., G.F. and L.L. calls within the Brigade Zone will be answered by all batteries when not engaged on barrage tasks.
   D/152 will receive these calls and transmit them direct to batteries and repeat to Brigade H.Q. so long as this battery has lateral communications with the 18 pdr batteries. When out of communication with 18 pdr batteries G.F. and L.L. calls will be sent to Brigade H.Q. and transmitted to the 18 pdr batteries at once.
   RATES OF FIRE.
   G.F. and L.L. calls, 3 rounds Gun fire.
   N.F. calls, 2 salvoes, to be repeated if call is repeated.

8. Acknowledge by wire.

R.W. Angell
Captain

Issued at 2.p.m.   Adjutant, 152nd Brigade.R.F.A.

Copies to all recipients of O.O.No.19.

SECRET COPY No. 10

Addendum No 2. to 152nd Brigade. R.F.A., O.O.19.

27th September, 1918.

1. Very small reconnoitring patrols only will be pushed out at H+10 mins to establish touch with the enemy.
   They will not proceed beyond the line A.1, A.2, A.3, A.4.
   Their ultimate position will be reported, and tables A & B will be amended as, and if, necessary before the main advance begins.
   The main advance will not begin by day till the enemy is definitely seen to be retiring or until batteries are available to cover a further advance, i.e. Not till after H+129 mins.
   BLUE Smoke signals will not be sent up until strong fighting patrols actually leave our lines.
   This, of course, does not affect the action of the Left Company, Left Battalion and the barrage covering them.

2. "J" day will be September 28th.
   "H" hour will be notified later.

R. W. Angell.
Captain.
Adjutant, 152nd Brigade. R. F. A.

Issued at 4.p.m.

Copies to all recipients of O.O.19.

WAR DIARY
or
INTELLIGENCE SUMMARY
(Erase heading not required.)

Army Form C. 2118.

Vol 33 October 1918

Place	Date	Hour			Summary of Events and Information	Remarks and references to Appendices
WERVICQ	1st	21.00	29.00	Dull	Brigade moved to KORTEWILDE area P13 b - Hostile fire very little.	AS1
	2nd		30.00	58 Fair	Brigade moved to take new line from 157 Bde (35 A.M.) ZANDVOORD area P3 (Sheet 28 SE) - Hostile fire active during day + during night.	2
	3rd	60.00	30.00	58 Fine	Brigade move to ZANDVOORD + took over from 157 Bde. HQ at P28 d8. Hostile fire active during day.	
	4th		29.00	58 Showery	Our fire - 100 rds night harassing. 100 rds day registration + observed targets. Two morning 18 pdrs out during night, 100 rds each on targets up to limit of range. Hostile fire - normal during day, above between 20.00 + mid-night, mostly in vicinity ZANDVOORD. Hostile bombing planes dropped about 30 bombs near ZANDVOORD between 21.00 and 23.00.	
	5th		30.02	58 Fine	Our fire - Two mornings out + night, 100 rds each on harassing night. 30 rds 18 pdr + 6 inch H.S. on day harassing + W.T. collect. Hostile fire - harassing throughout day + intermittently during night on roads, tracks, etc in P5 and ZANDVOORD.	
	6th		30.00	53 Fine	Our fire - Two morning firing out of night, 100 rds each on morning night. Hostile fire - Any firing throughout day hostile + 50 rds 5.9 Howitzer firing nights on roads, tracks + woods in P5, 10, 11, 16, 17 and ZANDVOORD.	
	7th		30.10	54 Fair	Our fire - Two morning firing out night, 100 rds each on morning night. Hostile fire - As same active as previous day, rather more active. Day observed shoots. 100 rds 4.5 how on field, batteries + wire.	
	8th		30.00	54 Fine	Our fire - 100 morning 18 pdr as previous night (100 rd.) Hostile fire - As same as previous day. Very active, also about 100 5.9 Burst on ZANDVOORD during night.	
	9th		30.10	55 Fine	Several enemy aeroplanes over our lines during the day. Our fire - Two morning 18 pdrs as previous night (200 rds), also two at 11th day. Hostile fire on small area as previous day, hill area mostly.	
	10th		30.20	58 Fine	Same above - two officers, two own L.G. during the morning. Our fire - Two morning 18 pdrs as previous night (200 rds on P13 area)	

Army Form C. 2118.

October 1918

WAR DIARY
or
INTELLIGENCE SUMMARY.
(Erase heading not required.)

Place	Date	Hour	Summary of Events and Information	Remarks and references to Appendices
SECTOR WERVICQ	10th (Contd)		Gunfire (Continued) 20 rds each 18 pdr + 4.5" how on T.M's at Q10 a 7.1. 20 rds 18 pdr day registration. Hostile fire – normal harassing during day. P5 + P6 also on our left, apparently enemy counter preparation. Enemy aircraft – Zero planes crossed our lines at 16.30 & brought down in flames. Three of our balloons – one of the three brought down by AA. Gunfire – 1 W.115 – 30 rds 4.5" how on T.M's at Q16.b.5.5 – 200 rounds 18 pdr on back areas during night, 300 rds on back areas.	
	11th	30.00		
		59 misty		
	12th	29.80	Gunfire 0100 JP0.27 – 2000 rds 4.5"hov, bombs 18/pr, barrage in connection with capture of full line at Q10.0.05 for identification – Operation successful. Hostile fire – below normal – harassing. 4000 rds 18/pr. – 2 min rapid gun ex all nights – 200 rds. Hostile fire – much blown normal. Batteries moved to battle positions A/152 – K31 C.5.5. B/152 – P27 b.9/o C/152 – P26.d.14.4/8. D/152 – P6.d.3/0 a/6, in connection with Operation order 28	(3)
		57 fine		
	13th	30.00	Gunfire – 1900 – 21.35 – 1000 rds R.B.3 (Gas shells – 18/pr) on to Q17.18.23 (12.13.19). Hostile fire – normal – light harassing over Bogaceum (no retaliation for our gas shoot).	(4)
		56 hot		
	14th	30.00	05.35 ZERO HOUR of 'J' DAY. Operation Order 28 – 102 Infantry Brigade on right, 103 Infantry Brigade on left, covered by 152, RFA on right, 160 RFA in centre & 96 AFB on left. Final objective of attack (Sheet 28 S.E. 1/20000) of 3 Div was line R.2.b. R18 f.d. R.18 b.d. Q.17 b. & c.1.2. All all 3rd Div objective on and left 30 Div on our left. This objective obtained at 08.10. Very little hostile fire during the hunt. Its reached to P6d.5.1 Battery moved forward. Machine in Q.8 + 9.	(4a)
		57 fine	16.00		
			18.00	200 rds harassing fire during night.	

WAR DIARY or INTELLIGENCE SUMMARY

Army Form C. 2118.

October 1918

Place	Date	Hour				Summary of Events and Information	Remarks and references to Appendices
MENIN	15th	29.90	59	Fool	18.00	HQ moved to K30 b 3.0 and batteries to positions L26 b 4.21 – K35 A 5.9.6.6 covering 101 Infantry Brigade on front L.33 d.1.14 – R.2 d.4.9. Hostile shelling very light. Enemy apparently moved back.	
	16th	29.90	58	hot	11.00	HQ moved to L26 d 6.3 and batteries to positions in L.34 & 35. covering 101 Infantry Brigade on front Pecq-Riv R.19 +18 – M.13. Hostile shelling very little. Enemy batteries again numerous. Gunfire – no rate W.5 How on Regt front. Rest also about 100 rds / gun. (Caplow gun) on front of the Regt.	
WEVELGHEM	17th	29.90	53	Fine	14.00	HQ moved to FLORA FARM L.34 D.1.6. Hostile shelling very light. Hostile aircraft active between 5.00 & 12.00	
	18	29.70	54	Fair	22.00	Op./DIV moved to MIRO T MYC. Hostile shelling very light. Bombardments EYNEGHEM	
BELLEGHEM	19	29.80	54	Fine	06.00	Bde HQ moves to LAUWE (A19b). Batteries moved two M25.a.0.5 – N20.b.6.6. A/155 north of D.R. covering 101 Infantry Bde. attacking two N25.0.5 – N20.b.6.6 A/155 north of D.R. attached 1.2/1st QUEENS. – No hostile shelling. – Gunfire about 100rds. Belleghem area.	
					heavy	Bde HQ moved to TRESHOEK M28a. Balloons in action covering 101 If Brigade attack.	
					22.00	BELLEGHEM (N.27) – N20 b.3.1 – No hostile shelling. Gunfire – nil. 162 Rf Brigade supporting 160 Bde RFA took over line from 101 Inf Brigade + 52 Bde RFA with two Batteries now in support.	
	20	29.90	54	Fair	dawn night	2i/C W.C. Beck and O. was to reconnoitre 11/8 Re.Lwn Arrived position at Jaargaten... 50 Bn. pushed through 34 Bn from head of the horse Roads. through N.35, N.29+17 N.22. 2° Bn. on out of the line. 152 Bde R.F.A. (Still attached to 101 Division) Pee George) Moved to and billets in N.25 b & N.26.c and 21 d Hostile shelling – our guns nil	
					11.00		
ROLLEGHEM	21	29.90	55	Showers		Brigade Staff in Rest Billets – No hostile shelling – our guns nil	
	22	30.00	S.e.	hot		– do –	
	23	29.90	SE	Fine		– do –	

WAR DIARY or INTELLIGENCE SUMMARY

Army Form C. 2118.

October 1918 (4)

Place	Date	Hour			Summary of Events and Information	Remarks and references to Appendices
KULLEGHEM	24	29.50	55	Fine 0900	Brigade moved to H.Q. O.32.a.0.9.5. Batteries O.8.b.1 to O.9.c.2 covering 102 Infantry Bde on front SCHELDT from BOSSUYT to AUTRYVE (V.13 to V.9)	(6)
MOEN	25	29.30	50	Fine 0900	102 Infantry Brigade (in conjunction with 41 Div. on left) attacked objectives near BOSSUYT-AUTRYVE - objective gained during cause of day. 152 Bde RFA supporting infantry - very little hostile shelling - no enemy planes over our lines.	(7) (8)
EELBEKE	26	29.80	52	Fine 0900	152 Bde RFA attached to 103 Infantry Group - Bde moved to EELBEKE area M2g end of line	
"	27	29.90	50	Fine 0900	152 Bde RFA moved to DEERLYCK area to rever 173 Bde RFA 30 K.Div. II Corps - covering 101 Infantry Bde in line (front J.33.c.6.8. - J.33.a.4.1. inclusive) 103 Infantry Brigade took over from 101 Inf. Bde on 28 inst. when 152 Bde was under latter. French infantry on our immediate left. Hostile shelling - intermittent harassing fire - one of our mg. Our Casualties - Nil - 1 OR killed, 1 OR wounded. Shellfire. Hostile shelling intermittent harassing fire - own fire nil.	
DEERLYK	28	29.70	52	Fine	Brigade moved to H.Q. I.36.207, Batteries J.31.a.7.6, covering 103 Infantry Brigade. Hostile shelling same as previous day - hostile aeroplanes active. Own fire nil.	
VICHTE	29	29.90	53	Fine	Hostile shelling - normal harassing fire - enemy planes also active - one of our balloons	(9) (9a)
"	30	30.10	50	Rain	Shot down. Own front 15.00 - 20.00, 120 rds 18 pdr harassing fire. 3rd Div attacked (103 Infy Bde, supported by 101 Infy Bde with 102 Infy Bde in reserve) both in? friends Div. on left - and 31 Div on right. 152 Bde RFA & 57 Bde RFA in Rapid Group and 160 Bde RFA & 113 Bde RFA on Left Groups. Covering own front. Objective of 3rd Div. was Road & Scuth of ANSEGHEM (J.30). One Section of B/152 (in?)	
"	31	29.80	50	Fine 05.25	Section joined Left Group Artillery, moved up in close supports of infantry. 03.00 - 05.25 - 120 5 inch 18 pdr. harassing fire in area south of attack moving on very little hostile shelling during our attack - objective attained about 10.00. Slight hostile shelling subsequently, hostile aero shining day. 152 Bde moved up to J34 Central.	

M. Davis Lieut. Col.
Commanding 152 Bde RFA

SECRET.   COPY No 7

<u>152 Brigade R.F.A. Operation Order No 20.</u>

<u>1st October 1918.</u>

<u>Map</u>: <u>Sheet 23/1-40000.</u>

1. The Brigade will move today to KORTEWILDE Area.
   <u>Route</u>. DICKEBUSCH, CAFE BELGE, VOORMEZEELE, ST ELOI, HOLLEBEKE ECLUSE No 6.
   <u>Starting Point</u>. Cross Roads N.34.a.1.8 at 1440.
   <u>Order of March</u>. Brigade H.Q, A, B, C and D.
   Units will pass starting point at following times.

H.Q.	1440
A.	1442
B.	1448
C.	1454
D.	1500

2. The Brigade is being followed by D.A.C. and No 1 Coy. Div: Train.

3. Acknowledge.

                                                        P.a. Angell.
                                                           Capt
Issued at 1020.   Adjt. 152nd Brigade. R.F.A

Copies to :- 1/. Batteries
              5. O.C. Signal Sub-section.
              6. This Office
              7/8. War Diary
              7. Spare.

DRAFT   COPY No 1

152nd Brigade.R.F.A. Operation Order No.21.

2nd October 1918.

Reference: Sheet 28.S.E. 1/20,000.

1. The 152nd Brigade.R.F.A. will relieve 157th Brigade.R.F.A. on the morning of 3rd October,1918. Relief of batteries to be complete by 06.00 in order to admit of relieved batteries moving before daylight.

2. A & D/152 will not take over the positions of A & D/157 but O's.C A & D/152 will inform O's.C. A & D/157 respectively by 05.30 that they will be ready to take over the line by 06.00.
B & C/152 will take over the positions of B & C/157 by 06.00.

3. Ammunition : 150 rounds 18 pdr per gun and 100 rounds 4.5" How per gun will be kept at the Gun position, and all echelons will be kept full. Batteries actually taking over positions of batteries of 157th Bde will take over ammunition left in those positions.

4. Battery positions on completion of relief will be as follows :-
   A/152.   P.5.c.6.3.
   B/152.   P.11.c.1.6.
   C/152.   P.10.d.9.4.
   D/152.   P.5.a.6.0.

5. S.O.S. lines will be on the following road junctions etc :-

   A/152.   B/152.
   2 guns. Q.15.a.65.05.   2 guns. Q.14.c.81.23.
   1 gun. Q.15.c.57.88.   1 gun. Q.20.a.73.70.
   1 gun. Q.15.c.35.50.   1 gun. Q.20.a.70.57.
   2 guns. Q.14.d.70.35.   2 guns. Q.20.b.45.80.

   C/152.   D/152.
   1 gun. Q.20.c.12.75.   1 gun. Q.15.c.75.60.
   1 gun. Q.20.c.21.33.   1 gun. Q.15.d.13.22.
   1 gun. Q.20.c.47.23.   1 gun. Q.20.b.38.53.
   1 gun. Q.20.c.5.1.   1 gun. Q.20.d.35.83.
   2 guns. Q.20.c.1.6.   1 gun. Q.20.c.80.25.
                                       1 gun. Q.20.c.9.1.

6. POLICY.
The policy in this Sector is not to attack further at present, consequently as soon as possible batteries will be split up into Active Sections and 4 Gun silent positions. Battery Commanders will reconnoitre for suitable positions as soon as possible, and will also select new Wagon Lines. Wagon lines should be moved on the night 3/4th Octbr to new sites at which they should arrive before it is sufficiently light on the morning of 4th October for movement to be seen by the enemy. It will probably be impossible to find good ground for Wagon lines out of range of the enemy's guns, and safety must be considered before comfort in this case, and every opportunity must be taken to improve the ground at once by leveling, draining, and putting in firm standings.

7. H.Q. 152nd Bde.R.F.A. will close at KORTEWILDE at 07.00 and re-open at P.3.d.3.5. at 08.30.

8. The Front line was reported to run as follows this afternoon, but since then an attack has been made with a view to advancing to the line of the ST JANSBEEK, with what result is not known.
Line. P.24.d.2.0. - 9.7. - P.19.a.0.1. - 5.9. - ONGEREET FM -
Q.13.b.2.0. - 5.6. - Q.8.c.0.0. - KLIJTMOLEN - Q.8.d.4.4.

9. Acknowledge.

R.W. Angell.
Captain
Adjutant, 152nd Brigade.R.F.A.

Issued at 2100.
Distribution: Copy 1/4. Batteries. 5. 157th Bde.R.F.A. 6.
7/8. War Diary. 9.Signals. 10.

BM 103rd Inf Bde
BM 94 DA

SECRET   COPY NO. 3

152nd Brigade R.F.A. Operation Order No. 27.

11th October, 1918.

Reference Sheet 28.S.E. 1/20,000.

1. A minor operation will be carried out by 4th.R.Sussex Regt on the night 11/12th October with a view to obtaining an identification.

2. Objective - Pill-box Q.10.c.0.5.

3. 152nd Brigade R.F.A. will co-operate as follows :-
   H to H + 15 mins.
       A/152. 4 guns cover the area Q.9.d.83.46 - Q.10.c.30.95. - Q.10.d.00.25. - Q.10.d.0.0. - Q.16.a.7.8. paying special attention to Pill-box Q.10.c.0.5.
       B/152. 2 guns cover the area Q.9.d.4.0. - Q.9.d.83.46. - Q.16.a.7.8 - Q.16.a.4.8.
       C/152. 2 guns cover the area Q.10.c.30.95. - Q.10.a.7.4. - Q.10.d.0.7. - Q.10.d.00.25.
       D/152. 4 hows shell QUARANTINE FARM, Pill-boxes about Q.10.c.9.7., FRENZY FARM and QUARTER COTTAGES.

   H + 15 to H + 35 mins.
       A/152. 2 guns barrage the line Q.10.c.0.0. - Q.10.c.4.2.
              2 guns barrage the line Q.10.c.4.2. - Q.10.c.55.70.
       B/152. 2 guns barrage Q.10.c.30.95. - Q.10.c.55.70.
       C/152. 2 guns barrage Q.9.d.6.2. - Q.10.c.0.0.
       D/152. As from H to H + 15.
       A/152. will sweep to cover the whole of their barrage line.

4. RATES OF FIRE.
       H to H + 15.   "RAPID".
       H + 15 to H + 20. "INTENSE".
       H + 20 to H + 30. "NORMAL".
       H + 30 to H + 35. "INTENSE".
       H + 35.   "STOP FIRING".

5. AMMUNITION. Shrapnel only will be fired by 18-prs., 4.5" Hows all "BX".

6. Watches will be synchronised by means of a watch sent out with these orders.

7. Zero hour (H) will be 01.00 12th October.
   The Infantry will take the opening of the Artillery fire as Zero hour.

8. ACKNOWLEDGE.

                                                   R.W. Angell.
                                                        Captain.
Issued at 16.00.   Adjutant, 152nd Brigade R.F.A.

Distribution : Copies 1 to 4. Batteries.
                        5.   101st Infy Bde.
                        6.   Office.
                        7/8.   War Diary.

SECRET   COPY No. 8

152nd Brigade R.F.A. Operation Order No 29.

Reference Sheet 28.S.E. 1/20,000.   12th October, 1918.

1. A Gas bombardment with "BB" (Mustard Gas) Shell will be carried out on October 13th : Zero hour 19.00.

2. The following batteries of 34th D.A. will be employed :- B/152, C/152, C/160.

3. The detail of targets and allotment of Ammunition for batteries of 152nd Brigade R.F.A. is as follows :-

B/152.

Target No.	Time.	Target.	Ammunition.
1.	19.00.	Cross roads COUCOU Village. Q.17.d.2.6.	150 rds.
2.	19.35.	SCOUT FARM. Q.23.b.3.4.	150 "
3.	20.00.	Houses Q.18.d.32.70.	200 "
4.	20.30.	SLUMBER FARM Q.22.d.9.8.	150 "
5.	20.55.	Houses Q.23.a.8.2.	100 "
6.	21.35.	Houses Q.24.a.1.7.	150 "

C/152.

1.	19.00.	RATHO Junction R.13.c.4.9.	150 rds.
2.	19.35.	Depot R.13.a.2.1.	200 "
3.	20.00.	RASCALS RETREAT. R.13.c.6.1.	200 "
4.	20.30.	Cross roads R.13.b.70.35.	100 "
5.	20.55.	MONGREL BRIDGE R.19.a.4.6.	100 "

4. RATE OF FIRE.
Commence on each target with 2 minutes Gun Fire, and then complete the full allotment at the rate of 2 rds p.g.p.m.

5. Attention is directed to the contents of S.S.217, and all ranks will be instructed in the precautions in handling "BB" shell.

6. A "BB" ranges similiarly to H.E. with 106 fuze.

7. All necessary ammunition for this bombardment will be drawn this evening and be at battle positions by dawn tomorrow.

8. To obtain the best concentration possible all guns should be laid on the central point of each target. The error of the gun will give quite sufficient distribution.

9. To enable this programme to be carried out B/152 and C/152 will take up their battle positions by dawn 13th instant. A/152 and D/152 will be in their battle positions ready to open fire at dawn on 14th instant.

10. ACKNOWLEDGE.

for O.C.
152nd Brigade R.F.A.

Issued at 11.30.

Distribution :- Copies to :-
    1 to 4.   Batteries.
    5.   102nd Infantry Brigade.
    6.   Captain. G.Fennie. M.C.(L.O. 102nd Infy Bde)
    7.   This office.
    8/9.   War Diary.

C.O.F.M No. 9

Amds No 3 to 152nd Brigade R.F.A., O.O. No.28.

13th October, 1918.

1. 152nd Brigade R.F.A. will fire a barrage on "J" day in accordance with 7th Corps Barrage map "A" and 34th D.A. O.O. No 35 (copies herewith to batteries only)

2. Special attention is directed to para 2 34th D.A. O.O. No 35. The barrage will commence on the line marked "O - 2" on the barrage map.

3. C/152 will be superimposed over the whole Brigade Front, and will answer GF and LL calls.
   A/152 will cover the Left half and B/152 the right half of the Brigade barrage zone.
   The boundary between A/152's and B/152's zones is shown by the black pencil line on barrage map "A".

4. One officer per battery will meet the Signal Officer at B & D/152nd Brigade R.F.A. Officer's Mess - Pill-box about P.6.d.5.0. at 17.50 on 13th instant - to synchronise watches. Each officer will take with him at least two watches.

5. D/152nd Brigade R.F.A. will form a jumping barrage on specified targets 300 x East of the 18-pdr barrage line.
   A special map and TABLE "A" is issued herewith to D/152 giving these targets and the times of lifting.

6. GF.LL Calls.   Three rounds Gun fire from all guns which can be brought to bear.

   GF Calls.
   AA.NF Calls.   Three rounds Gun fire from all guns when the target is in their own zone.

   ANF Calls, will not be answered by D.A. Units.

7. ACKNOWLEDGE.

R.W. Angell
Captain
Adjutant, 152nd Brigade R.F.A.

Issued at 09.00.
Distribution. Copies.
    1 to 4.   Batteries.
    5.   B.M. 102nd Infy Bde.
    6.   Signal Officer.
    7.   Liaison Officer.
    8.   This office.
    9-10.   War Diary.

SECRET   COPY No 9

152nd Brigade R.F.A. Operation Order No. 28

Reference Map "A" 1/20,000.
Sheets 28.N.E. & S.E. 1/20,000.
                                                          12th. October 1918.

1. The advance of the Second Army will be resumed on "J" day, (Not earlier than 14th October).
   The objective lines, Inter-Divisional Boundaries, and Infantry Starting line are shown on Map "A" attached (to batteries only).
   The advance will be divided into three phases:-
   1st Phase to BLACK Line.
   2nd Phase to BLUE and portions of BROWN Line.
   3rd Phase to Final Objective - BROWN Line.

2. The attack will be carried out by 102nd Brigade on the Right and 103rd Brigade on the Left.

   ARTILLERY PLAN.

3. The Division will be supported by 152nd Brigade R.F.A. on the Right, 160th Brigade R.F.A. in the Centre, and 96th Army Brigade R.F.A. on the Left, and a considerable amount of Heavy Artillery.
   1st Phase. The Advance will commence at H hour : at H - 2 the 18 pdr Batteries will put down a barrage on a line 300 x in front of the Infantry starting line and will commence to creep at H + 2, moving forward at the rate of 100 x in 2½ until it reaches a protective barrage line 200 x East of the BLACK line.
   2nd Phase. At H + 45 mins the barrage will again commence to creep at the same pace, moving forward till it reaches a line 250 x E of the BLUE Line where it will remain for 17 mins.
   The batteries of 152nd Brigade R.F.A. will not creep as far as this line, but will stop on the Final protective barrage line as they reach it.
   During the 1st and 2nd Phases Field Howitzers will fire a Jumping Barrage 300 x ahead of the 18-pdr Creeping barrage.
   During the first pause fire being concentrated on such portions of the Support and Front line and intervening wire of the TERHAND line, as safety conditions permit.
   During the second pause targets will be engaged 300 x East of 18-pdr protective barrage.
   152nd Brigade R.F.A. will probably take no part in the 3rd Phase.
   All fire will cease at an hour to be notified later except observed fire or fire ordered by 34th D.A. and the Infantry will push out patrols to the MENIN - WERVICQ Railway, one patrol being specially detailed to seize the KNOLL at R.3.c.0.0. to cover the flank of 41st Division.

4. During the 3rd Phase batteries of the Artillery covering 34th Division will be prepared to move forward in the following order :- 160th Brigade R.F.A., 96th Army Brigade R.F.A. when such batteries of 152nd Brigade R.F.A. as it will be necessary to move. No area for forward positions is allotted to this Brigade, but the following areas are allotted - To 160th Brigade. S of the MENIN Road (suggested Q.2.b.) : to 96th Army Brigade R.F.A. N of MENIN Road and W of GHELUWE.

5. A F.O.O. party under an Officer equipped with telephone and visual signalling equipment will be provided by the Brigade : also Liaison with the Right Infantry Brigade at SHEET Farm Q.J.d.9.5. These officers will be detailed later.

6. Barrage tables and detailed instructions will be issued later.

7. 103rd Infantry Brigade relieved the Left portion of 101st Infantry Brigade last night, and 102nd Infantry Brigade relieves the Right portion of 101st Infantry Brigade tonight.

8. ACKNOWLEDGE.
                                                          R. W. Angell.
                                                          Captain
                                        Adjutant, 152nd Brigade

COPY N. 9.

SECRET

Addenda No.1 to 152nd Brigade R.F.A. Operation Order No.28.

12th October, 1918.

1. **LIAISON.**

There will be no liaison officers with Battalions once the operations start.

Captain G. HENRY. M.C. will be Liaison Officer with 102nd Infantry Brigade H.Q. from 06.30 13th October at Q.1.d.0.0. He should take with him one telephone and a short length of wire to connect to the Infantry Brigade exchange.

A line to this place already exists.

The Liaison Officer of A/152 will go to the Right Battalion (1/7th Cheshire Regt.) when the relief takes place on the night of 12th/13th October, and will remain with the Battalion till the attack commences.

B/152 will find a Liaison Officer with the Left Battalion (1/4th Cheshire Regt.) from 06.30 13th October till the attack commences.

If the attack is postponed beyond 14th October, C/152 will be instructed to relieve the Liaison Officer with the Right Battalion on the evening of 14th October.

Battalion Liaison Officers will not take telephonists with them.

2. **F.O.O.**

D/152 will provide the F.O.O. for "Z" day. He must be provided with visual signalling equipment and telephone. He must report progress at least once an hour.

3. **SIGNALLING STATIONS.**

Before 2 hours of "Z" day a visual signalling station will be established at Brigade H.Q. (P.2.d.4.3.) to communicate with a visual station in the vicinity of the Brigade O.P. (Q.7.c.C2.92.). The latter station will be connected by telephone with the Brigade O.P. and with the Exchange used by B, C & D batteries.

These stations will be manned as follows:-

P.2.d.4.3. by 1 Signaller A/152, 1 Signaller B/152 1 lamp Bde H.Q.

Near the Brigade O.P. by 1 Signaller and 1 lamp C/152 and 1 Signaller D/152.

They will not be kept in action longer than necessary, and are only to be used as a subsidiary means of communication if telephone communication fails.

R.W. Angell
Captain,
Adjutant, 152nd Brigade R.F.A.

Issued at 09.00.

Distributed to all recipients of O.O.28.

SECRET.   Copy No. 9.

Addendum No 2 to 152nd Brigade R.F.A.
Operation Order No 25.

                                    12th October 1918.

1. "J" Day will be October 14th.
This is not to be communicated to
the troops or to any other person than
the recipients of this order until the
last possible moment.

2. The wagon lines of the 152nd Brigade R.F.A.
will remain in the present position, or
will be ready to move away, not after
H + 90 mins, at which time teams will be
harnessed up, but not loaded.

                            L.M. Paris Lt.Col. R.F.A.
                            Comdg 152nd Bde R.F.A.

Issued at 11.30.
Copies to:-
    1 - 4. Batteries.
    5.   102nd Brigade R.F.A.
    6.   Capt Ferris (L.O. 102nd Inf. Bde.)
    7.   Signals.
    8.   Office.
    9.10. War Diary.

SECRET   COPY No. 6

152nd Brigade R.F.A. Operation Order No.34.

Reference Sheet 29. 1/40,000.   23rd October 1918.

1. The Brigade will go into action tomorrow 24th instant in the area U.9.c. to cover the line of the SCHELDT from BOSSUYT to AUTRYVE.

2. Route.
   HELLINGHEM LE CHAT CABT (N.29.c.0.6.) - N.36.d.1.5. - N.35.b.9.2. - U.1.a.4.8. - O.31.c.8.1. - Wagon Lines.

3. Starting Point.   N.32.b.6.7.

4. Units will pass the starting point as follows :-
   H.Q.   10.30.   0900
   B/152.   10.38.   0903
   C/ "   10.41.   0911
   D/ "   10.49.   0919
   A/ "   10.57.   0927

5. Intervals.
   Intervals of 50 yards will be maintained between Sections and between the rear Section and the Transport of each battery.
   100 yards will be maintained between batteries.

6. Front line at present runs U.12.c. - U.5.d. - O.34.d. - O.27.a. - O.22.c. - O.23.a. - O.17.d.
   The line is at present held by 102nd Infantry Brigade.

7. Battery Commanders will meet the C.O. at Road junction O.31.c.8.1. at 09.30 to reconnoitre gun positions.
   One Officer per battery will meet the Orderly Officer at N.35.d.1.5. at 08.00 to reconnoitre Wagon lines.

8. Refilling same as today. Batteries will send guides to Refilling Point.

9. D.A.C. moves tomorrow to area N.31.

10. ACKNOWLEDGE.

                                                    R.W. Angell
                                                      Captain
Issued at 21.25.   Adjutant, 152nd Brigade R.F.A.

Copies to :-
       1/4.   Batteries.
       5.   This office.
       6/7.   War Dairy.

SECRET

COPY No 8

152nd Brigade R.F.A. Operation Order No 35.

Reference Sheets 29 S.W. & S.E. 1/20,000.   24th October 1918.

1. The 34th Division will attack in conjunction with 41st Division at an hour "H" on "J" day to be notified later.
   BOUNDARY. Between 34th Division and 41st Division.
   KNOKKE - HOSKE road, thence a straight line to V.9.a.0.0.

2. From H - 4 to H plus 62.
   18-pdr batteries of 152nd Brigade R.F.A. will barrage along the road from V.13.b.3.1. to V.7.a.5.0. all batteries covering the whole extent of the target and sweeping within its limits.

   From H plus 62 to H plus T (a time to be notified later)
   4 guns A/152. Houses in V.7.d. about V.7.d.75.95.
   4 guns B/152. Houses in V.8.c. about V.8.c.9.9.
   C/152, 2 guns of A/152 and 2 guns of B/152. Houses V.8.c.10.35. V.7.d.9.6.

   From H - 4 to H plus 62 D/152 will fire smoke as under :-
   3 Hows distributed along road from V.7.c.9.0. to V.7.c.7.6.
   3 Hows distributed along road from V.7.a.0.6. to U.6.d.7.0.

   From H plus 62 to H plus Y. (time to be notified later).
   D/152 will engage houses in the neighbourhood of V.8.a.2.9. with HE.

4. RATES OF FIRE.
   4.5"Hows firing smoke, one salvo per battery every three minutes.
   18-pdrs. H - 4 to H - 2. intense.
             H - 2 to H.   rapid.
             H to H plus 62. slow.
             H plus 62 to H plus 66. intense.
             H plus 66 to STOP. slow.
   4.5" Hows firing H.E., H plus 62 to H plus 66. intense.
                         H plus 66 to STOP. slow.

5. Ammunition.
   At least a full echelon will be available at each battery position at "H" hour.
   34th D.A.C. will deliver three wagon loads of smoke to D/152 tonight, if the smoke shell arrive in time. If these are not delivered D/152 will fire H.E. where ordered to fire smoke.

6. Medical.
   There are Aid posts at U.9.d.8.5. and at O.26.d.6.4.

7. Watches will be synchronized with the watch sent herewith.

8. ACKNOWLEDGE.

R.W. Angell

Captain
Adjutant, 152nd Brigade R.F.A.

Issued at 23.00.

Copies to :-
   1/4. Batteries.
   5.   102nd Infy Bde.
   6.   Signals.
   7.   Office.
   8/9. War Diary.

SECRET   C O P Y. No

152nd Brigade R.F.A. Operation Order No 37.

Reference Sheet 29. 1/40,000.   26th October 1918.

1. The Brigade will march to-morrow to the IInd Corps area, and will probably go into action in relief of a Brigade of 36th Division, or possibly to billets in the DESSELGHEM area.

2. <u>Starting point.</u>   LES TROIS ROIS CABT   N.18.c.7.1.

3. <u>Route.</u>   STE ANNE - X Roads N.7.c.2.3. - N.13.b.7.1. - WALLE - COURTRAI STATION - LOCK No 9 - STACKGHEM - HARLEBEKE - DESSELGHEM.

4. Order of march and times of passing Starting point :-
   H.Q.   09.25.
   D/152.   09.30.
   A/ "   09.37.
   B/ "   09.44.
   C/ "   09.51.

5. A distance of 50 yards will be maintained between Sections and at least 100 yards between batteries.

6. A halt of at least one hours duration will be made during the march for watering and feeding.

7. No troops are to enter the billetting area before 17.00.

8. Advanced parties of 1 Officer and 1 N.C.O. per battery will meet the Orderly officer at the Cross Roads SPRIETE (C.81.d.3.6.) at a time to be notified later.

9. In the event of the Brigade going into action tomorrow night batteries will march to Wagon Lines at present occupied by 36th Divl batteries, and their guns will be taken into action by the limbers of 36th Divl Batteries.

10. Steel helmets will not be worn, except forward of the Wagon Lines in the event of proceeding into action.

11. ACKNOWLEDGE.

                                                                    Captain
Issued at 21.40.   Adjutant, 152nd Brigade R. F. A.

Copies to .   1/4. Batteries.
              5.   O.C. Signals
              6.   War Diary.
              7.   Office.

6. AMMUNITION.
   18-pdrs. H to H plus 24.   50% "A" 50% "AX".
              H plus 24 to H plus 56. 100% "AX"
   These proportions will be followed as far as possible, and as much 106 fuze as available will be used.
   One 18-pdr per battery will fire smoke throughout the barrage.
   4.5" Hows will fire 50% "BX" 902 B.smoke throughout the barrage.

7. SYNCHRONISATION.
   Watches will be synchronised by means of a watch sent to batteries with these orders.

8. ACKNOWLEDGE.

                                                                       R.W. Angell.
                                                                          Captain

Issued at 19.45.   Adjutant, 152nd Brigade R.F.A.

Copies to :-
        1/4.   Batteries.
        5.   103rd Infy Bde.
        6.   L.O. 103rd Infy Bde.
        7.   Office.
        8/9.   War Diary.

SECRET

COPY No (9)

152nd Brigade R.F.A. Operation Order No 39.

Reference 152nd Bde. R.F.A. Instructions No 1, Map "A" (Barrage map) and Map "B" (4.5" How tasks to D/152 only)

30th October 1918.

1. **ATTACK.**
   (a) The 41st French Division will be on the Left of the 34th Division and not 164th as stated in Instructions No 1.
   (b) The attack of 103rd Infantry Brigade will be supported by two companies of Light French tanks.
   (c) The movement of the tanks when crossing their forming up line will be covered by machine gun and Artillery fire for which see para 4.

2. (a) The objective laid down in para 4, 152nd Bde R.F.A. Instructions No 1. is the FIRST OBJECTIVE. There will be a pause of two hours on this objective.
   (b) The advance will then be resumed by the 31st British Division on the Right and the 41st French Division on the Left under a creeping barrage.
   (c) The 103rd Infantry Brigade will resume its advance to its final objective which runs from K.25.a,1.5. to K.32.a,7.4. without a barrage but covered by 152nd Brigade R.F.A. and by the remainder of the Divisional Artillery as necessary.

3. **BARRAGE.**
   (a) The 18 pdr creeping barrage will come down on the initial barrage line shown on Map "A" at "H" and move forward in accordance with the timings shown on Map "A" till it reaches the protective barrage line. Zones of batteries are shown on Map "A".
   The Section of B/152 detailed for close support of the Infantry will not fire in the barrage.
   On reaching the protective barrage line only one gun per battery will fire.
   On lifting from the line marked plus 33 one section per battery will drop out of the barrage.
   On lifting from the line marked plus 45 only one section per battery will continue firing.
   Fire on the protective barrage line will cease at plus 66 mins.
   While the whole battery is firing one gun will fire smoke only, when less than six guns are firing one-sixth of the ammunition fired will be smoke.
   (b) D/152 will fire on the targets in the Brigade Zone shown in Map "B" lifting off them in accordance with the creeping barrage timings shown in Map "A" and maintaining a distance of 100 yards beyond the creeping barrage.
   NOTE.
   The times shown on Map "A" are those at which the 18-pdr barrage comes down on the lines, and consequently the times of lifting of 4.5" Hows from targets on those lines.

4. From 03.00 to "H" batteries will fire as follows, keeping up a steady rate of 1 round per battery per minute on roads and farms in the Brigade Zone to cover the sound of the tanks moving up to the starting line.
   A/152. 03.00 to 03.50. 50 rounds "A".
   C/152. 03.50 to 04.40. 50 rounds "A".
   B/152. 04.40 to "H".   45 rounds "A".

5. **RATES OF FIRE.**
   18-pdrs and 4.5" Hows.
   H to H plus 3.   INTENSE.
   H plus 3 to H plus 12. RAPID.
   H plus 12 to H plus 24. NORMAL.
   H plus 24 to H plus 30. RAPID.
   H plus 30 to H plus 51. NORMAL.
   H plus 51 to H plus 66. RAPID.
   H plus 66. STOP.

S E C R E T   COPY No 8

152nd Brigade R.F.A.   Instructions No 1.

Reference Sheets 29 N.W. & N.E. 1/20,000.
                                            30th October 1918.

ATTACK.
1. The 34th Division will attack at an hour "H" on a day "J" to be notified later, in conjunction with 164th French Division on the left and 81st Division on the right.
The attack will be carried out by the 103rd Infantry Brigade on a two Battalion front with one battalion in reserve. The 101st Infantry Brigade will be in support and 102nd Infantry Brigade in reserve.

2. BOUNDARIES.
The Northern Divisional boundary runs :-
K.32.a.8.0. - K.26.c.2.0. - K.25.central - J.24.d.3.0. - J.24.c.0.6. - J.23.a.0.4. - J.21.a.2.7. - J.16.c.0.0.
The Southern Divisional boundary runs :-
K.32.a.8.0. - J.34.c.4.0. - J.30.a.0.4.
Boundaries between Groups and Battalions will be notified later.

3. FORMING UP LINE.
J.16.d.7.1. - J.22.b.3.5. - J.22.d.8.5. - J.23.b.8.6. - J.29.a.0.0. - J.29.c.3.7. - J.35.a.3.2. - J.34.d.8.2. - P.4.b.9.6.

4. OBJECTIVE.
The FIRST objective for 34th Division will be
K.25.a.1.5. - K.25.c.0.8. - J.30.c.7.1. - J.35.c.3.0.

5. ARTILLERY.
(a) The attack will be supported by
152nd Brigade R.F.A.)
81st Brigade R.F.A.) On the Right.

160th Brigade R.F.A.)
112th Army Bde.R.F.A.) On the Left.

(b) The attack will be supported by a creeping barrage in accordance with a barrage map to be issued later.
One 18-pdr gun per battery will fire smoke.
4.5" How batteries will fire smoke and H.E. at selected localities. Details follow.

6. CLOSE SUPPORT.
O.C. B/152nd Brigade R.F.A. will provide one section under Lieut. F.C. Wilcock, and one other Officer to act in close support of the Infantry under orders issued separately to Lieut. F.C.Wilcock. This section will rejoin its battery at latest by dusk on "J" day.

7. No Artillery liaison officers are required with battalions.
Captain. D.M.McAlister will act as Liaison Officer with 103rd Infantry Brigade H.Q. (J.24.d.1.2.) and will report there with one telephone at 15 minutes after "H" hour.

8. On completion of the barrage 152nd Brigade R.F.A. will come under the orders of C.O.C. 103rd Infantry Brigade.

9. ACKNOWLEDGE.

                                for O.C.   Mordon Lt
Issued at 16.00.   152nd Brigade R. F. A.

Copies to:-
    1/4.   Batteries.
    5.   103rd Infy Bde.
    6.   Liaison Officer, 103rd Infy Bde.
    7.   Office.
    8/9.   War Diary.

WAR DIARY or INTELLIGENCE SUMMARY

Army Form C. 2118.

152 Bde R.F.A.
November 1918

Place	Date	Hour	Summary of Events and Information	Remarks and references to Appendices
SECTOR INGOYGHEM	1st	7am	152 Bde R.F.A. end of action, moved back to Mayndonine. J31 & I35 to await further orders. Mobile Arrilling. (Engineers for Sale of the Scheldt, however, INGOYGHEM-VICHTE road (J31)).	
	2nd	Noon	Brigade out of action - May. Shaps being employed shelling	
	3rd	Various	Brigade remains Reserve in Menin area. (R.u.t. 6 O.) end of action	
	4th 5th 6th 7th	Fine bad bad Fair	Brigade still no Reserve, end of action	
MENIN (WEVELGHEM)			152 Bde R.F.A. moved out (with 160 Bde R.F.A. & 2 Sections D.A.C.) to J27 & J33. to the attached to 35 Div (XIX Corps) in support of forthcoming attack	
DEERLYK	8th 9th	Wet Fine	Saw positions Reconnoitred in P21 & P27 - no hostile shelling	
			During the evening nothing over the Scheldt own anticipated attack cancelled -	
			152 Bde R.F.A. (with the above other 3rd Div units) returns to 3rd Div.	
	10th 11th	Fine	Brigade end of action - no hostile shelling or bombing.	
			HOSTILITIES CEASED at 11:00 under conditions of ARMISTICE	
MENIN (WEVELGHEM)	12th 13th 14th 15th 16th		Brigade moved back to WEVELGHEM area. HQ at Rut 6.80	
			Brigade in above area. Cleaning up, preparing to march with Germans.	
ST. GENOIS ARC AINIÈRES	17th		Brigade Commenced march, arrived at St Genois area. N.0 at O.20.2.18. (29,1,10,000).	
	18th		Brigade (with C/II R.G.A.) commenced march and arrived at ARC AINIÈRES area 14.00 - H.Q. 39/E with C.33	
	19th		Brigade at ARC AINIÈRE -	
			1 Section per Battery detached from Brigade (with some of ARC AINIÈRES taken over by XIX Corps	
OEUDEGHIEN	20/30		Brigade moved to OEUDEGHIEN AREA (H.7 - 38, 1:40,000) H.Q. at Grid 9.9	
		Changeable	Brigade Billets at OEUDEGHIEN	
			24th (Sunday) Divine Service held by Brit. Chaplain at Oudechien	
			28th - Brigade inspected by Divisional Commander	

A.M. Savill Lieut. Colonel
Comdg. 152 Bde R.F.A.

152 Brigade
R.F.A.

WAR DIARY
or
INTELLIGENCE SUMMARY.

(Erase heading not required.)

Army Form C. 2118.

November 1918

VOL 36

Instructions regarding War Diaries and Intelligence Summaries are contained in F. S. Regs., Part II. and the Staff Manual respectively. Title pages will be prepared in manuscript.

Place	Date	Hour	Summary of Events and Information	Remarks and references to Appendices
OEUDECHIEN	11th Nov	11.00	152 Brigade Still at OEUDECHIEN (Near LESSINES)	
"	11th–12th		Period preparation by Armoured Columns at Ends Chain	
OLLIGNIES	13th	10.00	152 Brigade moved to OLLIGNIES (SOIGNIES area)	
"	13th		at OLLIGNIES	
THORICOURT	14th	10.00	march to THORICOURT	
"	15th		at THORICOURT	
LA LOUVIERE	16th	10.00	march to LA LOUVIERE	
COURCELLES	17th	10.00	march to COURCELLES (CHARLEROI area)	
PONT DE LOUP	18th	10.00	march to PONT DE LOUP (CHATELET area)	
TRANIERE	19th	10.00	march to TRANIERE (NAMUR area)	
	20/3/4		Still at TRANIERE	
	21/3		Various (moved, demobilize appointed men) demobilized from 152 Brigade	
	21st		RE Signal Subsection returned to Armoured Sig. Coy.	

Reynoldson
Major
Commanding, 152 Bde RFA

WAR DIARY or INTELLIGENCE SUMMARY

Army Form C. 2118.

W.D. 36
152 Bde R.F.A.

Place	Date	Hour	Summary of Events and Information	Remarks and references to Appendices
FRANIERE			JANUARY 1919.	
	1/23		152 Bde R.F.A. still at FRANIERE FACTORY	
	1/24/26		152 Bde marched to NAMUR and entrained for TROISDORF (COLOGNE area), marched from TROISDORF to SIEGBURG and relieved 13 Canadian Field Artillery.	
			3rd Division took over C.R.D. Sub-sector of Cologne Bridgehead area to secure passage of the RHINE with 41st Division on our left, 32nd Division on our right. (in X Corps)	
			152 Bde RFA covering 101 Infantry Brigade (8th Sub-sector).	
			O.P's and gun positions selected:—	
			Advanced gun positions to cover BLANKENBERG - HENNEF - BÖDINGEN - ALLNER road. Main gun positions to cover Main road of defence between HENNEF & WOLPERATH opposite to ALLNER. Gun positions for reinforcing Artillery Brigades to cover main road of defence. Gun positions covering Support Line - NDR. PLEIS - KALDAUEN - HEIDE along road to ZEIT. Brigade H.Q. site near HEIDE.	
	27/31		2 Officers and 12 O.R's demobilized during January.	

M. Carlile
Lieut. Col.
Comdg. 152 Bde RFA

Army Form C. 2118.

WAR DIARY
or
INTELLIGENCE SUMMARY.

152 Brigade R.F.A.
February 1919.

No. 37

(Erase heading not required.)

Instructions regarding War Diaries and Intelligence Summaries are contained in F. S. Regs., Part II. and the Staff Manual respectively. Title pages will be prepared in manuscript.

Place	Date	Hour	Summary of Events and Information	Remarks and references to Appendices
Monthly to 28–2–1919			152 Bde R.F.A. at SIEGBURG forming part of the Rhine Army of occupation.	

A. M. Laird
Lieut Col.
Commdg. 152 Bde R.F.A.

Army Form C. 2118.

WAR DIARY
or
INTELLIGENCE SUMMARY.
(Erase heading not required).

MARCH 1919

Place	Date	Hour	Summary of Events and Information	Remarks and references to Appendices
SEIGBURG	22.3.19		Brigade billeted at SEIGBURG Germany - Cologne Bridgehead.	
	26.3.19.		G.O.C. Eastern Division Inspected Stables and Men's Billets.	
			R.A. Mounted Sports. The Brigade securing 3 first - 3 seconds.	
			The following Officers joined the Brigade during the month.	
			Major.S.E.L. TANNER, M.C.	
			Captain W.J. REID, M.C.	
			Number of O.R's demobilized during the month 29	
			" " " joined the Brigade during the month 101.	

[signature]
Lieutenant Colonel.
Commanding 152nd Brigade R.F.A.

Army Form C. 2118.

WAR DIARY
or
INTELLIGENCE SUMMARY.
(Erase heading not required.)

Instructions regarding War Diaries and Intelligence Summaries are contained in F. S. Regs., Part II. and the Staff Manual respectively. Title pages will be prepared in manuscript.

160th BRIGADE.
R.F.A.
No. MR 371
Date. 2.6.19

Place	Date	Hour	Summary of Events and Information	Remarks and references to Appendices
SIEGBURG			During the dates 1.5.19 to 31.5.19 the Brigade was in billets in SIEGBURG. Individual section and Battery training was carried out during this period.	
"	12.5.19		G.O.C. R.A. inspected Teams for WIESBADEN Horse Show.	
"	15.5.19		Lecture on the British Empire by Major. H. Hely-Pounds.	
"	19.5.19		Inspection by G.O.C./Xth Corps.	
TROISDORF	21.5.19		Lecture on "Bolshevism" at TROISDORF by Lieut.Col. Tysham.	
			Officers Joined the Brigade.	
	4.5.19		Lieut a/Capt. E.J. BARRETT.	
	4.5.19		2/Lieut. J.W. THOMPSON	
	12.5.19		T/Cap/A/Maj. W.G. PRINGLE, M.C.	
	15.5.19		Lieut a/Capt L.E. LEEMING	
	28.5.19		Major. D.J. FRASER, M.C.	
	28.5.19		a/Capt. T.H. HOLYOAK.	
			Officers Quitted the Brigade	
	7.5.19		2/Lieut. A. ROSS to Lancashire R.A.	
	8.5.19		2/Lieut. J.W. THOMPSON to Eastern D.A.C.	
	18.5.19		a/Capt. W.J. REID, M.C to 160th Brigade, R.F.A.	
	28.5.19		Lieut. P.C. YOUNG, M.C Demobilized.	14.5.19 Lieut. W.S.DYER Demobilized
			Other Ranks - Reinforcements.	
	12.5.19		Gunners — 11	
	16.5.19		Drivers — 21	
	17.5.19		Drivers — 13	
	18.5.19		Drivers — 11	
			Other Ranks - Demobilized.	
	3.5.19		Ftr/S/Sgt. 1 Ftr/Cpl 1 Sergt 1 Cpl/S/S 1 Cpls 3 Bdrs 3 Gnrs 4 Dvrs 2	
	8.5.19		Cpls 1 Bdrs 2 S/S 1 Whlr 1 Gnr 1	
	11.5.19		Sgt. 1 Cpls 1 Bdr 1 L/Bdr 1 Gnr 1 Dvr 1	
	23.5.19		Farr/Sgt 2 Sgt. 2 Cpls 1 Cpl/S/S 1 S/S 2 Saddlr 1 Gnrs. 8 Dvrs 2 Siglrs 1	
	25.5.19		Sgt. 1 Gnrs 2 Dvrs 3	

W.Kinnear Lieut. Col. R.F.A.
COMDG. 152nd (NOTTM) BDE, R.F.A.

Army Form C. 2118.

WAR DIARY
or
INTELLIGENCE SUMMARY.
(Erase heading not required.)

Instructions regarding War Diaries and Intelligence Summaries are contained in F. S. Regs., Part II. and the Staff Manual respectively. Title pages will be prepared in manuscript.

Place	Date	Hour	Summary of Events and Information	Remarks and references to Appendices
SIEGBURG	19th		From 1st to 18th June, the Brigade was in billets in SIEGBURG; training being carried out there. J-1 day. The Brigade moved to Race Course, HENNEF, where Col. KINNEAR assumed command of HQ., No. 1 Section, S.A.A. Section, D.A.C. & No. 1 Coy. Divisional Train, according to plan forming Col. KINNEAR'S Column.	
HENNEF	23rd		From 20th - 28th June, the Brigade remained in position of readiness. The Column held a Sports Meeting	
"	28th		Peace signed at 16.00 hours.	
"	30th		"A" Day. Inspection by G.O.C. Eastern Division at 09.30 hours. During the month, the following reinforcements joined the Brigade.	
SIEGBURG	2nd		1 Cpl. 1 a/Bdr.	
"	4th		2 Cpls. 4 Bdrs.	
"	14th		2 Bdrs.	
HENNEF	24th		17 Gnrs. 7 Dvrs.	

W. Kennear Cozen

for Lieutenant Colonel
Commanding 152nd Brigade, R.F.A.

Army Form C. 2118.

WAR DIARY
or
INTELLIGENCE SUMMARY.
(Erase heading not required.)

Instructions regarding War Diaries and Intelligence Summaries are contained in F. S. Regs., Part II. and the Staff Manual respectively. Title pages will be prepared in manuscript.

Place	Date	Hour	Summary of Events and Information	Remarks and references to Appendices
SIEGBURG	1.7.19 to 7.7.19		The Brigade was in Billets in SIEGBURG. Intensive training was carried out, preparatory for Practice Camp.	
WAHN	8.7.19		The Brigade marched to WAHN Barracks.	
	11.7.19		This was the first day's shoot, calibration being carried out.	
	14.7.19) 15.7.19) 16.7.19) 17.7.19)		During these four days, further practice was done.	
SIEGBURG	18.7.19 31.7.19		The Brigade returned to billets in the GESCHOSS FABRIK, SIEGBURG. On return from Practice Camp, time was devoted to the cleaning of vehicles etc., and work preparatory for the Eastern Divisional Horse Show, which was held on the 31.7.19 at SIEGBURG	
			The following Officers proceeded on leave during the month.	
			21.7.19 Capt. G.W. Brewitt, M.C. 24.7.19 Lieut.H. Witt. 25.7.1919 Lieut W.H. Atkins. 27.7.19 Lieut. J.T. Varley 28.7.19 Capt. R.S. Yates, M.C.	
	17.7.19 27.7.19		Lieut. J.S. Hoole-Lowsley-Williams proceeded on duty to U.K. and Capt. E.J. Wilson proceeded on leave to U.K. prior to embarking for RUSSIA.	
			No. of O.R's proceeded on leave during July to U.K. - 166 No. of O.R's demobilised during July - 12	
			The following reinforcements joined the Brigade - 25 gunners.	

Lieut. Col. R.F.A.
COMDG. 2nd. (NOTT'M) BDE. R.F.A.

www.ingramcontent.com/pod-product-compliance
Lightning Source LLC
Chambersburg PA
CBHW080816010526
44111CB00015B/2564